DEALING WITH DISAGREEMENT

MONOTHÉISMES ET PHILOSOPHIE
COLLECTION FONDÉE PAR CARLOS LÉVY ET
DIRIGÉE PAR GRETCHEN REYDAMS SCHILS

VOLUME 33

Dealing with Disagreement

The Construction of Traditions in Later Ancient Philosophy

Edited by
ALBERT JOOSSE AND ANGELA ULACCO

BREPOLS

© 2022, Brepols Publishers n.v., Turnhout, Belgium.

This is an open access publication made available under a
CC BY-NC 4.0 International License: https://
creativecommons.org/licenses/by-nc/4.0/. No part of this
publication may be reproduced, stored in a retrieval system,
or transmitted, in any form or by any means, for commercial
purposes, without the prior permission of the publisher, or as
expressly permitted by law, by licence or under terms agreed
with the appropriate reprographics rights organization.

D/2022/0095/326
ISBN 978-2-503-60284-4
eISBN 978-2-503-60285-1
DOI 10.1484/M.MON-EB.5.131817
ISSN 2295-0176
eISSN 2565-9839

Printed in the EU on acid-free paper.

Contents

Introduction
Albert Joosse and Angela Ulacco   7

The Early Peripatetic Interpreters of Aristotle's *Categories* and the Previous Philosophical Tradition
Riccardo Chiaradonna   19

È esistita un'eterodossia nel medioplatonismo?
Franco Ferrari   31

Galen on Disagreement. Sects, Philosophical Methods and Christians
Teun Tieleman   45

Γνῶθι σαυτόν and the Platonic Tradition in Clement of Alexandria
Albert Joosse   59

L'accusation de mauvaise entente (παρακοή) dans la polémique entre païens et chrétiens à la fin de l'Antiquité
Sébastien Morlet   81

Plato's Violent Readers. Pagan Neoplatonists against Christian Appropriations of Plato's *Timaeus*
Robbert M. van den Berg   111

Mythenkritik und Kultpolemik bei Firmicus Maternus
Helmut Seng   125

« L'âme est le lieu des formes ». Une réponse à l'argument du troisième homme à travers la *symphônia* de Platon et d'Aristote dans le *Commentaire à la Métaphysique* d'Asclépius de Tralles
Alexandra Michalewski   151

The Use of Stoic References in Simplicius' Discussion of Quality
Mareike Hauer   169

Bibliography   185

General index 209

Index locorum 217

Notes on Contributors 233

ALBERT JOOSSE AND ANGELA ULACCO

Introduction

One of the more characteristic aspects of ancient philosophy is its organization into distinct traditions and schools of thought. In some periods and in some areas, there were literal 'schools' whose members would meet in order to learn, investigate and discuss. More often, however, we can – to some extent – identify traditions by means of founding figures, texts or distinctive views. Speaking of traditions can be useful for us, modern scholars, as a means to structure and understand the varied world of ancient philosophy and philosophers. But many ancient thinkers too thought in terms of traditions: traditions with which they identified, traditions in which they included their opponents or colleagues, and traditions from which they sought to exclude others. But how did ancient thinkers build and conceive of traditions? This is the question which this volume seeks to address. Its focus, specifically, is on the way in which authors deal with opinions that they do not share and on how such 'dealing with disagreement' contributes to the formation of philosophical traditions.

The contributions to this volume were solicited for a conference held at the Freiburg Institute for Advanced Studies (FRIAS) on April 16–18, 2015, under the title 'Heterodoxy and Tradition: Conflict and Dialogue in Ancient Pagan and Christian Philosophy'. One of the premises of the conference was that Christian and pagan[1] intellectual activities should not be studied in isolation, if we are to understand ancient philosophical traditions properly. The contributions in this volume, we hope, bear out the fruitfulness of this approach. In its chronological scope the volume begins with the revival of Platonism and Aristotelianism in the first century BCE and ends with the last non-Christian generation of Platonist commentators in the 6th century CE. While late-antique studies has emerged as a field of its own, the developments in philosophy justify the inclusion of earlier centuries; hence our choice to employ the phrase 'later ancient philosophy' in the title.

---

1 We use the term 'pagan' for want of a better alternative. For discussion see Sághy/Schoolman (2017); Jones (2014).

Constructing traditions

In the first century BCE, the philosophical schools geographically tied to Athens dispersed. This is likely one of the factors that led to the development of text-based philosophy. In the absence of the living guidance of Athenian scholarchs, philosophers turned to the writings of the schools' founders and claimed to be returning to their original teaching. The texts of Plato, Aristotle, Epicurus and the early Stoics became a focus of philological study and philosophical exegesis.[2] To varying degrees, these texts and their authors served as authorities. It became common to appeal to the ancients as a way of rewriting one's philosophical pedigree and of providing support for one's philosophical convictions. By attributing authority to one set of texts rather than another, thinkers aligned themselves with distinct traditions.[3]

Moreover, as a result of this textual turn, the way philosophers dealt with disagreement also became more and more textual. The debates between Arcesilaus and Zeno, for instance, most probably occurred face to face. But from the first century BCE onward, responses to dissenters took the form of treatises and – increasingly – commentaries produced by leading philosophers.[4] By the same token, these texts increasingly became vehicles for the construction of traditions, whether through conscious strategies or other unconscious mechanisms. Such texts are therefore central to this volume.

Focusing on polemic, however, can easily obscure the extensive common ground between the different traditions in later ancient philosophy. This common ground includes the textual nature of philosophy we have just mentioned, but also a shared concern with emphasizing the antiquity of one's own tradition as evidence of its truth.[5] Moreover, we find many commonalities in the concepts employed by philosophers. As this volume aims to show, this common ground partly stems precisely from the polemic between schools.

These characteristics and mechanisms in the formation of traditions endured even when the dominant rival traditions were no longer the four Athenian ones, but the traditions we nowadays broadly identify as Neoplatonism and Christian

---

2 As argued by Pierre Hadot (1987), 14–17, 22–23.
3 See the seminal work by David Sedley (1989, 1997, esp. 116–129) and, more recently, Bryan/Wardy/Warren (2018), 1–19, as well as the Introduction in Erler/Heßler/Petrucci (2021). For a discussion of the very concept of epistemic authority in ancient textual traditions, see Opsomer/Ulacco (2016). As Baltzly has argued (2014), the authority which Neoplatonists attributed to Plato and his texts also involved the idea that these texts do not just express the truth but constitute a path to salvation for exegetes and students.
4 See the various contributions in Weisser/Thaler (2016); and cf. Niehoff's analysis of Neoplatonic *Timaeus* commentaries (with their view of creation as non-temporal) as pushbacks against Christian and Jewish attempts to claim this Platonic work (Niehoff 2007).
5 On the origin and importance of this motif see Boys-Stones (2001).

thought. This is only one of many reasons why it is essential to study later ancient philosophy and Christian thought side by side, as is increasingly being acknowledged.[6]

Disagreement and its uses

Before we turn to the individual papers in this volume, it may be useful to consider the different types of disagreement and the uses made of them. The problem with disagreement, according to ancient thinkers, is its incompatibility with knowledge. A central case, not specifically addressed in this volume, is the conflict between different beliefs simultaneously held by a person. This type of disagreement, diagnosed for instance by Socratic elenchus, disqualifies a person from claiming to be an expert. More to the point of this volume, disagreement plays an equally disqualifying role in communities. In the Platonic *First Alcibiades*, for instance, Socrates points out to Alcibiades that ordinary people are not suitable teachers of justice, since they disagree about what it means. This is a disagreement that is expressed in words, in the assembly. But it also manifests itself in behaviour: in conflicting actions and in war (*Alc. I* 111e11–112d3).[7] If disagreement is indicative of a lack of knowledge, then we should expect philosophical schools to avoid it. After all, they are communities of people striving for wisdom and knowledge. However, philosophers seem to find more value in disagreement than this conclusion would suggest.

Verbal disagreement may be diagnosed as merely verbal, when it conceals a substantial degree of agreement. Antiochus of Ascalon famously argued that the Stoics were in agreement with the Aristotelians and Academics; their disagreement was only verbal and due to Zeno's terminological innovations.[8] Where disagreement is not considered merely verbal, authors may choose to deal with it by passing it over in silence, whether because it is awkward in the specific context they are discussing or because they deem it to be of secondary importance. Compare for instance Proclus' and Olympiodorus' explanations of the passage

---

6 See, among many other contributions, Hirsch-Luipold et al. (2009); Mitchell/Van Nuffelen (2010); Karamanolis (2013); Rowe (2016); Petersen/van Kooten (2017); Riedweg et al. (2017), esp. Wyrwa (2017); Marmodoro/Cartwright (2018, on mind and body); Zambon (2019); and Brouwer/Vimercati (2020), on fate, providence and free will). The current volume studies the interactions between late-antique pagan philosophy and early Christian thought with a specific focus on the relation between disagreement and the construction of traditions.
7 Note that this phenomenon is often seen as indicating that there are no experts in the community at all. But this does not necessarily follow. This difficulty leads commentators to posit further requirements with respect to knowledge (e.g. that it be successful in convincing others); or to change the terms of the debate (Proclus denies that a sage is ever in disagreement with his fellow citizens – only they are in disagreement with him: *in Alc.* 268.12–16).
8 See e.g. Cicero, *Nat. D.* 1.16, along with Tsouni (2019). On the alleged agreement between Plato and Aristotle in the Platonic tradition, see Karamanolis (2006).

from the *First Alcibiades* we just considered. Proclus notes the objection that the presence of agreement in a community does not prove that its members possess knowledge. After all, the Christians agree amongst themselves in denying the existence of the Greek gods (*in Alc.* 264.3–6). Proclus points to the Christians' internal agreement to highlight their collective divergence from what he sees as the truth. Olympiodorus, however, when commenting on the same passage, avoids mentioning the Christians and refers to a much less tricky example: the Democriteans' agreement about the void (*in Alc.* 92.5–7). He chooses to gloss over the disagreement between Christians and the Platonic tradition. This more accepting attitude may be due to Olympiodorus' desire not to cause trouble in the face of Christian pressure on the Platonist school, or to his conviction that the disagreement between Christians and Platonists is only superficial and that the views on which they agree are much more essential.[9] In either case, Olympiodorus presents his own tradition as encompassing and less hostile toward Christianity.

When philosophers do diagnose or introduce a substantial disagreement, they can approach or use it in a range of different ways. In many cases, authors see disagreement as a bad thing. A common way of dealing with it is to attribute opposing views to some kind of deficient source. By doing so, authors can both explain the existence of the disagreement and disqualify their opponents. For instance, disagreements may be thought to result from a cognitive incapacity on the part of readers or hearers: Morlet discusses cases of misunderstanding (*parakouein*), a phenomenon which in *Theaetetus* 195c Socrates associates with a cognitive weakness of humankind in general. At other times, philosophers more specifically attribute the existence of opposing views to a moral failure: ambition or irrationality are frequently invoked in such cases, as shown in the contributions by Morlet, Van den Berg and Tieleman.

Negative uses of disagreement – when a thinker aims to discredit an opponent altogether or attributes his opponent's erroneous beliefs to serious moral shortcomings – may nevertheless have constructive motivations: thinkers wish to defend or even reinforce their own tradition. This approach is exemplified by Firmicus Maternus' criticism of pagan mythology. As Helmut Seng shows, this author's aim is to bolster the Christian tradition, which he has only recently joined. The same approach is also adopted, in a different way, by the Middle Platonists discussed by Franco Ferrari, who construct histories of the Academy to show that they represent Plato's true philosophy and that the Academic Sceptics have broken with this tradition.

But there are other ways of using disagreement to positive effect. Disagreement can serve as supporting evidence for one's own ideas or tradition, in at least five ways. In such instances disagreement may not be actively sought, but can still be employed in a positive way. First, interpretive disagreement can be

---

9 As argued by Griffin (2014).

seen as proof of the richness of a source text or of a founding thinker. In such cases disagreement is to be welcomed (especially when it concerns form rather than substance). Furthermore, dissenting views can be presented as likenesses or inferior versions of the truth. We may think here of the way in which Simplicius uses the Stoics' views to bring out the explanatory superiority of the Aristotelian scheme of categories, which Hauer discusses.[10]

A third way in which disagreement can be disarmed and used to bolster a tradition is by distinguishing between different domains of expertise. It is important to realize that ancient philosophers relate to the authorities they refer to in a variety of ways, which certainly do not always entail absolute and blind acceptance. Not agreeing with another philosophical tradition or with the theories of the masters of other schools does not *a priori* exclude the possibility of regarding them as authorities in certain domains, even though authors always tend to perceive the founder of their own tradition as the highest authority.[11] For instance, in order to explain the consistency of a Platonic theory, late-antique Platonists often found it necessary to appeal to other authorities, operating on different levels, to fill what could be perceived as gaps in Platonic thought. Such gaps could be seen to occur in those cases in which Plato had allegedly failed to formulate an idea clearly enough or had expressed a thought only from a single point of view. Platonists saw an opportunity to fill such gaps through a refined exegesis, sometimes by appropriating the theories of other schools. A case in point is the pseudo-Pythagorean text attributed to Timaeus of Locri, *On the Nature of the World and the Soul*.[12] Here we find the idea that the four elementary bodies mentioned in Plato's *Timaeus* primarily derive from form and matter.[13] This view is *de facto* a response to Aristotle's criticism that the *Timaeus*' mathematical approach cannot explain the constitution of physical bodies, since they actually derive from primary qualities (hot and cold, dry and wet) and not from primary triangles.[14] Timaeus Locrus appropriates Aristotle's hylomorphism, which at first glance is incompatible with Plato's views, and integrates it into the Pythagorean-Platonic tradition, which was in turn modified by this appropriation.[15]

---

10 See also Chiaradonna (2007) on the subordinated integration ('integrazione subordinata', p. 215) of theories and terminology of other schools within the Platonic tradition. In particular, Chiaradonna discusses the integration of the Stoic notion of 'common conceptions' (κοιναὶ ἔννοιαι) in Alcinous, Galen, Plotinus, and Porphyry. This integration, which is aimed at reinforcing Platonic philosophy as a coherent system, deeply modifies the original meaning of the Stoic concepts and subordinates them to Platonic philosophy.
11 Cf. Opsomer/Ulacco (2016), esp. 25–27; 37–42.
12 This text was probably composed between the 1st century BCE and the 1st century CE. On the nature and general aims of the pseudo-Pythagorean corpus and its reception by late-antique Platonic commentators, see Ulacco (2020).
13 Timaeus Locrus, *de univ. nat.* 215.13–15 Thesleff.
14 See, for instance, Aristotle, *DC* 3.8, 306a20–26.
15 Cf. Ulacco (2016).

Timaeus Locrus' text is also a good example of the fourth way of using disagreement in support of one's own tradition, i.e. by appealing to a 'grand tradition' that encompasses both one's primary authority and a secondary authority.[16] In the sixth century, we find Simplicius dealing with Aristotle's criticism of Plato by invoking this text. Simplicius regards it as authentic, i.e. as a Pythagorean source that inspired Plato as well as Aristotle. This premise allows Simplicius to maintain that Plato himself, like Aristotle, was committed to a hylomorphic explanation of elemental bodies, even if he did not state this explicitly.[17] Simplicius thus invokes a grand Pythagorean tradition to demonstrate the substantial agreement between Plato and Aristotle. We find similar strategies at work in early Christian texts that see Greek wisdom and Christian revelation as deriving from the same source. Clement of Alexandria's use of Platonic allusions, examined by Joosse, is a prominent example. Galen of Pergamum's work also makes ample use of this strategy, as Tieleman shows: he constructs a cross-disciplinary tradition of medicine and philosophy that predates division into schools and finds its origin in Plato and Hippocrates.

As a fifth positive use of disagreement one may mention later thinkers who use critical remarks against what they regard as authoritative texts as weapons to attack alternative interpretations of these texts, justifying their own interpretive tradition in the process. Simplicius' appeal to Timaeus Locrus can once more serve as an illustration. In responding to Aristotle's criticism of Plato, Simplicius not only argues for their substantial agreement but changes the intention of Aristotle's critical remarks, arguing that they target only the apparent meaning of the text, and thus refute inadequate readings of the *Timaeus*.[18] We find the same mechanism in the work of Simplicius' contemporary, Asclepius of Tralles. Michalewski's contribution to this volume shows how Asclepius succeeds in appropriating Aristotle as an authority for his version of Platonism by reinterpreting his statements in textually ingenious ways.[19] In doing so, he constructs a more precise profile of his own tradition by redirecting Aristotle's critiques to superficial readers of Plato.

In addition to approaches to disagreement that use it as evidence of the strength of one's own tradition, positive use of disagreement is made when thinkers reject their opponents' views but, – perhaps precisely for this purpose – adopt their terminology. One instance of this sort is Boethus' inclusion of Academic distinctions in his account of the categories, discussed by Chiaradonna. Another instance comes to the fore in Van den Berg's analysis. When Philoponus

---

16 See also Boys-Stones (2001).
17 Simplicius, *In DC*, 563.26–564.10.
18 Simplicius, *In DC*, 640.27–32.
19 For a discussion of the difference between the 'appropriation' of Aristotle's theories, which involves a selective reading and engagement with his texts and an actual 'integration', possible only after the commentary activity of Alexander of Aphrodisias in 2nd century CE and involving a deeper engagement with his works and arguments, see Falcon (2016b), 1–9.

charges Proclus with perverting the clear meaning of Plato's *Timaeus*, he is making the same accusation that pagan Neoplatonists regularly directed at Christians, namely: that moral depravity leads them to distort the text – violent interpretation, as Van den Berg calls it.

In parallel to the uses outlined above, we can also distinguish an important positive effect of disagreement, which need not result from conscious use: the emergence of not merely verbal but conceptual common ground across traditions. Conceptual common ground can result from the most intense polemics. A clear case in point is the charge of *parakoê* leveled at the Christians by Celsus and at Celsus by Origen, and which also features in further debates on and across both sides. Thus, the acknowledgment of partial truths can also involve an appropriation of the conceptual apparatus in which these are couched.

This subdivision of types and uses of disagreement can help to clarify the ways in which dealing with disagreement contributes to the formation of traditions. Here, we submit, fine-grained analyses are required, as it is impossible to identify general laws or make general claims that would accurately reflect such processes. For instance, both tolerant and intolerant attitudes toward disagreement can help construct traditions with strong identities, in different ways. A tolerant attitude can help build a tradition that sees itself as open to a variety of perspectives on the truth. The strength of the tradition may be bolstered by the inclusion of authorities from many different quarters. An intolerant attitude toward disagreement, expressed through frequent polemic, can give a tradition a clear and distinct identity. In order really to understand what makes particular traditions strong, we need to consider what concepts thinkers adopt or develop, in what ways, against what opponents, and in view of what interpretive constraints. There is no substitute here for detailed textual analyses.

Overview of the book

In his discussion of Andronicus of Rhodes and Boethus of Sidon, Riccardo CHIARADONNA argues that we should understand their view of the tradition in which they stand against the background of first-century BCE philosophy rather than that of the later Aristotelian tradition. Like contemporaries of theirs such as Antiochus of Ascalon and Eudorus of Alexandria, Andronicus and Boethus saw themselves as continuing the thinking of the 'ancients'. This group includes Plato as well as Aristotle, but also other 4th-century Peripatetics and Academics. Focusing on their interpretation of Aristotle's *Categories*, Chiaradonna argues that Andronicus and Boethus attempted to revive the philosophical project of these 4th-century thinkers, not to offer a faithful interpretation of the corpus of Aristotle. It is therefore unhelpful to describe these authors by using the terms 'orthodox' and 'heterodox', or generally to assess their thought on the basis of the degree to which they agree or disagree with the letter of Aristotle's texts. While this stance toward tradition is common in first-century BCE philosophy, differences between traditions remain. Just as Eudorus provides metaphysical readings of Aristotle to advance his Platonic-Pythagorean agenda, Andronicus and Boethus use Academic thought, adapted to a non-essentialist Peripatetic program.

Franco FERRARI surveys the major topics of discussion among the so-called Middle Platonists and concludes that no real consensus on any of these emerged. This realization applies to the problem of how to define the relation between the demiurge and the Form of the Good; to the theory of principles; to the problem of the origin of evil; and even to the question of whether Plato considered the cosmos to have originated in time. With respect to this last issue, Ferrari argues that we do not know enough of the developments between Eudorus and Taurus to settle the question: Plutarch's claim that most Platonists rejected the notion of a temporal origin only shows that he regarded this position as dominant and his own view as exceptional.

While all Middle Platonists were concerned with offering a systematic interpretation of Plato, the variety of theoretical options available makes it impossible to identify a common dogmatic core in this movement. From our perspective, therefore, it is impossible to speak of orthodox and heterodox positions. Ferrari points out, however, that these thinkers indeed thought in terms of true and deviant traditions. We can see a double motive behind this approach. On the one hand, the Middle Platonists turned to historiography in order to boost their claim to be true Platonists. From a historiographical perspective, it becomes possible to mark out particular thinkers as having broken up the tradition or at least distanced themselves from it. The Academic Sceptics, in particular, were considered to be heterodox (Plutarch is a partial exception here), even if the Middle Platonists did not use this term themselves. On the other hand, thinkers of this period increasingly developed their philosophy in the form of commentaries on Plato. This too encouraged thinking in terms of true and deviant Platonism: since prior Sceptical exegeses constituted an important challenge to any systematic reading of Plato's texts, the Middle Platonists needed to reject them. In fact, Ferrari suggests, their hostility to Academic interpretations may have the best claim to being the factor that unifies the Middle Platonists.

Teun TIELEMAN's contribution focuses on Galen of Pergamum's attitude to the earlier medical and philosophical tradition. Tieleman argues that Galen's synthesis can be characterized as an attempt to overcome the division into schools or sects (*haireseis*) prevalent in both philosophy and medicine. Galen extends his criticism of unnecessary sectarianism to the Christians and Jews, treating them as forming another sect comparable to a Greek philosophical school. According to Tieleman, what is key to Galen's strategy of defining his own position and criticizing what he sees as the sectarian behaviour of others is the conviction that scientific and moral progress consists in further developing the insights of a venerable tradition. Galen projects this tradition into a pre-sectarian past by arguing that it was founded by Hippocrates and Plato and further refined by philosophers from various epochs and schools. Galen's criticism is directed at philosophers and doctors who have turned away from this tradition, driven by desire for personal glory, and founded schools of their own. He seeks to remedy the situation by developing a method of demonstration modeled upon geometry, i.e. a deductive-axiomatic model of scientific procedure anticipated by Aristotle. Galen himself refuses to adhere to any one school, presenting himself as an independent-minded philosopher-doctor who feels free to select from each school what he believes to be the best theories. Tieleman shows that Galen's taste for controversy and disagreement allows him to harmonize his tradition of choice and to position himself within it.

Interaction across the Christian and Platonist divide is also addressed in Albert JOOSSE's chapter, which studies Clement of Alexandria's construction of a tradition of Christian philosophy. It zooms in on the Delphic injunction 'know yourself' as common ground across philosophical traditions. Joosse argues that Clement offers a sustained treatment of the Delphic maxim in the first book of his *Stromateis*, where he engages with Plato's and the Platonists' exegesis of it. Joosse argues that the very textual form of Clement's interpretations highlights structural parallels between Scriptural and Platonic phrases and ideas. Clement handles these parallels in such a way as to persuade his readers that the Christian tradition, as he construes it, is superior to the best the Hellenic tradition has to offer.

Sébastien MORLET's contribution is devoted to the accusation of misunderstanding (*parakouein*), employed by polemicists to explain the presence of false doctrines. The focus of his contribution is the polemic between Celsus and Origen, which furnishes most of the occurrences of this meaning of the word in the extant corpus of Greek literature. According to Celsus, the Christians have misunderstood both the myths of the Greeks and their philosophy. In his turn, Origen accuses Celsus and the Greeks in general of having misunderstood the biblical writings and the views of the church.

The polemic between Celsus and Origen turned the charge of *parakoê* into a weapon common to both pagan and Christian writers. The text which lies at the basis of this expression – Morlet shows – also provides an anthropological background for the accusation. In *Theaetetus* 195a, Socrates suggests that humans are cognitively so weak that they are prone to *parakouein* and misconceive most things (*pleista*). The connection between misunderstanding and *pleista* – Morlet suggests – facilitates, via the associations of *plêthos*, the later attribution of *parakoê* to incapacity and irrationality. In many of the passages Morlet discusses, an alleged moral deficiency similar to that examined by Van den Berg is said to cause interpreters to misunderstand their texts.

When it comes to the integration and differentiation of traditions, Morlet observes that a contrary effect underlies the common features of Celsus and Origen's polemic. For Celsus, to diagnose Christian error as a kind of misunderstanding is a way of excluding Christians from his pedigree of truth. For Origen, viewing pagan philosophy as a misunderstanding of biblical truth is a means to including it into his own tradition. The difference arguably results from the different statuses of the two traditions: for Origen, it is worthwhile to appropriate the prestige of

Greek philosophy for the Christian tradition. At the same time, as Morlet also points out in his contribution, a side-effect of Origen's use of the charge of *parakoê* is the exclusion of heretical Christian views from his own tradition. When Origen claims that Celsus' misunderstanding of biblical writings attests to his inability to grasp their spiritual meaning, this meaning also becomes a criterion of what counts as their tradition among those who self-identify as Christians. Moreover, some instances of Celsus' misunderstanding involve taking what Origen considers to be heretical views as representative of Christian thought. In both cases, then, Origen demarcates his Christian tradition internally by means of his polemic with Celsus.

Robbert M. VAN DEN BERG addresses cases in which different traditions appeal to the same authoritative texts but in order to draw very different conclusions. The focus of this contribution is the *Timaeus*, as interpreted by Neoplatonists and Christians. Each of the thinkers Van den Berg discusses – Plotinus, Proclus, and Philoponus – seeks to discredit his opponents' interpretation of key texts by means of a compound charge: these interpretations do violence to the text, or are expressed in an unclear way, because of a moral failure on the interpreters' part. Plotinus accuses the Gnostics of misunderstanding as well as plagiarizing Plato. According to him, they can successfully convey their interpretations only because their use of difficult and unclear jargon makes it hard for audiences to grasp their real meaning. Proclus argues that Christian interpreters of the *Timaeus* are incapable of using the word 'God' correctly, since they lack the virtue required to understand it in the first place. On the other side of the divide, Philoponus maintains that Proclus can deny Plato's clear proposition of a generated cosmos only by forcing an unnatural meaning onto the words 'principle' and 'generated'. Proclus does so, Philoponus claims, through an excessive love of the idea of an eternal cosmos.

The cases Van den Berg discusses clearly bring out the close connection between moral and hermeneutic rectitude which these thinkers assumed. Furthermore, in cases where the pedigree texts appealed to are the same for thinkers belonging to different traditions, the condemnation of readers' ability to interpret such texts becomes an important move in authors' overall strategy to distinguish and justify their own community vis-à-vis competing traditions. This move and the conceptual connection that justifies it establish common ground for the different traditions involved.

Conversion is the key word in Helmut SENG's account of Firmicus Maternus' *De errore profanarum religionum*. Firmicus, himself a recent convert to Christianity, takes pagan philosophical objections to Christian views and ritual and converts them into criticism of pagan myths and practices. He also embeds into his polemic existing, and widely shared, philosophical criticisms of pagan myths. And he converts pagan motifs which earlier Christian authors had used for apologetic purposes into tools for his polemic: rather than acknowledging the wisdom of the barbarians, Firmicus highlights their foolishness in their worship of the elements.

Seng shows that Firmicus is well aware of contemporary ritual practices and philosophical developments, and in some cases uses motifs that recur in later pagan authors. The *De errore* is an important example of the kind of Christian literature that departs from earlier apologetic intentions and advocates an intolerant attitude toward contemporary pagan religions and their practitioners. Firmicus' work attests to the way in which conceptual common ground is not only created by the polemic between traditions, but can also be used creatively by those eager to identify with a particular tradition.

Alexandra MICHALEWSKI shows that Asclepius harmonizes Aristotle and Plato by interpreting the former's comment about the soul being the place of the forms as indicating agreement with the theory of transcendent forms. By means of two other supposed citations from Aristotle, Asclepius reinterprets this comment as signifying that the divine intellect contains within itself the forms *qua* productive of reality. In this way, both Aristotle and Plato turn out to subscribe to the view that the divine intellect is not only the final but also the efficient cause of the cosmos.

A combination of tactics allows Asclepius to accomplish this purpose: he isolates Aristotelian phrases; he presents them in immediate succession, leaving it up to the reader to supply the necessary argumentative connections; he effectively suggests new readings of terms in earlier phrases based on the later phrases he quotes; and he presents as a quotation what is in fact a new formulation of his own.

In the process of demonstrating the harmony between Aristotle and Plato, Asclepius also emphasizes the purity of his own interpretation of Plato. Aristotle's objections against transcendent Forms must be interpreted as criticisms of a superficial interpretation of Plato. The incorporation of Aristotle into his Platonic pedigree therefore enables Asclepius to differentiate his own views from those of others who may call themselves Platonists, but are not true interpreters of Plato's works.

Mareike HAUER asks how and why Simplicius discusses the Stoic conception of quality. It is remarkable that Simplicius refers to Stoic ideas so often and so constructively, given that the Stoics were no longer in active competition with Simplicius' Platonic tradition. While these references likely go back to earlier Platonic commentators, Hauer argues that this assumption in itself is not sufficient to explain why Simplicius chose to include them in the first place.

To understand this inclusion, we ought to realize that Simplicius objected only to certain aspects of the Stoic theory but appreciated others. It is true that Simplicius objects to the corporeality of qualities and the existence of qualifieds without qualities. He agrees with the Stoics, however, that we may speak in terms of qualified things rather than qualities and that qualities have a formative function.

More importantly, by taking the Stoic discussion of quality seriously in this way, Simplicius presents it as a key part of their metaphysical theory and interprets the Stoic categories in general in parallel to the Aristotelian scheme of categories.

Simplicius' reason for rejecting the Stoic view is based on the assumption that the Aristotelian account has greater explanatory value. Simplicius represents the Stoic theory as a strong metaphysical position – Hauer argues – as a means to bring out his own account and his own tradition even more strongly.

As editors, we would like to thank those institutions and colleagues that have made this volume and its publication possible. First of all, we would like to thank the Freiburg Institute for Advanced Studies (FRIAS) for generously funding and hosting the 2015 conference through its junior researcher conference scheme. Work on this volume was supported by a grant from the Juniorprofessuren-Programm of Baden-Württemberg (Angela Ulacco) and by a VENI grant from NWO, the Dutch Research Council (research grant 275–220–049, Albert Joosse). The Open Access Books scheme of NWO has made it possible for this book to be freely accessible to all. The European Research Council (ERC–2019 AdG – Project Not Another History of Platonism. PlatoViaAristotle, PI Jan Opsomer, Grant agreement No. 885273, European Union's Horizon 2020 research and innovation programme) contributed to this volume by supporting Angela Ulacco's editorial work and the last revisions to Mareike Hauer's chapter.

We would like to thank all the contributors to the original conference, including Thomas Jürgasch, Jan Opsomer, and Georgia Tsouni for the constructive atmosphere and fruitful discussions in Freiburg. We are indebted to Bert van den Berg, Riccardo Chiaradonna, Jan Opsomer, and Teun Tieleman in particular for their suggestions during the conceptual stage of this volume. We are very grateful to the anonymous reviewers of the chapters for their time and acumen. We also thank Sergio Knipe for proofreading the chapters written in English and Dian Hulzebosch for her careful editing. Finally, we thank Gretchen Reydams-Schils for her comments on the introduction and for including this volume in the Monothéismes et Philosophie series.

RICCARDO CHIARADONNA

The Early Peripatetic Interpreters of Aristotle's *Categories* and the Previous Philosophical Tradition

The peripatetic commentators and the return to the ancients

The renaissance of interest in Plato and Aristotle is one of the major features of first-century BC philosophy. This aspect is famously connected to the genesis of an exegetical tradition on authoritative texts, which ultimately led to the great commentaries on Plato and Aristotle in Late Antiquity. The return to Plato and Aristotle was certainly also connected to a distinctive attitude to the past: the first century BC can be seen as an age of return to the ancients, as opposed to the anti-Classical attitude proper to the Hellenistic philosophical schools.[1] This holds true for Antiochus of Ascalon's return to Plato and the Old Academy and for Eudorus of Alexandria's return to Plato and Pythagoras.[2]

Here I will try to reconstruct how Andronicus of Rhodes and Boethus of Sidon, the two most prominent Peripatetic commentators on Aristotle's *Categories* in the first century BC, fit with this picture.[3] As I aim to show, their approach to Aristotle can best be assessed against the distinctive backdrop of first-century philosophical debates. Andronicus and Boethus come across as somewhat surprising figures, if compared to later Aristotelian commentators such as Alexander

---

1 On this see e.g. Gerson and Inwood (1997), xvi: 'on the crucial issues both the Stoics and the Epicureans set themselves deliberately and consciously against what they took to be the views of Plato and Aristotle'. The Hellenistic philosophers consciously bypassed Plato and Aristotle to return to the early Greek thinkers (Democritus or Heraclitus are prime examples of this tendency).
2 There is a vast literature on these issues. I would only refer to the classical discussion in Frede (1999). On the ongoing debate, see the papers collected in Schofield (2013); Griffin (2015).
3 Details about Andronicus and Boethus' lives are extremely scanty. On Boethus, see now Chiaradonna and Rashed (2020a) (collection of fragments with essays). Philoponus (*In Cat.* 5.15–20) says that Andronicus was Boethus' teacher: for details, see Griffin (2015), 32–33 and Chiaradonna and Rashed (2020b), 1–5. A survey can be found in Falcon (2016b).

Dealing with Disagreement, ed. by Albert Joosse and Angela Ulacco, Monothéismes et Philosophie, 33 (Turnhout: Brepols, 2022), pp. 19–30
BREPOLS ☙ PUBLISHERS   10.1484/M.MON-EB.5.132745
This is an open access article made available under a CC BY-NC 4.0 International License.

of Aphrodisias. As we shall see below, Andronicus and Boethus' positions are somewhat idiosyncratic, as they do not refrain from emending certain aspects of Aristotle's philosophy; moreover, both Andronicus and Boethus appropriate doctrines from the Old Academy. Scholars are sometimes inclined to assess these aspects against the background of the later Aristotelian commentary tradition: it is argued that in their time no standard Aristotelian position had been established yet and that this explains why their attitude to the authorities was rather free if compared to the subsequent approach to the same authorities. A passage from Michael Frede's authoritative survey of post-Hellenistic philosophy is revealing of this approach:

> This vagueness and indefiniteness about what it is to belong to a certain school must have reinforced greatly the process by which the founders of a school turned into authorities and their writings became authoritative texts that to some extent defined the school. What came to unify a school more and more was the special status the schools accorded to their respective founder or founders. At the beginning of the period it still had been possible for a Peripatetic to take issue with Aristotle, even though Aristotle was an authority. Thus Andronicus does not accept Aristotle's doctrine of categories, and Xenarchus writes against Aristotle's assumption of a fifth element. But it seems that in the course of time the explication and defence of Plato's or Aristotle's views became more and more important.[4]

It seems to me that this outline is potentially misleading in that it presents the early commentators in a quasi-teleological way: their work is seen as a first approximation of the full systematisation which was to be achieved later on. Here I will follow a different approach and will investigate whether the specific philosophical situation during the first century BC can explain certain features of Andronicus and Boethus' distinctive approaches and in particular their attitude to the previous philosophical tradition.

Focusing on the early commentators on Aristotle's *Categories* can help shed light on some crucial aspects of first-century BC philosophy. Aristotle's *Categories* was the 'star treatise', so to speak, of the ancient commentary tradition. This at least partly depended on Andronicus' arrangement of the Aristotelian corpus. Andronicus probably placed the *Organon* at the very beginning of his list of Aristotelian writings because he took the study of logic to be a prerequisite for the rest of philosophy (see Philop., *In Cat.* 5.19–20).[5] It is possible too that within the *Organon* he placed the *Categories* first because this treatise focuses on terms rather than on propositions.[6] It is likely that those who wanted to study Aristotle, even only to refute his views, started from the *Categories* – and, more often than not, stopped at it, for the other treatises were difficult and long enough to discourage

---

4 Frede (1999), 793.
5 See Griffin (2015), 225.
6 See Bodéüs (2001), XI–XXIV.

any further engagement.[7] As a matter of fact, both Aristotelian commentators and philosophers from other schools soon critically engaged with the treatise. Simplicius (*In Cat.* 159.32) draws a list of 'ancient exegetes' of the *Categories*, which provides something like a map of school debates during the first century BC. It includes three Peripatetics (Andronicus of Rhodes, Boethus of Sidon, and Ariston of Alexandria), one Academic philosopher (Eudorus of Alexandria), and one Stoic (Athenodorus). So the interpretation of Aristotle's *Categories* provides a privileged perspective to assess philosophical school debates in the first century BCE.

The early commentators and the previous tradition

Both Andronicus and Boethus have much to disconcert those who equate the genesis of the commentary tradition with the creation of some kind of 'orthodoxy' based on allegiance to authoritative texts. Andronicus, for example, criticised Aristotle's division of the categories as redundant and sided with Xenocrates' bipartition of *per se* and *relative* (Simpl., *In Cat.* 63.22–24). Boethus, on the other hand, claimed that the hylomorphic form must be placed outside substance, if we accept the definition of substance as a primary subject of inherence set out in the *Categories* (Simpl., *In Cat.* 78.4–20). And Boethus was apparently sympathetic to the Old Academy. So he argued that Aristotle's distinction of homonyms, synonyms, and paronyms in the first chapter of the *Categories* omits what the moderns (i.e. the Stoics) call synonyms, and Speusippus called polyonyms (e.g. a plurality of names for the same thing, where their account is one and the same) (Simpl., *In Cat.* 36.28–31). Boethus referred to Speusippus' account of 'onymies' positively: for (unlike Aristotle's account, we may add) that of Speusippus is a division that includes all names (Simpl., *In Cat.* 38.19–39.2). Indeed, this entails a further departure from Aristotle. For Aristotle's homonyms, synonyms, and paronyms are things, whereas Boethus apparently construed this division as a division of names and of their properties.[8] In addition to this, Boethus was certainly familiar with Plato and he aimed to show that certain features of Aristotle's thought had somehow been anticipated by his master. So, according to Simplicius, Boethus discussed Aristotle's initial definition of the relative in *Cat.* 7, 6a36–7 (relatives are those 'which are said to be what they are "of" other things') and traced it back to Plato (see *Republic* IV.438a7–b1; *Sophist* 255 d; Simpl., *In Cat.* 159.10–15).[9]

---

7 There is an extensive literature on Andronicus' arrangement of Aristotle's treatises. Recent contributions include Griffin (2015), 29–32; Griffin (2016); Hatzimichali (2016); Perkams (2019); Rashed (2021).
8 On this, see Barnes (2012), 298–302. For further details on Boethus' views on semantics, see Chiaradonna (2020a).
9 On Boethus' account of relatives, see Rashed (2020).

Some of these changes may be seen as hardly significant. But others certainly *are* significant and it is very interesting for example that Simplicius reports that Andronicus and Xenocrates endorsed the bipartite categorial division between 'per se' and 'relative', and had reservations (αἰτιῶνται) about the redundancy of Aristotle's division (*In Cat.* 63.22–24). If we possessed nothing but this fragment from Andronicus, we might infer that he was a Platonising follower of Xenocrates rather than a Peripatetic. Furthermore, Andronicus' sympathy for Xenocrates was not limited to the *Categories*. Themistius reports that Andronicus accepted Xenocrates' definition of the soul as a self-moving number and attempted to reconcile this definition with the view that the soul is the harmony of the constituents of the underlying body (*In De An.* 32.22–31).[10] Apparently, Andronicus held that Xenocrates' definition refers to the role played by soul as the cause of the ratio in the mixture of the primary elements of the body.[11] This is a very partial survey of the evidence and it is limited to the interpretation of Aristotle's *Categories* (so, for example, I omit Xenarchus' discussion of Aristotle's physics).[12] That said, even this partial survey suffices to draw a provisional conclusion. It seems to me that it is somewhat misleading to say that the early commentators were slowly and imperfectly approaching a standard reading of Aristotle similar to that developed by the later exegetes, i.e. a reading which is based (to put it very roughly) on the idea that the authoritative texts are both always true and always consistent with one another. We simply don't find this general idea in the surviving evidence. Should we therefore infer that the early commentators were heterodox? Indeed, they are such if seen from the later commentators' perspective. In a series of contributions, Marwan Rashed has persuasively shown that Alexander of Aphrodisias' reading of Aristotle was construed as a response to the earlier interpretations by Andronicus and Boethus.[13] As a matter of fact, Boethus' controversial arguments in Simplicius are sometimes followed by replies by Porphyry who, in turn, probably relied on previous material (possibly on Alexander) (see e.g. Simpl., *In Cat.* 78.20–24 = Porph., 58F. Smith against Boethus' account of hylomorphic form). If we take Alexander's exegetical project to imply the creation of an Aristotelian orthodoxy, then we can certainly regard Andronicus and Boethus as his heterodox counterparts.

It is, however, far from clear that Alexander is an orthodox Aristotelian whereas Andronicus or Boethus are heterodox. Actually, confessional notions such as those of 'allegiance', 'orthodoxy', and 'heterodoxy' should be used with caution when reconstructing philosophical debates and are perhaps best avoided. Rashed has argued persuasively that both Boethus and Alexander were Aristotelian philosophers who developed different possible readings of Aristotle's

---

10 See Sharples (2010), 239–240 and 247. On Andronicus' attitude to Xenocrates, see Rashed (2004).
11 For further details, see Rashed (2004), 47 n. 82.
12 See Falcon (2012).
13 See, in particular, Rashed (2004); (2007); (2013).

works and philosophy (different 'possible Aristotelianisms').[14] It is worth quoting Rashed's remarks:

> Alexander's opposition to Boethus allows us to see more clearly in what sense Boethus' ontology is neither a piece of 'Aristotelian orthodoxy' nor un-Aristotelian, but nothing but a possible way of reading Aristotle. The main interest of the commentators is precisely to construct, out of different possible doctrines latent in the Master's corpus, a coherent interpretation.[15]

Furthermore, Andronicus and Boethus' approaches were not unprecedented. The early disciples of Aristotle in the Lyceum regarded themselves as somehow contributing to their master's philosophical and scientific enterprise rather than interpreting his authoritative works. So they did not refrain from emending certain aspects of Aristotle's thought. Now, if assessed from the perspective of later Peripatetic scholasticism, this attitude can obviously be seen as critical or even polemical. And in fact an extensive scholarly debate focuses e.g. on Theophrastus' criticism of Aristotle's physics. But nothing compels us to see the work of the early Peripatetics from this perspective. For example, David Lefebvre characterises Theophrastus' attitude as follows: 'Theophrastus' work in fact testifies more to a desire to explore and apply its Aristotelian theoretical inheritance than to criticise it. Of all Aristotle's successors, Theophrastus is the only one whose work suggests a global research project, potentially comparable to Aristotle's'.[16] Besides, this was a common situation within the philosophical schools in Athens: for example, the debates among the Stoic scholarchs offer ample evidence of the same situation. So we should not take Theophrastus and Eudemus' work on Aristotle's logic, for example, as a criticism of Aristotle and a departure from his views, but rather as further work on a research area already explored by their master. This situation was not limited to logic but included the revision of some crucial aspects of Aristotle's physics and psychology. One example is particularly interesting for the present investigation. Among the early Peripatetics, both Aristoxenus and Dicaearchus equated the soul with the harmony of the constituents of the underlying body (though with different nuances).[17] Aristotle famously discards this view in his treatise *On the Soul* (I.4, 407b34–408a5) and his criticism is based on his hylomorphic ontology, which sees the form inherent in the body as both a substance and something causally efficacious: the form, while supervenient upon the body, cannot be reduced to the physical properties of the underlying body.[18] Apparently, Aristotle's early disciples did not find these aspects of his physics and ontology very appealing. And, indeed, the interpretation of Aristotle's soul in Aristoxenus and Dicaearchus can be read against a wider background, since

---

14 See Rashed (2007), 1–31.
15 Rashed (2013), 61.
16 Lefebvre (2016), 17.
17 The authoritative discussion is Caston (1997).
18 For further details, I can only refer to Caston (1997), 326–332.

none of the early Peripatetics were apparently very interested in developing Aristotle's account of substantial form and his essentialist ontology (Theophrastus' *Metaphysics* offers a famous example of this).

Now, if we keep this background in mind, then Andronicus and Boethus' philosophical positions become much less surprising. Andronicus actually takes up the early Peripatetic view and reads Xenocrates' definition of the soul as number against this background. So, apparently, Andronicus regarded Xenocrates' reference to 'number' as actually designating the harmony of constituents of the underlying body (see Them., *In De An.* 32.22–31). Boethus' rejection of the substantial status of form seems like the obvious consequence of this general view once it is adopted in the exegesis of Aristotle's *Categories*. For if form is nothing but the arrangement of the underlying body, then we must assume that it is just a quality inherent in the body and so that it must fall outside substance. Furthermore, we know that Boethus addressed some objections to Plato's *Phaedo* and these are closely reminiscent of Strato's earlier discussion.[19]

From this picture it emerges that the early commentators were probably reviving the philosophical stances and methods that characterised the early Peripatos during the fourth century BC. There is a major difference, however, since they combined these positions with exegetical work on Aristotle's treatises and this reflects a new situation. Scholars have convincingly argued that the genesis of a commentary tradition on Plato and Aristotle was somehow connected to the end of the philosophical schools in Athens and to the decentralisation of philosophy. Since there was no longer any institutional continuity with the scholarchs, Platonic and Aristotelian philosophers had to comment on their normative texts in order to justify their philosophical allegiance.[20] Commenting on Plato and Aristotle was an effective way to construe systematic readings of Plato and Aristotle capable of competing with Stoicism.[21] Finally, the genesis of commentary traditions certainly reflects the philosophical climate characterised by a return to the ancients which marked the decline of the Hellenistic schools.[22]

Platonists and Peripatetics in the 1st century BC

Andronicus and Boethus aim not only to reaffirm Aristotle's authority, but also to revive the philosophical traditions and debates of the fourth century BC. Interestingly, Boethus mentions the 'ancients' and he uses this expression to refer to

---

19 On Strato, see Dam. (?), *In Phaed.* versio I.433 and 442 = Fr. 80.8–11 and 33–35 Sharples. On Boethus, see [Simpl.], *In De An.* 247.23–26. Discussion in Trabattoni (2011) and (2020).
20 See Sedley (2003).
21 See Donini (1994).
22 See Frede (1999), 784.

Aristotle:[23] this move is somewhat parallel to Antiochus' famous references to the 'ancients'. This does not entail that Aristotle was regarded as an infallible authority: as noted earlier, the early Peripatetic debates on Aristotle did not rule out criticisms and emendations. Furthermore, if my discussion thus far is plausible, early engagement with the ancients was not limited to Aristotle but extended to the early Peripatetics and, at least to a certain extent, to Plato and the Old Academy. From this point of view, all the various revivals of interest in Plato and Aristotle during the first century BCE shared some common ideological features (whatever of their philosophical interests). That there actually was some common ground between Platonic and Aristotelian philosophers at that time is interestingly shown by some well-known lines of Philodemus' *Index Academicorum* (xxxv.11–16) which report that Ariston and Cratippus, two students of Antiochus' and of his brother Aristus', 'became Peripatetics' (ἐγένοντο. Περιπατη[τι-/καὶ ...: xxxv.14–15).[24] It is at least possible that Ariston and Cratippus' move from Antiochus' Academy to the Peripatos was not perceived as a traumatic event and that it may even have been inspired by Antiochus' favourable attitude to Aristotle.[25] Such a conclusion lends further support to the idea that the philosophical panorama of the first century BC was fluid and that the boundaries between Platonism and Aristotelianism were permeable since, after all, both philosophical movements were characterised by the revival of fourth-century philosophical traditions.

Eudorus of Alexandria's interest in Aristotle can be read along the same lines.[26] His attitude was not so much that of an anti-Aristotelian opponent, as that of an opinionated reader of Aristotle who aimed to incorporate Aristotle's thought and works into a Platonist-Pythagorean background. Such an approach certainly did not rule out the presence of particular criticisms and objections, but by no means implied a rejection of Aristotle similar to what we can find in the anti-Aristotelian Platonist philosopher Atticus two centuries later. The second-century AD Platonist approach to Aristotle is certainly marked by the *querelle* about the harmony or disagreement between Plato and Aristotle: this debate apparently continued down to Ammonius Saccas, Plotinus' master in Alexandria (see Hierocles *apud*

---

23 See Simpl., *In Cat.* 41.28–29: 'Boethus says that for the ancients only thoughts [νοήσεις] are said and signified [ὁ δὲ Βόηθος μόνα λεγόμενα καὶ σημαινόμενα τὰς νοήσεις εἶναί φησι παρὰ τοῖς ἀρχαίοις]'. The reference here is to Arist., *De An.*, III.6, 430a26–28 (see also Dexippus, *In Cat.* 9.27–10.1). Further discussion in Menn (2018), 28–29. In Simpl., *In Cat.* 38.19–24 Boethus says that he understands 'synonyms' 'according to the usage of the ancients'. Here 'ancients' refers to Aristotle (and probably Speusippus), as opposed to the Stoics.
24 Text after Blank (2007); see also Chiaradonna and Rashed (2020a), 2–3.
25 See Chiaradonna (2013), 38–39. On Cratippus, see now Dorandi and Verde (2019).
26 See Chiaradonna (2009a) and (2013). The relevant sources are now collected and discussed in Boys-Stones (2018), 418–436 (Texts 15A–Q). An updated survey of the reception of Aristotle in Middle Platonism can now be found in Michalewski (2016). The reference discussion can be found in Karamanolis (2006).

Phot., *Bibl.* cod. 251, col. 461a24–39 = Ammonius T. 15 Schwyzer).²⁷ Alexander of Aphrodisias' reading of Aristotle can (at least partly) be seen as a systematic attempt to develop an interpretation of Aristotle capable of countering Platonic objections such as those raised by Taurus and Atticus. This is consistent with the fact that Alexander parted company with readings that dangerously blurred the distinction between Aristotle and the Old Academy: this explains his criticism of Xenocrates, which can be read as a tacit response to Andronicus.²⁸

As a matter of fact, nothing really suggests that the same debates took place in the first century BC. At this time, I would argue, the discussion between Platonists and Aristotelians focused not so much on the differences between Plato and Aristotle, but rather on the different ways in which one could revive the philosophies of the 'ancients', in an effort to compete with the Hellenistic schools and particularly with the Stoics.

From these remarks, however, we should certainly not infer that Peripatetic and Platonic philosophers held the *same* views in the first century. Indeed, their ways of reviving the past were probably very different. To put it very simply, Eudorus of Alexandria and his followers adapted (and thus subordinated) Aristotle's philosophy to their Platonic-Pythagorising metaphysics. This is nicely shown, for example, by Ps.-Archytas' treatise *On the Universal Account*, which probably stems from Eudorus' milieu. The author argues that 'Man-in-itself' receives Aristotle's first category, i.e. the τὸ τί ἐστιν κατὰ τὰν ἰδέαν ([Arch.], *Cat.* 30.23–31.5).²⁹ Some later Platonising references to Aristotle's metaphysics as 'Aristotle's epoptics' in Plutarch and Clement of Alexandria possibly stem from the same philosophical *milieu*.³⁰ What happens in the early Peripatetic commentators is different or rather the reverse. Apparently, they incorporated Plato and the Old Academy and adapted them to a Peripatetic philosophical background, so that Plato and the Academy were actually subordinated to Aristotle. More precisely, they incorporated Plato and the Old Academics into a philosophical background shaped by an anti-essentialist reading of Aristotle, which was based on the approach developed by the early Peripatetics in the fourth century BC (i.e. the approach of philosophers like Aristoxenus, Dicaearchus, and Strato).

The clearest example of this situation is the testimony regarding Andronicus' view on the nature of the soul. This view apparently strips Xenocrates' theory of all its metaphysical implications and takes it to express the belief that the soul is the harmony of the constituents of the underlying body (to be more precise, Andronicus espouses a more sophisticated version of this view: see also Gal., *Quod animi mores* 4.26.9–27.1 Bazou = IV.782–783 Kühn = 4.44.12–20 Müller).³¹ Even

---

27 For details, see now Michalewski (2016), 232–234, with further references. Hierocles' report is possibly based on Porphyry and raises a number of problems: see Chiaradonna (2016).
28 See Rashed (2004).
29 For a recent discussion, see Ulacco (2016), 206–210.
30 See Plut., *V. Alex.* 7.668A–B; Clem. Alex., *Strom.* I.28.176. See also Chiaradonna (2017).
31 For details, see Rashed (2004), 47 n. 82 and Sharples (2010), 247.

Andronicus' argument in favour of the bipartion of categories should probably be seen as implying not so much a rejection of Aristotle's division but rather a reform of it.[32] As for Boethus, his reference to Plato was ultimately meant to show the superiority of Aristotle's distinctive second definition of the *pros ti*. And Boethus' positive references to Speusippus were meant to supplement Aristotle's discussion of the 'onymies' and not to endorse Speusippus' metaphysical views. Scanty as it is, our extant evidence suggests that Boethus rejected Eudorus' metaphysical reading of the *Categories* and refused to read Aristotle's substance against the background of Plato's metaphysics.[33]

Boethus and the monad

These remarks can perhaps shed light on a very difficult fragment from Boethus' lost commentary on the *Categories*. The passage comes from Simplicius' commentary on the *Categories*. There Simplicius focuses on some objections against the alleged completeness of Aristotle's list of categories. Among these objections, he mentions the one concerning the categorial status of the monad and the point. After mentioning Alexander's solution (the monad and the point should be placed among the relative), Simplicius says:

> If, however, number is twofold – one incorporeal, the other corporeal – then, as Boethus too would say, the monad will also be twofold: one which is substance, and is in intelligible number – Aristotle also thinks that this one exists – and one which is a relative or quantified item. Later, however, Boethus says that perhaps it is better to call it a quantified item, for as whiteness is to white, so the dyad is to two. If, therefore, the former are both qualified, the latter are also quantified. (Simpl., *In Cat.* 65.19–24)[34]

Paul Moraux had already remarked that this passage is somewhat troublesome. Boethus' philosophical views cannot easily be reconciled with a theory of ideal numbers such as that which Simplicius seems to attribute to Boethus in these lines. Moraux, however, regards Simplicius' report as trustworthy and suggests that Boethus followed Speusippus also on this issue.[35] Unfortunately, Simplicius'

---

32 See Reinhardt (2007), 521–522. On Andronicus' distinctive Aristotelian reception of Xenocrates, see now Granieri (2019).
33 See Boethus *apud* Simpl., *In Cat.* 78.4–5. Discussion in Chiaradonna (2009a), 104.
34 Trans. Chase (2003). Εἰ δὲ διττὸς ὁ ἀριθμός, ὁ μὲν ἀσώματος, ὁ δὲ σωματικός, ἔσται, ὡς καὶ ὁ Βόηθος ἂν φαίη, καὶ ἡ μονὰς διττή, ἡ μὲν οὐσία, ἡ ἐν τῷ νοητῷ ἀριθμῷ (τοῦτο δὲ καὶ Ἀριστοτέλει δοκεῖ), ἡ δὲ πρός τι ἢ ποσόν. ὕστερον δέ φησιν ὁ Βόηθος μήποτε ἄμεινον εἶναι ποσὸν φάναι· ὡς γὰρ λευκότης ἔχει πρὸς λευκόν, οὕτως καὶ ἡ δυὰς πρὸς τὰ δύο· εἰ οὖν ἐκεῖνα ἄμφω ποιόν, καὶ ταῦτα ποσόν.
35 See Moraux (1973), 155. For further details on the scholarly debate, see Griffin (2015), 127. See now Chiaradonna (2020b).

words (ὡς καὶ Βόηθος ἂν φαίη: Simpl., *In Cat.* 65.20) do not help to settle the matter and it remains uncertain whether his paraphrase can completely be trusted or not.

Simplicius refers to two different solutions proposed by Boethus. According to the first solution, Boethus distinguished between a substantial monad, which is in the realm of intelligible number, and a relative or quantified monad, which should obviously be placed in the sensible world. According to a second solution set out 'later', however, Boethus said that perhaps it is better to call 'it' a quantified item, for the dyad is to two as whiteness is to white. Accordingly, if both whiteness and white are qualified, then both the dyad and two are quantified. The Greek text at Simpl., *In Cat.* 65.14 runs as follows: ὕστερον δέ φησιν ὁ Βόηθος μήποτε ἄμεινον εἶναι ποσὸν φάναι. The subject of εἶναι ποσόν can plausibly be identified as the monad (more on this below). If this is the case, according to Boethus' second solution both the monad and the dyad are quantified items. Thus, given a couple of particulars, the dyad is the quantity that corresponds to the quantified predicate 'two'; given a single particular, the monad is the quantity that corresponds to the quantified predicate 'one'.

A first reading of Simplicius' passage would credit Boethus with a quasi-Speusippean doctrine that regards the intelligible monad as a substantial intelligible number. If the words τοῦτο δὲ καὶ Ἀριστοτέλει δοκεῖ (Simpl., *In Cat.* 65.21) stem from Boethus, then he suggested that Aristotle too held this view.[36] As for the sensible monad, Boethus first suggested that it should be equated with a relative or quantified item; then, on a second approach (ὕστερον), he suggested to regard it as a quantified item (thus ruling out the hypothesis that it is a relative). Note that according to this reading the subject of εἶναι ποσόν would be the *sensible* monad (as opposed to the intelligible and substantial one), which is first seen as a relative or a quantified item, and then is set in parallel with the dyad and seen as a quantified item. If this interpretation is correct, Boethus would be incorporating an Academic theory of intelligible numbers into his reading of Aristotle's *Categories*. An objection to this interpretation comes from another well-known passage where Simplicius reports that Boethus rejected the view that Aristotle's account of substance refers to the οὐσία νοητή: so he regarded the investigation of those who brought intelligible substance into the exegesis of Aristotle's *Categories* as redundant (Simpl., *In Cat.* 78.4–5). It is difficult to suppose that Boethus held this view but, at the same time, took Aristotle's substance to include intelligible numbers.

I would suggest, then, a different reading of the passage. Simplicius, or rather his source (Porphyry or Iamblichus), may be reporting Boethus' interpretation misleadingly. The first part of the fragment would thus contain not Boethus' view

---

36 Kalbfleisch (1907) *in app.* refers to Arist., *A.Post.* I.27, 87a36 (there Aristotle mentions the definition of the monad as οὐσία ἄθετος). Chase (2003), 147 n. 733 suggests that Simplicius' reference may instead be to Aristotle's lost *On the Good*: this hypothesis would be supported by the reference to the dyad in what follows.

about the intelligible monad and the sensible, but a view reported by Boethus and later rejected in his commentary. According to this view, Aristotle's division of categories can account for the distinction between the intelligible and the sensible monad: the former is a substance while the latter is a quantity or a relative. This reading is similar to that in Ps.-Archytas' treatise, where 'Man-in-itself' is said to receive Aristotle's first category, i.e. the τὸ τί ἐστιν κατὰ τὰν ἰδέαν. I would suggest that both readings have the same origin, i.e. the exegesis of Aristotle in Eudorus' circle.[37] If this is the case, Simplicius' words τοῦτο δὲ καὶ Ἀριστοτέλει δοκεῖ (Simpl., In Cat. 65.21) would ultimately reflect the position of Boethus' opponents, i.e. those interpreters who did not refrain from ascribing a theory of intelligible numbers to Aristotle (but it could indeed be the case that these words reflect Simplicius' position, influenced by Iamblichus' Pythagorising reading of the Categories). Boethus' second solution would actually be Boethus' response to this reading. So, if not according to Simplicius, at least according to Boethus' original argument, we should identify the subject of εἶναι ποσόν not as the sensible monad (as distinct from the intelligible and substantial one), but with the monad *as such*. Boethus would be rejecting the rival interpretation according to which there are two levels to the monad (a substantial level and a quantified or relative level): against this view, Boethus claims that the monad is nothing but a quantified item. This reading can perhaps explain a puzzling detail in this passage, i.e. Boethus' reference to the dyad. In order to show that the monad is a quantified item, Boethus actually says that whiteness is to white as the dyad is to two. We would rather expect a reference to the monad. But if Boethus is rejecting a Pythagorising interpretation of the categories, then his reference to the dyad acquires an interesting polemical nuance. For Boethus would indirectly be suggesting that there is actually no difference between the status of the monad and that of the dyad. Both are quantified items that stand to the predicates 'one' and 'two' in the same way as whiteness stands to the predicate 'white'. Far from endorsing a reading of Aristotle along Platonic-Pythagorean lines, Boethus would actually be rejecting such a reading.

I would tentatively suggest that the second interpretation – speculative as it undoubtedly is – is the correct one. Indeed, we are forced to suppose that Simplicius (or his source) actually misunderstood Boethus' original argument. But the passage acquires a more satisfying meaning, which can both account for the reference to the dyad and be consistent with Boethus' general interpretation of the Categories. If this is the case, Simplicius' arrangement of the text may be

---

37 According to Eudorus' outline of the Pythagorean doctrine of principles (Simpl., In Phys. 181.7–30 = 3O Boys-Stones), there exist two levels of principles. The highest level is that of the One, later called *archê* and God. The secondary level is that of the Monad and the Dyad, later specified as *stoicheia*, See Bonazzi (2013), 171–179. Boethus' argument would focus on the second level of Eudorus' metaphysics and would critically equate the status of the monad and that of the dyad: both of them would be somewhat ironically downplayed to the status of quantified items.

somewhat misleading. Boethus would not exactly be responding to the objections of those who found no place for the monad in Aristotle's system.[38] Rather, Boethus would be countering those who aimed to incorporate Aristotle's list of categories into a Pythagorean account of principles. To be more precise, I would suggest that those Pythagorising interpretations (by Eudorus or someone else) run more or less as follows. Aristotle's division of categories needs to be supplemented, since there is no mention in it of the monad. From this perspective, Aristotle's list is certainly insufficient. However, Aristotle's division can be adapted and therefore incorporated into the Pythagorean account of principles, since the intelligible monad is actually a substance and the sensible monad is a relative or a quantified item. In doing so, Eudorus and his followers possibly aimed to integrate Aristotle's categories, while at the same time showing the superiority of their metaphysical views. Boethus adopts the opposite approach, since he makes use of Aristotle's account of quantified items in order to downplay the status of Pythagorean principles (the monad and the dyad): as a matter of fact, these are nothing else than quantified items that correspond to predicates of sensible objects ('one', 'two').

If the present discussion is correct, during the first century BC Platonic and Peripatetic philosophers tried to revive the legacy of fourth-century BC philosophy and to build – from different philosophical perspectives – something like a common front of ancient philosophers against the Hellenistic schools. This does not mean, however, that Platonic and Peripatetic philosophers held the same positions, for their ways of reviving the ancient traditions were very different and even opposite. Eudorus and his followers aimed to show the superiority of their Platonic-Pythagorean metaphysics when integrating Aristotle's doctrines into it. Andronicus and Boethus, instead, stripped their references to Plato and the Academics of theological and metaphysical connotations. Furthermore, Boethus probably criticised some Pythagorising readings of Aristotle. Andronicus and Boethus' readings of Aristotle and their attitude to the previous tradition are best explained against this background and should not be assessed against the background of later discussions.[39]

---

38 My interpretation, then, is different from that in Griffin (2015), 122–124; 189 n. 34, who regards this passage as one of Boethus' replies to the 'Lucians' (i.e. the followers of Lucius), the Platonic-Pythagorean opponents of Aristotle, who found no place in Aristotle's system for the Monad. In his response, Boethus would be willing to acknowledge the reality of intelligible beings, such as intelligible numbers.

39 A fuller discussion of Boethus' passage on the Monad can be found in Chiaradonna (2020b). On Eudorus and the early reception of Aristotle's treatises, see also Chiaradonna (2019). I would like to thank the anonymous referee for some valuable comments on a previous draft of this chapter.

FRANCO FERRARI

È esistita un'eterodossia nel medioplatonismo?

Un campo di battaglia

All'interrogativo formulato nel titolo di questo contributo sembra inevitabile fornire una risposta inequivocabilmente negativa: nel medioplatonismo, ossia tra gli autori platonici che tra il I secolo a.C. e gli inizi del III secolo d.C. reagirono allo scetticismo imperante durante l'epoca ellenistica,[1] non si fece strada un atteggiamento eterodosso per la semplice ragione che nel corso di questa fase della storia del platonismo non prese forma una vera e propria ortodossia dottrinaria alla quale opporsi.

Come spesso accade, tuttavia, una simile risposta è ancora troppo generica e richiede alcune precisazioni, che queste pagine si propongono di fornire. Non c'è dubbio che durante l'arco di tempo che va da Antioco di Ascalona o da Eudoro di Alessandria, ossia i due autori che la storiografia è solita collocare agli inizi della reazione antiscettica, a Plotino non si affermò tra i platonici un sistema filosofico unitario e omogeneo, che potesse ambire a profilarsi come la versione ortodossa di questo indirizzo. La stessa chiusura dell'Accademia, intorno all'inizio del secondo decennio del I secolo a.C., finì per privare coloro che si professavano platonici di un importante punto di riferimento istituzionale.[2] Questa circostanza spiega, almeno in parte, quella proliferazione di immagini diverse e contrastanti della filosofia platonica che caratterizzò il periodo che divide il tramonto dello scetticismo accademico dalla composizione delle *Enneadi* di Plotino.

Quella medioplatonica fu dunque un'epoca segnata dalla presenza di platonismi diversi e spesso in aperto conflitto tra di loro. Se è vero infatti che quasi tutti gli autori platonici attivi in questo periodo furono accomunati dall'intento di

---

1 Sull'origine e sul significato storiografico della nozione di «medioplatonismo» cf. Donini (1982), 9–30.
2 Sulle vicende che portarono alla chiusura dell'Accademia e dunque all'interruzione della catena delle successioni rimane fondamentale Glucker (1978), 159–225, 330–356; cf. anche Donini (1982), 31–39.

trasformare la filosofia del maestro in un *sistema*, ossia di costruire (o ri-costruire) sulle macerie dello scetticismo accademico un impianto dottrinario unitario e coerente, è altrettanto vero che la realizzazione di un simile compito richiese il ricorso ad «alleati» esterni, che furono diversi nei vari autori. La conseguenza di una simile situazione fu che accanto a un platonismo di impronta stoicizzante, come quello propagandato da Antioco e poi da Attico, prese forma un platonismo disposto a recepire dottrine pitagoriche o pitagorizzanti, che ebbe in Eudoro il suo primo sostenitore e in Numenio il rappresentante più illustre e influente, e poi un platonismo incline ad accogliere concezioni aristoteliche, come quello sviluppato da Alcinoo, da Apuleio e da altri.[3] E a ben vedere, anche alcune tracce dei temi cari allo scetticismo continuarono, sia pure in forma tutto sommato marginale, a sopravvivere, come i casi di Plutarco e Favorino sembrano testimoniare.[4]

I secoli che precedettero la stesura delle *Enneadi* videro affrontarsi i platonici come in un «campo di battaglia», secondo la celebre immagine di Heinrich Dörrie.[5] Molti di loro, allo scopo di legittimare la propria interpretazione del pensiero del maestro, arrivarono a comporre scritti di «storiografia filosofica» nei quali ricostruivano una storia della tradizione che fosse omogenea a un determinato punto di vista filosofico. Così Antioco, in polemica con lo scetticismo probabilista di Filone e disgustato dalle tesi contenute nei «libri romani» di quest'ultimo, sostanziò il suo appello a *remigrare in domum veterem e nova* (Cic., Ac. post. 13 = Baust. 19.3 Dörrie-Baltes), ossia a tornare all'insegnamento dell'Accademia antica ancora non contaminato dallo scetticismo, attraverso una ricostruzione della storia del platonismo incline a enfatizzare le convergenze tra Platone, i primi Accademici, Aristotele e lo stoicismo, e a deprecare la svolta scettica impressa da Arcesilao.[6]

Sulla stessa linea di Antioco, ma con esiti molto più radicali, si mosse poco meno di due secoli dopo Numenio, il quale compose uno scritto dal significativo titolo *Sul distacco degli Accademici nei confronti di Platone* (Περὶ τῆς τῶν Ἀκαδημαϊκῶν πρὸς Πλάτωνα διαστάσεως), nel quale arrivava ad accusare tutti i successori di Platone, compresi i suoi immediati allievi, cioè Speusippo, Senocrate e Polemone, di essersi allontanati dall'insegnamento del maestro, ossia di

---

3 Sull'esistenza di immagini concorrenti della filosofia platonica cf. Donini (1994), 5030–5035 e Bonazzi (2015), 76–80. Sui reciproci influssi tra platonismo e stoicismo cf. Bonazzi/Helmig (2007); sulla tradizione del platonismo pitagorizzante si veda Bonazzi/Levy/Steel (2007); mentre sulla complessa vicenda del rapporto tra platonismo e aristotelismo è fondamentale Karamanolis (2006).

4 La sopravvivenza di elementi scettico-accademici nel medioplatonismo è stata indagata in maniera approfondita da Opsomer (1998).

5 Cf. Dörrie (1976); vedi anche Michalewski (2014), 31–45.

6 Sulla ricostruzione della storia della filosofia proposta da Antioco cf. Sedley (2012). Più in generale sulla tendenza a considerare il pensiero platonico come la fonte della filosofia successiva, in particolare di quella peripatetica e stoica, sono importanti le riflessioni di Boys-Stones (2001), 99–122.

averne tradito l'originaria eredità:[7] per Numenio costoro, pur non avendo ancora promosso una vera e propria svolta paragonabile a quella impressa da Arcesilao, sono responsabili di avere tradito la πρώτη διαδοχή di Platone, che era stato invece capace di comprendere pienamente e di valorizzare in maniera adeguata la dottrina di Pitagora, cui era così legato da giustificare il conio per lui del verbo «pitagorizzare», che significa appunto «fare filosofia secondo un'attitudine di matrice pitagorica»: ὁ δὲ Πλάτων πυθαγορίσας (fr. 24.57 des Places).

Nel dibattito relativo alla storia del platonismo non mancò chi tentò di propagandare un'immagine complessivamente unitaria dello sviluppo della scuola. Dopo Filone, la cui ricostruzione unitarista suscitò l'irritata reazione di Antioco, anche Plutarco propose uno schema storiografico nel quale la fase scettica non costituiva una soluzione di continuità nei confronti del periodo precedente. Il titolo di un suo scritto andato perduto, *Sul fatto che è una l'Accademia di Platone* (Περὶ τοῦ μίαν εἶναι τὴν τοῦ Πλάτωνος Ἀκαδημίαν: n. 63 Catalogo Lampria), manifesta gli intenti dell'autore, il quale doveva presumibilmente reclamare allo scetticismo accademico una certa continuità con alcuni motivi già presenti in Platone (la critica alle pretese conoscitive della sensazione, una certa cautela nei confronti della possibilità di accedere a una conoscenza sicura della sfera divina ecc.), premurandosi contemporaneamente di distinguere l'attitudine moderata dell'Accademia ellenistica dallo scetticismo radicale dei Pirroniani.[8]

Il quadro delle dispute sull'eredità di Platone e sulla legittimità delle affiliazioni con altri orientamenti si arricchì grazie alla stesura del celebre scritto di Attico, il quale si scagliò con toni veementi contro quei platonici che si servivano di Aristotele per interpretare Platone (Πρὸς τοὺς διὰ τῶν Ἀριστοτέλους τὰ Πλάτωνος ὑπισχνουμένους), rivendicando con energia l'assoluta irriducibilità del pensiero di Platone a quello del suo allievo.[9] È evidente che Attico opponeva la propria attitudine, ortodossa e fedele all'insegnamento platonico, all'eterodossia di coloro che avevano introdotto nel cuore del platonismo teoremi ad esso sostanzialmente estranei.

Questi pochi accenni alla produzione storiografica riconducibile agli autori medioplatonici[10] testimonia di quanto frastagliato fosse il quadro al cui interno essi si muovevano, ma dimostra anche quanto avvertita fosse la questione dell'eredità dell'insegnamento del maestro. Filosofi come Antioco, Attico e Numenio

---

7 Numen. fr. 24.5–16 des Places. Sullo scritto dedicato al distacco degli Accademici da Platone cf. Frede (1987), 1040–1050.
8 Sull'unitarismo storiografico di Plutarco cf. Bonazzi (2003), 213–236 e soprattutto Bonazzi (2012); utili riflessioni si trovano anche in Corti (2014), 184–198. Più in generale sul dibattito circa la natura dello scetticismo e la distinzione tra «accademici» e «pirroniani» si veda Tarrant (1985).
9 Sull'antiaristotelismo radicale di Attico cf. Karamanolis (2006), 150–179, il quale sembra tuttavia incline a ritenere che la formula riportata non corrispondesse al titolo dello scritto di Attico, ma semplicemente all'argomento in esso dibattuto.
10 Sulla produzione storiografica dei platonici cf. Baltes (1993), 243–250.

rivendicavano a se stessi il compito di restaurare la filosofia platonica, contro i guasti prodottisi nella tradizione (soprattutto accademica). Sebbene non venissero esplicitamente evocate, la nozione di «ortodossia», e quella complementare di «eterodossia», dovevano esercitare un peso rilevante all'interno di queste dispute. Del resto l'uso della categoria di «distacco», «allontanamento» (διάστασις) presupponeva in un autore come Numenio l'invito a ritornare alla forma ortodossa del pensiero di Platone, contro gli scivolamenti eterodossi dei successori, visti come eredi del tutto illegittimi.

Sembra dunque di poter dire che, sebbene il medioplatonismo non abbia prodotto nessuna forma di ortodossia dottrinaria, gli autori attivi in questo periodo reclamavano a sé il merito di avere compreso in maniera corretta l'insegnamento del maestro. Ciascuno di loro, in modo diverso e spesso in polemica con gli altri, pretendeva di ritornare all'autentica *doxa* di Platone, accusando, in forma esplicita o implicita, gli avversari di eterodossia.

La svolta dogmatica e l'eresia accademica

Si è già avuto modo di osservare che il denominatore che accomuna quasi tutti i platonici attivi nei primi secoli dell'epoca imperiale è rappresentato dall'opzione sistematica, dall'obiettivo cioè di restituire alla filosofia platonica il profilo sistematico che essa avrebbe avuto all'origine, ossia prima della parentesi scettica.[11]

Il raggiungimento di un simile obiettivo fu perseguito in forme e modi differenti, ma non c'è dubbio che autori come Antioco, Attico, Alcinoo, Numenio, Apuleio, Tauro, e per più di un aspetto anche Plutarco (il quale mantenne nei confronti dello scetticismo ellenistico un'attitudine molto più benevola), potevano vantare, ciascuno in modo autonomo, la realizzazione del programma appena menzionato. Attico, ad esempio, arrivò a reclamare con forza a Platone il merito di avere per primo ricondotto ad unità le parti della filosofia e di avere finalmente trasformato quest'ultima in un «corpo, cioè in un vivente completo» (fr. 1.19–23 des Places), vale a dire di avere costruito un edificio dottrinario completo, dal quale non mancava nulla (fr. 1.32–37).[12]

Uno dei modi attraverso i quali i filosofi medioplatonici, o almeno alcuni di loro, si proposero di sottolineare l'importanza del richiamo a Platone contro le deviazioni intervenute successivamente e di segnare una rottura nei confronti dell'interpretazione ellenistica fu rappresentato dalla scelta di sostituire la denominazione ἀπὸ τοῦ τόπου con quella ἀπὸ τοῦ διδασκάλου, definendosi non più ἀκαδημαϊκοί, aggettivo riservato agli interpreti scettici, bensì πλατωνικοί.[13]

---

11 Sul carattere sistematico della filosofia di Platone, la quale sarebbe già una forma di «platonismo», cf. Gerson (2013), 3–33.
12 Donini (1994), 5033; Ferrari (2001), 537–538, e Ferrari (2010), 55.
13 Si veda in proposito Glucker (1978), 206–225 e Bonazzi (2003), 208–211.

Non c'è dubbio che al programma di sistematizzare Platone e di presentarne la filosofia come un organismo unitario, coerente e soprattutto «dogmatico», ossia propositivo, sembrava opporre una tenace resistenza la natura stessa dei suoi scritti, che sono *dialoghi* e non trattati. Si tratta di opere spesso diverse per ambientazione drammatica e contenuto filosofico; molte delle quali presentano un profilo aperto, se non proprio aporetico; inoltre i personaggi che le animano sono tra loro diversi per doti morali e competenze intellettuali ed esprimono punti di vista filosofici tra loro irriducibili. Tutto ciò rende molto difficile il compito di individuare la posizione dell'autore, e perfino la sua attitudine filosofica.

Con la natura polifonica e straordinariamente diversificata dei dialoghi dovettero fare i conti tutti gli interpreti impegnati a sistematizzare Platone. Antioco dimostra di essere perfettamente consapevole di questa situazione quando riconosce che Platone *varius et multiplex et copiosus fuit.*[14] Non deve sorprendere la circostanza che alla polifonia degli scritti platonici e all'esito aporetico di molti di essi poterono appellarsi gli interpreti scettici dell'Accademia ellenistica per attribuire al fondatore della scuola un'attitudine antidogmatica.

Il compito che avevano di fronte i platonici «dogmatici», ossia la maggior parte dei filosofi medioplatonici, era dunque arduo. Ma ciò non significa che fosse destinato a un inevitabile naufragio, come del resto l'esito positivo di questo processo dimostra ampiamente. Autori come Plutarco, Attico, Numenio, Tauro, Arpocrazione, Albino, Severo, Alcinoo e Apuleio approntarono un raffinato complesso di tecniche esegetiche finalizzate a operare quella sistematizzazione di Platone cui essi ambivano. In effetti la filosofia del medioplatonismo si profila come sostanzialmente *philologisch orientierte*, vale a dire focalizzata intorno alla pratica del *commento*, diretto o indiretto, ai testi del maestro.[15] Solo per mezzo di un accurato lavoro esegetico operato sui testi, parve possibile dimostrare l'unità e la coerenza del pensiero contenuto nei dialoghi. Il giudizio con il quale Seneca lamentava la trasformazione della filosofia in filologia (*quae philosophia fuit facta philologia est*),[16] sebbene non si riferisse direttamente ai pensatori platonici, ad essi sembra certamente applicabile. Un simile rimprovero non si discosta da quello che, qualche tempo dopo, Plotino muoverà al «medioplatonico» Longino, colpevole di concentrarsi sul dettato del testo smarrendone l'autentico significato filosofico, di essere cioè φιλόλογος μέν ... φιλόσοφος δὲ οὐδαμῶς.[17]

Gli autori medioplatonici furono dunque coinvolti in un grandioso programma di sistematizzazione del pensiero di Platone, che essi attuarono in larga parte per mezzo dell'esegesi dei testi del maestro. Dall'assunzione di una simile attitudine conseguì quasi inevitabilmente l'attribuzione all'interpretazione

---

14 Cic., *Ac. post.* 17 = Baust. 21 Dörrie-Baltes. Cf. in proposito Baltes (1999b), 223-224.
15 Sull'importanza della pratica del commento si veda Barnes (1992) e soprattutto Baltes (1993), 162-226.
16 *Epist.* 108.23. Si veda quanto scrivo in Ferrari (2010), 71-73.
17 Porph., *Vita Plotini* 14.19-20. Cf. in proposito Maennlein-Robert (2001), 142-145 e Ferrari (2012a), 78-79.

scettico-aporetica di un profilo eterodosso. In effetti sembra di poter affermare che, se i filosofi medioplatonici non proposero un'unica interpretazione della filosofia di Platone e se di conseguenza non sarebbe affatto corretto parlare di una versione ortodossa del platonismo, essi furono accomunati, con la parziale eccezione di Plutarco (e forse dell'Anonimo commentatore del *Teeteto*),[18] dall'ostilità nei confronti dell'esegesi scettica, considerata una forma di *eterodossia*.

Prospettive divergenti

I medioplatonici non svilupparono dunque una concezione filosofica unitaria. Questo non significa però che non siano individuabili nei testi di questi autori alcune tendenze di fondo, declinate in maniera autonoma dai singoli pensatori. Sostanzialmente in tutti i platonici dei primi secoli dell'epoca imperiale si assiste a un rinnovato interesse per la dimensione della trascendenza e in generale per i temi metafisici. Ugualmente diffusa sembra poi la tendenza ad accentuare la centralità del motivo teologico nei confronti di quello squisitamente ontologico. La primarietà generalmente attribuita alla divinità demiurgica (o meta-demiurgica) costituisce senza dubbio uno degli aspetti nei quali questa tendenza prese forma. Alla medesima impostazione sembra riconducibile la propensione a subordinare le idee alla divinità, sebbene questa subordinazione non assunse sempre, come invece si tende erroneamente a credere, la forma della concezione delle idee come «pensieri di dio» (e quest'ultimo aspetto rappresenta un ulteriore indizio dell'assenza di una vera e propria ortodossia dottrinaria).[19] Anche la tendenza a costruire modelli ontologici di tipo gerarchico, nei quali la contrapposizione platonica tra la sfera trascendente e quella sensibile è arricchita dall'introduzione di livelli intermedi (si pensi alle forme immanenti, agli enti matematici, ai demoni ecc.),[20] presenta un certo grado di diffusione tra i medioplatonici, così come il tentativo di collegare la teoria dei principi (Uno e Diade indeterminata), attribuita a Platone dalla tradizione indiretta, alla concezione delle cause ricavabile dai dialoghi e in particolare dal *Timeo*.

In generale i motivi appena richiamati convergono nel decretare il ruolo fondamentale giocato dal *Timeo*, che fu indubbiamente il dialogo intorno al quale si focalizzò il programma di sistematizzazione della filosofia platonica promosso da questi autori.[21] Accanto al *Timeo*, che poteva vantare in forma quasi immediata

---

18 Cf. Anon., *In Theaet*. 54.38–55.13, dove l'autore arriva a sostenere che anche gli Accademici, ossia gli scettici, avrebbero professato «dottrine» (δόγματα) e che dunque esiste un'unica Accademia. Si veda su questo importante testo Bastianini/Sedley (1995), 539–541.
19 Sui principali caratteri della metafisica e della teologia medioplatonica mi permetto di rinviare a Ferrari (2015). Sulla concezione medioplatonica delle idee come «pensieri di dio» cf. Dillon (2011) e Michalewski (2014), 69–96.
20 Sulla demonologia medioplatonica cf. Timotin (2012), 99–241.
21 Sulle ragioni della preminenza di questo dialogo rinvio a Ferrari (2012b), 85–89.

un profilo sistematico, soprattutto in ragione dell'impianto monologico che ne caratterizza l'andamento, gli interpreti medioplatonici si concentrarono sul VI libro (e in misura minore sul X) della *Repubblica*, su alcune sezioni del *Sofista* e del *Politico*, sul *Simposio*, sulla psicologia contenuta in dialoghi quali il *Fedone* e il *Fedro*, sul X libro delle *Leggi*, oltre che su alcuni passaggi del *Parmenide* e delle *Lettere II, VI* e *VII*.[22]

Le principali questioni intorno alle quali ruotò il dibattito filosofico di questo periodo attengono ai rapporti tra l'intelletto demiurgico, l'idea del bene e il mondo delle idee e in generale all'articolazione interna della sfera trascendente, all'esistenza di un principio attivo del male e del disordine, al tema della provvidenza (e del determinismo), ai generi di vita, alla legittimità di integrare la logica e alcuni aspetti della fisica di Aristotele nel sistema platonico, e naturalmente al problema della natura della generazione dell'universo descritta nel *Timeo*. A proposito di molte di queste topiche non si può parlare di ortodossia e di eterodossia, perché i medioplatonici assunsero punti di vista diversi, senza che nessuno di essi arrivasse a imporsi in forma veramente egemone, tanto da venire considerato «ortodosso». Vale la pena menzionare alcuni esempi.

Un tema sul quale gli autori platonici procedettero in ordine abbastanza sparso è quello del rapporto tra il demiurgo del *Timeo*, concepito come un intelletto divino, e l'idea del bene della *Repubblica*. Alla cosiddetta *konservative Richtung des mittleren Platonismus*, testimoniata da Plutarco e Attico, i quali identificarono il bene e l'intelletto demiurgico ammettendo una sola divinità dotata di funzioni efficienti, paradigmatiche e teleologiche, si oppose il punto di vista di coloro che, come Alcinoo e in misura più netta Numenio, distinsero chiaramente l'idea del bene, identificata con il primo dio e il primo intelletto (e l'Uno), e il demiurgo, concepito come secondo dio e secondo intelletto.[23] Nessuna delle due opinioni si impose chiaramente sull'altra tanto da meritarsi l'etichetta di «ortodossa», ma non c'è dubbio che mentre l'identificazione del demiurgo con il bene sembra esprimere un certo conservatorismo esegetico, la posizione di un autore come Numenio precorre modelli gerarchici destinati a imporsi nel neoplatonismo e

---

22 Le testimonianze relative ai dialoghi direttamente interessati dall'attività esegetica dei platonici sono raccolte da Baltes (1993), Baust. 78–81.
23 In Plutarco l'identificazione (implicita o esplicita) tra la divinità demiurgica e il bene (o la totalità del paradigma eidetico) è presupposta in *Is. et Os.* 372E-F, 373E-F, *Def. orac.* 435F–436F, *De E* 393A–C, *Ser. num. vind.* 550D ecc.; Attico identifica esplicitamente il demiurgo e il bene in fr. 12 des Places; Numenio articola il suo modello gerarchico fondato sulla distinzione tra l'idea del bene (primo dio, primo intelletto e demiurgo dell'essere) e il demiurgo (secondo dio, secondo intelletto e demiurgo della generazione) in frr. 11.11–14, 12.1–14, 15.1–5, 16.1–12, 17.1–8, 19.8–13, 21.1–10, 22.1–5 ecc. Per un quadro generale della questione rinvio a Opsomer (2005), 51–56, 73–83, 87–96 e Ferrari (2015), 323–329; sulla posizione di Attico cf. Zambon (2002), 159–160 e ora Michalewski (2014), 75–78; su Numenio si veda Frede (1987), 1054–1070, Müller (2011), 60–67 e ancora Zambon (2002), 221–230. La formula *die konservative Richtung des mittleren Platonismus* è dovuta a Baltes (1999a), 84.

può dunque considerarsi tendenzialmente più incline a una certa audacia interpretativa.[24]

L'assunzione di un approccio differente nei confronti dell'esistenza di una gerarchia di entità divine si riverbera nel modo in cui Numenio e Plutarco interpretano il celebre passo di *Timeo*, 28c3–5, dove il personaggio principale del dialogo riconosce la difficoltà di trovare l'artefice e il padre di questo universo, e addirittura l'impossibilità di parlarne a tutti: τὸν μὲν οὖν ποιητὴν καὶ πατέρα τοῦδε τοῦ παντὸς εὑρεῖν τε ἔργον καὶ εὑρόντα εἰς πάντας ἀδύνατον λέγειν. I due autori medioplatonici fornirono spiegazioni radicalmente diverse del significato dei due appellativi presenti nel testo platonico, ossia πατήρ e ποιητής, che entrambi, comunque, misero in relazione alla sfera divina, cui a ben vedere non si fa però menzione nel passo: per Numenio essi si riferiscono rispettivamente al primo dio, cioè all'idea del bene (πατήρ), e al secondo dio, vale a dire al demiurgo (ποιητής); viceversa Plutarco ritiene che essi indichino due attività del medesimo dio, che sarebbe «artefice» del corpo cosmico e «padre» dell'anima del mondo.[25]

Anche a proposito della teoria dei principi e delle cause la situazione appare piuttosto fluida e non sarebbe sensato pretendere di indicare una versione per così dire canonica. La convinzione, piuttosto diffusa tra gli studiosi, che la cosiddetta «dottrina dei tre principi», ossia dio–idee–materia, costituì la concezione standard nel medioplatonismo andrebbe abbandonata o quantomeno assai relativizzata. Essa conosce la sua formulazione canonica nel *Didascalicus* di Alcinoo e nel *De Platone et eius dogmate* di Apuleio, e si ritrova con significative varianti in Attico e Plutarco, i quali tuttavia propongono solitamente una teoria delle cause e dei principi differente, incentrata oltre che su dio (che incorpora le idee) e sulla materia anche sull'anima precosmica irrazionale.[26] In altri autori, come Eudoro, Numenio e nella stessa fonte di Seneca (*Epist.* 65.2–10 = 116.2 Dörrie-Baltes),

---

24 Per una recente analisi del *dossier* mi permetto di rinviare a Ferrari (2020).
25 Numen. fr. 21 des Places (Baust. 197.4 Dörrie-Baltes) e Plut., *Plat. quaest.* II.1001B–C (202 Dörrie-Baltes). Per un esame più dettagliato delle interpretazioni del passo platonico devo rimandare a Ferrari (2014b), in cui si trovano anche gli opportuni riferimenti bibliografici.
26 Alcin., *Didasc.* 163.11–14 (Baust. 113.3 Dörrie-Baltes); Apul., *De Platone*, 190 (123.2 Dörrie-Baltes); in Plut., *Quaest. Conv.* VIII.2, 720A–C (110.1 Dörrie-Baltes) la teoria dei tre principi (presentata come una διαίρεσις ricavata dal *Timeo*) emerge in maniera piuttosto bizzarra come soluzione 'matematica' all'interrogativo sul perché Platone sia solito geometrizzare. La concezione 'canonica' di Plutarco, ripresa poi da Attico (fr. 23 des Places), fa invece appello all'ipotesi dell'anima precosmica irrazionale, che forma insieme alla materia e a dio (che incorpora in sé anche il mondo delle idee) la triade dei principi e delle cause della realtà (cf. per esempio *An. procr.* 1015A–B = 114.1 Dörrie-Baltes, *Is. et Os.* 370E–371A = 114.2 Dörrie-Baltes). Sulle differenti versioni della teoria dei principi cf. Baltes (1996), 387–489; sulla complessa articolazione della concezione medioplatonica delle cause si veda Ferrari (2014c); sulla teoria dei tre principi di Apuleio (dio-materia-idee) cf. Moreschini (2015), 219–259; sulla concezione dell'anima precosmica irrazionale sostenuta da Plutarco e Attico si veda Deuse (1983), 12–43, 51–61 e Ferrari (2014a), 258–265; infine sulla teoria dei principi di Attico cf. Zambon (2002), 142–151.

vengono presentate dottrine sostanzialmente diverse rispetto a quella che si è soliti considerare come ortodossa.

Strettamente connesso alla dottrina dei principi e delle cause dovette poi essere il dibattito intorno alla questione dell'origine del male, al quale presero parte autori come Plutarco, Attico, Numenio, Massimo di Tiro ecc. Anche in questo caso non sembra emergere un punto di vista canonico, sebbene la tendenza ad attribuire genericamente alla materia la causa del male si impose, forse in forma implicita, nella maggioranza dei platonici dell'epoca. È proprio in polemica contro una simile posizione, la quale finisce per assegnare a un'entità priva di qualità (ἄποιος) come la materia la causa del male, Plutarco introdusse l'ipotesi dell'anima precosmica irrazionale, che sconvolge la materia prima dell'intervento cosmopoietico del demiurgo. L'origine del disordine e dunque del male viene individuata da Plutarco (e dopo di lui da Attico e in misura più oscillante da Numenio) nel movimento caotico prodotto dall'anima precosmica, vale a dire quella stessa anima alla quale Platone avrebbe accennato nel X libro delle *Leggi*.[27]

La posizione di Plutarco e Attico fu parzialmente accolta da Numenio, il quale sembra in effetti avere ricondotto l'origine del male non alla materia bensì alla *anima silvae*, vale a dire all'anima della materia. Essa tuttavia non si impose tra i platonici dell'epoca (Massimo di Tiro riconduce la causa del male prevalentemente al πάθος ὕλης), e fu senz'altro respinta da Plotino, il quale nel trattato I.8 tornò a individuare nella materia l'origine primaria del male.[28] Le riflessioni di Plotino sono profonde e originali e non possono venire collocate sullo stesso piano delle proposte avanzate dagli autori medioplatonici. Non c'è comunque dubbio che neppure la questione dell'origine del male ammetteva tra i platonici attivi prima di Plotino una risposta univoca e canonica.

Gli esempi che possono confermare l'assenza nel platonismo medio di una vera e propria ortodossia dottrinaria sono davvero molti e non sarebbe ragionevole menzionarli tutti. Del resto la stessa condizione istituzionale di questo indirizzo filosofico, vale a dire il venire meno di una scuola ufficiale, rendeva di per sé difficile l'instaurazione di una dottrina ortodossa.[29]

---

27 Plut., *An. procr.* 1014D–1015F; Attic. fr. 23 des Places. Sulla dottrina dell'origine del male di Plutarco cf. Jourdan (2014a). Sulla connessione precosmica tra materia e anima irrazionale rimando ancora a Ferrari (2014a), 258–265.
28 L'accenno all'anima della materia (*anima silvae*) è attestato per Numenio in fr. 52.92–93 des Places; Plotino ha dedicato al tema del male l'*Enn.* I.8, dal titolo *Quali sono e da dove vengono i mali*. Sulla dottrina di Numenio cf. Jourdan (2014b); mentre sul trattato di Plotino si vedano Schäfer (2002), 51–167 e la discussione di O'Meara (2005).
29 Anche in un settore della filosofia medioplatonica caratterizzato da un quadro dottrinario generalmente più unitario come l'etica (incentrata intorno alla ripresa della psicologia tripartita platonico-aristotelica, alla concezione della μετριοπάθεια e alla dottrina del τέλος come ὁμοίωσις θεῷ), non mancarono opzioni autonome, spesso legate alla ricezione di motivi provenienti da altre tradizioni, in particolare quella stoica (Antioco e Attico) e pitagorica (Eudoro). Sui differenti orientamenti dell'etica medioplatonica cf. Linguiti (2015).

La *querelle* intorno alla natura della generazione dell'universo: l'eterodossia di Plutarco

Esiste tuttavia una questione a proposito della quale sembra effettivamente essersi formata un'opinione consolidata, in grado forse di ambire a venire considerata come ortodossa. Così dovette almeno apparire a un suo avversario come Plutarco, il quale all'inizio del trattato *De animae procreatione in Timaeo* giustifica la stessa stesura dello scritto appellandosi all'esigenza di opporsi alla posizione della maggioranza dei platonici (1012B). Come si sarà certamente intuito, si tratta del problema della generazione del cosmo e dell'anima descritta nel *Timeo*, vale a dire della questione che più ha coinvolto gli esegetici antichi di Platone, tanto da giustificare la celebre affermazione di Matthias Baltes, secondo il quale «keine andere Frage hat die Interpreten des *Timaios* so stark bewegt wie die, ob Platon in seinem Spätdialog eine reale Schöpfung der Welt lehre oder nicht».[30]

I termini della questione sono fin troppo noti perché valga la pena riprenderli analiticamente in questa sede. Basterà ricordare che gli allievi di Platone si divisero subito tra i sostenitori di un'interpretazione letterale e temporale del racconto di Timeo e i fautori di un'esegesi metaforica e didascalica: per i primi, tra i quali va annoverato Aristotele, le parole di Platone vanno prese alla lettera e indicano che l'universo ha avuto un inizio «temporale», è sorto cioè in virtù di un atto istantaneo, unico e circoscritto (tesi che ad Aristotele appare del tutto inaccettabile); mentre per i secondi, tra i quali si segnalano Speusippo, Senocrate e poi Crantore, la descrizione della «generazione» del cosmo rappresenta un artificio attraverso il quale Platone ha inteso, per esigenze didattiche (διδασκαλίας χάριν) e di chiarezza (σαφηνείας ἕνεκα), esporre in forma temporale, cioè come se si trattasse di un «evento» (o di una serie di eventi), la condizione ontologica dell'universo, che risulta «generato» (γενητός) non perché ha avuto un inizio temporale, bensì perché rappresenta un'entità soggetta al divenire (un γιγνόμενον), e dipendente da un sistema di cause e di principi.[31]

All'epoca in cui Plutarco compose il *De animae procreatione* l'esegesi didascalico-metaforica, forse minoritaria durante l'ellenismo, dovette avere ormai preso il sopravvento, se l'autore si lamenta proprio della circostanza che i commentatori più degni di stima, sia tra coloro che avevano accolto l'interpretazione numerica della struttura dell'anima del mondo avanzata da Senocrate, sia tra coloro che avevano accettato l'esegesi epistemologica proposta da Crantore, ritengono che tanto l'anima quanto il corpo del mondo non hanno avuto un vero e proprio inizio, ossia un'origine, ma costituiscono realtà eterne, e che Platone ne ha descritto in forma temporale la nascita per esigenze espositive (θεωρίας ἕνεκα), vale a dire allo scopo di renderne più chiara la costituzione ontologica (*An. procr.* 1013A–B).

---

30 Baltes (1976), 1. Sul dibattito relativo al significato della cosmogenesi esposta nel *Timeo* cf. da ultimo Petrucci (2015), cui si rinvia anche per gli aggiornamenti bibliografici.
31 Un'accurata ricostruzione di questo dibattito viene fornita da Centrone (2012).

È probabile che l'affermazione dell'esegesi didattico-metaforica sia dovuta all'influenza esercitata dal commento di Eudoro di Alessandria, il quale costituisce anche la principale fonte da cui Plutarco ricavò le informazioni relative alle interpretazioni precedenti. Ad ogni modo i termini con cui Plutarco presenta la questione inducono a ritenere che l'esegesi didascalica della cosmogenesi e della psicogenesi del *Timeo* rappresentasse ormai una sorta di dogma accettato dalla maggioranza dei platonici dell'epoca. Egli scrive infatti:

Ὅ γε μὴν οὗτοί τε κοινῇ καὶ οἱ πλεῖστοι τῶν χρωμένων Πλάτωνι φοβούμενοι καὶ παραμυθούμενοι πάντα μηχανῶνται καὶ παραβιάζονται καὶ στρέφουσιν, ὥς τι δεινὸν καὶ ἄρρητον οἰόμενοι δεῖν περικαλύπτειν καὶ ἀρνεῖσθαι, τήν τε τοῦ κόσμου τήν τε τῆς ψυχῆς αὐτοῦ γένεσιν καὶ σύστασιν, οὐκ ἐξ ἀιδίου συνεστώτων οὐδὲ τὸν ἄπειρον χρόνον οὕτως ἐχόντων.

> In ogni caso, costoro [scil.: Senocrate e Crantore], unitamente alla maggior parte di quelli che studiano Platone, temono fino ad esserne sconvolti un punto, e perciò manipolano, forzano e capovolgono tutte le cose, pensando appunto di dovere nascondere e negare qualcosa di terribile e indicibile, vale a dire il carattere generato e composto del cosmo e della sua anima, che non esistono dall'eternità e non si trovano nello stato presente per un tempo infinito. (*An. procr.* 1013E).

Plutarco sembra dunque perfettamente consapevole dell'eccentricità della sua interpretazione, la quale si oppone a un punto di vista così diffuso e consolidato da apparire ormai ortodosso. E in effetti nel corso del trattato egli è costretto a ricorrere a tutte le sue qualità esegetiche e a un'invidiabile conoscenza dei testi platonici per tentare di propagandare l'esegesi letterale del racconto contenuto nel *Timeo*, per sostenere cioè che, secondo Platone, il cosmo (e la sua anima) è generato (Περὶ τοῦ γεγονέναι κατὰ Πλάτωνα τὸν κόσμον), per menzionare il titolo di un suo scritto andato perduto (n. 66 Catalogo di Lampria). Opponendosi all'ortodossia eternalista, Plutarco si propone di ristabilire la corretta esegesi di Platone, ossia di ripristinare l'autentica «ortodossia» platonica.

Lo sforzo di Plutarco non dovette risultare completamente vano, se qualche decennio dopo di lui un altro medioplatonico, Lucio Calveno Tauro, si sentì in dovere di comporre un commento al *Timeo* (ὑπόμνημα εἰς τὸν Τίμαιον), finalizzato a raccogliere, riformulare e codificare i principali argomenti in favore dell'esegesi didascalico-metaforica, evidentemente messa in discussione dagli scritti plutarchei. Il commento di Tauro è andato perduto, ma i frammenti disponibili, per lo più conservati nello scritto *De aeternitate mundi* (*Contra Proclum*) del filosofo neoplatonico cristiano Giovanni Filopono, ci consentono di acquisire un'idea abbastanza precisa delle tesi contenute nell'opera.[32]

---

32 La più recente raccolta dei frammenti e delle testimonianze relativi a Tauro si trova in appendice di Petrucci (2018).

Non è possibile in questa sede esporre nel dettaglio gli argomenti «eternalisti» proposti da Tauro, molti dei quali riprendono tesi già avanzate da Senocrate, Crantore e forse Eudoro.[33] Vale però la pena spendere due parole su uno dei motivi (αἰτίαι) che, secondo Tauro, indussero Platone a presentare in forma temporale la generazione del cosmo, sebbene egli fosse certo della sua eternità. Si tratta della devozione (εὐσέβεια) nei confronti della divinità, e in particolare del riconoscimento dell'esistenza della provvidenza: secondo Tauro, Platone era consapevole del fatto che la maggioranza degli uomini non è in grado di comprendere l'esistenza di una relazione causale, se quest'ultima non viene formulata in termini temporali, cioè in modo che la causa preceda temporalmente l'effetto (αἴτιον τὸ προτεροῦν χρόνῳ); ma il mancato riconoscimento della causalità divina finisce per determinare la negazione della provvidenza, vale a dire dell'azione di dio nei confronti del cosmo; per questo motivo Tauro attribuisce a Platone la decisione di esprimere in forma temporale, ossia secondo la scansione πρότερον/ὕστερον, rapporti di dipendenza di natura ontologica (e non temporale). In altre parole Platone avrebbe per esigenze di chiarezza espositiva temporalizzato relazioni tra entità simultanee, ma caratterizzate da una relazione di priorità/posteriorità ontologica. Filopono ricostruisce nei seguenti termini il ragionamento di Tauro:

> Sapendo infatti che i più considerano causa soltanto ciò che è anteriore nel tempo (αἴτιον τὸ προτεροῦν χρόνῳ) e non credono nell'esistenza di una causa di diverso tipo, e che da questo deriva il pericolo che essi si oppongano all'esistenza della provvidenza, Platone, volendo difendere la dottrina secondo la quale il cosmo è retto dalla provvidenza, fa comprendere tacitamente a coloro che sono in grado di intendere anche in diverso modo che il cosmo non è generato nel tempo (ἀγένητος ὁ κόσμος κατὰ χρόνον), mentre a coloro che ne sono incapaci spiega che esso è generato, e prega che essi vi credano, perché abbiano fede al tempo stesso anche nella provvidenza.[34]

Tauro attribuisce a Platone la decisione di affidare all'espediente narrativo (μῦθος) il compito di trasferire sul piano temporale rapporti di dipendenza di natura ontologica. Anticipando un'attitudine tipica dell'ermeneutica neoplatonica, egli presuppone la distinzione tra due tipi di lettori, l'uno filosoficamente profondo, in grado di comprendere relazioni complesse, cioè rapporti di dipendenza metafisica (anche se non formulati in termini temporali), l'altro superficiale e filosoficamente più ingenuo, capace di cogliere la dipendenza metafisica solo se espressa in forma di anteriorità/posterità temporale.

---

33 Per una presentazione generale dello scritto di Tauro e per una valutazione della consistenza dei suoi argomenti in favore dell'interpretazione eternalista della cosmogonia platonica è fondamentale Petrucci (2018), 26–75; si veda anche Ferrari (2014d). Sull'esegesi di Tauro resta imprescindibile Baltes (1976), 105–121.

34 Philop., Aet. Mundi 187.6–15 Rabe = Test. 23 B Lakmann = T. 27 Petrucci = Baust. 138.2 Dörrie-Baltes. Su questo fondamentale documento si veda il commento di Baltes (1998), 428–435; cf. anche Ferrari (2014d), 329–330.

Vale la pena osservare che anche i sostenitori dell'interpretazione temporale della cosmogenesi si appellavano al tema della provvidenza, sostenendo che l'unico atteggiamento in grado di salvaguardarne la presenza nel cosmo consiste nell'ammettere che quest'ultimo rappresenta il prodotto di un atto demiurgico reale, espressione della provvidenza della divinità.[35]

Non c'è dubbio che il commento al *Timeo* di Tauro esercitò un'influenza enorme nel dibattito sull'interpretazione della cosmologia platonica e giocò un ruolo decisivo nell'affermazione dell'esegesi metaforica, che tra i filosofi neoplatonici pagani venne accolta in maniera sostanzialmente unanime. Quello di autori come Plutarco, Attico e Severo fu forse l'ultimo tentativo di arginare la corrente eternalista, inaugurata da Senocrate e Crantore, rilanciata da Eudoro e codificata in via quasi definitiva da Tauro. Ma anche in questo caso è difficile dire se l'esegesi metaforica del racconto di *Timeo* e l'attribuzione a Platone di una cosmologia eternalista costituisse tra i filosofi medioplatonici una tesi veramente ortodossa. Quello che possiamo affermare è che in questi termini essa fu recepita, e per questo accanitamente combattuta, da Plutarco.

Conclusioni

Il quadro dottrinario del platonismo medio si presenta, come si è cercato di mostrare nelle pagine precedenti, quanto mai fluido. Accanto ad alcune tendenze di fondo presero forma opzioni personali che rendono di fatto impossibile individuare una vera e propria ortodossia filosofica.

In un importante saggio risalente alla fine del secolo scorso Matthias Baltes, allora il più autorevole studioso del platonismo antico, si propose di dimostrare che dalla dottrina dell'immortalità dell'anima, accolta da tutti i filosofi platonici, è possibile dedurre alcuni «dogmi» fondamentali, i quali definirebbero i contorni di una sorta di ortodossia del platonismo antico (del medio e soprattutto del neoplatonismo).[36] Secondo Baltes, dalla concezione della immaterialità e dell'immortalità dell'anima si possono ricavare in particolare a) la tesi della libertà dell'anima contro il determinismo stoico; b) la dottrina dell'eternità dell'universo; c) la concezione dell'anima come viandante cosmico e meta-cosmico; d) la gerarchizzazione della realtà; e) la collocazione metafisica delle idee.

Rinuncio in questa sede a riportare gli argomenti attraverso i quali Baltes corrobora la sua tesi, limitandomi però a constatare a) che l'opzione eternalista non è stata accolta in maniera unanime dai filosofi platonici; b) che la gerarchizzazione della realtà, certamente comune a molti medioplatonici, presenta nei vari autori declinazioni differenti (basti pensare all'esistenza o meno di una distinzione tra il

---

35 Cf., per esempio, Attic. fr. 4 des Places. Sull'implicazione in Attico tra provvidenzialismo e interpretazione temporale della generazione dell'universo cf. Zambon (2002), 152–153 e soprattutto Michalewski (2014), 84–86.
36 Baltes (1999b), 235–241.

primo e il secondo dio); c) che la collocazione delle idee costituisce un problema destinato a venire risolto in via definitiva solo da Plotino con la sua celebre concezione dell'insediamento delle idee nell'intelletto (*Enn.* V.5). L'ipotesi di Baltes dunque descrive bene la situazione del neoplatonismo, mentre non sembra adattarsi completamente anche agli autori medioplatonici.

Queste ultime considerazioni intendono confermare quanto arduo, e probabilmente destinato a un inevitabile naufragio, sia ogni tentativo di individuare un medioplatonismo ortodosso al quale si sarebbe contrapposta una linea eterodossa. L'assenza di un'istituzione ufficiale incoraggiò certamente la proliferazione di immagini diverse e contrapposte della filosofia platonica.

Come si è visto, non mancarono tendenze condivise che accomunarono molti degli autori platonici attivi da Antioco a Plotino. Ma non si affermò una vera e propria ortodossia dottrinaria, perché mancarono forse le condizioni, interne ed esterne, per il verificarsi di un simile fenomeno. Su alcune questioni, come abbiamo visto, alcuni autori presentarono il loro pensiero come una reazione a una determinata *communis opinio* affermatasi tra i platonici dell'epoca: è il caso di Plutarco (e Attico) a proposito dell'interpretazione didascalico-metaforica della cosmogenesi del *Timeo*, cui essi opposero le ragioni del letteralismo. Anche la vivace polemica di Attico contro i platonici inclini a integrare concezioni aristoteliche all'interno del sistema platonico testimonia che questa tendenza doveva essere certamente diffusa. In generale, tuttavia, nelle dispute filosofiche gli autori medioplatonici non sembrano presupporre l'esistenza di una dottrina ortodossa, da confermare o eventualmente da respingere, quanto piuttosto quella di una corretta interpretazione dei testi del maestro contro i fraintendimenti nei quali sono incorsi i rivali.

Del resto la straordinaria ricchezza del pensiero filosofico di Platone è forse la causa prima di quella proliferazione di immagini contrastanti che ha attraversato i primi secoli della nostra èra.

TEUN TIELEMAN

Galen on Disagreement

Sects, Philosophical Methods and Christians

Introduction

The doctor-cum-philosopher Galen of Pergamum (129–c. 213 CE) disagreed with many people on many things. He devoted separate treatises to refuting particular philosophers or doctors, e.g. the Academic philosopher Favorinus of Arelate (in his *On the Best Method of Teaching*) and the doctors Lycus and Julian.[1] His taste for controversy furnishes one of the principles of arrangement in his bio-bibliography *On My Own Books*: we have sections listing many treatises (most of them lost) against the Hellenistic doctor and medical scientist Erasistratus of Ceos (ch. X), the Empiricists, a medical school or sect (ch. XII), the Methodist school of medicine (ch. XIII), as well as the Stoics (ch. XIII). But there are more examples. In his great work *On the Doctrines of Hippocrates and Plato* he vindicates Plato's tripartite model of the mind (which he also ascribes to Hippocrates) through a broadside against Stoic 'monist' psychology in no less than five books. Sideswipes are also ubiquitous in expository or constructive treatises. Unsurprisingly, he has been called a controversialist.[2] But his acrimony should not be dismissed as a less attractive trait of his character. Rather, it reflects a particular factor at play: the traditional 'identity politics' pursued in both philosophy and medicine, with schools defining themselves in opposition to their competitors no less than through self-presentation. We may consider here the polemical treatises composed by Plutarch against the Stoics and Epicurus or the evidence for philosophical invective and indeed slander to be found in the pages of Diogenes Laertius–styles of posturing and arguing that go back to the time when the phenomenon of schools emerged, esp. the early Hellenistic period (3rd century BCE). Seen in the proper historical light, then, Galen's critical attitude becomes more comprehensible and less exceptional, given his wish to carve out a

---

1 *Opt. Doctr.* I.40–52 Kühn (hereafter K.), later published by A. Barigazzi in *Corpus Medicorum Graecorum* series (hereafter *CMG*) V.1.1; *Adv. Lyc.* XVIIIA.196–245 and *Adv. Iul.* XVIIIA.246–299 K., both later published in *CMG* V.10.3 (E. Wenkebach).
2 Hankinson (2008), XV.

Dealing with Disagreement, ed. by Albert Joosse and Angela Ulacco, Monothéismes et Philosophie, 33 (Turnhout: Brepols, 2022), pp. 45–58
BREPOLS ❧ PUBLISHERS   10.1484/M.MON-EB.5.132747
This is an open access article made available under a CC BY-NC 4.0 International License.

niche for himself in both philosophy and medicine, by combining these two fields in a special way. There is moreover another, harmonizing side to the way in which he positions himself. Galen projects into the past a tradition of good medicine and philosophy that has Hippocrates and Plato as its fountainheads.[3] Scientific and moral progress consists in further developing the insights from this grand tradition, to which – Galen argues – medical scientists and philosophers from various periods and schools have contributed.[4] His criticism therefore concerns those who fall outside this tradition, such as Epicurus and Thessalus of Tralles, the founder of the Methodist school of medicine. Galen's syncretic project can be characterized as an attempt to overcome the division of both philosophy and medicine into schools or sects (*haireseis*).[5] Galen refuses to adhere to any one school, presenting himself as an independent-minded eclectic who feels free to select from each school what he deems best.[6] His attitude comes with an insistence on scientific demonstration and with a firm rejection of the authority principle.[7] This makes Galen a fascinating observer and critic of the phenomenon of schools in the Greco-Roman world, with its characteristic distinction between orthodoxy and heterodoxy in relation to both past and present. This chapter considers the ways in which Galen justifies his own position and criticizes what he sees as the sectarian behaviour of others, including – most interestingly –, Jews and Christians.

The lamentable phenomenon of sects: its nature and a possible remedy

A passage from Galen's bio-bibliography *On My Own Books* brings together several features of Galen's position on sectarian divisions. Although it is anatomy and medical schools that are at issue here, what he says is, *mutatis mutandis*, also applicable to philosophical schools. The context is a chapter (I) in which Galen discusses the works he wrote during his first stay in Rome (162–166 CE). When

---

[3] Vegetti (1986) and Tieleman (1996), xxviii–xxxvii.
[4] See Hankinson (1994).
[5] On the idea of sects and on medical sects see Von Staden (1988).
[6] On Galen's eclecticism see Hankinson (1992), Tieleman (1996), xvii–xxi, and Asmis (2014); on ancient eclecticism in general see Donini (1988) and Hatzmichali (2011).
[7] On Galen's rejection of authority in science and philosophy see Walzer (1949), Tieleman (1986), 16–17, 21–23, and Tieleman (2010), esp. 130, 140; cf. Flemming (2017). Galen classed the mere appeal to witnesses such as authoritative thinkers or poets as a 'rhetorical' practice, foreign to scientific procedure (using Aristotle's term ἔνδοξα): see *PHP* III.3.8–9, 10–11; II.4.3 (offering a fourfold classification: demonstrative, dialectical, rhetorical and sophistical premises or arguments), with Tieleman (1986), 12–23. On the role actually played by authority in ancient philosophy see Sedley (1989) and the studies collected more recently in Bryan/Wardy/Warren (2018) and (on the Platonist tradition in particular) Erler/Heßler/Petrucci (2021); cf. also Opsomer/Ulacco (2016).

Galen was making his mark as an anatomist, he attracted the attention of an adherent of the school of Erasistratus of Ceos (active in Alexandria in the first half of 3rd century BCE), Martialios, a prominent anatomist at the time, whose Erasistratean views Galen attacked during his public performances as a dissector (cf. *Lib. prop.* 1.11, 139.1–3 Boudon).[8] The passage that should concern us most runs as follows:

> [Martialios] was malicious and quite contentious (φιλόνεικος), although he was more than seventy years old. Having learned that my public lectures and teachings on an anatomical issue had been highly praised by those who had followed them, he inquired of one of my friends to which school (αἱρέσεως) I belonged. He was told that I call slaves those who present themselves as Hippocratics or Erasistrateans or Praxagoreans or in general name themselves after some man (τινος ἀνδρός),[9] and that I select (ἐκλέγοιμι) what is sound (τὰ καλά) from each of them. He then asked a second question: whom of the ancients (τῶν παλαιῶν) did I praise most? Having learned that I praised Hippocrates, he said that for him Hippocrates did not constitute a subject for anatomical study at all, whereas Erasistratus was marvellous in anatomy as well as in other parts of his science. Because of him, then, I wrote, in a rather emulous vein (φιλοτιμότερον), *On the Anatomy of Hippocrates*, in six books, and *On the Anatomy of Erasistratus*, in three books (*Lib. prop.* I.8–10, 138.6–21 Boudon = I, p. 94.26–95.14 Müller = XIX.13–14 Kühn; my translation).

Preferring or praising Hippocrates does not make one a Hippocratic. Indeed, the distinction indicated here is crucial. Hippocratics are no better than Erasistrateans and Praxagoreans (named after the 4th-century BCE doctor Praxagoras of Cos), as each group is and behaves like a sect. Galen presents his attitude as different in that he has an independent mind and selects and combines what he deems best in each of the schools: he is a self-conscious eclectic. So if Galen considers Hippocrates the greatest, this is because he finds that this physician has said the best things about medicine (including, rather startlingly, anatomy). We will presently turn to Galen's criterion of selection. Here we should note that he presents Martialios as morally flawed (i.e. malicious and contentious). This is typical of how he views the sectarian attitude: it does not seek truth but victory and honour, motives that should have no place in science. A striking and rather untypical element is that Galen presents *himself* as having shown too much of the same

---

8 On the Martialios episode in the context of Galen's practice of performing anatomical demonstrations, see Boudon (2012), 143–146 and Salas (2020), 192; cf. 53, 82.
9 Boudon and others – not inappropriately – translate this as 'authority'. Galen's literal expression, which is retained in this translation, seems to suggest that a human being should not be made central to the study of Nature.

attitude (φιλοτιμότερον, 'in a rather emulous vein')[10] when attacking Martialios in some of the books written around that time: he deliberately provoked the old man, who was esteemed for his anatomical knowledge and anatomical treatises. Love of honour (φιλοτιμία) is the motive Galen usually imputes to the founders of new sects.[11] He may be implying that this is the kind of brash and vindictive behaviour typically shown by a man in his mid-thirties, as he was at the time, i.e. one still at the early stages of his career yet already making his mark. Martialios is called contentious too, but it suited him less precisely because of his advanced age.

Contentiousness is also the moral flaw typical of those who proclaim themselves followers of a particular sect or school (αἵρεσις):

> [The adherents of the various schools] cling to their own assumption and pretend to put firm trust in what they unwarrantably say in support of some dogma of those of their own school (αἱρέσεως), just as others have no qualms about lying to refute some doctrine of those who hold a different view (ἑτεροδόξων). Those who proclaim themselves the adherents of some school feel duty-bound to mount a fight over all the doctrines of their school, even in those cases where there is no logical need to do so in view of the core of their teaching, as with the debate on the soul (*PHP* IX.7.5–6, 586.27–34 De Lacy; my transl.).

In other words, the adherents of a school show a 'right or wrong, my country' attitude: instead of being focused on the truth, they compulsively attack those with different views. The Greek word used for their adversaries, ἑτεροδόξων, seems broader than its later Christian use would suggest. Given the plurality of schools confronting Galen, he uses the term primarily to refer to disagreements *between* rather than within sects (although, as we shall see, he is well aware of that phenomenon too: see below, pp. 50–51); he never uses the opposite term 'orthodoxy'.[12] But Galen's picture of sectarian behaviour does involve the idea of a system of tenets that should be accepted as a whole by the adherents of the

---

10 Singer translates 'in this rather combative vein', Boudon 'surtout par amour de la gloire'. Both elements are present in Galen's notion of φιλοτιμία. Singer's translation draws attention to the tone of the books written by Galen to refute Erasistratus and thus, indirectly, Martialios.
11 See (e.g.) *Nat. Fac.* II.34 K.; *Aff. Dig.* V.51; *PHP* III.8.39, 232.25 De Lacy; and *Typ.* VII.476.
12 For similar uses see *PHP* II.5.65, 140.18 De Lacy (the Stoic Chrysippus against Plato and the Platonists), *Loc. aff.* VIII.314 K., and *Cris.* X.670 (medical sects). At *PHP* V.6.5, 326.25–26 De Lacy we have ὀρθοδοξοῦσιν in a quotation from Posidonius (F 187 EK) presented by Galen as aimed at other Stoics in a debate on moral philosophy; but these opponents remain anonymous in the Posidonian passage, and Galen's reports about Posidonius disagreeing with his fellow Stoics should be treated with suspicion: see *infra*, n. 14. The degree to which philosophical schools expected or enforced the acceptance of a set of distinctive or 'orthodox' doctrines varied; for instance, the Stoics were more liberal about this than the Epicureans; cf. e.g. Sedley (1989).

school in question.[13] In the second half of the passage he indicates that there is no logical need for this. As he goes on to explain in what follows, there is no need for philosophers to quarrel about the seat of the ruling part of the soul, since this issue does not affect moral issues, such as the differences between virtues or moral progress (whereas it is necessary for doctors to know where the intellect resides with a view of applying certain remedies in the case of cognitive disorders, *ibid.* 7–8). In other words, it is often possible and indeed preferable to do what Galen presents himself as doing in the above-quoted passage from *On My Own Books*, namely: to select what is best from each school. In the lines preceding the passage under discussion, Galen is in fact concerned with the tools required to make this selection: logical methods such as distinguishing between similar things – notably between what is plausible and what is true – and a criterion of truth to which these matters can be referred. An epistemological foundationalist, Galen refers here to the Stoic criterion of truth, the evident, 'kataleptic' presentation, which he is all too happy to identify with the Academics' idea of the presentation that is persuasive to the highest degree (by being also 'incontrovertible' and 'viewed from all sides'). Thus, Galen does away with the epic, protracted battle on precisely this point between the two schools in the Hellenistic period. Clearly, he is seeking to establish a common ground here: what is needed is sound reason that is properly trained to do more specialized work; various schools have articulated this insight in their own way (the method of distinguishing between similar things is ascribed by Galen to Plato) (*ibid.* 1–4). This, then, is not selecting what is best from individual schools, but rather syncretically combining their doctrines.

Before looking more closely at Galen's ideas on knowledge, let us dwell a little more on his response to the sectarian state of mind. A felicitous exception to the picture drawn by Galen above is the Stoic philosopher Posidonius of Apamea (130–*c.* 55 BCE), who was brave enough to diverge from the monist psychology of Chrysippus and the majority of Stoics.[14] Indeed, he had dared to criticize them:

> It was precisely these points of Stoic philosophy that were criticized by Posidonius too, the most scientific of all the Stoics. He deserves great praise precisely where he is taken to task by all the other Stoics: they would have persuaded themselves to betray their country rather than the Stoic line; Posidonius preferred the truth to a Stoic dogma (*QAM* 11.85.8–86.2 Bazou = 11.77.17–78.2 Müller = Posid. T58 EK transl. Kidd).

---

13 Cf. the definition of a school at Diog. Laert., 1.20, among others: αἵρεσιν … πρόσκλισιν δόγμασιν ἀκολουθίαν ἔχουσιν. Cf. Gal., *Loc. Aff.* VIII.5, 158.17–159.9 K.
14 I have argued that Galen distorts Posidonius' real position, which represents a development of the Chrysippean one he inherited, rather than a deviation from it in Tieleman (2003), ch. 5. But the issue remains controversial. For the history of the scholarly discussion and more publications see now *Oxford Bibliographies in Classics*, s.v. Posidonius, section 'Moral Psychology' (T. Tieleman).

Here Galen summarizes a point he had developed at great length in books IV and V of *On the Doctrines of Hippocrates and Plato*, where we find the following passage:

> Posidonius, because in my opinion he had been trained in geometry and was accustomed to follow demonstrative proof more than any other Stoic, was ashamed of the conflict with evident facts and the self-contradictions found in Chrysippus. But all the other Stoics somehow or other put up with following the errors of Chrysippus rather than choosing the truth (*PHP* IV.4.38, 258.19–25 De Lacy = Posid. T83, T59 EK; transl. Kidd).

Here Galen presents Posidonius as the embodiment of his ideal (a role he more often gives to himself), viz. that of the independent truth-seeker, who moreover shares Galen's interest in geometry as a model for proper procedure.

At the beginning of *On the Order of My Books* Galen observes that many doctors and philosophers join a particular school out of admiration for other doctors and philosophers without having studied their doctrines or having any proper training in demonstrative knowledge (ἐπιστήμην ἀποδεικτικήν). Whether one becomes an Empiricist, Methodist or Dogmatist in medicine or a Platonist, Peripatetic, Stoic or Epicurean in philosophy is often a matter of chance: it depends on the beliefs of one's own father or of the person who happened to have gathered a following in one's own home town (*Ord.Lib.Prop.* 1.3–4, XIX.50 K.). A little further on Galen reports that he devoted a separate treatise to remedying the flaws of the sectarian condition: *On the Best Sect*,[15] which in contrast with usual practice did not come out in favour of any one particular school, but provided a method by which to judge existing schools and construct the best one (*ibid.* 51). This last point must refer to the independent and eclectic procedure he indicated in the above-quoted passage from *On My Own Books*. The theory of demonstration one needs in order to follow this procedure successfully was set out by Galen in his *On Demonstration*, which he goes on to recommend as a starting point (ibid. 52). This work is no longer extant, but Galen's theory can be reconstructed from many passages scattered throughout his preserved works.[16]

The motivation behind *On Demonstration* is also explained in chapter XIV of *On My Own Books*. Here Galen provides a piece of intellectual autobiography, stating that the controversies among philosophers motivated him to study logic and methodology with philosophers from various schools. Their theories, however, proved useless or contrary to natural notions. Moreover, disagreement was rife not just between but within sects, which – it is implied – was only to be

---

15 The tract *On the Best Sect to Thrasyboulos* printed in the *Opera Omnia* edition by Kühn (vol. I, 106–223) is generally regarded as spurious. Galen also called for independent judgement in works with similar titles: *The Best Method of Teaching*, against Favorinus (who omitted to teach a criterion of truth to his pupils, so that they could not judge things properly) and *On Recognizing the Best Physician*. On this passage see also Havrda (2020), 84–87.

16 See Müller (1897), Barnes (1993), Chiaradonna (2009b), Havrda (2015).

expected, given their lack of a proper method. The Peripatetics were divided among themselves to a lesser extent than the other schools, not least because they had modelled their theory on geometrical proofs. In fact, Galen sees geometrical procedure as what saved him from falling into 'the impasse of the Pyrrhonists', i.e. from suspending judgement, the standard Sceptical response to disagreement (διαφωνία) (*Lib. Prop.* XIV.1–8, 164.1–165.23 Boudon = XIX.116–117 K.). In sum, Galen represents one of the two main options intellectuals saw from the first century BCE onwards to respond to the disagreement among schools: syncretism and Scepticism. His syncretic solution comes with an appeal to common (or natural) and obvious notions inspired by Euclidean geometry and the useful and efficacious arts based on it – an idea and a predilection which Galen sees as a family tradition.[17] The appeal to the geometrical model, however, is by no means confined to Galen. His no doubt stylized story of a quest for wisdom involving various schools, none of which is chosen in the end, is also traditional.[18]

Paradise lost – and regained?

But how did sects and sectarian disagreements arise in the first place? Galen answers that the problem is moral in origin:

> The early philosophers, in their desire to be of benefit to mankind, not only originated and produced theories about things which are clearly known, but also attempted to find out about many things which are not clear; and hence in those times, on the basis of their findings, the growth of knowledge made its greatest progress. However, some of the doctors and philosophers who succeeded them wanted to make their reputation and despairing of ever achieving it in a just manner, they resorted to charlatanry. And those who were unable to refute the sophisms they posed reacted in one of two ways: either they believed them to be true, or else they thought that the best course was to remain in doubt about everything (*CP* 1.1–3, 170.1–13 H. Transl. Hankinson).

Here, in speaking of the early philosophers, Galen may be thinking of those whom he elsewhere refers to as the ancients: Plato and Aristotle (and perhaps pupils of theirs such as Theophrastus) and their immediate predecessor Socrates rather than the Presocratics.[19] There was consensus, collaboration, progress, and a high-minded moral purpose: to benefit humankind. Intellectually and morally

---

17 Cf. *Indol.* 58–59, 18–19.10 Boudon-Jouanna.
18 On geometry as a model of method in Galen see Lloyd (2005); cf. Menn (2003), who pays considerable attention to Galen.
19 See Tieleman 2022. In *HNH* Galen presents the Presocratics and especially monists as inferior to Hippocrates. On the more widespread tendency to see what is old as good, see Pilhofer (1990).

inferior philosophers and doctors who wanted to make a name for themselves then resorted to charlatanry and sophistry. People were unable to refute them, so some accepted their claims while others turned into Sceptics. Here, it seems, we have reached what we call the Hellenistic period.

So Galen's story of philosophical and moral decline comes with an evocation of original pre-sectarian bliss. In other words, he projects his ideal back into the past, thereby providing it with time-honoured and venerable credentials. Progress is not so much a matter of surpassing these ancients but of proving them right and making up for their omissions:

> Now I, for my part, as I have already said, have not set myself the task of stating what has already been demonstrated so well by the ancients (οἱ παλαιοί), since I cannot surpass these men either in intelligence or in style. However, there are things they have said without demonstration, as being self-evident, because they could not suspect that there would be some evil sophists who would despise the truth contained in their words; and there are other things which they completely omitted. It is these things which I think it right to discover and demonstrate (*Nat. Fac.* 2.8, II.116–117 K. Transl. Brock, modified).

The ancients could not have foreseen the moral decline that was to set in after them and which made sophists lose all respect for the truth: once again the problem is essentially a moral one. Here Galen's attitude to the ancients is one of modesty, although he also refers to omissions on their part. He appears to claim a somewhat bigger role for himself in the following two passages:

> I say that the best accounts of demonstration were written by the old philosophers, Theophrastus and Aristotle in their *Posterior Analytics* (*PHP* II.2.4, 104.3–5 De Lacy). What premises ought one to seek as appropriate and proper to the problem at hand? These have been discussed at length, both in the rather unclear and brief statements made by the ancients, and in what we wrote in our clear and full explanation of those statements [scil. in *On Demonstration*] (*ibid.* II.3.1, 108.21–25 De Lacy; transl. De Lacy).

Here, then, Galen's role is not merely to underpin the true statements of the ancients or to add what they left unsaid, but rather to improve on their theories in terms of clarity and explanatory power. Even so, Galen presents Aristotle and Theophrastus as the ancients who wrote the best accounts of demonstration and whom he follows. They are part of the same collaborative effort or tradition that includes Plato and Hippocrates. Galen did not turn a blind eye to those cases where Aristotle deviated from Plato, for instance concerning the seat of the ruling part, or intellect, in the body. But he includes Aristotle wholeheartedly whenever he can: in addition to logic and the theory of demonstration, Aristotle followed Plato and Hippocrates as far as the theory of physical elements is concerned. Indeed, Galen explains the Hippocratic references to 'the hot' and 'the cold' in Aristotelian terms as pertaining not to elementary qualities but to the elements as analyzable into qualities (the formal aspect) and matter. (Here Plato's account of the elements in geometrical terms, so-called geometrical atomism,[20] was not an option open to him and is passed over in silence.)

The physical elements provide Galen with the opportunity of taking the Stoics on board too. At the beginning of his *Method of Healing* (*MM*) he confronts the Methodist physician Thessalus by invoking this tradition of sound thinking about the most basic constituents of physical reality: 'I would beg you choose Zeno, Chrysippus and all their followers. None of them, most insolent Thessalus, condemned Hippocrates' doctrines on the nature of man ...' (*MM* I.9–10). But this is by no means the only passage of this kind.[21] It might be supposed that in these passages, forgetting about his rejection of the authority principle, Galen simply relies on these great names to trump Thessalus. But in fact Galen does not appeal to authority here. He assumes that the truth offers itself to various thinkers who have no morally questionable reason to deny it and have found confirmation of the four-element theory by working out their own physical theories. Their broad consensus on this point, then, is significant in itself. Galen is not just dropping names but rather engaging in the dialectical grouping of authorities as a way of ordering a debate.[22]

Christians: the ultimate sectarians?

The picture of intellectual life emerging from the pages of Galen's work is a rather disheartening one. As we have seen, it is ridden with sectarian disagreements caused by and perpetuating moral flaws. In response many have lapsed into Scepticism, which offers no real hope for moral and scientific progress either. To be sure, there is an element of dramatization in all this, designed to bring out Galen's own role as a saviour leading us out of these troubles. Nonetheless, his concern is real and so is the prevalent division between sects. But so far the problem has involved philosophical and medical schools. Galen extends it to include Christians, effectively treating them as another sect comparable to the Greek philosophical schools. Galen's relevant observations on Christian beliefs and practices (which may include Jewish ones, given Galen's response to the book of *Genesis*, see below) are extremely interesting, coming as they do from an early pagan witness

---

[20] See Plato, *Tim.* 53b5–57d6.
[21] Galen, *Adv. Jul.* XVIIIA.257–259 (*SVF* 2.771): Zeno and Chrysippus, like Aristotle and Theophrastus, always explained diseases by reference to an imbalance between the elementary qualities or the four humours, as is proven by many passages. Cf. ibid. 268. *Nat. fac.* II.92 (Hippocrates + Aristotle + Stoics on mixture); *PHP* 5.3.18 (Chrysippus and Stoics + Aristotle + Plato + Hippocrates); *HNH* XV.37 (Hippocrates' conception of the mixture of the four elements accepted by Aristotle and the Stoics); *Hipp. Off. Med.* XVIIIb.658 (Hippocrates as the source of dogmatic philosophies).
[22] *Pace* Flemming (2017), 185–186. On the use of doxographic schemes (and Galen's own schemes, inspired by the doxographic genre), see Tieleman (2018).

to the new creed.[23] Galen seems to be a comparatively well-informed observer, who not only criticizes the Christians but also compliments them for their morals. For our purposes it is worth noting the specific similarities and differences with respect to Galen's response to the Greek medical and philosophical sects.

The first passage is part of an even longer section[24] from Galen's *On the Functionality of Parts* and is made even more interesting by the fact that shows Galen's familiarity with the creation story from the first chapter of *Genesis*:

> It is precisely this point in which our own opinion and that of Plato and the other Greeks who follow the right method in science differ from the position taken by Moses. For the latter it seems enough to say that God simply willed the arrangement of matter and instantaneously it was arranged; for he believes everything to be possible with God, even should he wish to make a bull or a horse out of ashes. We however do not hold this; we say that certain things are impossible by nature and that God does not attempt such things at all but that he chooses the best out of the possibilities of becoming (*UP* XI, ch. 14 = Vol. II, 158–159 Helmreich; my transl.).

What Galen here objects to is not the idea of *creatio ex nihilo* – according to a common reading of Genesis I, which would certainly go against the postulates of Greek philosophy of any variety – but rather Moses' belief that the material for this creation is indifferent: his God does not face the constraints and dilemmas familiar from Plato's creation story in the *Timaeus*. Moses' account is deficient in terms of the causal theory underlying this Platonic work, and later formalized by Aristotle in his fourfold division of causes. Although Moses recognizes the efficient cause – God – he fails to pay attention to the material cause. God can create everything from anything.[25] Although Galen presents the Greeks as superior on the whole, Moses' account is not unworthy of comparison in the context of his discussion of sects. In what follows, the Greek Epicurus receives a jab: Moses' account is superior to his insofar as it recognizes the efficient cause, viz. the divine Creator, whereas Epicurus believes that matter suffices to explain creation.[26] Furthermore, we have a typical emphasis on the need for a proper *method*. Moses explains creation by reference to what God wills and orders. What seems to be implied here is the idea that he fails to produce a proper explanation

---

23 The study of the relevant testimonies starts from the collection by Walzer (1949), to be supplemented with some further Arabic evidence discussed by Gero (1990). Discussions in Tieleman (2005), Tieleman (2013), Van der Eijk (2014), and Flemming (2017); cf. Alexander (1994) and Barnes (2002).
24 For a full discussion see Tieleman (2005).
25 Galen's examples here echo particular passages from the New Testament: see further Tieleman (2010), 128–138.
26 For a similar use of the Christian attitude to deal a blow at Greek sectarians who should have known better, consider the following passage: 'One might more easily teach novelties to the followers of Moses and Christ than to the physicians and philosophers who cling fast to their schools' (*Diff. Puls.* III.3 = VIII.657 K. ~ Reference 3 Walzer; transl. Walzer).

of why the world was created and why it possesses the features it does (as, again, Plato does in the *Timaeus*). This assumption can be shored up a bit further by looking at some additional testimonies:

> They compare those who practice medicine without scientific knowledge to Moses, who framed laws for the tribe of the Jews, since it is his method in his books to write without offering proofs, saying 'God commanded, God spake' (Ibn al-Matran, *Life of Galen*, vol. I.77 Müller (~ Reference 1 Walzer; transl. Walzer).

Galen appears to have seen God's speech-act as a characteristic and striking feature of the Mosaic story, which replaces a proper demonstrative account. It may be recalled that Galen also referred to the Greek ancients as sometimes having omitted a demonstration when they felt that their thesis was clear and readily acceptable (see above, p. 52). Later followers, including Galen, had to add demonstrations, but this was because of the attacks suffered by the ancient accounts at the hands of uncharitable critics. By Galen's time Moses could also be seen as a representative of ancient wisdom, even by Greeks.[27] But here Moses' case seems different, and his procedure lacks the credibility that Galen is willing to ascribe to Greek ancients such as Hippocrates and Plato. It is the lack of proper proof that Galen finds fault with, as also witnessed by the following two testimonies:

> In order that one should not at the very beginning, as if one had come into the school of Moses and Christ, hear talk of undemonstrated laws, and that where it is least appropriate (*Diff. Puls.* II.4, VIII.579 K. ~ Ref. 4 Walzer; transl. Walzer).

> If I had in mind people who taught their pupils in the same way as the followers of Moses and Christ teach theirs – for they order them to accept everything on faith – I should not have given you a definition (Ibn al-Matran, *Life of Galen*, vol. I.77 Müller ~Ref. 5 Walzer; transl. Walzer).

In Christianity and, it appears, Judaism the authority principle is even more prominent and common – and indeed widely accepted – than it is in the philosophical and medical sects criticized by Galen. In their case it is Galen who exposes them as relying on authority. It is not as if they do not try to demonstrate their doctrines. It is just that their bias and emotions stand in the way of accepting other views when these are supported by better arguments: they have lost their capacity for independent judgement. For Christians, however, accepting things on faith is the right thing to do. Even so, Galen qualifies his objection in a particular way. Having already hinted at morality by reference to the laws accepted by Jews and Christians, he makes the following observation:

---

27 Clement for instance cites Galen's contemporary Numenius of Apamea as calling Plato an Atticizing Moses (Euseb. *Praep. Ev.* XI.10.14, fr. 8.13).

> Most people are unable to follow any demonstrative argument consecutively; hence they need parables, and benefit from them – and he [*scil.* Galen] understands by parables tales of rewards and punishments in a future life – just as now we see the people called Christians drawing their faith from parables [and miracles], and yet sometimes acting in the same way [as those who philosophize]. For their contempt of death [and of its sequel] is patent to us every day, and likewise their restraint in cohabitation. For they include men but also women who refrain from cohabiting all through their lives; and they number also individuals who, in self-discipline and self-control in matters of food and drink, and in their keen pursuit of justice, have attained a pitch not inferior to that of genuine philosophers (from the *Summary of Plato's Republic*, as quoted by Abu'l-Fida', *Universal Chronicle*, 108 Fleischer; transl. Walzer 1949).[28]

How one faces death is the ultimate test for any Greek philosopher. We do not know whether Galen refers here to the courage shown by those Christians who were persecuted under Marcus Aurelius in particular or to their general courage in the face of death (cf. the reference to 'every day'). Likewise he praises other main virtues displayed by them: moderation with regard to food, drink and sex – a feature much appreciated by Galen, we may assume – as well as justice, which may refer to Christian charity. Interestingly, Galen recognizes that technical philosophy and particularly demonstrative argumentation is not for everyone. Those who cannot follow it are better served with stories and images, which, as the Christians prove, can be quite effective in producing the same kind of virtuous behaviour that is expected of philosophers in the more formal sense. The bottom line here is that Christians are free from the moral flaws Galen detects in sectarian doctors and philosophers – and this may help explain why he is making this observation in the first place.[29] It may be due to Galen's nuanced and interested approach that some later Christians' were sensitive to his criticism about their lack of a proper logical method.[30]

---

28 On Walzer's translation of Arabic *rumūz* as 'parables' see Gero (1990), 403–405, who prefers 'signs', 'indications', i.e. σημεῖα).
29 See *supra*, n. 26 with text thereto.
30 Cf. Euseb. PE I.1.3d; transl. Walzer 54: 'Some have supposed that Christianity has no reason (λόγος) to support itself but that those who desire the name confirm their opinion by an unreasoning faith and an assent without examination; and they assert that no one is able by clear demonstration to furnish evidence of the truth of what is promised, but that they require their converts to adhere to faith alone, and the reason why they are called the faithful lies in their uncritical and untested faith'. See further Barnes (2002) and Chiaradonna (2009b).

Conclusion

Galen explains the lamentable phenomenon of disagreeing schools, both philosophical and medical, in predominantly moral terms: the ancients (i.e. mainly Hippocrates and Plato) laid the foundations for real progress. But instead of building on their work, some philosophers and doctors, driven by desire for personal glory, turned away from them and founded schools of their own. With their newfangled theories they attracted large followings, particularly since most people were unable to assess the claims of these new authorities for lack of proper training. This situation has persisted until Galen's own day, if not deteriorated further. The authority principle has supplanted an unbiased and independent attitude, which is why schools are often named after a person such as Epicurus or indeed Plato or Hippocrates. This makes the disagreement between the various schools particularly hard to overcome. Galen seeks the remedy in a method of demonstration modelled upon geometry, i.e. a deductive-axiomatic model of scientific procedure of the kind anticipated by Aristotle. It is ultimately based on the natural criteria of reason and experience, which should be further developed, refined and trained. Thus we will acquire the skills needed for philosophical and scientific inquiry, which should be based on rational and experiential methods (i.e., respectively, reason and experience as 'technical criteria'). If properly applied, this method exposes many issues which keep the schools divided as speculative and insoluble (and, in any case, they are useless for scientific and moral progress).[31]

Among existing schools, then, there is no 'best sect' – not even the Platonist school or the Hippocratean one qualifies as such. To put it differently, the best sect is the community of scientists/philosophers working in the great tradition founded by Hippocrates and Plato but devoid of the flaws of sects in the ordinary sense.[32] Galen's Hippocrates and Plato are not authorities beyond all criticism: they can be proved correct or at least be shown to be on the right track, but many of their ideas are still undeveloped or have yet to be fully articulated. Galen does not effectively add a new, medico-philosophical school of his own to the existing ones. What he provides is rather the identification of a pedigree for what is sound in the progress of medicine and philosophy, without the authority principle but

---

[31] On Galen's epistemology see the pioneering study by Frede (1981), who argues that Galen's combination of reason and experience resulted from his response to the conflict between the Empiricist and Rationalist sects, and the recent collection of studies in Hankinson & Havrda (2022). In Bibliography: R. J. Hankinson and M. Havrda, eds. *Galen's Epistemology: Experience, Reason, and Method in Ancient Medicine* (Cambridge: CUP 2022). On common and technical criteria see Tieleman (2011), esp. 85–89. On useless dogmas see Tieleman (2018).

[32] Galen's position here is comparable to that of the Pyrrhonian Sceptics as typified by Sextus Empiricus: they are united by a common attitude but not a school in the ordinary sense of sharing a set of tenets. See Sext., *P.H.* VIII.16–18: 'Does the Sceptic have a School (αἵρεσιν)?'.

with considerable strategic advantages: Galen can thus anchor his innovations in these ancients who are esteemed yet still leave sufficient room for innovation.

Galen's syncretistic project is by no means unparalleled: we may compare it to the philosophy of Antiochus of Ascalon (c. 130–c. 68 BCE),[33] who updated Platonism in the light of Stoicism, or to Neoplatonism, i.e. the phase of Platonism initiated by Plotinus (205–270 CE), shortly after Galen's lifetime. In many ways this kind of project, usually supported by a revisionist view of the history of philosophy, represented an alternative to Scepticism as a way of responding to the disagreement among philosophers and their division into schools. Galen, for his part, transferred the syncretistic response to medicine, providing it with an appropriate pedigree, too. What he arrived at was a merging of medicine and the useful parts of philosophy, a medical philosophy or philosophical medicine aimed at human well-being, both physical and mental. It would have been a stroke of historical irony if in doing so Galen had founded a school liable to the very objections that he himself had levelled at others. He may have had apprentices or pupils.[34] But this is not tantamount to founding a school. His legacy is of a different sort: far from establishing another school, Galen laid the foundations for medicine as a unitary art, or science, based on the consensus of its participants about its aims and methods. In other words, his synthesis of medical knowledge based, in Hippocrates' name, on the principles of reason and experience put an end to the variety of medical schools. This, in turn, paved the way for the institutionalization of medicine, which we now take largely for granted. Galen's occasional criticisms of Christian beliefs and practices did not prevent him from becoming, alongside Hippocrates, the dominant medical authority in the European world of later centuries. The same thing happened in the Islamic world. This canonization may have discouraged disagreement with Galen for too long, but when it arose it was also clear that critics such as the anatomist Andreas Vesalius (1514–1564) and an innovator such as William Harvey (1578–1657) stood on his shoulders.[35*)]

---

33 On the similarities between the epistemologies of Antiochus and Galen, see Hankinson (1997).
34 Galen refers to his ἑταῖροι, a term that may refer to companions or friends but also to pupils or followers, e.g. AA II.620 K., HNH XV.2 K., Hipp. Epid. XVIIB.224 K. Cf. Xen., Mem. 2.8.1, Arist., Pol. 1274a28). Galen dedicated some of his books to what may have been pupils but also friends or colleagues of his. In much of his corpus – and not merely in works specifically intended for students ('beginners') – he adopts the role of a teacher; cf. also his On the Best Method of Teaching, referred to supra, p. 45 and n. 15. But this does not solve the question in one way or the other. See Scarborough (1981) and Boudon-Millot (2012), 195–197.
35 I am grateful to Dr Aistė Čelkytė and the anonymous reviewer for their helpful comments on the presentation of my argument.

ALBERT JOOSSE

Γνῶθι σαυτόν and the Platonic Tradition in Clement of Alexandria

Traditions form through the transmission and modification of what is seen as some kind of heritage. In the case of philosophical traditions, this heritage will often include doctrines, arguments, texts and the veneration of exemplary thinkers. People who (whether consciously or not) contribute to the formation of a tradition can do so by affirming ideas that they take to be central to their world-view or by repudiating ideas they take to be characteristic of relevant rivals. But they can also do so by appropriating shared elements: shared with rival movements, or even within the wider culture. What is shared is not any one movement's exclusive property, and hence the very manner in which authors incorporate such shared elements within their own teaching becomes significant, as it says much about how they position their own tradition with respect to their cultural environment.[1]

The focus of this contribution is on a phrase that can be considered just such a piece of shared heritage: the maxim 'know yourself'. The phrase is strongly associated with the oracle at Delphi and so has a clear Greek stamp to it. But beyond that, it is not anyone's particular preserve. It is common currency for anyone who can identify with the Greek language and culture in some way. At the same time, it is not a phrase like any other, but a philosophically salient one: its very words seem to invite philosophical interpretation and thus appropriation into particular philosophical traditions. This offers us a methodological opportunity insofar as we can illustrate more general mechanisms of tradition-building and of ways to deal with disagreement by means of the particular case of 'know yourself'.

It is impossible to offer a complete overview of ancient philosophical uses of the maxim within the confines of this chapter. This has been done admirably by Pierre Courcelle (1974).[2] Instead, I will zoom in on a particular moment in the

---

[1] It is important to emphasise, with Reydams-Schils (2020), 131–132, that terms and ideas which are widely shared have not for that reason become empty or loose from their context of origin. Their significance in being employed in new contexts depends on the interplay of old and new, as this chapter too serves to show.

[2] See also Wilkins' useful classification (1917).

Dealing with Disagreement, ed. by Albert Joosse and Angela Ulacco, Monothéismes et Philosophie, 33 (Turnhout: Brepols, 2022), pp. 59–80
BREPOLS 🕮 PUBLISHERS   10.1484/M.MON-EB.5.132748
This is an open access article made available under a CC BY-NC 4.0 International License.

history of uses of this maxim and consider Clement of Alexandria's incorporation of it into the first book of his *Stromateis*. My choice of Clement is motivated by his importance in the formation of a Christian philosophical tradition. After the generation of apologists, Clement's œuvre is the first attempt to offer a systematic account of Christian insights on the basis of Greek philosophy. The most prominent Greek philosophical tradition against the background of, or within which, Clement saw himself operating is Platonism.[3] The importance attached to the maxim 'know yourself' in the Platonic tradition makes this an especially promising lens through which to study Clement's attitude towards the Platonic tradition and the manner in which he positions the Christian philosophical movement with respect to it.

What I offer here is a case study. It is not a representative case of ancient treatments of 'know yourself'. Platonic interpretations of the maxim are of course not necessarily representative of the wider culture. And even within the Platonic tradition one can find other interpretations which are less relevant to this chapter's study of Clement – one might point, for instance, to some authors' insistence on the phrase as a means to observe one's role in society.[4] What follows here, however, is a case study in the sense that it studies a privileged treatment of the maxim that can illustrate more general mechanisms in the construction of tradition.

The chapter is set up as follows. I first offer a brief sketch of the treatment of 'know yourself' in the Platonic tradition. Plato's writings, in particular the *Protagoras*, *Phaedrus*, and *First Alcibiades*, set the agenda for discussions in later authors. Cicero and Porphyry give us some insight into these discussions within the Platonic tradition. I will then turn to Clement's *Stromateis* and in particular to three passages in book 1 of that work. These passages are all related, as I will show, and offer a progressive understanding of what is involved in self-knowledge and the way for the reader to obtain it. In the course of developing his ideas on self-knowledge, Clement effects a transposition of Platonic ideas and phrases, highlighting their parallels with the Christian tradition and signalling important disagreements.

---

3 See Wyrwa (1983) for an in-depth study of Platonic texts and ideas in Clement, including their role in the composition of Clement's work. Lilla 1971 emphasises the presence of Middle- and even Neoplatonic ideas in Clement (alongside gnostic ideas and the influence of Philo).
4 e.g. Plutarch, *Adulator* 49B, 65F; *De capienda* 89A.

'Know yourself' in the Platonic tradition

The Platonic corpus

The Platonic corpus includes the phrase γνῶθι σεαυτόν in many places.[5] Five dialogues offer discussions that are particularly relevant for understanding later Platonists and Clement: the *Protagoras*, *Philebus*, *Charmides*, *Phaedrus*, and *First Alcibiades*. In the *Protagoras*, the phrase appears in the wake of Socrates' praise of Sparta (and Crete): philosophy is oldest there, he claims tongue-in-cheek, and the city contains many sophists (342a7–b1), even if the Spartans (Socrates claims) hide this fact. Evidence of the Spartans' wisdom is their pithiness (342e2–4). The Seven Sages recognised this Spartan quality.[6] They were all champions of Spartan education, and at some point convened to offer to Apollo their own creations in this Spartan tradition of brevity. These included 'know yourself' and 'nothing in excess' (343a6–b5), Socrates says. The maxim here serves as an example of pithy wisdom, while the Seven Sages themselves are cast not as the pioneers of wisdom or philosophy, but as students of the Spartans.

The *Philebus* mentions 'know yourself' when Socrates explains what makes someone ridiculous and the object of comedy (at 48c10). We consider someone ridiculous when he exhibits one of three forms (εἴδη, 48e8) of self-ignorance: ignorance with respect to his possessions, body, or soul. It is characteristic of this occurrence of 'know yourself' that it plays a relatively subservient role and has a broad range of meaning accorded to it.

The *Charmides*' treatment of self-knowledge (164c–175c) is complex and subtle. It is beyond the scope of this chapter to discuss it in any detail. There is no need to do so, however, since, in the strict context of discussions of 'know yourself', later authors do not seem to have engaged much with the difficult epistemological discussion that occupies the second half of the dialogue.[7] Two things are nonetheless important to note. First, Critias reinterprets the phrase 'know yourself' (164d3–165b4). According to him the phrase means σωφρόνει, 'be temperate'. Second, he ascribes the phrase to a person other than the god (an authorial allusion, perhaps, to his image as a sceptic about traditional religion). This other person successfully hid his own authorship because of the enigmatic character of the phrase, which invites people to think that the god Apollo himself authored it. Its enigmatic nature also justifies Critias' effort at reinterpretation.

---

5 In addition to the five texts discussed here, the phrase is also touched upon in *Tim.* 72a5, *Leg.* 923a4–5, *Anter.* 138a7; mere mention of it is made in *Hipp.* 228e2. On self-knowledge in Plato, see Courcelle (1974), 14–18; Annas (1985); Tsouna (2001); Moore (2015); Ambury and German (2019).

6 This is in fact the first extant passage to give seven names of sages, but the tradition predates Plato. See Christes (2006).

7 But there were plenty of later treatments of the *Charmides*' conundrum of self-intellection. See Crystal (2002).

The *Phaedrus* features what is perhaps the most famous occurrence of the phrase 'know yourself' in the Platonic corpus. Socrates is made to utter this phrase when Phaedrus asks him what he thinks the right interpretation of the myth of Boreas might be. Socrates says that he has no time for such questions. The type of demythologizing interpretation that his contemporaries propose requires an amount of leisure that Socrates says he does not have. He is therefore content to stick to the traditional stories while he devotes his time to what he thinks is a much more urgent concern, namely getting to know himself, in obedience to the Delphic inscription (229e4–230a6). In later writers, this call for intellectual restraint is picked up frequently. Mostly, however, the type of endeavour that is deferred in favour of the project of obtaining self-knowledge is not the sophistic explanation of myths, but natural science: knowledge of the causes and mechanisms of physical processes and of cosmological phenomena, like the movements of heavenly bodies.[8]

Socrates' suggestion that there might be a θεία μοῖρα in him, however, keeps open a possibility that is explored much more boldly in the *Alcibiades I*. This dialogue also contains the longest discussion of the Delphic injunction and of its meaning. The discussion starts[9] when Socrates asks Alcibiades whether self-knowledge is easily obtained – and whether the author of 'know yourself' was a nobody (τις ἦν φαῦλος, 129a3) – or a very difficult thing to achieve. It is very difficult indeed (παγχάλεπον, 129a6), Alcibiades agrees. So, a little later, he asks how (ὄντιν' ἂν τρόπον, 132b4–5, c7–9) this may be achieved. Socrates comments that the real meaning of 'know yourself' is easily obscured by one's first grasp of it (132c9–10): 'have we not understood the Delphic inscription which we just mentioned?'[10]

According to Socrates, the real meaning of the injunction is that we should get to know our souls (130e8–9). This follows from the identification of each human being with his soul rather than with his body. In support of this identification, the dialogue offers the famous argument that human beings are the users of their bodies and that it is precisely the soul which uses the body (129e3–130c3). In a move that highlights what they are actually doing in conducting their dialogue, Socrates argues that this means that he is not addressing his words to Alcibiades' face, but that they are having a conversation soul to soul (130d8–e5).

---

8 e.g. Philo, *De migr. Abr.* 136–138, 184–186; *De somn.* 1.54–58; Gregory of Nyssa, *In Cant. hom.* 2.2; cf. Augustine, *Conf.* 10.15.
9 This is not the first mention of the phrase 'know yourself' in the text, which occurs at 124a8–b1: γνῶθι σαυτόν, ὅτι οὗτοι ἡμῖν εἰσιν ἀντίπαλοι. Socrates points out to Alcibiades that the Spartans and Persians are his actual rivals, not other Athenian citizens, as Alcibiades seems to think. The phrase is functional to Socrates' exhortation that Alcibiades must be more ambitious, in striking contrast to the traditional association of 'know yourself' with awareness of human mortality and limitations (cf. Wilkins (1917), 12–40, 52–59).
10 ἆρα πρὸς θεῶν εὖ λέγοντος οὗ νυνδὴ ἐμνήσθημεν τοῦ Δελφικοῦ γράμματος οὐ συνίεμεν;

As a more precise (ἐναργέστατα, 132c7) description of self-knowledge, Socrates offers a famous analogy between eyes and souls. If Apollo told your eye to see itself, he asks, what would the eye have to do? It would have to look into a mirror or into something like a mirror, preferably another eye (132e7–133a2).[11] Analogously, souls must look into souls to get to know themselves, especially into the highest part of the soul, where wisdom arises (133b7–c3). 'It is to the god, then, that this part of the soul is similar, and if someone looks into it and has come to know all the divine, god and wisdom, he will also know himself most in this way' (133c4–6).[12]

It turns out that knowing yourself involves much: knowing god and 'all the divine'. This grand perspective is open to Alcibiades only if he keeps in view the wisdom in a soul – and by that soul Socrates here clearly means his own soul. Alcibiades affirms this when he vows, at the end of the dialogue, to follow Socrates. Compared to the *Phaedrus* perspective, then, the *Alcibiades I* offers a surprising reversal: knowledge of oneself is consequent upon knowledge of 'all the divine'.

Three elements from this text are important to bear in mind when considering the later Platonic tradition and Clement: the origin of γνῶθι σαυτόν as an indication of its meaning; the idea of looking at your teacher to know yourself; and the combination of knowing yourself and knowing, ultimately, everything.

Later Platonists

The rich textual foundation of the phrase 'know yourself' in Plato's corpus was sure to lead later Platonists to engage with it. We also have evidence of other philosophers doing so. Aristotle is said to have discussed it, as Plutarch tells us – referring to it, incidentally, as one of Aristotle's 'Platonic works' (*adv. Colotem* 1118C).[13] It is also likely that the old Stoics engaged with it. After all, their theory of οἰκείωσις is centrally concerned with a kind of self-knowledge. Little evidence of direct exegesis of the maxim survives, however. Later Stoics such as Seneca,

---

11 This preference is implied in Socrates' failure to engage with Alcibiades' suggestion that the eye may see itself in a mirror, instead proposing that there is such a mirror in another eye. The philosophical reason for this preference is that the mirror in the other eye, the pupil, is itself a seeing thing and so much more like the eye that wishes to see itself than any old mirror. For this point see Gill (2007), 108 and Joosse (2014), 3–6.
12 Τῷ θεῷ ἄρα τοῦτ' ἔοικεν αὐτῆς, καί τις εἰς τοῦτο βλέπων καὶ πᾶν τὸ θεῖον γνούς, θεόν τε καὶ φρόνησιν, οὕτω καὶ ἑαυτὸν ἂν γνοίη μάλιστα (my trans.).
13 καὶ τῶν ἐν Δελφοῖς γραμμάτων θειότατον ἐδόκει τὸ 'γνῶθι σαυτόν', ὃ δὴ καὶ Σωκράτει τῆς ἀπορίας καὶ ζητήσεως ταύτης ἀρχὴν ἐνέδωκεν, ὡς Ἀριστοτέλης ἐν τοῖς Πλατωνικοῖς εἴρηκε· (text from Einarson/De Lacy (Loeb)). The attribution of this citation to περὶ φιλοσοφίας is based on Porphyry's reference to the work in fragment 275 Smith (discussed below, pp. 64–65). Among the works preserved in the Aristotelian corpus, the *Rhetoric* refers to it as a platitude to be avoided or even contradicted by a skilled orator (1395a21); and the *Magna Moralia* refers to it less explicitly in 1213a13, as a difficult thing to achieve.

Epictetus and Marcus Aurelius mention the maxim frequently in connection with their ethical focus on what is up to us, and with the realization that our reason is the core of our being.[14] Some of this Stoic theorizing may have been formative for Clement as well. The scope of this chapter, however, is limited to Clement's use of Platonic motifs.

Seven aspects stand out in Platonic uses of 'know yourself'. First, there are uses of 'know yourself' as injunctions to remember that one is mortal. In *On the E at Delphi*, Plutarch presents γνῶθι σαυτόν as the god's answer to the human greeting of εἶ: the latter emphasizes the god's eternity, the former human mortality and frailty. Plutarch here offers a degree of philosophical background for the traditional association of 'know yourself' with human limits and mortality.[15]

More often, however, we find the contrary. In line with the *Alcibiades I*, Platonic authors view 'know yourself' as an invitation to understand the tight connection between human souls and the divine. This is sometimes formulated as the strong claim that the human mind itself is, or contains, a god or something divine (e.g. Cicero, *Leg.* 1.58–59, *Rep.* 6.26).[16]

In connection with the divine aspect of human souls we often also find the idea that human beings are their souls. In a passage that closely follows the *Alcibiades I*, Cicero says that when the Delphic maxim enjoins us to know ourselves, it enjoins us to know our souls (*Tusc.* 1.52: *cum igitur: Nosce te, dicit, hoc dicit: Nosce animum tuum*). But the picture here is by no means absolute. Elsewhere, Cicero connects 'know yourself' to knowledge of soul as well as body (*Fin.* 5.44).[17] In his treatise *On 'Know Yourself'*, Porphyry[18] alludes to both the *Philebus* and the *Alcibiades I* to offer a wider and tiered understanding of what it means to know

---

14 See Courcelle (1974), 49–64. It is unclear to me to what extent the Roman Stoics' view on 'know yourself' continues old-Stoic trends or incorporates Platonic elements.
15 392A, 394C. Plutarch is credited with a treatise περὶ τοῦ γνῶθι σαυτὸν καὶ εἰ ἀθάνατος ἡ ψυχή in the so-called *Lamprias catalogue*.
16 I treat Cicero as a Platonic author for the purposes of this chapter. It has been clearly established, in my view, that he is reflecting Platonic views in the passages discussed in this section (see Boyancé (1963); Courcelle (1974), 34–38; Renaud and Tarrant (2015), 110–125). The passages' strong textual links to the *Alcibiades I* and the dense use of other Platonic texts in *Tusc.* 1.52–58 are strong indications of this.
17 Michel (1984), 131–133 does not think this difference is significant and considers it amply explained by the difference in context. Renaud and Tarrant opt for a similar approach, suggesting that the two positions may correspond to different 'levels of knowledge' (2015), 122. That Cicero was aware of at least some substantive differences between his works emerges from *Tusc.* 5.32, where the interlocutor refers to *Fin.* book 4.
18 A note on my use of Porphyry: although he was born 20 years after Clement died, he is nevertheless a valuable witness to the Platonic views of an earlier generation. This is not only due to his general historiographic interest, but also to the fact that the fragments of his treatise on the Delphic maxim explicitly discuss earlier views.

oneself: to know one's soul, but also to know one's body and even to know one's possessions (fr. 275F Smith).[19]

A fourth aspect of Platonic uses of 'know yourself' is the way in which it serves as a bridge to grasp the whole of philosophy. According to some people, Porphyry says, it means that 'from what is present within us we reach conclusions about what is in the whole [cosmos] and through examining and discovering ourselves we advance more easily to a contemplation of the universe' (fr. 274F Smith, 580.19–22 Hense).[20] He himself is prepared to go further and to identify the true knowledge of our essence with the attainment of wisdom itself (581.10–14 Hense). Cicero too on the one hand speaks of the *adumbratae intellegentiae* which the mind has conceived as divine elements allowing us to gain knowledge of the whole of reality (*Leg.* 1.59); and, on the other hand, considers the maxim to be fulfilled to a wonderful extent when we have come to know the universe (*Leg.* 1.61).[21]

For related reasons, the maxim is often also associated with the beginning of philosophy. Porphyry, again, mentions the view according to which 'know yourself' is an exhortation to practice philosophy, based on the idea that the human being is a microcosm (fr. 274F Smith, 580.12–16 Hense).[22] The context shows that Plutarch agrees when he cites the above-mentioned passage from Aristotle's *On Philosophy*, according to which Socrates made 'know yourself' the beginning of his philosophical quest (*adv. Colotem* 1118C).[23] The *Alcibiades I*, with its central consideration of the maxim, is mentioned as the ideal starting point for Platonic teaching in general by Albinus (*Prologos* 5).[24]

---

19 Porphyry calls the latter τὰ ἡμέτερα and τὰ τῶν ἡμετέρων, terminology adopted from *Alc. I* 133c22–e3. On a possible exegesis of *Alc. I* that may underlie the whole of this passage see Renaud and Tarrant (2015), 162–164.

20 ὅτι μὲν ἀπὸ τῶν ἐν ἡμῖν συλλογιζόμεθα καὶ περὶ τῶν ἐν τῷ ὅλῳ καὶ ἡμᾶς ἐτάζοντες καὶ εὑρίσκοντες ῥᾷον μεταβαίνομεν ἐπὶ τὴν τοῦ παντὸς θεωρίαν, *On 'Know Yourself'* fr. 274F Smith.

21 *in hac ille magnificentia rerum atque in hoc conspectu et cognitione naturae, dii inmortales, quam se ipse noscet, quod Apollo praecepit Pythius!*

22 Porphyry himself made one of the chronologically last treatises of Plotinus – one that deals extensively with self-knowledge and the Platonic *Alcibiades I* – the first in his edition (*Enn.* I.1 [53]). Plotinus refers to the maxim at the beginning of IV.3 [27], as something he is obeying in beginning his examination of the human soul.

23 Plutarch elsewhere compares the maxim, and other Delphic maxims, to a σπέρμα and a γόνιμος λόγος (*De E* 385D).

24 Iamblichus was later to organise or consolidate the Neoplatonic curriculum into two cycles of ten and two dialogues, respectively, the former starting with the *Alcibiades I*. Proclus offers theoretical support for this, which may largely derive from Iamblichus, connecting this pole position explicitly to the Delphic 'know yourself' (*in Alc.* 5.1–6.7). We may have traces of this already in Cicero (who may be following Antiochus of Ascalon here, cf. Boyancé (1963)): in *Leg.* 1.58–62 and *Tusc.* 5.70–72, he presents the acquisition of Delphic self-knowledge as the beginning (and in some ways also the completion) of a trajectory through the three parts of philosophy. Cf. Boyancé (1963); Pépin (1971), 55–62; Courcelle (1974), 27–38; Lévy (1992), 451–494. Renaud and Tarrant (2015), 122–124 revisit this curricular question and agree that

Apart from different proposals about what it means to know oneself, Platonic authors also thematise the maxim itself and the difficulty of obeying it. As in the *Charmides* and *Alcibiades I*, they ask about its author as a way of underlining its importance, often opting for a divine origin in the end. For instance, the first preserved fragment of Porphyry's *On 'Know Yourself'* opens with the question 'what and whose was the sacred command in Delphi?', continues with a long list of possible attributions, and ends by stating that it was 'said by god or not without god' (fr. 273F Smith). (See also Cicero, *Leg.* 1.58, *Fin.* 5.44, *Tusc.* 1.52; Plutarch, *Dem.* 3.2).

Finally, in Cicero specifically, we find the dialogic aspect of the *Alcibiades I* in some passages that deal with 'know yourself'. In *Tusculan Disputations* 1.52, the speaker is made to exhort his interlocutor by drawing attention to the personal implication of the idea that human beings are their souls: *neque nos corpora sumus, nec ego tibi haec dicens corpori tuo dico* ('nor are we bodies, nor do I, in saying this, say it to your body').[25]

Clement's transposition of the Platonic 'know yourself' in *Stromateis* 1

Self-knowledge in the context of *Stromateis* 1

The *Stromateis* is the most ambitious of Clement's preserved works in scope as well as aim. While his aim in the *Protrepticus* had been to exhort fellow Christians and in the *Paedagogus* to show the Greeks that Christianity is the true philosophy, the *Stromateis* seems to pursue both goals at once.[26] Moreover, it also offers the advanced Christian the elements needed to reach a state of deep, knowledgeable faith, which Clement calls *gnôsis*. This choice of word indicates an ulterior aim of the work: to show that Clement can offer the sort of intellectual salvation that some of his rivals, the gnostics, offer, but within the boundaries – as Clement claims – of the established church. Polemic, exhortation, integration: the *Stromateis* serves different purposes with respect to different audiences. The scope of the work matches this multiplicity. Its seven books discuss ethics, epistemology

---

it is plausible to think that already in Cicero's time, the *Alc. I* was treated as the first dialogue to be read when studying Plato, much as it was in the Neoplatonic curriculum from Iamblichus onwards.

25 The same dialogic aspect is present in a closely parallel passage in which, however, the maxim is not mentioned explicitly: *Rep.* 6.26, in which Scipio's grandfather tells Scipio: *Tu uero enitere et sic habeto, non esse te mortalem, sed corpus hoc; nec enim tu is es, quem forma ista declarat, ... non ea figura, quae digito demonstrari potest.* Outside the Platonic tradition we find a similar dialogic element connected with the maxim in the Aristotelian *Magna Moralia* (1213a10–26).

26 Cf. Méhat (1966), 134. On the place of the *Stromateis* among Clement's works see Osborn (2005), 5–15.

and metaphysics, making use of an exceptionally broad range of both biblical and Greek philosophical and poetic texts. It contains clear and plain passages as well as sections that are very difficult to understand indeed. Most of the text is dense with allusions that require knowledge of the original contexts of the passages cited to appreciate the full sense of what Clement is trying to convey.[27]

In the course of the seven books, Clement invokes the maxim 'know yourself' for two main reasons. First, he uses it repeatedly to illustrate the Greeks' habit of resorting to symbols, including gnomic expressions, to express hidden truths. The reason this matters to him is that he wishes to claim that the Hebrew Scriptures riddlingly convey the true Christian philosophy. If Clement can show that the Greeks themselves, and other peoples too for that matter, are in the habit of using such means of communication, this will make his claim plausible in the eyes of his Greek readers. The use of symbols at play in 1.60 (to be discussed below), in 2.70.4, 5.23.1 and in 5.45.4. Second, Clement also refers to 'know yourself' in order to to tie this old Greek maxim to his beliefs as a Christian. In 4.27.2 he says that to know oneself is to find one's soul, which he has just explained is what happens when you repent of your sins. In 7.20.7–8 he connects 'know yourself' to obedience to God's commandments as the purpose of our existence.[28]

In this chapter I will focus on the three passages in the first book that mention the maxim, because through them Clement aims to do something more than connect an old maxim to new content or to provide an illustration of concise communication. Clement's successive comments about the maxim in book one, I will argue, show that he uses it programmatically: they offer a progressive account of what is meant by self-knowledge and, in doing so, chart the ideal development of his reader. The three passages together offer an encompassing notion of self-knowledge, taking the reader from the un-Greek beginnings of 'know yourself' to the Mosaic and epoptic vision of truth that crowns philosophical development. Such a programmatic use of the maxim in the first book fits its Platonic association with the beginning of philosophy,[29] an association with which Clement is familiar, as the first of the passages discussed below shows. Our three passages come at significant moments in the book: the first occurs when Clement first turns to the content of early Greek philosophy; the second expands on this after Clement has demonstrated the temporal priority of Moses' wisdom over

---

27 That context would have been very familiar to many of Clement's readers. His use of τὰς συνήθεις ... δόξας τε καὶ φωνάς is also meant to attract their attention, as he says in 1.16.2. But note that the φιλοσοφίας δόγματα also serve to hide the truth as a nut is enveloped by its shell (1.18.1). For discussion see Méhat (1966), 125–135.
28 See Courcelle (1974), 77–80 for an overview of these texts.
29 See p. 65 above, and the *Alcibiades I*. See n. 24 for the programmatic status of self-knowledge for the Neoplatonists from Iamblichus onwards, who placed the *Alcibiades I* at the head of the ten plus two Platonic dialogues of the curriculum mainly because of its treatment of self-knowledge. On this, see Renaud and Tarrant (2015), 170, 178–180.

Greek philosophy; and the third reveals Clement's reorientation of the notion of self-knowledge near the end of book one.

Clement's handling of the maxim of 'know yourself' shows that he is intent on pursuing a two-sided project: in the very same passages and sometimes even in the very same words, he aims to evince deep parallels between Platonic and Christian motifs and texts while signalling the superiority of Christian truth. In the process, he can encourage Christian readers to have philosophical respect for their own tradition and invite Platonic readers to see Christian thought as a continuation of what they hold dear.

The origin of 'know yourself'

Let us briefly consider the run-up to the first passage. The first book opens with a defence of writing (in clear response to the *Phaedrus*' criticism of it)[30] and then offers an apology of philosophy, which essentially runs along three lines: Clement argues that philosophy too is a gift from God, one that was even given to the Greeks as a preparation for faith (1.20–21, 1.25–38); he distinguishes true philosophy from the type of activity that focuses on victory in debate or on technicalities (1.22–24, 1.39–42, 1.47–51); and he argues that philosophy is necessary for a full understanding and articulation of the Christian faith (1.43–46, 1.51–54).[31] In 1.55–56, Clement returns to a topic addressed in the prologue, emphasising his own trepidation in communicating true wisdom and reiterating the need to purify our ears in order to receive it.

1.57–58 is a section that marks a transition towards a consideration of Greek philosophy in relation to Hebrew wisdom. Clement describes this relation as that between a whole and its parts: Greek philosophical schools (just like other religious traditions) have torn off parts of the truth, claiming that these are the whole truth. Clement thinks that while it would be a mistake to believe this claim, the truth that the schools do possess can be appreciated and explored. In the long section that follows, from 1.59 onwards, Clement elaborates in detail on his claim that the earliest Greek sages were conscious or unconscious imitators of Hebrew wisdom.

Clement's plan in 1.59 and the following paragraphs, then, is to showcase both what truth the Greeks have obtained and to argue that this truth was derived from the truth that God revealed to Moses and the Hebrews.[32] In doing so, he engages

---

30 On this defence and its relation to the *Phaedrus*, see Osborn (1959); Wyrwa (1983), 30–46; Itter (2009), 114–121.
31 On the place of philosophy in relation to faith for Clement, see Osborn (2005), 199–203; Méhat (1966), 346–394.
32 The argumentative strategy of deriving legitimacy from anteriority was not an exclusively Christian; Greek-Jewish writers had written about Moses' seniority with respect to Greek wisdom, and in the Greek tradition itself the link between chronological age and worth is clearly present from Hecataeus onwards, as Pilhofer (1990) shows. See Boys-Stones (2001) for the more

with the content (rather than status) of Greek philosophy for the first time in this work.[33] He begins with the Seven Sages, the first to be considered famous on the basis of their wisdom. He lists them and comments on some of the differences in the lists by later writers. He then goes on to say (*Str.* 1.60, II.38.11–22 Stählin):

> Let us now look into the characteristic style of the philosophy they practised, as it is Hebraic and enigmatic. They welcomed brevity: it is exhortative and very useful indeed. Plato himself says that it was because of [its/their] seriousness that there was this style in early times, generally among all the Greeks, but especially among the Spartans and Cretans, the most lawful peoples. The phrase 'Know yourself', in any case, some have taken to be by Chilon, Chamaileon in *On the Gods* to be by Thales, and Aristotle by the Pythia. It means to enjoin us to pursue knowledge, since without the being of the whole it is impossible to know its parts; we must therefore concern ourselves with the coming to be of the cosmos, through which it will be possible fully to understand human nature as well.[34]

Clement here argues that the first Greek philosophers exhibit a style (τρόπος) that betrays the Hebrew origin of their philosophy. This directly supports his case. As if to show this in more detail, Clement starts to discuss a number of old maxims that are often associated with the Seven Sages, 'know yourself' being the first of them.

Clement makes two different comments about the phrase 'know yourself'. First, he comments on the authorship of the phrase, pointing out that there is disagreement among earlier authors about who exactly said or wrote it. Second, he adds a comment on what it means. As the passage continues, Clement mentions other maxims associated with the Seven Sages. In each case, he mentions the

---

specific form of the argument which sees disagreements between schools of philosophy as signs of deviation from a unified and ancient tradition of truth; Boys-Stones argues that this form of the argument was developed by thinkers often referred to as Middle Platonists and adopted by Christian writers. For a recent discussion of this theme in Clement's work, see Gibbons (2019), ch. 2.

33 Clement does mention Greek views in earlier paragraphs, of course, but they are either statements about the status of philosophy and of sophistry, or views which Clement considers sophistic and rejects. Examples of the latter can be found for instance in 1.50–51, where Clement explains that Paul's negative comment about 'philosophy' in *Col.* 2.8 is directed only at views like Epicurean hedonism or Stoic materialism, which Clement associates with sophistry and qualifies as 'childish' (1.51.2).

34 ὁ δὲ τρόπος τῆς παρ' αὐτοῖς φιλοσοφίας, ὡς Ἑβραϊκὸς καὶ αἰνιγματώδης, ἤδη ἐπισκεπτέος. βραχυλογίαν γοῦν ἠσπάζοντο τὴν παραινετικήν, τὴν ὠφελιμωτάτην. αὐτίκα Πλάτων πάλαι διὰ σπουδῆς γεγονέναι τόνδε τὸν τρόπον λέγει, κοινῶς μὲν πᾶσιν Ἕλλησιν, ἐξαιρέτως δὲ Λακεδαιμονίοις καὶ Κρησὶ τοῖς εὐνομωτάτοις. Τὸ μὲν οὖν «γνῶθι σαυτὸν» οἳ μὲν Χίλωνος ὑπειλήφασι, Χαμαιλέων δὲ ἐν τῷ περὶ θεῶν Θαλοῦ, Ἀριστοτέλης δὲ τῆς Πυθίας. δύναται δὲ τὴν γνῶσιν ἐγκελεύεσθαι μεταδιώκειν. οὐκ ἔστι γὰρ ἄνευ τῆς τῶν ὅλων οὐσίας εἰδέναι τὰ μέρη· δεῖ δὴ τὴν γένεσιν τοῦ κόσμου πολυπραγμονῆσαι, δι' ἧς καὶ τὴν τοῦ ἀνθρώπου φύσιν καταμαθεῖν ἐξέσται. Translations are mine unless otherwise indicated.

candidates for authorship of the phrase, but he adds no explanation of what the respective phrase means – this happens only in connection with 'know yourself'.

According to Clement, γνῶθι σεαυτόν is a command to pursue knowledge. The word for 'knowledge' here is γνῶσις, which not only corresponds to the verb γνῶθι but is also the word that Clement uses for the fullest kind of understanding, available only to the Christian who has deepened his faith by combining it with philosophy. 'Know yourself' stands at the beginning of philosophy as Clement sees it. This is because knowing oneself inevitably involves (or perhaps consists in) knowing what a human being is. And since human beings are parts of the whole that is the cosmos, and one cannot know a part without knowing the whole, knowledge of oneself will require knowledge of the cosmos.

How does this passage engage with Platonic treatments of 'know yourself'? It is clear that *Protagoras* 342–343 was on Clement's mind or in his hands when he wrote this passage. Just before the beginning of the section cited above, Clement gives a list of the Seven Sages which differs from Plato's in the *Protagoras* in featuring Periander of Corinth instead of Myson of Chen. Clement himself comments on this difference: 'Plato inserts Myson of Chen instead of Periander, whose having been a tyrant made him unworthy of wisdom'.[35] Clement also makes use of another element of the *Protagoras* passage, the idea that concision (βραχυλογία) is a mark of archaic philosophy.[36] He exploits the fact that Plato drives a wedge between philosophy as it was known in his own days and its origin: first, Socrates departs from standard accounts of the beginning of philosophy and attributes it to the Spartans and Cretans, whom the Athenians considered to be unphilosophical. Moreover, Plato has Socrates present this origin as a hidden one: the Spartans and Cretans were unwilling to communicate it to others. Both factors render the origin of philosophy open to reinterpretation, which allows Clement to introduce yet another origin for philosophy. Like Plato, he demotes the Seven Sages to the status of epigones, but they turn out not to be students of the Spartans but ultimately of Moses. In an adroit transposition of the original motif, Clement treats the βραχυλογία which Plato says characterises early philosophy as an indication of this Hebrew origin of philosophy.

To the same purpose, Clement finds new use for the Platonic practice of underlining the significance of 'know yourself' by raising the question of its

---

35 Πλάτων δὲ ἀντὶ Περιάνδρου ὡς ἀναξίου σοφίας διὰ τὸ τετυραννηκέναι ἀντικατατάττει Μύσωνα τὸν Χηνέα (38.8–9 St.). The motivation Clement offers does not occur in the *Protagoras*. *Republic* 336a5 mentions Periander among four possible authors of the definition of justice as helping one's friends and harming one's enemies; what unites the four is that they are rich and think that they μέγα δύνασθαι. This may have been a common connection in Platonic exegesis, but it is implausible to suggest that Clement here did not base himself directly on the *Protagoras* (pace Wyrwa (1983), 72–73).

36 cf. βραχυλογία in *Str.* 1.60.2 (38.12–13 St.) and *Prot.* 343b5, τρόπος in 1.60.1–2 (38.11–14 St.) and *Prot.* 343b4; and αἰνιγματώδης in 1.60.1 (38.12 St.) with αἰνιγματωδέστερον in *Chrm.* 164e6.

origin. When he introduces the phrase as the first of the statements by the Seven Sages, he too makes explicit mention of the uncertainty of its attribution. This common element in Platonic treatments of 'know yourself' lends support to his view: for Clement, the fact that Platonic authors thematise the difficulty they have in attributing the phrase only shows that the Greeks are deeply ignorant of where their wisdom comes from, namely from the Hebrews.

The content of 'know yourself'

In *Str.* 1.60.3–4, Clement also gives a first characterisation of the meaning of the Delphic injunction: he describes it as a command to pursue wisdom. In view of the connection of 'know yourself' and the different parts of philosophy, it is clear that Clement here makes use of a common Platonic element. He agrees particularly with the idea that the phrase is protreptic, an exhortation to engage in philosophy. As we have seen, Clement thereby joins cause with those who regard 'know yourself' as the beginning of philosophy. This interpretation also agrees well with the presence of the theme of self-knowledge in the first book of *Stromateis*.[37]

It is also revealing that Clement associates the phrase with the question of human nature (ἡ τοῦ ἀνθρώπου φύσις, II.38.21 St.). The pursuit of self-knowledge is not a matter merely of the moral awareness of one's own limits and potential (for instance), but is rather an anthropological question. This too is a familiar element from the Greek philosophical tradition. It is particularly associated with the *Alcibiades I*, which was also known by its subtitle, περὶ φύσεως ἀνθρώπου.[38]

The anthropological question itself is tied closely to a cosmological question in *Str.* 1.60.4. In other words, from his first mention of 'know yourself', Clement interprets the phrase as a question involving knowledge of the cosmos. In doing so, he works along Platonic lines, as described above (p. 65). At the same time, Clement's approach is in strong contrast to Socrates' attitude in the *Phaedrus*, where he says that he cannot occupy himself with (myths about) questions of natural philosophy before he has achieved self-knowledge.[39]

In Clement, the cosmological question is more specifically a cosmogonical one. Clement signals his Christian position by speaking of the γένεσις of the cosmos as the object of study for anyone wishing to get to know himself. This is an idea that returns in our second passage from Clement, *Str.* 1.94 (cited below,

---

37 This is not to say that it is not present in other books, see p. 67.
38 Clement's familiarity with the *Alc. I* is beyond doubt: he explicitly quotes from it in *Str.* 2.22.5 (II.124.18–20 St.) and 5.17.2 (II.336.29–337.1–4 St.).
39 This may explain why Clement uses the word πολυπραγμονεῖν, which in Clement's classical models has the negative connotation of interfering with things that are not your business. It is as if Clement, in the very act of recommending that human beings study the universe, feels compelled to make at least a verbal concession to the *Phaedrus* paradigm. I thank Bert van den Berg for highlighting Clement's lexical choice here.

p. 73). There, Clement specifies that we must come to know God as the creative cause, which in our third passage *Str.* 1.178 (cited below, pp. 76–77) is described as the father of the all. Although Greek philosophers could also speak of the divine as the maker of the universe (think of literal interpretations of the *Timaeus* or of the Stoic notion of pneuma as πῦρ τεχνικόν), Clement emphasises this idea to an extent that distances him from the Greek philosophical tradition.

The way to 'know yourself': the divine within

Clement's reinterpretation of Platonic patterns to suit his Christian message is most conspicuous in his description of the method by which we can come to know ourselves. We have seen that the Platonic tradition tightly links knowledge of the universe and self-knowledge. But how exactly is self-knowledge in a narrower sense connected to knowledge of the universe? The *Alcibiades I* contains the idea that knowing all of the divine is prior to knowing ourselves, and that the connection between the two is to be found in the fundamental similarity between them (ἔοικεν, 133c4), which consists in their being divine. As noted above, this model is very different from that of the *Phaedrus*, where Socrates seems to be much more modest epistemically and to posit self-knowledge as prior to any attempt to study physics. Related to the notion of similarity is what we found in Porphyry: that we can pass from knowledge of ourselves as human beings to knowledge of the cosmos because the human being is a microcosm and so contains on a smaller scale all that can be found in the cosmos at large. But, at the same time, Porphyry himself seems hesitant; he agrees that there is a connection between knowing oneself and knowing the universe, but he speaks of it as an epistemic transition that is made *easier*, without suggesting that the two kinds of knowledge are one and the same thing. In Cicero, similarity also seems to play an important role, insofar as both soul and universe are divine.[40] But Cicero also speaks of a different connection between knowing oneself and knowing the universe, a connection established through the concepts in the human mind. In *De Legibus* 1.59 Cicero suggests that we can come to understand ethics, physics and logic on the basis of the *adumbratae intelligentiae* which have formed in our minds.

Clement is not unsympathetic to such ideas. In *Str.* 1.60.4, he agrees with the thought that we need to have knowledge of the universe before we can understand human nature as part of the whole. But the main method to obtain self-knowledge that he proposes in *Stromateis* 1 is markedly different, as our second passage,

---

40 *Rep.* 6.26 posits a comparison (*tam ... quam*) between the human soul which governs the human body and the eternal god who governs the world; the suggestion is that this thought helps understand that the human soul too is divine because it engages in the same activities as god. However, the passage does not explicitly state that one needs to know the whole in order to know oneself.

Str. 1.94, shows.[41] After 1.60, Clement first continues his discussion by tracing the chronology of Greek philosophy after the Seven Sages, distinguishing three schools of philosophy and providing an account of the successions within these schools. He also shows that Greek philosophers themselves at various points acknowledge inspiration from non-Greeks, and that there are all kinds of arts as well as cultural and technological achievements whose inventors are 'barbarians'. Having thus established the priority of non-Greek wisdom over Greek philosophy (and culture), Clement returns to the question of how one should evaluate the Greeks' derivation of their wisdom from others. In 1.81–87, for instance, he gives a nuanced response to the suggestion that it ought to be considered a case of theft.

In 1.94, Clement considers four alternative explanations of why Greek philosophers were able to formulate (part of) the truth. In his view, each of these explanations implies that God is the ultimate cause, whether the proximate cause be (i) chance (περίπτωσις, συντυχία), (ii) a kind of natural knowledge (φυσικὴ ἔννοια, κοινὸς νοῦς), (iii) prophecy (προαναφώνησις, συνεκφώνησις), or (iv) some kind of reflection of the truth (ἔμφασις ἀληθείας).[42] Clement discusses the last of these at greater length (1.94.3–7, II.60.22–61.5 St.):

> Indeed, others claim that some things were said by the philosophers by an appearance of truth. The divinely sounding apostle writes about us: 'for now we look as if through a mirror', knowing ourselves by reflection in it and in so doing, on the basis of what is divine in us and to the extent that we can, contemplating our productive cause as well. It is written: 'for you have seen your brother, you have seen your God'. I think the Saviour is named God for us here. But after putting aside the flesh, 'face to face'; [we will see] definitely and cognitively when our heart becomes pure. And those among the Greeks who have been precise in their philosophy see through to God by appearance and transparency. For of this kind are the impressions of truth through weakness, the way an impression sees what is seen in water or through transparent and clear bodies.[43]

---

41 For a complementary account of the ἀνάβασις of the soul see Rizzerio (1996), 271–290. Rizzerio, whose focus is not on self-knowledge, distinguishes three phases in this process, in which physics occupies the second rung and the third involves the intervention of the Son.
42 On this passage and its division into four possible origins see Molland (1936), especially 65–71. See also Lilla (1971), 12–16 (but note that Lilla combines elements which in Clement seem to belong to distinct explanations).
43 ναὶ μὴν κατ' ἔμφασιν ἀληθείας ἄλλοι θέλουσιν εἰρῆσθαί τινα τοῖς φιλοσόφοις. ὁ μὲν οὖν θεσπέσιος ἀπόστολος ἐφ' ἡμῶν γράφει· «βλέπομεν γὰρ νῦν ὡς δι' ἐσόπτρου», κατ' ἀνάκλασιν ἐπ' αὐτοῦ ἑαυτοὺς γινώσκοντες κἀκ τοῦ ἐν ἡμῖν θείου τὸ ποιητικὸν αἴτιον ὡς οἷόν τε συνθεωροῦντες· «εἶδες γάρ», φησί, «τὸν ἀδελφόν σου, εἶδες τὸν θεόν σου.» τὸν σωτῆρα οἶμαι θεὸν εἰρῆσθαι ἡμῖν τὰ νῦν· μετὰ δὲ τὴν τῆς σαρκὸς ἀπόθεσιν «πρόσωπον πρὸς πρόσωπον», τότε ἤδη ὁριστικῶς καὶ καταληπτικῶς, ὅταν καθαρὰ ἡ καρδία γένηται. καὶ κατ' ἔμφασιν δὲ καὶ διάφασιν οἱ ἀκριβῶς παρ' Ἕλλησι φιλοσοφήσαντες διορῶσι τὸν θεόν· τοιαῦται γὰρ αἱ κατ' ἀδυναμίαν φαντασίαι ἀληθείας, ὡς φαντασία καθορᾷ τὰ ἐν τοῖς ὕδασιν ὁρώμενα καὶ τὰ διὰ τῶν διαφανῶν καὶ διαυγῶν σωμάτων. – The MS reading of the last sentence must be emended: τοιαῦται γὰρ αἱ κατ' ἀδυναμίαν φαντασίαι

This is a remarkable but difficult passage.[44] The length of the account of this fourth explanation suggests that Clement is favourably disposed towards it.[45] For our purposes, we should note a number of apparently unmotivated shifts in the type of knowledge described here. First, the passage starts out by explaining that the Greeks possessed at least some wisdom because they saw some kind of appearance of the truth: here Clement uses ἔμφασις in a general sense.[46] But he proceeds by taking ἔμφασις in a much narrower sense, as the reflection in a mirroring surface. He produces and underlines this shift by citing Paul's pronouncement to the Corinthians that we now look as if into a mirror.[47] Second, from a consideration of the general truths articulated by Greek philosophers, Clement moves on to a much more specific kind of knowledge: self-knowledge. What we seemed to be talking about up until and including the citation from Paul were appearances in mirrors as a means of indirect vision: the Greeks were able to see the truth which they could not see directly, while Paul speaks of our inability to see God directly but only via the surface of a mirror. It is Clement himself who, in his comments after the citation, connects the image of the mirror to the issue of seeing and knowing *oneself*. In this double restriction of his fourth explanation, Clement is activating in his reader's mind the text of the *Alcibiades I*, in which the mirror is indeed a way of knowing oneself and in which knowledge of oneself is connected to knowing the whole of the divine.[48] When Clement continues by referring to τὸ ἐν ἡμῖν θεῖον, therefore, he initially invites his philosophically schooled reader – especially those among his audience who see themselves as Platonists – to identify this as our intellect.

ἀληθεῖς, ὡς φαντασία καθορᾶται ἐν τοῖς ὕδασιν ὁρῶμεν καὶ τὰ διὰ τῶν διαφανῶν καὶ διαυγῶν σωμάτων. I have translated the reading of the fourth edition of Stählin/Früchtel/Treu, but this too is cumbersome. The general sense is clear, however. Clement seems to be alluding to *Resp.* 510a1–2, the things seen in the lowest rung of the divided line.

44 (i) The citation from Paul is from 1 *Cor.* 13.12, where our text reads βλέπομεν γὰρ ἄρτι δι' ἐσόπτρου ἐν αἰνίγματι, τότε δὲ πρόσωπον πρὸς πρόσωπον· ἄρτι γινώσκω ἐκ μέρους, τότε δὲ ἐπιγνώσομαι καθὼς καὶ ἐπεγνώσθην. (ii) The saying (*logion*) is cited also at *Strom.* 2.70.5 (as the origin of γνῶθι σεαυτόν); and by Tertullian, *De Oratione* 26; and in the *Apophthegmata patrum* Ammonathas 3 (PG 65:136). It is included as *agraphon* 144 in Resch's collection. It is the object of study in Bauer (1989); see also Cain (2013), 352 n. 19. (iii) Seeing god is for the καθαροὶ τῇ καρδίᾳ in *Matth.* 5.8. (iv) The expression ἐμφάσεις καὶ διαφάσεις ... τῆς ... ἀληθείας occurs in Xenocrates, who speaks of the view of the truth about daemons that is preserved in the mysteries (fr. 227 Parente, preserved in Plutarch, *De def. or.* 416d; also used in *De Is. et Os.* 354c). The talk of mirrors and knowing oneself is also meant to allude to the *Alc. I*, as I will suggest below (NB that Socrates thematises ἀκριβῶς philosophising in *Alc. I* 130c8–9).
45 It is also plausible to see a climax in the four explanations offered, as Molland (1936), 71–72 argues.
46 On ἔμφασις in Clement see Molland (1936) 72–75.
47 On the role of this citation in Clement's epistemology see Mortley (1976), especially 114–118 on this passage.
48 The activation of the *Alc. I* as an intertext is also assisted by Clement's invocation of Paul's phrase 'πρόσωπον πρὸς πρόσωπον'. Osborn (1957), 163 identifies the face of God with the Son.

In a third and double shift, however, Clement purposefully modifies this understanding of τὸ ἐν ἡμῖν θεῖον. He first adds that we are able to 'study' our creative cause 'alongside' (συνθεωροῦντες) ourselves: knowledge of the creator turns out to be closely connected to self-knowledge, as it was in 1.60. He then continues by citing the saying of Jesus (*logion*) 'you have seen your brother, you have seen your God' and by specifying that this citation concerns the 'Saviour'. Here, the divine ἐν ἡμῖν is no longer the human intellect but the divine *among us*, the Saviour who was both fellow human and God.[49] The figure of a mirror in which we can see ourselves gives way to the figure of the brother. From the context of *Alc. I* 132c–133c, we can understand why Clement identifies another human being as the mirror into which one might want to look in search of self-knowledge. Indeed, as we saw in Cicero, the dialogic element of the process of self-knowledge remained present in the Platonic tradition. But Clement gives a clearly Christian twist to this motif by speaking of a 'brother' and particularly by identifying this brother with God.[50] In the course of this passage, then, Clement alludes to a model for the attainment of self-knowledge which is prominent in the Platonic tradition, and then reinterprets key phrases of that model (κάτ-/εἴσοπτρον, τὸ ἐν ἡμῖν θεῖον) to construct an alternative route to self-knowledge for his own Christian tradition, i.e. via the brother-God of the *logion*.[51]

A final shift worth noting in 1.94 is from the Greek philosophers to a group that includes Clement and his fellow Christians. From the citation from Paul onwards, Clement no longer ascribes a particular epistemic condition only to the Greek philosophers, but speaks of 'we'. He includes himself and potential Christian readers in the group of those who, by looking at the brother-God, will be able to see God. The ἔμφασις which allows the most precise of Greek philosophers (ἀκριβῶς φιλοσοφήσαντες) to see the real object of their desire for wisdom, i.e. God, is the same mechanism by which the Christian gnostic too obtains

---

49 Molland (1936), 70 considers the *logion* and its application to the σωτήρ a 'digression', dealing with *revelatio specialis* in a context otherwise concerned with *revelatio generalis*, to which Clement returns in the sequel. But this interpretation plays down the transposition Clement effects here. Mortley (1976), 117–118 also points to the 'Christological' interpretation of τὸ ἐν ἡμῖν θεῖον; however, in leaving no room for the traditional, Platonic, reading of it, he effectively rules out the transposition from the Platonic to the Christian interpretation of the phrase.

50 Pépin (1971), 192 also draws attention to the close links of this passage with *Alc. I* 132d–133c; however, overlooking the identification of the brother with God, he is led to posit knowledge of ourselves as an intermediary link between knowledge of one's neighbour and knowledge of God; the divine in us, on this reading, remains what it was in the Platonic tradition, one's own intellect.

51 Note that the commandment to love one's neighbour is in the background here, too. On the relational aspect of the good life in Clement, see Reydams-Schils (2020), 134–137.

knowledge of God (before he has reached the final stage of mystical, face-to-face contemplation). In this sense, the passage is part of Clement's exhortation to his readers to pursue knowledge.[52]

The guide to 'know yourself': the Son superior to Socrates

The transposition of meaning which we have just studied in the phrase τὸ ἐν ἡμῖν θεῖον is not isolated, as becomes clear from our third passage, 1.178. This passage is part of the penultimate section of book one (1.176–179). From 1.151 onwards, Clement focuses first on Moses' life and qualities and then on his greatest achievement, the law which he gave. This gives Clement the opportunity, in 1.176–179, to offer a description of the 'philosophy of Moses', which he identifies with dialectic and which generates the sort of wisdom he is really after.[53] This can plausibly be seen as the climax of this first book, before Clement ends with another reaffirmation of the anteriority of Hebrew to Greek wisdom.[54] Clement starts with the claim that Mosaic philosophy has four parts: the historical and the legislative parts, which are comparable to ethics in the Greek division of philosophy; the ceremonial (ἱερουργικόν), which can be compared to physics; and the fourth part, called 'theology' and 'epoptics'. This fourth is the highest part of philosophy. Clement explicitly credits Aristotle and Plato with having recognised it under different names, but points out that it is already contained in the Mosaic law.[55] This highest wisdom is true dialectic (*Str.* 1.178.1–2, II.109.19–29 St.):

> It [dialectic] alone leads us by the hand towards true wisdom, which is a divine power, which knows the things that are as they are, which has perfection, which is released from all passion, not without the Saviour who by the divine word draws down from off the seeing part of our soul the mist-like ignorance, poured over it by a poor way of life, and restores what is best, 'in order that we know both god and man'. It is he who truly demonstrates how

---

52 The passage may be compared with *Str.* 7.56–57, where sight through mirrors is finally left behind by the gnostic souls who journey up to the highest places. On this theme see Osborn (1957), 162–163.
53 On Clement's view of dialectic see Osborn (2005), 62–68 (66 for a paraphrase of our passage); cf. Mondésert (1944), 124–126 on the role of dialectic in scriptural exegesis.
54 Clement underscores this anteriority by citing Plato's *Timaeus* 22b4–8, where the Egyptian priest tells Solon that the Greeks have no ancient wisdom. As Wyrwa has pointed out (1983: 83–87, 100, 131–133), this citation closes (at 1.180.1, II.110.13–15 St.) a string of Platonic citations from 1.165 onwards, just as an earlier string of Platonic citations in 1.66.3–69.3, used to demonstrate Plato's dependence on barbarian wisdom, also closes with *Tim.* 22b4–8. This supports the idea that in terms of content, our passage constitutes the climax in book 1 of Clement's Christian appropriation of Platonic wisdom, including self-knowledge.
55 Van den Hoek (1988), 48–68 shows that Clement systematically uses and adapts Philo's *De Vita Moysis* in his treatment of Moses (1.151–182). On the Platonic and Stoic background of 1.151–182, see also Gibbons (2015).

we may know ourselves, he who reveals the father of the whole to whom he wishes, as far as human nature is able to advance: 'for no one knows the Son but the Father, nor the Father but the Son and to whomever the Son reveals him.'[56]

At the beginning of this passage, Clement offers a description of dialectic in terms that one might also expect to find in a non-Christian text: it is a wisdom that knows all beings for what they are and that has been purified of all πάθος.[57] Clement next makes the transition to explicitly Christian content by means of an abrupt transitional phrase, οὐκ ἄνευ – this wisdom, Clement clarifies, is inseparable from the Son of God. He calls him the Saviour, who dispels the mist from the mind's eye and gives what is best, i.e. knowledge of things human and divine, as the citation from Homer (*Il.* 5.128) seems intended to convey (more on this below).[58] In this passage, much as in 1.94, we get a fairly sudden transition to self-knowledge, with a focus here on the method by which this may be obtained. Based on the juxtaposition with the statement that the Saviour reveals the Father of the universe, it is plausible to interpret Clement as pointing to knowledge of the Father as being this method by which we may come to know ourselves.[59]

Before we look at the Christian transposition of Platonic ideas that Clement produces in this passage, let us consider the elements, in addition to the theme of self-knowledge, which tie 1.178 back to 1.60 and 1.94, in thought and wording. Let me mention three. First, the suffix -τέον in γνωστέον ἑαυτούς makes it clear that Clement is thinking of the Delphic imperative γνῶθι σεαυτόν. This calls to mind 1.60, where Clement introduced this imperative. Second, in 1.60 he suggested that this maxim implies that we ought to know the essence of the whole (ἡ τῶν ὅλων οὐσία) and therefore the coming to be of the cosmos (ἡ γένεσις τοῦ

---

56 καὶ μόνη αὕτη ἐπὶ τὴν ἀληθῆ σοφίαν χειραγωγεῖ, ἥτις ἐστὶ δύναμις θεία, τῶν ὄντων ὡς ὄντων γνωστική, τὸ τέλειον ἔχουσα, παντὸς πάθους ἀπηλλαγμένη, οὐκ ἄνευ τοῦ σωτῆρος τοῦ καταγαγόντος ἡμῶν τῷ θείῳ λόγῳ τοῦ ὁρατικοῦ τῆς ψυχῆς τὴν ἐπιχυθεῖσαν ἐκ φαύλης ἀναστροφῆς ἄγνοιαν ἀχλυώδη καὶ τὸ βέλτιστον ἀποδεδωκότος, 'ὄφρ᾽ εὖ γινώσκοιμεν ἠμὲν θεὸν ἠδὲ καὶ ἄνδρα'. οὗτός ἐστιν ὁ τῷ ὄντι δείξας ὅπως γνωστέον ἑαυτούς, οὗτος ὁ τῶν ὅλων τὸν πατέρα ἐκκαλύπτων, ᾧ ἂν βούληται, ὡς οἷόν τε τὴν ἀνθρωπίνην φύσιν χωρῆσαι· 'οὐδεὶς γὰρ ἔγνω τὸν υἱὸν εἰ μὴ ὁ πατήρ, οὐδὲ τὸν πατέρα εἰ μὴ ὁ υἱὸς καὶ ᾧ ἂν ὁ υἱὸς ἀποκαλύψῃ'.

57 For being ἀπηλλαγμένη of passions, cf. *Phd.* 70a7, 81a8. On the Platonic background of Clement's description of dialectic in 1.177–178 see Pépin (1972), esp. 379–383; and cf. Itter (2009), 81–87, esp. 84.

58 The passage emphasises insight as a gift given by God – on this aspect see Völker (1952), 322–325; and Mondésert (1944), 106. For Osborn (2005), 79, not the least among the things which the Saviour clears is the mind of the exegete himself. On this passage as a protreptic from Platonism to Christianity, see Wyrwa (1983), 131; and Völker (1952), 323 ('Tendenz propagandistisch').

59 The mention of the Son's revelation of the Father does not make the epistemic process much more transparent. As Méhat put it in 1966: 'Le rapport du Père au Fils […] c'est un point où la pensée de Clément reste encore pour nous bien obscure. Pour lui aussi peut-être…' (440). See also Osborn (1957), 38–40 and Osborn (2005), 122–136.

κόσμου). In this passage, he specifies that knowing oneself is made possible by the revelation of the father of the universe (ὁ τῶν ὅλων πατήρ). The connection to 1.60 seems a firm one. But the reference to the γένεσις of the cosmos also links 1.178 to 1.94, where we saw knowledge of oneself being paired with knowledge of the creative cause (of us? of the cosmos?). Third, 1.178 mentions human nature (τὴν ἀνθρωπίνην φύσιν, 109.27 St.) in close connection to self-knowledge, inviting comparison with the human nature in 1.60 (τὴν τοῦ ἀνθρώπου φύσιν). But this similarity actually marks an important distinction between the two passages: in 1.60, the idea is that we may understand the creation of the world and as a result know about our own nature, whereas in 1.178 human nature is adduced as a limitation on our power to know.

1.178 also continues the narrative from 1.94 in elaborating on the brother-God who provides the way to self-knowledge. Again, Clement here points to the Saviour as the guide who allows us to see and know ourselves. He thus comes to play the role that in Plato, and the *Alcibiades I* specifically, is reserved for Socrates.[60] Two elements of the text in particular connect Clement's description to the relationship between Socrates and Alcibiades. Clement describes the Saviour as freeing the eye of our soul from the misty (ἀχλυώδη) ignorance that now covers it.[61] As a result, we will be able to know god and man, as Clement adds with the citation from *Il.* 5.128. The idea to apply this line from Homer and to interpret the mist (the ἀχλύς of which Homer speaks in 5.127) as the ignorance of the philosophically unilluminated is not new. It first occurs, in fact, at the end of the *Alcibiades II* (150d6–e3), where Socrates identifies himself as the person who is able to dispel the mist of ignorance from Alcibiades' eyes.[62]

The second element of 1.178 which links this passage to Socrates and Alcibiades is the phrase that follows immediately after the citation. The Saviour is 'he who truly (τῷ ὄντι) demonstrates how we may know ourselves (γνωστέον ἑαυτούς, 109.25 St.)'. As we just saw, the last two words are meant to bring the Delphic phrase to mind. Note that the *Alcibiades I* emphasises the *method* of self-knowledge: Alcibiades asks Socrates how he may know himself and Socrates

---

60 Courcelle reaches the same conclusion in his succinct commentary on Clement, (1974), 79–80. See also Völker (1952), 323–324. In view of the presence of Moses in the sections preceding our passage, it is clear that Clement also demotes Moses from the status he had in Philo; see Van den Hoek (1988), 48–68, 218–219, 228–229.
61 Cf. *Protr.* 114.1, where Clement exhorts the readers themselves to take away (καταγαγόντες) the ἀχλύς from their sight in order to see the true God.
62 For most ancient readers, the fact that two different texts discuss the same philosophical relationship creates a much more significant unity between them than the modern habit of isolating texts as distinct literary units would allow. The case in point here is of course that of the *Alc. I* and *Alc. II*, but the same happens for instance with the *Alc. I* and the *Smp.* For discussion of this point see Tarrant (2000), 36–38. – Using ἀχλύς as an image for ignorance is common in the Platonic tradition. Clement takes the extra trouble of returning to the Homeric citation in *Alc. II*.

points to himself as the soul into which Alcibiades should look. τῷ ὄντι is Clement's way of indicating that the Son is a better guide than Socrates.

Closer inspection of the respective forms of the Homer citation in *Alcibiades II* and in Clement reveals a further aspect of the Christian transposition of Socratic pedagogy. In Homer, mist is on Diomedes' eyes as a result of an arrow wound he received. Athena comes down to clear his eyes, in order, as she says, that Diomedes may be able to distinguish men and gods on the battlefields. This is because she explicitly orders him to refrain from fighting against gods. In adopting this image in his philosophical discourse, the Socrates of *Alcibiades II* reinterprets the recognition of gods and men as the recognition of good and bad (150d9, e3: ἠμὲν κακὸν ἠδὲ καὶ ἐσθλόν). Clement stays closer to the letter of Homer's ἠμὲν θεὸν ἠδὲ καὶ ἄνδρα, but reinterprets this phrase in an important way: it now refers to the brother-God, who is not god *or* man but unites the two categories. The Saviour dispels the mist from our eyes in order that we may recognise *him* as God-man.

Conclusion

When read together, the three passages from *Stromateis* 1 in which Clement discusses self-knowledge constitute a progressive account of what is meant by it and how it can be achieved. Leading his reader from 'know yourself' as an exhortation to wisdom, via the Son as the brother-God, to dialectic as the highest part of philosophy, in which self-knowledge and knowledge of God coincide, Clement progressively unfolds his Christian interpretation of the Delphic injunction, showing the reader the path of philosophical development. This is a first conclusion that we can draw.

A second conclusion concerns how Clement's view of the way to know yourself relates to Platonic views. There is agreement between them about the initially exhortative character of the phrase and about the subsequently all-encompassing character of its fulfilment. But there is disagreement about the way in which this fulfilment can be achieved. In Clement, the Son is the referent of the phrase τὸ θεῖον ἐν ἡμῖν as well as the substitute for Socrates; he is the real means by which we may come to know ourselves. The connection between knowledge of the cosmos and self-knowledge in the narrow sense is not based on similarity between the human intellect and the divine governance of the world, although such similarity indeed exists. Ultimately, the connection is based on the coincidence of humanity and divinity in the Son, as well as on the Son's 'revelation' (ἐκκαλύπτων, ἀποκαλύψῃ) of the Father. The Greek injunction to know oneself thus becomes a deeply Christian epistemic quest in which knowing oneself is bound up with knowing the Creator and the Saviour, the cosmos and the incarnate deity.

This disagreement, however, is couched in terms that highlight the parallels between the traditions while at the same time revealing their differences. Clement makes subtle use of available Platonic motifs, texts and phrases. He also replaces them with Christian passages and references to signal ideas that he thinks have received a more profound treatment in Scripture than in Platonic texts. Particularly significant is the technique which he brings to bear on such substitutions. Clement moulds and combines his Christian texts in such a way that they follow established Platonic patterns to a great extent. The movement of thought we saw in 1.94, for instance, with its reference to mirroring, its combination of self-knowledge and knowledge of the divine, and its inclusion of one's fellow human being as instrumental to the attainment of this self-knowledge, bears a structural resemblance to the mirror passage of the *Alcibiades I*. This allows Clement to activate an intertext that provides a specific illustration of the Greeks' ability to state what is true (and which, as such, furnishes evidence of what he is claiming) and at the same time to highlight what is distinctive about his Christian views. This technique also allows him to turn the Christian texts he cites into suitable vehicles for Platonic ideas, thus to some extent supplanting the original Platonic formulations in their role as classic expressions of truth. In the case of 1.94, Paul's description of seeing through a mirror evokes ideas associated with the *Alcibiades I*, but it is Paul, not Plato, who is cited.

This manner in which Clement shapes his text has implications for the contribution that he makes to the development of a Christian tradition – and this is a fourth conclusion that we can draw. In transposing Platonic ideas into a Christian context and in constructing and exploiting the structural similarities between Platonic and Christian texts, Clement has a message for two potential audiences. For Platonic readers, Clement showcases the agreement of Christian doctrine with their deepest philosophical convictions and positions the Christian tradition as a meaningful continuation of the Platonic one. For readers who see themselves as Christians, Clement's treatment can stimulate confidence in the philosophical respectability of their own views and encourage a broad appreciation of the value of Greek culture and education. But it also assures them that their Christian tradition brings to light deeper truths than Greek philosophers were able to formulate and that their divine guide, the source of their tradition, is superior to the best of the Greek teachers.

SÉBASTIEN MORLET

L'accusation de mauvaise entente (παρακοή) dans la polémique entre païens et chrétiens à la fin de l'Antiquité

L'accusation de rupture avec la tradition compte parmi les accusations les plus anciennes et les plus importantes que les Grecs et les Romains aient formulées contre les chrétiens. Dans les Actes des apôtres, Paul doit déjà affronter les critiques de philosophes qui lui reprochent d'introduire des divinités étrangères (ξένων δαιμονίων), comme Socrate l'avait été avant lui par ses accusateurs (Ac 17, 18). De Celse à Damascius, les chrétiens seront constamment accusés d'avoir innové, c'est-à-dire d'avoir rompu avec les traditions ancestrales en introduisant sur le monde ou sur Dieu des idées fausses[1].

Mais comment les Grecs expliquaient-ils cette innovation (καινοτομία) ? L'explication la plus commune consistait à voir dans le christianisme une apostasie : les chrétiens étaient accusés de s'être *détournés* des traditions. Celse, au IIe s., formule plusieurs fois ce reproche. Il accuse les chrétiens d'avoir quitté l'hellénisme pour le judaïsme[2], puis de s'être détournés du judaïsme[3]. Eusèbe de Césarée, au début du IVe s., reproduit des accusations semblables :

> À quel châtiment ne serait-il pas légitime de les livrer, ces hommes qui ont déserté les mœurs ancestrales pour se faire les zélateurs des fables étrangères et universellement décriées des juifs ? Quoi ! N'est-ce pas le dernier degré de la perversité et de la versatilité que d'abandonner d'un cœur égal les institutions nationales pour adopter, avec une foi exempte de logique et d'examen, celles d'un peuple impie en guerre avec toutes les nations ? Et ne pas même s'en remettre au dieu lui-même qui est honoré chez les juifs selon les traditions en usage chez eux, mais tracer pour eux-mêmes un sentier nouveau et solitaire

---

1 Voir par exemple Morlet (2014a), 54–55.
2 Voir Origène, *Contre Celse* I.23 ; V.41.
3 *Ibid.* II.4 ; V.33.

qui ne respecte ni les traditions des Hellènes ni celles des juifs[4] ? (tr. J. Sirinelli – É. des Places)

On retrouve dans ce texte l'allusion à la double apostasie des chrétiens : apostasie à l'égard de l'hellénisme, puis du judaïsme. Le christianisme n'apparaissait donc pas seulement aux yeux des Grecs comme *barbare*, mais également comme quelque chose de *nouveau*, qui ne respectait *aucune* tradition. L'accusation « païenne » reproduite par Eusèbe évoque quelques facteurs psychologiques pour expliquer cette double apostasie : des facteurs d'ordre éthique – la perversité (μοχθηρία) et la versatilité (εὐχέρεια : litt. le laisser aller, le relâchement) – ou d'ordre intellectuel – l'irrationalité. Le texte d'Eusèbe passe, depuis U. von Wilamowitz-Moellendorff, pour un fragment du traité de Porphyre contre les chrétiens[5], mais son origine n'est pas aussi sûre[6]. Nous avons nous-même proposé d'y voir plutôt un propos artificiel, inspiré avant tout par les attaques de Celse, et servant à Eusèbe d'*annonce* de sa démonstration, consacré à l'apostasie à l'égard de l'hellénisme, dans la *Préparation*, puis à l'apostasie à l'égard du judaïsme, dans la *Démonstration*.

Or, dès la polémique de Celse, la καινοτομία chrétienne est aussi envisagée d'une autre façon. Celse ne dit pas seulement que les chrétiens se serait *détournés* des traditions. Il revient plusieurs fois sur l'idée qu'ils les auraient mal comprises, c'est-à-dire *déformées*[7]. L'innovation chrétienne apparaît alors, non tant comme une apostasie, que comme le résultat d'un contresens, d'une déformation de l'hellénisme. Il ne s'agit pas à proprement parler d'une accusation de plagiat[8]. Le plagiat consiste à reproduire textuellement une source sans le dire. Il correspond à une imposture qui revient à présenter comme nouveau ce qui, en réalité, existe déjà. Celse connaît ce genre d'accusation contre les chrétiens : il leur reproche par exemple de s'en remettre aux traditions des juifs, dont la circoncision serait, selon lui, la reprise d'un rite égyptien[9]. Mais l'accusation de παρακοή consiste à prêter aux chrétiens l'attitude inverse de celle d'un plagiaire : il ne s'agit pas de dénoncer la *reproduction* occulte d'une source, mais au contraire sa *déformation*. Ce qui est

---

4 *Préparation évangélique* I.2.1–4.
5 Wilamowitz-Moellendorff (1900), 101–105. L'argumentation du savant a convaincu von Harnack (1916) de faire de ce texte le fr. 1 de son édition des fragments du *Contra Christianos*.
6 Voir nos remarques critiques (2009), 41–48, et celles de Johnson (2010), 53–58.
7 Andresen (1955), 144–166, parle à ce propos d'une « Depravationstheorie » de Celse, dont il discerne deux aspects : les chrétiens auraient falsifié (παραχάραττειν, παραφθείρειν) la vérité ; ils auraient mal compris (παρακούειν) les textes grecs. Il cherche à comparer l'argument de Celse à la « Dekadenztheorie » de l'époque impériale (165–166), dont la constitution serait, pour lui, imputable avant tout à Posidonios d'Apamée (248–249). Notre étude montre plutôt le contexte immédiat de l'argument de la παρακοή, qui est celui des polémiques entre écoles sous le Haut-Empire. Voir également, sur l'accusation de rupture avec la tradition chez Celse, Fédou (1988), 496–503 (« Le débat sur la Tradition »).
8 Sur l'accusation de plagiat dans l'Antiquité, voir l'étude canonique de E. Stempflinger (1912), et plus récemment G. Aragione (2010), 1–2.
9 Voir Origène, *Contre Celse* I.22.

en cause, ce n'est pas la reprise à l'identique, mais le contresens, l'incapacité à comprendre et à transmettre correctement.

Cette accusation est systématiquement exprimée par Celse au moyen du verbe παρακούειν et de ses dérivés. Le verbe παρακούειν ne signifie pas dans ce contexte « désobéir » comme c'est souvent le cas en grec, mais « entendre mal », « entendre à côté ».

Or, dans tout l'ensemble de la littérature grecque, on constate que la plupart des occurrences de cet emploi de παρακούειν se trouvent dans la polémique de Celse et d'Origène, c'est-à-dire dans le *Discours vrai* du philosophe, puis dans le *Contre Celse* du chrétien. C'est dire l'importance historique de cet échange polémique dans l'histoire de ce type d'accusation.

Nous étudierons d'abord la façon dont l'accusation est formulée par Celse, puis par Origène, avant de nous interroger sur son arrière-plan intellectuel et sa postérité.

L'accusation de παρακοή chez Celse

Il faut d'abord signaler un emploi marginal de l'accusation, qui concerne les évangiles, que Celse accuse d'être des παρακούσματα, c'est-à-dire des récits issus de traditions mal comprises :

> Cels. II.30 : Παρέρριψε δ' ὁ Κέλσος καὶ τό· Θεὸν δὲ καὶ θεοῦ υἱὸν οὐδεὶς ἐκ τοιούτων συμβόλων καὶ παρακουσμάτων οὐδ' ἐξ οὕτως ἀγεννῶν τεκμηρίων συνίστησιν.
>
>> Celse a lancé encore cette attaque : Personne n'établit une divinité ou une filiation divine par de tels indices mêlés d'histoires mal entendues et d'aussi médiocres preuves[10].

Ce fragment est le seul dans lequel l'accusation de παρακοή soit utilisée à propos des évangiles.

De manière générale, le verbe παρακούειν et ses dérivés (παρακοή, παράκουσμα) sont utilisés par Celse pour accuser plutôt la doctrine chrétienne – et non les textes évangéliques – d'être le résultat d'une mauvaise compréhension des traditions :

> Cels. V.65 : Μετὰ ταῦτά φησι· Φέρ' οὖν, εἰ καὶ μηδεμίαν ἀρχὴν τοῦ δόγματος ἔχουσιν, αὐτὸν ἐξετάσωμεν τὸν λόγον· πρότερον δὲ ὅσα παρακηκοότες ὑπ' ἀγνοίας διαφθείρουσιν, οὐκ ἐμμελῶς ἐν ἀρχαῖς εὐθὺς ἀπαυθαδιαζόμενοι περὶ ὧν οὐκ ἴσασι, λεκτέον· ἔστιν δὲ τάδε.
>
>> Après quoi, il déclare : Eh bien ! même si leur religion n'a aucun fondement, examinons la doctrine elle-même. Il faut d'abord lire tout ce

---

10 Nous reprenons la traduction Borret, souvent très modifiée.

qu'ils ont mal compris et gâté par l'ignorance, la présomption les faisant aussitôt trancher à tort et à travers sur les principes en des matières qu'ils ne connaissent pas. En voici des exemples.

Ces traditions sont toujours dans l'esprit de Celse les traditions *grecques*. D'un côté, elles correspondent aux traditions mythologiques, de l'autre, aux traditions philosophiques.

Les doctrines des chrétiens comme déformation des mythes

Cette première thèse est exprimée dans un fragment transmis par le livre III du *Contre Celse* :

> Cels. III.16 : Ἀλλὰ καὶ ἐπὰν λέγῃ ὅτι τὰ τοῦ παλαιοῦ λόγου παρακούσματα συμπλάττοντες τούτοις προκαταυλοῦμεν καὶ προκατηχοῦμεν τοὺς ἀνθρώπους ὡς οἱ τοὺς κορυβαντιζομένους περιβομβοῦντες…
>
> De plus, puisqu'il dit que, forgeant les déformations de l'antique tradition, nous commençons avec elles par étourdir les hommes aux sons de la flûte et par les instruire, comme ceux qui battent du tambour autour des gens qu'on initie aux rites des Corybantes…

Dans les fragments conservés, Celse évoque plus précisément les croyances eschatologiques et accuse les chrétiens de tirer leur doctrine du jugement dernier d'une mauvaise compréhension des traditions sur le déluge et sur l'embrasement de l'univers :

> Cels. IV.11 : Μετὰ ταῦτα βουλόμενος ἡμᾶς παραδεῖξαι μηδὲν παράδοξον μηδὲ καινὸν λέγειν περὶ κατακλυσμοῦ ἢ ἐκπυρώσεως, ἀλλὰ καὶ παρακούσαντας τῶν παρ' Ἕλλησιν ἢ βαρβάροις περὶ τούτων λεγομένων ταῖς ἡμετέραις πεπιστευκέναι περὶ αὐτῶν γραφαῖς, φησὶ ταῦτα· Ἐπῆλθε δ' αὐτοῖς καὶ ταῦτα ἐκείνων παρακούσασιν, ὅτι δὴ κατὰ χρόνων μακρῶν κύκλους καὶ ἄστρων ἐπανόδους τε καὶ συνόδους ἐκπυρώσεις καὶ ἐπικλύσεις συμβαίνουσι, καὶ ὅτι μετὰ τὸν τελευταῖον ἐπὶ Δευκαλίωνος κατακλυσμὸν ἡ περίοδος κατὰ τὴν τῶν ὅλων ἀμοιβὴν ἐκπύρωσιν ἀπαιτεῖ· ταῦτ' αὐτοὺς ἐποίησεν ἐσφαλμένῃ δόξῃ λέγειν ὅτι ὁ θεὸς καταβήσεται δίκην βασανιστοῦ πῦρ φέρων.
>
> Ensuite, il veut montrer que nous ne disons rien de remarquable ni de neuf sur le déluge et l'embrasement, bien plus, que c'est pour avoir mal compris ce qu'on en dit chez les Grecs ou les barbares que nous avons cru au récit qu'en font les Écritures, et il déclare : Pour avoir mal compris ces doctrines, il leur est venu l'idée qu'après des cycles de longues durées et des retours et des conjonctions d'étoiles ont lieu des embrasements et des déluges, et qu'après le dernier déluge au temps de Deucalion, le retour périodique selon l'alternance de l'univers exige un embrasement. De là vient l'opinion erronée qui leur fait dire : Dieu va descendre en bourreau armé de feu.

L'argument est repris plus loin (*Cels*. IV.11) : Καὶ μὴ νοήσαντας τὰ περὶ ἐκπυρώσεως εἰρηκέναι ὅτι ὁ θεὸς καταβήσεται δίκην βασανιστοῦ πῦρ φέρων (Et, sans comprendre ce qui concerne la conflagration, ils disent que Dieu descendra à la manière d'un bourreau armé de feu).

Dans un autre texte, Celse reproche à la doctrine de Satan d'être inspirée d'une mauvaise compréhension des récits de guerres divines :

> *Cels*. VI.42 : Εἶθ' ἑξῆς τούτοις <ἐκτίθεσθαι> βουλόμενος τὰ αἰνίγματα, ὧν οἴεται παρακηκοότας ἡμᾶς τὰ περὶ τοῦ Σατανᾶ εἰσάγειν…
>
> Aussitôt après, il veut indiquer les énigmes que, dit Celse, nous aurions mal comprises dans notre doctrine sur Satan…

Le passage présente ensuite la doctrine de Satan comme la déformation des guerres divines rapportées par Homère, Héraclite et Phérécyde (les Titans contre les Géants, ou Typhon, Horus et Osiris). Origène reproche à Celse de ne pas expliquer la corrélation entre la doctrine biblique et les mythes grecs :

> *Cels*. VI.42 : Εἶτ' ἐκθέμενος τὰ τοιαῦτα καὶ μὴ παραμυθησάμενος, τίνα τρόπον ἐκεῖνα μὲν λόγου ἔχεται κρείττονος ταῦτα δέ ἐστιν ἐκείνων παρακούσματα, διαλοιδορεῖται ἡμῖν λέγων…
>
> Après la citation, sans expliquer comment ces mythes contiennent une doctrine supérieure, et comment nos doctrines en sont des déformations, il continue à nous injurier, en disant…

Les doctrines des chrétiens comme déformation de la philosophie

La plupart du temps, Celse utilise l'argument de la παρακοή pour accuser les chrétiens d'avoir mal compris non les mythes mais la philosophie, et notamment Platon. Il évoque au moins quatre cas, tous fondés sur des références plus ou moins précises à des textes platoniciens.

1) En *Cels*. VI.7, Origène rapporte que son adversaire accusait les chrétiens de tenir leur doctrine ésotérique d'une mauvaise compréhension de la Lettre 7 (341d) :

> Οἵτινες οὐχ, ὡς οἴεται Κέλσος, παρακούσαντες τοῦ Πλάτωνος τοιαῦτ' εἰρήκασι.
>
> Ils étaient loin d'avoir dit cela pour avoir compris Platon de travers, comme le croit Celse.

2) En *Cels*. VI.15, Origène affirme que Celse considérait la conception chrétienne de l'humilité comme une mauvaise compréhension (παράκουσμα) des *Lois* 715e–716a :

Εἶτα μετὰ ταῦτα ὁ Κέλσος ὡς περιηχηθεὶς τὰ περὶ ταπεινοφροσύνης καὶ μὴ ἐπιμελῶς αὐτὴν νοήσας βούλεται μὲν τὴν παρ' ἡμῖν κακολογεῖν, οἴεται δ' αὐτὴν παράκουσμα εἶναι τῶν Πλάτωνος λόγων, ὅς φησί που ἐν τοῖς Νόμοις.

> Et puis après cela, comme s'il avait entendu parler de la doctrine de l'humilité sans avoir pris soin de la comprendre, Celse veut décrier la nôtre. Il croit que c'est une déformation de ce que Platon dit quelque part dans les *Lois*.

3) D'après *Cels.* VI.19, le philosophe accusait le culte chrétien, consacré à un Dieu supérieur au ciel, d'être inspiré par une mauvaise compréhension de Platon, probablement la Lettre 2, 312e–313a évoquée plus haut par Origène :

Ἑξῆς δὲ τούτοις φησὶν ὁ Κέλσος παρακούσαντάς τινας Χριστιανοὺς πλατωνικῶν λέξεων αὐχεῖν τὸν ὑπερουράνιον θεόν, ὑπεραναβαίνοντας τὸν Ἰουδαίων οὐρανόν.

> Celse dit ensuite : Pour avoir mal compris les expressions platoniciennes, certains chrétiens exaltent le Dieu supracéleste et s'élèvent même au-dessus du ciel des juifs.

4) En *Cels.* VII.32, enfin, Origène rapporte que Celse accusait la doctrine de la résurrection d'être une mauvaise compréhension de l'idée de metensomatose, ce qui peut être une nouvelle allusion à Platon (*Phèdre* ?) :

Χρήσιμον πρὸς τοῖς ἀνωτέρω εἰρημένοις ἡμῖν περὶ τούτου τοῦτο μόνον ὑποσημειώσασθαι πρὸς τὸν λόγον, ὅτι οὐχ, ὡς οἴεται Κέλσος, τῆς μετενσωματώσεως παρακούσαντες τὰ περὶ ἀναστάσεώς φαμεν ...

> Il sera utile d'ajouter à ce que j'en ai dit plus haut cette simple observation sur la doctrine ; ce n'est pas, comme le croit Celse, pour avoir compris de travers la doctrine de la métensomatose que nous parlons de résurrection.

Bien sûr, les rapprochements mis en avant par Celse sont purement polémiques. Ils ont pour but de dénoncer dans le christianisme une *déformation* de l'hellénisme, soit parce que Celse est vraiment convaincu que le christianisme est issu de l'hellénisme, soit parce qu'il cherche à *exclure* les chrétiens de l'hellénisme, et qu'on ne peut exclure qu'en ayant préalablement intégré.

On peut se demander en revanche si, à travers ces parallèles entre Platon et la doctrine chrétienne, Celse ne cherche pas à retourner l'argument des apologistes, et notamment de Justin, selon lequel la philosophie serait inspirée par l'Écriture[11]. Parmi les textes platoniciens convoqués par Celse, Justin citait justement la Lettre

---

11 Voir Justin, *Apologie* I.44.9 : « Tout ce que philosophes et poètes ont dit de l'immortalité de l'âme, des châtiments après la mort, de la contemplation des choses célestes et des doctrines semblables, c'est pour en avoir repris les principes chez les prophètes qu'ils ont pu le concevoir et l'exposer. » Cf. Andresen (1955), 159 et Cook (2004), 96, émettent avec raison l'hypothèse selon laquelle Celse cherche peut-être à répondre à l'argument apologétique qui consiste à rapprocher Bible et sagesse grecque.

2, qu'il mettait en parallèle avec la doctrine chrétienne de Dieu[12]. Nous avons vu plus haut que Celse reprochait aux chrétiens d'avoir déformé les traditions sur le sort de l'âme après la mort. S'il évoque peut-être des traditions mythologiques, il peut aussi faire référence à Platon. Or Justin mettait justement le mythe final du *Gorgias* en parallèle avec la croyance des chrétiens en un jugement de Dieu[13]. Andresen a remarqué également que les attaques de Celse contre le culte des chrétiens adressé au Dieu « supracéleste » trouvait un écho précis dans le *Dialogue* de Justin (56.1)[14] et que ses propos concernant la « déformation » des traditions sur la fin rappelle le rapprochement que Justin opère, mais dans l'autre sens, et sans parler de παρακοή, entre l'eschatologie chrétienne et la doctrine stoïcienne de la conflagration, qui en serait inspirée (*Apologie* I.20.4)[15].

L'accusation de παρακοή dans la réponse d'Origène

Origène, dans sa réponse, plus tardive (v. 248), accorde une grande importance à l'accusation de Celse. Sa réaction est double : elle consiste d'une part à *répondre* à la thèse de son adversaire pour en montrer l'absurdité, mais elle consiste aussi à *retourner* l'argument contre le philosophe.

Les réponses d'Origène concernant la παρακοή des chrétiens

La première réponse d'Origène consiste à opposer à la thèse de la déformation, celle d'un *accord* des chrétiens avec les Grecs et avec les juifs. Sur la question des destinées de l'âme après la mort, il note que les uns et les autres sont tous d'accord :

> Cels. III.16 : Ἀλλὰ καὶ ἐπὰν λέγῃ ὅτι τὰ τοῦ παλαιοῦ λόγου παρακούσματα συμπλάττοντες τούτοις προκαταυλοῦμεν καὶ προκατηχοῦμεν τοὺς ἀνθρώπους ὡς οἱ τοὺς κορυβαντιζομένους περιβομβοῦντες, φήσομεν πρὸς αὐτόν· ποίου παλαιοῦ λόγου παρακούσματα ; Εἴτε γὰρ τοῦ ἑλληνικοῦ, καὶ διδάξαντος περὶ τῶν ὑπὸ γῆν δικαστηρίων, εἴτε τοῦ ἰουδαϊκοῦ, μετὰ τῶν ἄλλων καὶ περὶ τῆς ἑξῆς τῷ βίῳ τούτῳ ζωῆς προφητεύσαντος, οὐκ ἂν ἔχοι παραστῆσαι ὅτι ἡμεῖς ἐν παρακούσμασι γενόμενοι τῆς ἀληθείας, ὅσοι γε πειρώμεθα μετὰ λόγου πιστεύειν, πρὸς τὰ τοιαῦτα ζῶμεν δόγματα.
>
> De plus, puisqu'il dit que, forgeant les déformations de l'antique tradition, nous commençons avec elles par étourdir les hommes aux sons de la flûte par les instruire, comme ceux qui battent du tambour autour des gens

---

12 *Apologie* I.60.7.
13 *Apologie* I.8.4.
14 Andresen (1955), 159.
15 Andresen (1955), 161.

> qu'on initie aux rites des Corybantes, je lui répondrai : les déformations de quelle antique tradition ? De la tradition grecque, qui a enseigné aussi l'existence de tribunaux sur la terre ? De la tradition juive, qui a prédit entre autres l'existence d'une vie qui suit la vie présente ? Il serait bien incapable de prouver que nous déformons la vérité, nous tous du moins qui nous efforçons d'avoir une foi réfléchie, quand nous accordons notre vie à de telles doctrines.

À l'accusation de παρακοή, Origène répond ici par l'argument de la συμφωνία. Il s'agissait d'un argument classique dans l'apologétique chrétienne, au moins depuis Justin, et Origène avait lui-même consacré un ouvrage perdu, les *Stromates*, à confirmer les doctrines chrétiennes à l'aide des philosophes (Platon, Aristote, Numénius, Cornutus, et les stoïciens au moins)[16]. Dans le *Contre Celse*, il lui arrive encore d'utiliser plusieurs fois cet argument[17].

L'argument de la συμφωνία n'est cependant pas celui qu'utilise normalement Origène pour répondre à l'accusation de παρακοή. Partout ailleurs, il cherche au contraire à montrer que, si les chrétiens n'ont déformé ni les mythes ni Platon, c'est parce que ces derniers ne peuvent pas avoir servi de sources aux chrétiens. D'abord, Moïse et les prophètes étaient antérieurs, tant aux traditions mythiques des Grecs que de Platon :

> *Cels.* IV.11 : Ἀρχαιότερος ἦν Μωϋσῆς τῶν κατὰ χρόνων μακρὰς περιόδους κατακλυσμοὺς καὶ ἐκπυρώσεις φησάντων γίνεσθαι ἐν τῷ κόσμῳ.
> *Cels.* VI.7 : Οἵτινες οὐχ, ὡς οἴεται Κέλσος, παρακούσαντες τοῦ Πλάτωνος τοιαῦτ' εἰρήκασι. Πῶς γὰρ οἷόν τ' ἦν τοῦ μηδέπω γενομένου αὐτοὺς ἀκηκοέναι ;

> Moïse était plus ancien que ceux qui ont dit qu'il y a dans le monde après de longues périodes de temps des déluges et des embrasements.
> Ils étaient loin d'avoir dit cela pour avoir compris Platon de travers, comme le croit Celse : comment eussent-ils pu entendre celui qui n'était pas encore né ?

Origène note par ailleurs l'*invraisemblance* de la thèse de Celse, qui suppose que les auteurs sacrés, qui étaient des simples, aient pu connaître les textes de Platon : « Vois s'il n'est pas d'emblée invraisemblable de dire que Paul le fabricant de tentes, Pierre le pêcheur, Jean qui a laissé les filets de son père, aient transmis une

---

16 Voir la description laissée par Jérôme, Lettre 70.4 : *Origenes decem scripsit Stromateas, christianorum et philosophorum inter se sententias conparans, et omnia nostrae religionis dogmata de Platone et Aristotele, Numenio, Cornutoque confirmans.* Les témoignages essentiels sont regroupés par Nautin (1977), 293-302. Voir encore Moreschini (1987), 36-43. H. D. Saffrey (1975a), 46-51, pensait que l'œuvre avait pu inspirer la comparaison de l'Écriture et de la philosophie dans la *Préparation évangélique* d'Eusèbe (XI-XIII). Nous avons à plusieurs reprises montré que cette hypothèse était tout à fait envisageable : (2004), 127-140 ; (2013), 107-123 ; (2014a), 213-252.
17 Voir par exemple V.15 ; V.20-21 ; V.43 ; V.57 ; VII.3 ; VII.30-31 ; VIII.35.

telle doctrine sur Dieu pour avoir compris de travers les propos de Platon dans ses lettres ! »[18]

En d'autres termes, les auteurs sacrés ne peuvent avoir lu les philosophes, ou bien parce qu'ils leur étaient antérieurs (auteurs de l'Ancien Testament), ou bien parce qu'ils étaient des simples (auteurs du Nouveau Testament). Origène simplifie l'argumentation de Celse, car ce dernier ne s'en prend pas uniquement aux auteurs sacrés, mais aux chrétiens eux-mêmes et, sur ce point, il n'apporte aucune réponse.

Mais Origène n'en reste pas là et retourne l'argument de Celse : pour lui, les parentés entre les Grecs et les chrétiens ne s'expliqueraient pas parce que les juifs ou les chrétiens auraient mal compris les Grecs, mais parce que *les Grecs* auraient mal compris les traditions bibliques : « Car il suffit de signaler seulement que Moïse et certains prophètes, qui vivaient en des temps très reculés, n'ont pas repris à d'autres ce qui concerne la conflagration de l'univers, mais, s'il faut s'exprimer après avoir considéré les temps, c'est plutôt d'autres qui les ont mal compris et qui, sans avoir de connaissance précise de ce qu'ils disaient, ont forgé des identités pour chaque période et immuables dans leurs caractéristiques propres et dans les accidents eux-mêmes. »[19]

Et ailleurs, écrit-il : « Mon propos était uniquement de montrer que notre doctrine sur la terre sainte ne doit rien aux Grecs ni à Platon. Ce sont eux qui, venus bien après le très ancien Moïse et même la plupart des prophètes, soit ont mal compris certains termes énigmatiques employés par eux à ce sujet, soit ont lu les Écritures sacrées et ont imité ces propos en disant certaines paroles de ce genre à propos de la terre supérieure. »[20]

Dans ce texte intéressant, la παρακοή est clairement *distinguée* du plagiat, qui suppose une *intention* frauduleuse (celle d'*imiter* délibérément un texte). Elle apparaît au contraire comme le signe d'une *impuissance* à comprendre un texte.

Mais la rétorsion de l'argument va plus loin encore puisqu'elle conduit Origène à accuser Celse lui-même de mal comprendre ses sources.

La rétorsion de l'argument contre le philosophe

Origène retourne contre Celse l'accusation de παρακοή de deux manières : Celse aurait lui-même commis des contresens à propos des chrétiens, et ce ne seraient pas les chrétiens qui auraient déformé les doctrines des Grecs, mais ces derniers qui auraient déformé les Écritures.

D'abord, donc, Origène accuse Celse, à propos des juifs et des chrétiens, de s'en être remis à des sources qu'il aurait été, selon Origène, incapable de

---

18 *Cels.* VI.7.
19 *Cels.* VI.12.
20 *Cels.* VII.30.

comprendre. Celse accuse les juifs d'adorer le ciel et les anges. Origène relève la méprise de son adversaire, qui ignore que les juifs n'adorent pas les anges :

> Cels. V.6 : Ἐν τούτοις δὲ δοκεῖ μοι συγκεχύσθαι ὁ Κέλσος καὶ ἀπὸ παρακουσμάτων ἃ μὴ ᾔδει γεγραφέναι·
>
> Ici, Celse me semble avoir confondu et avoir écrit ce qu'il ne connaissait pas à partir de mauvaises compréhensions.

Origène reproche à son adversaire d'attribuer aux chrétiens la croyance selon laquelle Dieu ne se soucierait que des hommes et non du monde en général et que les hommes seraient des « vers » à ses yeux :

> Cels. IV.29 : Τάχα δέ τινων παρήκουσεν ὁ Κέλσος ὅτι ὁ θεός ἐστιν, εἶτα μετ' ἐκεῖνον ἡμεῖς, οὓς ὠνόμασε σκώληκας.
>
> Peut-être a-t-il mal compris une phrase de certains : 'Il y a Dieu, et ensuite nous, qu'il a nommés vers'.

Il existe, note Origène, de nombreux êtres entre les hommes et Dieu, tels les Trônes, les Dominations, les Principautés, les Puissances, et nul homme n'est considéré comme un vers parmi les chrétiens. Origène reproche à Celse de s'en être remis à une source peu fiable, comme si, pour dénoncer toute une école philosophique, il s'était appuyé sur les dires d'un homme qui ne l'aurait fréquenté que trois jours. Origène fait donc l'hypothèse d'une source qui aurait elle-même mal compris la doctrine correcte en supposant qu'après Dieu viennent directement les hommes :

> Ibid. : Εἰ δέ τις τὸ λεγόμενον ὑπό τινων, εἴτε τῶν νοούντων εἴτε τῶν μὴ συνιέντων ἀλλὰ παρακουσάντων λόγου ὑγιοῦς, φάσκοι, ὅτι ὁ θεός ἐστιν, εἶτα μετ' ἐκεῖνον ἡμεῖς· καὶ τοῦτό γ' ἂν ἑρμηνεύοιμι, τὸ ἡμεῖς λέγων ἀντὶ τοῦ οἱ λογικοὶ καὶ ἔτι μᾶλλον οἱ σπουδαῖοι λογικοί.
>
> Que si l'on maintient les propos de certains qui, intelligents ou stupides, ont mal compris une saine doctrine : 'Il y a Dieu, et immédiatement après, nous', même cela, je l'interpréterais en disant : 'nous' désigne les être raisonnables, et mieux encore les êtres raisonnables vertueux.

Celse, donc, s'en serait bien remis à une source chrétienne, mais une source émanant des « simples ».

En V.61, Origène accuse Celse d'imaginer l'existence, dans l'Église, de « sibyllistes ». Ce terme, explique-t-il, provient peut-être d'un malentendu concernant ceux qui croient au don prophétique de la Sibylle :

> Cels. V.61 : Εἶπε δέ τινας εἶναι καὶ Σιβυλλιστάς, τάχα παρακούσας τινῶν ἐγκαλούντων τοῖς οἰομένοις προφῆτιν γεγονέναι τὴν Σίβυλλαν καὶ Σιβυλλιστὰς τοὺς τοιούτους καλεσάντων.

Il ajoute : Parmi eux, il y a encore des Sibyllistes, peut-être pour avoir compris de travers des gens qui blâment ceux qui croient au don prophétique de la Sibylle et les ont appelés Sibyllistes.

En VI.24, Origène accuse son adversaire de prêter aux chrétiens dans leur ensemble des croyances ésotériques qui sont plutôt celles des Ophites, qu'il aurait de plus mal comprises :

Δοκεῖ δέ μοι καὶ ἐκ τούτων ἐκ παρακουσμάτων ἀσημοτάτης αἱρέσεως Ὀφιανῶν οἶμαι ἐκτεθεῖσθαι τὰ τοῦ διαγράμματος ἀπὸ μέρους.

À en juger par ces paroles, je crois pouvoir conjecturer qu'il a tiré en partie sa description du diagramme des doctrines mal comprises de la secte fort obscure des Ophites.

En VI.27, Origène reproche à Celse de parler du rite du Sceau d'une façon tellement fantaisiste qu'il exclut ici formellement la possibilité qu'il ait même pu disposer de sources, mêmes déformées :

Ἑξῆς δὲ τοῖς περὶ τοῦ διαγράμματος μηδὲ παρακούσας τῶν περὶ τῆς καλουμένης παρὰ τοῖς ἐκκλησιαστικοῖς σφραγῖδος...

Après ces remarques sur le diagramme, ce qu'il dit ne provient même pas d'une mésintelligence de ce que, dans l'Église, on appelle le "Sceau"...

En VI.34, le chrétien reproduit la présentation polémique que Celse donne de l'ensemble de la doctrine chrétienne et conclut :

Ἐν τούτοις δὲ δοκεῖ μοι φύρειν τὰ παρακούσματα ὁ Κέλσος. Εἰκὸς γὰρ ὅτι, εἴ τι ἤκουσεν οἱασδηποτοῦν αἱρέσεως λεξείδιον, μὴ τρανώσας αὐτὸ κἂν κατὰ τὸ βούλημα ἐκείνης ἀλλὰ τὰ ῥημάτια συμφορήσας, ἐπεδείκνυτο ἐν τοῖς μηδὲν ἐπισταμένοις μήτε τῶν ἡμετέρων μήτε τῶν ἐν ταῖς αἱρέσεσιν ὡς ἄρα πάντα τὰ Χριστιανῶν γινώσκοι.

Celse me paraît ici confondre les idées qu'il a mal comprises. On dirait un homme qui, ayant saisi quelques bouts de phrase prononcés dans une secte ou l'autre sans en avoir compris le sens et l'intention, en a rassemblé les bribes pour donner à ceux qui ne savent rien ni de nos doctrines ni de celles des hérésies l'impression qu'il connaît toutes les doctrines du christianisme.

En VI.35, Origène relève que Prunicos, dont Celse veut faire une vierge mentionnée dans la doctrine chrétienne, ne concerne pas l'Église, mais les doctrines valentiniennes :

Προυνικὸν δέ τινα σοφίαν οἱ ἀπὸ Οὐαλεντίνου ὀνομάζουσι κατὰ τὴν πεπλανημένην ἑαυτῶν σοφίαν, ἧς σύμβολον εἶναι βούλονται καὶ δώδεκα ἔτεσιν αἱμορροοῦσαν· ἣν παρακούσας ὁ ἅμα πάντα φύρων τὰ Ἑλλήνων καὶ βαρβάρων καὶ τῶν ἐν ταῖς αἱρέσεσιν εἶπε τό· Προυνικοῦ τινος δύναμιν ῥέουσαν παρθένου.

Le nom de Prunicos est celui que donnent les Valentiniens à une certaine sagesse, dans l'égarement de leur propre sagesse symbolisée d'après eux par l'hémorroïse depuis douze ans malade ; se méprenant sur le sens et brouillant toutes les opinions des Grecs, des barbares et des hérésies, Celse a dit que d'une certaine vierge Prunicos émane une vertu.

En VI.38, Origène donne sa version du diagramme ophite et conclut :

Καὶ ταῦτα δὲ παρειλήφαμεν εἰς τὸν κατὰ Κέλσου λόγον, ἵνα παραστήσωμεν τοῖς ἐντυγχάνουσι τρανότερον ἐκείνου ἐγνωκέναι καὶ οὐκ ἐκ παρακουσμάτων τὰ καὶ ὑφ' ἡμῶν κατηγορούμενα.

J'ai inséré ces remarques dans mon discours contre Celse pour montrer aux lecteurs que je connais plus clairement que lui, et non sur de vagues on-dit, les doctrines que j'attaque moi aussi.

En VI.51, de nouveau, Origène accuse certains propos de Celse d'être des malentendus dérivés des idées des hérétiques :

Παρακούσας δ' οἶμαι μοχθηρᾶς αἱρέσεώς τινος καὶ κακῶς διηγησαμένης τὸ «γενηθήτω φῶς» ὡς εὐκτικῶς ὑπὸ τοῦ δημιουργοῦ εἰρημένον εἶπεν· Οὐ γὰρ δὴ καθάπερ οἱ τοὺς λύχνους ἐκ γειτόνων ἐναυόμενοι φῶς ὁ δημιουργὸς ἄνωθεν ἐχρήσατο. Καὶ ἄλλης δ' ἀσεβοῦς αἱρέσεως παρακούσας εἶπε καὶ τό· Εἰ μὲν ἐναντίος τις ἦν τῷ μεγάλῳ θεῷ θεὸς κατηραμένος ὁ ταῦτα ποιῶν παρὰ γνώμην τὴν ἐκείνου, τί αὐτῷ τὸ φῶς ἐκίχρα ;

Mais pour avoir mal compris, je pense, une secte pernicieuse qui explique à tort le mot *Que la lumière soit !* comme exprimant un souhait de la part du Créateur, Celse ajouta : ce n'est tout de même pas de la même manière dont on allume sa lampe à celle du voisin que le Créateur a emprunté d'en haut la lumière ! Et, pour avoir avoir mal compris une autre hérésie impie, il dit encore : S'il y avait un dieu maudit ennemi du grand Dieu, créant contre sa volonté, pourquoi lui prêterait-il sa lumière ?

En VI.53, Origène reproche au philosophe d'utiliser contre les chrétiens des critiques utilisées contre Marcion par certains chrétiens inintelligents :

Εἶτ' οἶμαι φύρων αἱρέσεις αἱρέσεσι καὶ μὴ ἐπισημειούμενος ὅτι τάδε μὲν ἄλλης αἱρέσεώς ἐστι τάδε δὲ ἄλλης, τὰ πρὸς Μαρκίωνα ὑφ' ἡμῶν ἀπορούμενα προφέρει, τάχα καὶ τούτων παρακούσας ἀπό τινων εὐτελῶς καὶ ἰδιωτικῶς ἐγκαλούντων λόγῳ, οὐ μὴν πάνυ συνετῶς.

Ensuite il mélange les hérésies, je pense, et ne précise pas les doctrines d'une hérésie et celles d'une autre. Ce sont nos propres critiques à Marcion qu'il nous oppose ; peut-être les a-t-il mal comprises de la bouche de certains qui s'en prennent à la doctrine d'une manière vulgaire et triviale, et assurément sans aucune intelligence.

En VI.74, Origène accuse Celse de faire une présentation déformée de la doctrine de Marcion :

> Εἶθ' ἑξῆς ἐπαναλαμβάνει πολλάκις ἤδη εἰπὼν τὰ περὶ τῆς γνώμης Μαρκίωνος, καὶ πῇ μὲν ἀληθῶς τὰ Μαρκίωνος ἐκτίθεται πῇ δὲ κἀκείνων παρήκουσεν· πρὸς ἣν οὐκ ἀναγκαῖον ἡμᾶς ἀπαντᾶν ἢ καὶ ἐλέγχειν.

> Il revient ensuite au système de Marcion déjà maintes fois abordé, et en donne un exposé en partie fidèle, en partie déformé. Il n'est pas nécessaire d'y répondre ou même de le réfuter.

En VIII.14, Origène reproche à son adversaire d'avoir, une nouvelle fois, confondu les idées hérétiques avec les idées correctes de l'Église :

> Εἰ δέ τινων παρήκουσε Κέλσος, μὴ ὁμολογούντων τὸν υἱὸν τοῦ θεοῦ υἱὸν εἶναι τοῦ δημιουργήσαντος τόδε τὸ πᾶν, αὐτὸς ἂν εἰδείη καὶ οἱ συγκατατιθέμενοι τοιούτῳ λόγῳ.

> Que Celse ait pu se méprendre sur le refus de certains d'identifier le Fils de Dieu avec celui du Créateur de cet univers, cela le regarde lui et les adeptes de cette doctrine.

Une seconde manière de retourner l'accusation de παρακοή contre Celse consiste à soutenir qu'il aurait mal compris les Écritures. Origène propose ici une rétorsion parfaite de l'argument de son adversaire. À ce dernier, qui accusait les chrétiens d'avoir déformé les traditions mythologiques et les textes philosophiques, Origène oppose l'argument selon lequel ce serait, non seulement les Grecs, mais encore Celse lui-même, qui auraient mal compris la Bible. La plupart des textes mentionnés par Origène se trouvent dans le Pentateuque ou les épîtres de Paul. Il n'évoque qu'une fois les évangiles, à propos de la confusion qu'il prête à Celse entre les mages et les chaldéens :

> *Cels.* I.58 : Ὅρα οὖν ἐν τούτῳ τὸ παράκουσμα τοῦ οὐ διακρίναντος μάγους Χαλδαίων μηδὲ τὰς ἐπαγγελίας διαφόρους οὔσας αὐτῶν θεωρήσαντος καὶ διὰ τοῦτο καταψευσαμένου τῆς εὐαγγελικῆς γραφῆς.

> Vois donc ici la méprise d'un homme qui des Chaldéens ne distingue pas les mages, qui ne s'est pas avisé de la différence des doctrines qu'ils professent, et en conséquence a falsifié le texte évangélique !

Au nombre des sources vétérotestamentaire de Celse figurerait d'abord Gn 1.26 :

> IV.30 : Δοκεῖ δέ μοι παρακηκοέναι ὁ Κέλσος καὶ τοῦ «Ποιήσωμεν ἄνθρωπον κατ' εἰκόνα καὶ ὁμοίωσιν ἡμετέραν» καὶ παρὰ τοῦτο πεποιηκέναι τοὺς σκώληκας λέγοντας ὅτι ὑπὸ τοῦ θεοῦ γεγονότες πάντῃ ἐσμὲν αὐτῷ ὅμοιοι.

> C'est, à mon sens, pour avoir mal compris encore la parole : *faisons l'homme à notre image et ressemblance*, que Celse a imaginé des vers disant : "créés par Dieu, nous sommes entièrement semblables à lui".

En V.29, Origène reproche au philosophe de ne pas avoir compris le sens de la répartition des anges en Dt 32 :

> Δοκεῖ δή μοι παρακηκοέναι τινῶν ὁ Κέλσος περὶ τῆς διανεμήσεως τῶν ἐπὶ γῆς μυστικωτέρων λόγων.

> Celse me paraît donc s'être mépris sur quelques-unes des raisons mystérieuses du partage des régions terrestres.

En V.32, Origène accuse plutôt son adversaire de s'en être remis à d'autres, qui auraient mal compris le passage biblique :

> Ἀλλ' ὡς προείπομεν, ταῦτα ἡμῖν ἐπικεκρυμμένως λελέχθω, παριστᾶσιν ὧν παρήκουσαν οἱ φήσαντες τὰ μέρη τῆς γῆς ἐξ ἀρχῆς ἄλλα ἄλλοις ἐπόπταις νενεμημένα, κατά τινας ἐπικρατείας διειλημμένα, ταύτῃ διοικεῖσθαι· ἀφ' ὧν καὶ ὁ Κέλσος λαβὼν τὰς ἐκκειμένας εἶπε λέξεις.

> Mais, comme on l'a dit, cette histoire doit être présentée par nous avec un sens caché pour établir les vérités déformées par ceux qui ont dit : les différentes parties de la terre ont été dès l'origine attribuées à différentes puissances tutélaires et réparties en autant de gouvernements ; et c'est la manière dont elles sont administrées. C'est à eux que Celse a emprunté les paroles citées.

En VI.35, Origène accuse Celse de prêter aux chrétiens une doctrine des cercles cosmiques (« cercles sur cercles »). Il commence par supposer que l'expression viendrait des Ophites, avant d'imaginer que Celse ait pu déformer un propos de l'Écriture :

> Τάχα δὲ καὶ ἀπὸ τοῦ Ἐκκλησιαστοῦ ἐστι παράκουσμα λέγοντος· «Κυκλοῖ κυκλῶν πορεύεται τὸ πνεῦμα, καὶ ἐπὶ κύκλους αὐτοῦ ἐπιστρέφει τὸ πνεῦμα.»

> Ou peut-être a-t-il mal compris cette parole de l'Ecclésiaste : *Tourne, tourne, s'en va le vent, et à ses cercles revient le vent* (Eccl 1.6)

En VI.62, Origène reproche au philosophe de critiquer trop facilement les anthropomorphismes divins dans la Bible :

> Πάλιν τε αὖ ὁ Κέλσος τάχα μὲν παρακούσας τοῦ «Τὸ γὰρ στόμα κυρίου ἐλάλησε ταῦτα» τάχα δὲ καὶ τῶν ἰδιωτῶν προπετευσαμένων περὶ τῆς τῶν τοιούτων διηγήσεως, μὴ νοήσας τε, ἐπὶ τίνων τάσσεται τὰ ὀνόμασι σωματικῶν μελῶν ἐπὶ τῶν δυνάμεων τοῦ θεοῦ λεγόμενα, φησίν· Οὐδὲ στόμα αὐτῷ ἐστιν οὐδὲ φωνή.

> Peut-être par une méprise sur le sens des mots : *car la bouche du Seigneur a proféré ces paroles* (Is 1.20), ou peut-être à cause de l'interprétation téméraire donnée par les simples à de pareils textes, Celse n'a pas saisi en quel sens on applique aux puissances de Dieu ce qu'expriment les noms des membres du corps, et il dit : Dieu n'a ni bouche ni voix.

En V.54, Origène reproche à Celse de vouloir mettre vainement les chrétiens en contradiction avec eux-mêmes en soutenant que « beaucoup sont déjà venus ». Origène pense qu'il fait allusion à la descente des anges chez les hommes rapportée dans le livre d'Enoch, qu'il aurait mal comprise :

Πολλῷ δὲ πλέον οὐ προσήσεται ἅπερ ἔοικε παρακούσας ἀπὸ τῶν ἐν τῷ Ἐνὼχ γεγραμμένων τεθεικέναι ὁ Κέλσος. Οὐδεὶς τοίνυν ἐλέγχει ἡμᾶς ψευδομένους καὶ τὰ ἐναντία τιθέντας, ὅτι τε μόνος ἦλθεν ὁ σωτὴρ ἡμῶν καὶ ὅτι, ἐπεὶ ἄλλοι πολλοὶ πολλάκις ἐληλύθασι. Πάνυ δὲ συγκεχυμένως ἐν τῇ περὶ τῶν ἐληλυθότων πρὸς ἀνθρώπους ἀγγέλων ἐξετάσει τίθησι τὰ ἀτρανώτως ἐλθόντα εἰς αὐτὸν ἀπὸ τῶν ἐν τῷ Ἐνὼχ γεγραμμένων· ἅτινα οὐδ' αὐτὰ φαίνεται ἀναγνοὺς οὐδὲ γνωρίσας ὅτι ἐν ταῖς ἐκκλησίαις οὐ πάνυ φέρεται ὡς θεῖα τὰ ἐπιγεγραμμένα τοῦ Ἐνὼχ βιβλία·

> À bien plus forte raison refusera-t-il d'admettre (Apelles) le passage que Celse paraît avoir cité du livre d'Enoch sans l'avoir compris. Personne donc ne nous convainc de mensonge et de contradiction, comme si nous disions que notre Sauveur est venu seul et que cependant il en est souvent venu d'autres. C'est avec une confusion totale, quand il discute la venue des anges vers les hommes, qu'il cite des passages obscurs tirés du livre d'Enoch. Il ne semble ni l'avoir lu, ni avoir su que le livre intitulé Enoch n'est pas généralement tenu pour divin dans les Églises.

Les autres rapprochements textuels concernent les épîtres pauliniennes. En V.17, Origène reproche à Celse de faire un résumé incorrect de la doctrine du jugement dernier :

Εἶτα τούτοις ἑξῆς παρακούσας ἤτοι τῶν ἱερῶν γραμμάτων ἢ τῶν μὴ νενοηκότων τὰ ἱερὰ γράμματα φησιν ὑφ' ἡμῶν λέγεσθαι μόνους διαμενεῖν κατὰ τὸν καιρὸν τοῦ ἐπαχθησομένου τῷ κόσμῳ διὰ πυρὸς καθαρσίου οὐ μόνον τοὺς ζῶντας τότε ἀλλὰ καὶ τοὺς πάλαι ποτὲ ἀποθανόντας· οὐχ ὑπολαβὼν μετά τινος ἀπορρήτου σοφίας λελέχθαι παρὰ τῷ ἀποστόλῳ τοῦ Ἰησοῦ τό· « Οὐ πάντες κοιμηθησόμεθα, πάντες δὲ ἀλλαγησόμεθα ἐν ἀτόμῳ, ἐν ῥιπῇ ὀφθαλμοῦ, ἐν τῇ ἐσχάτῃ σάλπιγγι· σαλπίσει γάρ, καὶ οἱ νεκροὶ ἐγερθήσονται ἄφθαρτοι, καὶ ἡμεῖς ἀλλαγησόμεθα.»

> Ensuite, pour avoir mal compris les saintes Écritures, ou entendu ceux qui ne les avaient pas pénétrées, il nous fait dire que seront seuls à survivre au moment où la purification par le feu sera infligée au monde non seulement les vivants d'alors, mais même ceux qui seront morts depuis longtemps. Il n'a pas saisi la sagesse cachée qu'enferme la parole de l'Apôtre de Jésus : *Nous ne mourrons pas tous, mais tous nous serons transformés, en un instant, en un clin d'œil, au son de la trompette finale ; car la trompette sonnera, les morts ressusciteront incorruptibles, et nous, nous serons transformés* (1 Cor 15.51–52).

En V.64, Origène affirme que, lorsque Celse parle de chrétiens appelés « cautères de l'oreille », il déformerait un propos de l'Apôtre :

Παρακηκοέναι δέ μοι φαίνεται τῆς τε ἀποστολικῆς λέξεως φασκούσης· «Ἐν ὑστέροις καιροῖς ἀποστήσονταί τινες τῆς πίστεως, προσέχοντες πνεύμασι πλάνοις καὶ διδασκαλίαις δαιμονίων, ἐν ὑποκρίσει ψευδολόγων, κεκαυστηριασμένων τὴν οἰκείαν συνείδησιν, κωλυόντων γαμεῖν, ἀπέχεσθαι βρωμάτων, ἃ ὁ θεὸς ἔκτισεν εἰς μετάληψιν μετ᾽ εὐχαριστίας τοῖς πιστοῖς», παρακηκοέναι δὲ καὶ τῶν ταύταις τοῦ ἀποστόλου ταῖς λέξεσι χρησαμένων κατὰ τῶν παραχαραξάντων τὰ χριστιανισμοῦ· διόπερ εἶπεν ὁ Κέλσος ἀκοῆς καυστήριά τινας ὀνομάζεσθαι παρὰ Χριστιανοῖς.

> Celse a mal compris, me semble-t-il, cette parole de l'Apôtre : *Dans les derniers temps, certains s'écarteront de la foi pour s'attacher à des esprits trompeurs et à des doctrines diaboliques, séduits par des menteurs hypocrties marsués au fer rouge dans leur conscience : ils interdisent le mariage et l'usage d'aliments que Dieu a créés pour être pris avec actions de grâce par les croyants* (1 Tim 4.1–3). Il a mal compris encore les gens qui citent ces paroles de l'Apôtre contre ceux qui altèrent les vérités du christianisme : aussi dit-il que, parmi les chrétiens, certains sont appelés les cautères de l'oreille.

En VI.12, Origène reproche à Celse de ne pas comprendre Paul (1 Cor 3.19) et de confondre sagesse humaine et sagesse du monde :

Διὸ μεταβαίνομεν ἐπ᾽ ἄλλην Κέλσου κατηγορίαν, οὐδὲ τὰς λέξεις ἡμῶν εἰδότος ἀλλ᾽ ἐκ παρακουσμάτων φήσαντος ὅτι φαμὲν τὴν ἐν ἀνθρώποις σοφίαν μωρίαν εἶναι παρὰ θεῷ, τοῦ Παύλου λέγοντος· «Ἡ σοφία τοῦ κόσμου μωρία παρὰ θεῷ ἐστι.»

> Je passe donc à une autre accusation de Celse. Il ne connaît même pas nos textes, mais, par suite de méprises, nous accuse de soutenir que la sagesse humaine est folie devant Dieu, alors que Paul dit : *La sagesse de ce monde est folie devant Dieu.*

En VI.36, Origène reproche au philosophe d'accuser vainement les chrétiens de parler de résurrection de la chair par le bois et d'avoir sur ce point commis un nouveau contresens sur les textes pauliniens :

Νῦν δ᾽ οὐκ ἀρκεσθεὶς τοῖς εἰρημένοις φησὶ λέγεσθαι ἀνάστασιν σαρκὸς ἀπὸ ξύλου, παρακούσας οἶμαι τοῦ συμβολικῶς εἰρημένου, ὅτι διὰ ξύλου θάνατος καὶ διὰ ξύλου ζωή, θάνατος μὲν κατὰ τὸν Ἀδὰμ ζωὴ δὲ κατὰ τὸν Χριστόν.

> Ici, non content de ce qu'il a déjà dit, il ajoute qu'il est question de la résurrection de la chair par le bois, faute d'entendre, je pense, l'expression figurée : *c'est par le bois que vint la mort, et par le bois la vie ; la mort en Adam, la vie dans le Christ* (Rm 5.12–14 ; 1 Cor 15.21–22).

On le voit, la thèse d'Origène consiste à prêter à Celse une connaissance de textes bibliques précis, ou de propos émanant de chrétiens, ou simples ou hérétiques, qui ne les auraient pas compris. Cette thèse soulève la question de savoir dans quelle mesure Celse connaissait les Écritures[21]. On notera qu'Origène, comme à son habitude, manifeste une certaine prudence et présente cette thèse seulement comme l'explication la plus probable pour expliquer les erreurs de Celse. Dans certains cas, la démonstration d'Origène paraît fiable et peut nous aider à identifier quelques-unes des sources bibliques du philosophe : ainsi, lorsqu'il met en relation le propos de Celse sur la « sagesse humaine » et le texte de Paul sur la « sagesse du monde » (1 Cor 3.19). Dans d'autres cas, en revanche, le propos paraît plus douteux : par exemple, lorsqu'Origène accuse Celse d'avoir mal compris 1 Tim 4.1–3 dans son allusion aux « cautères de l'oreille », ou de s'être mépris sur un passage d'Enoch. Concernant le premier point, les hérésiologues évoquent en effet l'habitude de certains gnostiques de marquer au fer rouge leur doctrine sous le lobe de l'oreille[22]. Celse fait probablement allusion à ces gnostiques, beaucoup plus qu'au texte de Paul que, selon toute vraisemblance, il ne connaît pas. Il n'y a par ailleurs aucune preuve que Celse ait pu connaître le passage du Livre d'Enoch auquel pense Origène[23].

Fondés ou non, les rapprochements textuels d'Origène répondent à une intention analogue à celle de Celse : montrer que son adversaire ne comprend pas les textes qu'il est censé utiliser. Mais Origène ne se situe pas tout à fait au même niveau que son adversaire : son but n'est pas de l'exclure d'une tradition, mais de discréditer sa posture d'attaquant et de l'identifier, lorsqu'il s'agit de l'Écriture, à un mauvais exégète, dont il associe l'interprétation à celle des simples ou des hérétiques. Le philosophe sert ainsi de faire-valoir à la mise en évidence du sens spirituel : si Celse n'a pas compris, c'est en effet souvent, pour Origène, parce qu'il aurait manqué l'intention spirituelle des textes[24]. Le dialogue différé qu'Origène entretient avec le philosophe lui permet donc de montrer, à son lectorat chrétien, combien les païens sont incapables de saisir le sens des Écritures, c'est-à-dire combien importent la foi et l'éducation chrétienne, et combien, réciproquement, toute exégèse qui manque le sens spirituel, parce qu'elle est simple ou hétérodoxe, se ramène finalement à une forme d'incapacité *païenne* à accéder à la vérité des textes.

Cette rétorsion *ad hominem* de l'argument est intéressante, mais elle n'aura guère de postérité. En revanche, le premier niveau de la rétorsion de l'accusation de Celse, celle qui consiste à retourner contre *les Grecs* les reproches que Celse adresse aux chrétiens, aura, nous le verrons, une postérité dans la littérature chrétienne. Or, on ne peut qu'être frappé par la façon dont le discours sur la παρακοή fait irruption dans les textes chrétiens avec Origène, et notamment le *Contre Celse*, qui totalise toutes les occurrences des mots de la famille de παρακούειν chez Origène au sens de « mal entendre », à l'exception d'une seule, sur laquelle

---

[21] Pour une évaluation de la connaissance que Celse pouvait avoir de la Bible, voir G. Rinaldi (1997), 107–118 ; Cook (2004) 55–149.
[22] Irénée, *Haer.* I.25.6 ; Hippolyte, *Elenchos* VII.32.8 ; Épiphane, *Panarion* 27.5.9.
[23] *Cels.* V.54 (voir Cook (2004), 92, qui émet des doutes sur l'hypothèse d'Origène).
[24] Voir notamment V.19.

nous reviendrons. Dans les textes chrétiens, on ne trouve que trois occurrences de παρακούειν au sens de « mal entendre » avant Origène[25]. C'est bien le *Contre Celse* qui a introduit dans la réflexion chrétienne le thème du contresens des Grecs, et ce thème apparaît comme une réaction à l'argumentation de Celse. Il reste à savoir d'où provient cette dernière.

L'arrière-plan intellectuel de l'accusation de παρακοή

L'accusation de παρακοή, chez Celse, renvoie à un double contexte. Le premier est platonicien. Platon est le premier auteur grec chez qui apparaisse le sens « comprendre de travers » de παρακούειν. Le philosophe l'utilise assez souvent avec cette signification. Le texte du *Théétète* 195a présente de ce point de vue un intérêt particulier. À propos des hommes, Socrate remarque qu'ils « sont lents, se brouillent en leurs attributions et voient de travers, entendent de travers, conçoivent de travers la plupart du temps » (βραδεῖς τέ εἰσι καὶ ἀλλοτριονομοῦντες παρορῶσί τε καὶ παρακούουσι καὶ παρανοοῦσι πλεῖστα). Ce texte important présente la possibilité du παρακούειν (mal entendre) comme un fait constitutif de la nature humaine, associé à celle du παρορᾶν (mal voir) et du παρανοεῖν (mal concevoir). Il suppose que la ligne de partage entre la foule (indiquée indirectement par le mot πλεῖστα) et le philosophe se fait autour de ces trois actions.

Le platonicien Celse connaît sûrement ce texte. On peut donc faire l'hypothèse que, dans son esprit, l'accusation de παρακοή renvoie à cette incapacité du vulgaire à saisir correctement la vérité sans la déformer. Elle est une autre façon de dénoncer l'*irrationalité* des chrétiens. Les chrétiens apparaissent, de ce point de vue, comme l'incarnation par excellence du vulgaire selon Platon.

L'œuvre de Platon témoigne par ailleurs déjà de cas de malentendus philosophiques. Dans le *Protagoras* 330e, Socrate affirme ainsi : « Τὰ μὲν ἄλλα ὀρθῶς ἤκουσας, ὅτι δὲ καὶ ἐμὲ οἴει εἰπεῖν τοῦτο, παρήκουσας » (Pour le reste, tu nous as bien entendu ; mais où tu fais erreur, c'est quand tu m'attribues cette opinion).

La *Lettre 7* (338d) évoque ceux qui, à Syracuse, avaient l'esprit plein de propos philosophiques mal compris (« Il y avait aussi à Syracuse des gens qui avaient entendu des entretiens de Dion, d'autres qui les tenaient de ces derniers, et ils avaient la tête farcie de propos philosophiques mal compris »[26]). Un peu plus loin, le texte mentionne plus précisément le cas du tyran Denys, parmi ceux qui « étaient pleins de doctrines mal comprises » (τοῖς τῶν παρακουσμάτων μεστοῖς). La *Lettre 7*, on s'en souvient, faisait partie des textes platoniciens opposés par Celse aux chrétiens.

On ne trouve ensuite plus rien dans les textes jusqu'à l'époque impériale (1ᵉʳ–IIᵉ s.). C'est le second contexte qu'il faut évoquer pour comprendre la genèse de

---

25 Chez Clément d'Alexandrie (voir *infra*).
26 Συρακούσαις ἦσαν Δίωνός τε ἄττα διακηκοότες καὶ τούτων τινὲς ἄλλοι, παρακουσμάτων τινῶν ἔμμεστοι τῶν κατὰ φιλοσοφίαν.

l'accusation de παρακοή chez Celse. Ce type d'accusation devient alors fréquent dans les polémiques entre écoles. Plutarque reprend le cas de Denys et de ses malentendus platoniciens (τοῖς Πλάτωνος παρακούσμασι)[27]. Épictète s'en prend à ceux qui ne comprennent pas (οἱ παρακούοντες) les propos stoïciens sur la volonté et qui en tirent des conclusions indues[28].

Diogène Laërce, de même, évoque ceux qui identifient à tort le bien suprême selon Démocrite au plaisir :

> Le bien suprême est l'égalité d'humeur, qui n'est pas identique au plaisir, comme certains l'ont compris par l'effet d'un malentendu, mais qui est une manière d'être où l'âme mène sa vie dans le calme et l'équilibre, sans être troublée par aucune crainte, superstition ou quelque autre passion[29]. (tr. M.-O. Goulet-Cazé *et alii*)

Artémidore dénonce encore les contresens commis sur Aristote et d'autres philosophes à propos des animaux :

> Beaucoup, d'ailleurs, d'après les œuvres d'Aristote sur les animaux, et celles d'Archélaos et de Xénocrate d'Aphrodisias, ayant mal compris ce qui guérit chaque créature, ce qui lui fait peur et ce qui lui plaît le plus, se sont hasardés à forger prescriptions et cures[30]. (tr. J.-Y. Boriaud)

L'œuvre de Galien représente, avec la polémique de Celse et d'Origène, le corpus où apparaît le plus souvent l'accusation de παρακοή : le médecin évoque notamment des cas de contresens sur Hippocrate ou sur Aristote[31]. On sait qu'il existe d'autres points communs entre l'argumentation de Celse et celle de Galien[32], ainsi qu'entre Galien et Origène[33].

---

27 *Dion* 18.3.
28 *Entretiens* II.15.4.
29 IX.45 : τέλος δ' εἶναι τὴν εὐθυμίαν, οὐ τὴν αὐτὴν οὖσαν τῇ ἡδονῇ, ὡς ἔνιοι παρακούσαντες ἐξεδέξαντο, ἀλλὰ καθ' ἣν γαληνῶς καὶ εὐσταθῶς ἡ ψυχὴ διάγει, ὑπὸ μηδενὸς ταραττομένη φόβου ἢ δεισιδαιμονίας ἢ ἄλλου τινὸς πάθους.
30 *Onirocriticon* IV.22 : πολλοὶ δὲ καὶ ἐκ τῶν Ἀριστοτέλους περὶ ζῴων καὶ Ἀρχελάου καὶ τῶν Ξενοκράτους <τοῦ> Ἀφροδισιέως παρακηκοότες ὑφ' οὗ ἕκαστον ζῷον θεραπεύεται καὶ τί ἕκαστον φοβεῖται καὶ ᾧ μάλιστα χαίρει, εἰς συνταγὰς καὶ θεραπείας ἀναπεπλάκασι.
31 Voir, parmi ces très nombreuses références, *De temperamentis* I.523 ; 535 ; 622 Kühn.
32 Notamment l'accusation de foi irrationnelle dirigée contre les chrétiens (voir Walzer (1949), et plus récemment Boudon-Millot (2015), 133–144 ; cf. la contribution de Tieleman). On s'est parfois demandé si Celse était identique au Celse épicurien connu de Galien, mais ce ne semble pas être le cas.
33 Voir Grant (1983), 533–536, qui pense qu'Origène a lu Galien et qu'il lui doit notamment l'idée que Celse pourrait être épicurien (cf. Galien, *De libris propriis* 19.3, 173.3 Boudon = 16.124.6 Müller). Sur Galien, voir, dans ce volume, l'exposé de Teun Tieleman.

L'accusation de παρακοή était utilisée également par les auteurs de commentaires de textes littéraires, comme l'atteste une scholie sur Pindare[34] :

> *Lorsque, à Pylos* (Olympiques 9.31) : parce qu'il n'a pas compris Homère quand il dit : *en pylô en nekuessi* (Iliade V.397). C'est pourquoi il a évoqué le mythe de la Pylos de Nestor. Or Homère ne dit pas qu'il combat dans la cité de *Pylos*, mais dans la *porte* d'Hadès[35].

L'auteur de ce commentaire reproche à Pindare d'avoir prêté à Héraclès un séjour à Pylos. Il aurait mal compris un passage d'Homère, où il aurait lu le mot *pylos* comme un nom propre au lieu d'y voir le nom commun signifiant « porte ».

Porphyre, à propos de Paulinos, l'un des élèves de Plotin, écrit qu'il était « plein de propos mal entendus » (παρακουσμάτων πλήρη)[36]. Le même Porphyre évoque les doctrines « bâtardes et mal entendues » (νόθα καὶ παρηκουσμένα) de ceux qui se réclament de Pythagore sans pourtant comprendre sa pensée. Il met ces malentendus au compte de l'obscurité du philosophe[37]. Dans l'*Ad Gaurum*, il s'en prend de même à des objecteurs anonymes qu'il accuse de se méprendre sur un passage du *Phèdre*[38]. Il reprenait peut-être l'argumentation de Celse dans son *Contre les chrétiens*, mais les fragments conservés ne permettent pas de le dire : ils ne contiennent aucune accusation concernant une quelconque παρακοή des chrétiens. Porphyre était convaincu de l'antiquité de Moïse et des prophètes[39]. On peut donc imaginer que, s'il reprenait l'argument de Celse, il en donnait une version plus prudente, consistant peut-être à accuser *les chrétiens*, mais sans doute pas Moïse et les prophètes, d'avoir déformé les traditions des Grecs. Mais, encore une fois, il n'existe aucune trace de l'argument dans les fragments conservés. La persistance de ce type d'accusation, chez les néoplatoniciens postérieurs à Porphyre (voir *infra*), pourrait cependant nous conduire à penser que ce dernier en avait bien fait usage, car les néoplatoniciens des Ve et VIe s. ne connaissaient sûrement plus le *Discours vrai*. Porphyre lui-même ne le connaissait peut-être qu'à travers le *Contre Celse* d'Origène.

Quant aux accusations de Celse concernant la façon dont les chrétiens auraient mal compris les mythes, elles trouvent au moins un précédent dans un texte de Plutarque, qui évoque un mythe égyptien qui serait le résultat d'une παρακοή de la tradition :

---

34 Dans ce volume, Bert van den Berg fait allusion à d'autres aspects de la présence, dans les textes philosophiques, des termes de la critique des textes.
35 *Scholia uetera in Pindarum*, sur Olympique 9, scholie 46 (éd. Drachmann) : ἀνίκ᾽ ἀμφὶ Πύλον· ὅτι παρακήκοεν Ὁμήρου λέγοντος (Ε397)· ἐν πύλῳ ἐν νεκύεσσι. διὸ καὶ μεμυθολόγηκε τὰ περὶ τὴν Πύλον τοῦ Νέστορος. Ὅμηρος δὲ οὐκ ἐν Πύλῳ λέγει τῇ πόλει, ἀλλ᾽ ἐν πύλῃ τῇ τοῦ Ἅιδου φησὶν αὐτὸν μάχεσθαι.
36 *Vie de Plotin* 7.
37 *Vie de Pythagore* 53.
38 *Ad Gaurum* 9.4.
39 Voir notamment le fr. 40 du *Contra Christianos* et son commentaire par Goulet (1977), 137–164 = (2001), 245–266.

Pour expliquer le fait qu'une fois par an, pendant la pleine lune, ils sacrifient et mangent un porc, ils (= les Égyptiens) racontent que Typhon poursuivait un sanglier à la lueur de la lune en son plein lorsqu'il découvrit le coffre de bois où gisait le corps d'Osiris, qu'il démembra et dont il dispersa les morceaux. Mais tous n'acceptent pas cette version, y voyant une déformation tardive de la tradition, parmi tant d'autres[40].

Ces quelques parallèles montrent que la critique de Celse s'inscrit dans un contexte intellectuel qui est typique du Haut-Empire. Le philosophe a appliqué à la polémique avec les chrétiens un argument-type des polémiques doctrinales de l'époque.

La réponse d'Origène s'inscrit probablement dans le même contexte. On n'a aucune raison de croire en effet qu'il ignorait l'arrière-plan lettré que nous avons rappelé, et il est en général un bon représentant de la culture de son temps. Le seul autre texte de son œuvre conservée qui témoigne d'un emploi de παρακούειν au sens de « mal entendre » se trouve dans son *Commentaire sur Jean*. À propos d'Héracléon, qui suppose que la substance du diable diffère de la substance des être raisonnables, Origène écrit :

> Il me paraît être en cela dans les mêmes dispositions que celui qui affirmerait qu'autre est la substance de l'œil qui voit mal et autre celle de celui qui voit bien, autre la substance de l'oreille qui entend mal de celle qui entend bien. De même qu'en ces organes la substance n'est pas différente, mais qu'un accident a été la cause de la mauvaise ouïe et de la mauvaise vue, de même, en tout ce qui est de nature à suivre la raison, la substance qui peut la suivre est la même, qu'elle accepte la raison ou qu'elle s'y refuse[41].

Ce texte associe mauvaise ouïe (παρακούειν) et mauvaise vue (παρορᾶν), et suppose un parallèle implicite entre le domaine physique et le domaine intellectuel. Ces deux raisons tendent à montrer qu'Origène a sans doute ici à l'esprit le texte du *Théétète* 195a.

Son usage de l'accusation de παρακοή peut cependant renvoyer aussi à un arrière-plan juif et chrétien, mais sur ce point, les textes sont beaucoup moins documentés.

Philon d'Alexandrie connaît le texte du *Théétète* 195a. Il l'évoque au moins à cinq reprises :

1) *De plantatione* 84 : « Car, comment se ferait-il que l'on vît, que l'on entendît ou que l'on comprît de travers, si les perceptions répondant à chaque organe

---

40 *De Iside et Osiride* 354a.
41 *Commentaire sur Jean*, XX.23.199 : Ὅμοιον δὲ ἐν τούτῳ μοι πεπονθέναι φαίνεται τῷ ἑτέραν οὐσίαν φάσκοντι ὀφθαλμοῦ παρορῶντος καὶ ἑτέραν ὁρῶντος, καὶ ἑτέραν οὐσίαν ἀκοῆς παρακουούσης καὶ ὑγιῶς ἀκουούσης. Ὡς γὰρ ἐν τούτοις οὐχ ἡ οὐσία διάφορος, ἀλλά τι αἴτιον ἐπισυμβέβηκεν τοῦ παρακούειν καὶ τοῦ παρορᾶν, οὕτως παντὸς τοῦ πεφυκότος λόγῳ παρακολουθεῖν ἡ παρακολουθητικὴ οὐσία ἡ αὐτή ἐστιν, εἴτε παραδέχεται τὸν λόγον εἴτε ἀνανεύει πρὸς αὐτόν.

étaient fichées en lui au lieu que ce fût Dieu qui semât en chacun d'eux la certitude[42] ? » (tr. J. Pouilloux)

2) *De ebrietate* 158 : « Le contraire de l'ignorance, la science, est, d'une certaine façon la vue et l'ouïe de l'âme. Elle fixe l'attention sur ce qui est dit, contemple la réalité des objets, ne permet pas de voir ou d'entendre à côté, observe et regarde autour d'elle tout ce qui mérite d'être entendu et vu[43]. » (tr. J. Gorez modifiée)

3) *Quis rerum diuinarum heres sit* 109 : décrit l'homme qui vit selon la sensation, « indifférente aux sages conseillers qu'elle ne voit pas, qu'elle n'entend pas, car elle rejette avec mépris tout ce qu'ils peuvent dire à son bénéfice. » (tr. M. Harl)[44]

4) *De specialibus legibus* IV.53 : (à propos du refus d'entendre un témoignage unique) « Car, premièrement, une personne unique peut avoir mal vu, mal entendu, mal compris, ou s'être laissée abuser ; de fait, les opinions erronées sont légion et légion les raisons qui les font se produire[45]. » (tr. A. Mosès)

5) *De uirtutibus* 173 : (à propos de l'arrogant en matière de science) : « s'il regarde, il ne le fait que de travers, et, s'il entend, il n'entend que d'une oreille[46] » (tr. P. Delobre et alii).

Du côté chrétien, on ne peut citer que trois textes antérieurs à Origène qui utilisent le mot παρακούειν au sens de « mal entendre ». Ils se trouvent tous chez Clément d'Alexandrie.

Le premier passage intervient dans une critique de la communauté des femmes selon l'hérétique Carpocrate. Clément suppose que cette doctrine hérétique est la déformation de la doctrine de la *République* :

> Il me semble avoir mal compris Platon, qui dit, dans la *République*, que les femmes sont communes pour tous, voulant dire qu'elles sont communes, celles qui, avant le mariage, font partie de celles qui vont être demandées en mariage de même que le théâtre est commun aux spectateurs, mais que chacune appartient à celui qui l'a prise en premier, et que celle qui est mariée n'est plus commune[47].

---

42 πῶς γὰρ ἂν παρορᾶν ἢ παρακούειν ἢ παρανοεῖν συνέβαινεν, εἴπερ ἐν τούτοις πάγιαι ἦσαν αἱ ἀντιλήψεις ἑκάστου, ἀλλὰ μὴ ἐπ' αὐτῶν θεοῦ σπείροντος ;

43 καὶ γὰρ τῇ ἀγνοίᾳ τὸ ἐναντίον, ἡ ἐπιστήμη, τρόπον τινὰ ψυχῆς καὶ ὀφθαλμοὶ καὶ ὦτά ἐστι· καὶ γὰρ τοῖς λεγομένοις προσέχει τὸν νοῦν καὶ καταθεᾶται τὰ ὄντα καὶ οὐδὲν οὔτε παρορᾶν οὔτε παρακούειν ὑπομένει, πάντα δ' ὅσα ἀκοῆς καὶ θέας ἄξια περισκοπεῖ καὶ περιβλέπεται.

44 ἀλογοῦσαν τῶν σωφρονιστῶν, ὡς παρορᾶν καὶ παρακούειν καὶ ὅσα ἂν ἐπ' ὠφελείᾳ διεξέρχωνται παραπτύειν.

45 πρῶτον μὲν ὅτι ἐνδέχεται ἕνα καὶ παριδεῖν τι καὶ παρακοῦσαι καὶ παρενθυμηθῆναι καὶ ἀπατηθῆναι, δόξαι γὰρ αἱ ψευδεῖς μυρίαι καὶ ἀπὸ μυρίων εἰώθασι προσπίπτειν.

46 καὶ ὁρῶν παραβλέπει πλαγίαις ὄψεσι καὶ ἀκούων παρακούει...

47 *Str*. III, 2.10.2 : δοκεῖ δέ μοι καὶ τοῦ Πλάτωνος παρακηκοέναι ἐν τῇ Πολιτείᾳ φαμένου κοινὰς εἶναι τὰς γυναῖκας πάντων, κοινὰς μὲν τὰς πρὸ τοῦ γάμου τῶν αἰτεῖσθαι μελλόντων, καθάπερ καὶ τὸ θέατρον κοινὸν τῶν θεωμένων φάσκοντος, τοῦ προκαταλαβόντος δὲ ἑκάστην ἑκάστου εἶναι

Plus haut, Clément présente clairement Carpocrate comme un platonicien qui aurait fait lire l'œuvre du philosophe à son fils Épiphane[48]. C'est, jusqu'à Origène, à notre connaissance, le seul emploi de l'accusation de παρακοή à l'encontre d'un hérétique. Clément connaît visiblement la possibilité de cette accusation dans les polémiques entre écoles et l'applique, pour la première fois, à la polémique antihérétique.

Le second texte intervient dans le cadre d'un propos sur le pédagogue chrétien. Clément lui conseille de ne pas introduire aux doctrines difficiles ceux qui en sont incapables, de peur qu'ils ne se méprennent sur le sens des paroles :

> Ainsi, de peur qu'un de ceux-là, fourvoyé dans la connaissance que tu enseignes et incapable de tenir la vérité, n'entende de travers et ne fasse une chute, ne commets pas d'erreur, dit le texte, dans l'usage de la parole ; pour ceux qui s'approchent de façon irrationnelle, ferme la source vive des profondeurs et n'offre à boire qu'à ceux qui ont soif de vérité[49].

On sent dans ce texte le poids de la tradition platonicienne, issue de *Théétète* 195a. Il suppose que la vérité est réservée à ceux qui en sont dignes. Il est donc inutile de la proposer à ceux qui l'approchent de façon irrationnelle, car ils sont voués à se *méprendre*. Comme chez Celse, la παρακοή est liée à l'irrationalité.

Le troisième texte de Clément est un passage du *Stromate VI* dans lequel l'Alexandrin évoque les différentes modalités par lesquelles les vérités bibliques ont été connues des Grecs :

> Ces doctrines, dérobées à la grâce donnée par Dieu aux barbares, sont parées de langue grecque. Certaines, ils les ont volées, mais en les comprenant de travers ; pour les autres, tantôt ils ont parlé sous une incitation, mais sans mener à bien leur travail, tantôt ils ont agi par conjecture et raisonnements humains, et là aussi ils tombent à côté. Ces gens-là croient atteindre parfaitement la vérité, mais, d'après ce que nous saisissons d'eux, ils ne le font que de manière partielle[50].

À travers peu d'emplois du verbe παρακούειν au sens de « comprendre de travers », Clément témoigne donc déjà, avant Origène, de trois cas possibles de

---

καὶ οὐκέτι κοινὴν τὴν γεγαμημένην. For Clement, we use the texts and translations printed in Sources chrétiennes.

48 *Str.* III, 2.5.3.

49 *Str.* V, 8.54.2 : ἵνα οὖν μή τις τούτων, ἐμπεσὼν εἰς τὴν ὑπὸ σοῦ διδασκομένην γνῶσιν, ἀκρατὴς γενόμενος τῆς ἀληθείας, παρακούσῃ τε καὶ παραπέσῃ, ἀσφαλής, φησί, περὶ τὴν χρῆσιν τοῦ λόγου γίνου, καὶ πρὸς μὲν τοὺς ἀλόγως προσιόντας ἀπόκλειε τὴν ζῶσαν ἐν βάθει πηγήν, ποτὸν δὲ ὄρεγε τοῖς τῆς ἀληθείας δεδιψηκόσιν.

50 *Str.* VI, 7.55.4 : ἃ καὶ αὐτά, ἐκ τῆς βαρβάρου κλαπέντα θεοδωρήτου χάριτος, Ἑλληνικῷ κεκόσμηται λόγῳ· τῶν μὲν γὰρ κλέπται, ὧν δὲ καὶ παρήκουσαν· ἐν δὲ τοῖς ἄλλοις ἃ μὲν κινούμενοι εἰρήκασιν, ἀλλ' οὐ τελείως ἐξειργάσαντο, τὰ δὲ ἀνθρωπίνῳ στοχασμῷ τε καὶ ἐπιλογισμῷ, ἐν οἷς καὶ παραπίπτουσιν· ἐπιβάλλειν δ' οἴονται τῇ ἀληθείᾳ οὗτοι μὲν τελείως. ὡς δ' ἡμεῖς αὐτοὺς καταλαμβανόμεθα, μερικῶς.

contresens : le contresens, fait par un hérétique, à partir de Platon ; le contresens que pourrait faire un élève non préparé sur la doctrine ; le contresens, enfin, des Grecs par rapport aux doctrines qu'ils sont censées avoir dérobées aux Écritures.

Ces quelques textes de Philon et de Clément montrent que, au-delà d'un possible arrière-plan philosophique et platonicien, il est tentant de renvoyer aussi l'accusation de contresens, chez Origène, à un contexte alexandrin. La présence de l'explication par la παρακοή dans une scholie sur Pindare montre aussi qu'il a pu être familiarisé à cet argument par sa connaissance de la littérature grammaticale – Eusèbe affirme qu'il fut lui-même un *grammatikos*[51].

L'accusation de παρακοή dans la polémique entre chrétiens et païens après Origène

On ne peut pas dans le cadre de cet article recenser toutes les occurrences de l'accusation de contresens jusqu'à la fin de l'Antiquité. Quelques remarques nous aideront simplement à illustrer la permanence et les évolutions de ce type d'accusation des deux côtés.

Après Celse, l'accusation de παρακοή reparaît une fois dans les fragments du *Contre les Galiléens* de Julien :

> *La circoncision sera sur ta chair*, dit Moïse (cf. Gn 17.13[52]). C'est pour avoir mal compris cela qu'ils disent : 'nous nous circoncisons le cœur'[53].

On le voit, Julien innove par rapport à Celse. Il n'accuse pas les chrétiens d'avoir déformé la philosophie, mais le texte juif, dont ils se réclament. Ce propos peut être mis en relation avec un texte d'Eusèbe dans lequel les juifs étaient présentés comme accusant les chrétiens de mal entendre (παρακούειν) les Écritures :

> Et si les Écritures contiennent par ailleurs d'assez flatteuses perspectives, elles aussi sont exprimées à l'intention des juifs et nous sommes malhonnêtes en les détournant de leur sens[54].

Julien connaît-il Eusèbe ? Les deux auteurs dépendent-ils d'un argument de Porphyre qui n'aurait pas été transmis à la postérité (accusation de παρακοή par rapport au judaïsme) ? Eusèbe ne dépend en tout cas sûrement pas d'une accusation juive « véritable ». Comme c'est souvent le cas lorsqu'il prétend transmettre une accusation, qu'elle soit juive ou grecque, il la construit à partir

---

51 *Histoire ecclésiastique* VI.2.15.
52 La citation est très lointaine.
53 *Contre les Galiléens* fr. 86 Masaracchia : «ἡ περιτομὴ ἔσται περὶ τὴν σάρκα σου», <ὁ Μωυσῆς> φησι. παρακούσαντες τούτου «τὰς καρδίας» φασὶ «περιτεμνόμεθα».
54 *Préparation évangélique* I.2.6 : εἴτε τινὰ ἄλλα φαιδρότερα περιέχουσιν αἱ γραφαί, καὶ ταῦτα Ἰουδαίοις ἀναφωνεῖσθαι, ὧν οὐκ εὖ πράττοντας παρακούειν ἡμᾶς. Translation : Sources chrétiennes.

de ses propres intérêts apologétiques. On peut donc penser, ou bien qu'il dépend d'une source païenne perdue (Porphyre) ou bien qu'il est lui-même l'inventeur de cette accusation soi-disant juive qui, si elle correspond sur le fond à un type d'argument que des juifs pouvaient utiliser (les chrétiens se servent de textes qui ne sont pas à eux et leur donnent un sens incorrect), est *formulée* dans des termes qui renvoient à un contexte grec et dont la source peut être le *Contre Celse*. Nous avons, en effet, montré ailleurs combien la polémique d'Origène, dans le *Contre Celse*, a inspiré celle qu'Eusèbe engage avec le judaïsme et l'hellénisme dans la *Préparation* et la *Démonstration évangélique*[55].

Après Julien, l'accusation de παρακοή apparaît de nouveau dans les *Vies des sophistes*, d'Eunape, à travers la courte notice qu'il consacre à Plotin :

> Plotin était un philosophe originaire d'Égypte. Et puisque j'ai écrit "originaire d'Égypte", je vais aussi ajouter sa patrie. On l'appelle Lycô. Ce point, pourtant, Porphyre, le divin philosophe, ne l'a pas consigné, lui qui affirme avoir été son disciple et l'avoir fréquenté pendant toute sa vie, ou la plus grande partie de sa vie. De ce Plotin, les autels sont aujourd'hui encore chauds. Et ses livres, non seulement les gens éduqués les ont entre les mains et les placent plus haut que les écrits de Platon, mais même le grand nombre plie le genou devant eux, s'il vient à entendre, quoique de travers, quelqu'une de ses doctrines. Porphyre a fait connaître l'ensemble de la vie de Plotin, si bien qu'il était[56] impossible à quiconque d'ajouter quoi que ce soit. Plus encore, il est manifeste qu'il a interprété de nombreux livres de Plotin[57].

On ne peut pas en être certain, mais l'allusion au grand nombre pourrait renvoyer aux chrétiens, que le « grand nombre » représente dans l'esprit d'Eunape une catégorie *englobante* dont les chrétiens ne seraient qu'une partie, ou qu'il soit une façon de renvoyer *exclusivement* aux chrétiens, de manière occulte[58]. L'accusation de contresens sur Plotin pourrait alors s'expliquer par la façon dont les chrétiens, à partir d'Eusèbe, puis chez les Cappadociens, utilisaient le philosophie[59].

---

55 *La Démonstration évangélique d'Eusèbe de Césarée. Étude sur l'apologétique chrétienne à l'époque de Constantin*, Paris (2009).
56 Ou : qu'il serait.
57 Eunape, *Vies des sophistes*, 1–5 : Πλωτῖνος ἦν ἐξ Αἰγύπτου φιλόσοφος. τὸ ἐξ Αἰγύπτου νῦν γράφων, καὶ τὴν πατρίδα προσθήσω. Λυκὼ ταύτην ὀνομάζουσιν· καίτοι γε ὁ θεσπέσιος φιλόσοφος Πορφύριος τοῦτο οὐκ ἀνέγραψε, μαθητής τε αὐτοῦ γεγενῆσθαι λέγων, καὶ συνεσχολακέναι τὸν βίον ἅπαντα ἢ τὸν πλεῖστον. τούτου Πλωτίνου θερμοὶ βωμοὶ νῦν, καὶ τὰ βιβλία οὐ μόνον τοῖς πεπαιδευμένοις διὰ χειρὸς ὑπὲρ τοὺς Πλατωνικοὺς λόγους, ἀλλὰ καὶ τὸ πολὺ πλῆθος, ἐάν τι παρακούσῃ δογμάτων, ἐς αὐτὰ κάμπτεται. τὸν βίον αὐτοῦ πάντα Πορφύριος ἐξήνεγκεν, ὡς οὐδένα οἷόν τε ἦν πλέον εἰσφέρειν· ἀλλὰ καὶ πολλὰ τῶν βιβλίων ἑρμηνεύσας αὐτοῦ φαίνεται.
58 Selon le procédé, courant chez les néoplatoniciens sous l'Empire chrétien, des allusions cryptées : voir sur ce point Saffrey (1975b), repris dans (1990), 201–211 ; Hoffmann (2012).
59 Eusèbe est le premier à citer Plotin comme témoin grec de la doctrine de la Trinité (*Préparation évangélique* XI.9–10). Chez les Cappadociens, l'œuvre de Plotin imprègne le traité *Sur le*

Ce type d'accusation reste persistant jusqu'à la fin de l'Antiquité, comme en témoigne l'œuvre de Simplicius. Son commentaire au *De caelo*, par exemple, contient au moins trois passages dans lesquels certains (τινες) sont accusés de mal entendre (παρακούειν) Platon ou Aristote. Le philosophe dénonce par exemple ceux qui pensent que les réalités célestes sont de même nature que les réalités sublunaires sous prétextes qu'elles seraient constituées comme elles des quatre éléments :

> Ἀλλ' ὅτι μὲν καὶ οἱ ἐκ τῶν τεσσάρων στοιχείων εἰπόντες, εἰ παρακούειν οὕτως τινὰς ἀσεβῶς ὑπελάμβανον ὡς ὁμοφυῆ διὰ τοῦτο τὰ οὐράνια τοῖς ὑπὸ σελήνην νομίσαι, οὐκ ἂν οὕτως προήγαγον τὸν λόγον, πρόδηλον[60].

> Mais il est évident que même ceux qui disent (que le ciel est composé) des quatre éléments, s'ils imaginaient que certains commettent un contre sens tellement impie qu'ils pensent pour cette raison que les réalités célestes sont de même nature que celles qui se trouvent sous la lune, n'avanceraient pas ainsi leur discours.

Simplicius évoque ici probablement la doctrine du *Timée* (31b *sqq*.). Ceux qu'il accuse ont le tort de déformer le propos de Platon en lui faisant dire que, parce que le ciel (ou le monde) serait composé des quatre éléments, il ne serait pas foncièrement différent dans sa nature des réalités sublunaires. On peine à résister à l'idée que Simplicius vise ici les chrétiens, qui ne font pas de distinction entre les réalités physiques créées par Dieu.

Ailleurs, Simplicius critique les malentendus (παρακοάς) de ceux qui pensent que, parce qu'Aristote a dit, dans le *De caelo* (278b3–4 et 279a7–9), que le ciel était matériel (ἔνυλον), il était constitué de la matière qui est au fondement des êtres périssables. Non, répond Simplicius, Aristote ne confirme pas l'idée que le ciel soit périssable. S'il l'a nommé « matériel », c'est uniquement en tant qu'il est affecté d'un mouvement[61]. Il est difficile, une fois encore, de résister à l'idée que Simplicius dénonce ici une façon chrétienne d'utiliser Aristote pour étayer la thèse du caractère périssable du monde, bien que son propos puisse être plus large.

Du côté chrétien, l'accusation de παρακοή se retrouve d'abord chez Eusèbe de Césarée. Comme pour retourner l'argument de Celse, qui suppose que les chrétiens auraient déformé les traditions mythologiques grecques, Eusèbe affirme, dans la *Préparation évangélique,* dans le droit fil d'Origène, que ce sont les mythes

---

Saint-Esprit de Basile de Césarée comme le *De anima et resurrectione* et les *Homélies sur le Cantique* de Grégoire de Nysse.
60 Simplicius, *In Aristotelis quattuor libros de caelo commentaria*, 90.25–28 Heiberg.
61 *In Aristotelis* 135.18–21 : κἂν λέγῃ οὖν ἐν τῇ Περὶ οὐρανοῦ τὸν οὐρανὸν ἔνυλον εἶναι, ὡς καθ' ἕκαστα αὐτὸν καὶ αἰσθητὸν λέγει, οὐ μέντοι ὡς τὴν τοῖς γενητοῖς καὶ φθαρτοῖς ὑποκειμένην ὕλην ἔχοντα, ἀλλὰ μόνον τὴν κατὰ τόπον κινητήν· Voir encore 139.6–13 sur le même sujet, et sur les malentendus (παρακοάς) qu'il faut éviter sur Aristote.

grecs qui seraient le résultat d'une mauvaise compréhension des mythes étrangers. Commentant un passage du Ps 21, l'évêque de Césarée écrit ainsi :

> Mais il descend jusque là et s'avance jusqu'à ce point, je veux dire, jusqu'au sabre qui est dans l'Hadès et la main de celui qui est dit là-bas 'chien' (il est vraisemblable que c'est de là que les Grecs, au prix d'un contresens, décrivent un chien de la mort à trois têtes)[62]...

Le mythe de Cerbère serait donc un contresens sur le Ps 21 (*Sauve... ton fils premier-né de la main du chien*)...

Dans la première partie de l'apologie, Eusèbe avait accusé les Grecs d'être dépendants de traditions égyptiennes mal comprises :

> Les traditions vénérées de la théologie égyptienne ont pris le tour que l'on a exposé ; or celles des Grecs n'en sont que les lambeaux et les échos mal compris, ainsi qu'il a été bien des fois et que l'attestent les auteurs que nous avons cités[63].

C'est la reprise d'un thème apologétique ancien : les Grecs devraient leurs traditions aux barbares[64]. Mais l'usage du verbe παρακούειν rappelle ici plus précisément la polémique d'Origène contre Celse[65].

Après Eusèbe, Chrysostome évoquera encore les malentendus des Grecs à propos des doctrines bibliques (παρακουσμάτων τῶν παρ' ἡμῖν), qui les auraient conduits à imaginer les mythes qu'ils attachent au sort de l'homme après sa mort[66]. Ce genre d'accusation pourra à l'occasion être utilisé contre des « hérétiques » : Cyrille de Jérusalem, dans ses *Catéchèses*, accuse ainsi les manichéens, qui pensent que la résurrection du Christ fut une illusion, de s'être mépris sur les propos de Paul (παρακούοντες Παύλου τοῦ γράφοντος...)[67].

---

62 *Démonstration évangélique* X.8.92 (à propos du Ps 21.21 : *sauve mon âme du sabre, et sauve ton fils unique de la main du chien*) : ἀλλὰ γὰρ ἐπὶ τοσοῦτον κατελθὼν καὶ μέχρι τούτου φθάσας, λέγω δὴ μέχρι τῆς ἐν τῷ ᾅδῃ «ῥομφαίας», καὶ τῆς «χειρὸς» τοῦ αὐτόθι λεγομένου «κυνός» (ὅθεν καὶ παῖδας Ἑλλήνων εἰκὸς τοιοῦτόν τινα, παρακούσαντας, κύνα θανάτου καὶ τοῦτον τρικέφαλον ἀναζωγραφεῖν)...
63 *Préparation évangélique* II.1.53 : τὰ μὲν δὴ σεμνὰ τῆς Αἰγυπτίων θεολογίας τὸν προεκτεθέντα περιείληφε τρόπον, τὰ δὲ Ἑλληνικὰ ὅτι τούτων αὐτῶν ἀποσπάσματα καὶ παρακούσματα τυγχάνει προείρηται μὲν πολλάκις καὶ διὰ τῆς τῶν προτεθέντων συγγραφέων διαγνώσεως.
64 Voir par exemple Clément d'Alexandrie, *Stromates* I.15.
65 Quant au texte de *Théétète* 195a, il y en a peut-être une allusion dans la *Préparation évangélique* XIV.20.10, mais à travers une citation d'Aristoclès.
66 *Aduersus oppugnatores uitae monasticae* II.10 (PG 47.347.23–26).
67 *Catéchèses* 14.21.

Conclusion

L'accusation de mauvaise entente (παρακοή) a représenté, à la fin de l'Antiquité, une explication possible à la genèse de l'innovation, ou simplement de l'erreur, en matière doctrinale. Le concept de παρακοή permet de comprendre comment l'erreur peut naître de la vérité, comment la déviance peut naître de la tradition. Le fondement anthropologique de cette accusation se trouve dans le texte du *Théétète* 195a : il existe dans la plupart des hommes une faiblesse constitutive qui les fait se méprendre (ils voient mal, entendent mal et conçoivent mal). La παρακοή apparaît ainsi comme une faute inévitable, inscrite dans la nature humaine : il y a des contresens parce que tous les hommes ne sont pas capables de philosopher. Cette méprise intellectuelle, propre à la masse des hommes, caractérise par là-même, aux yeux des platoniciens, les chrétiens qui, dès Celse, c'est-à-dire avant l'époque où les chrétiens deviendront majoritaires, représentent déjà le vulgaire, le πολὺ πλῆθος, dont ils incarnent tous les travers.

L'accusation utilisée pour la première fois par Celse contre les chrétiens s'inscrit dans le sillage des discussions entre écoles caractéristiques de l'époque impériale. À partir d'Origène, elle devient un bien commun partagé tant par les païens que par les chrétiens : une explication utilisée dans des termes analogues par les uns et les autres pour penser l'innovation dans l'histoire de la vérité. Ce cas particulier montre combien la polémique est ici responsable de la circulation d'un même argument dans les textes païens et chrétiens.

Dans les deux cas, l'argument présente un paradoxe. La παρακοή conduit à la διαφωνία. Elle écarte de la tradition. Mais pour qu'il y ait écart, il faut qu'il y ait, au départ, une même tradition partagée. Accuser l'adversaire de παρακοή, c'est donc à la fois l'exclure et l'intégrer. Ce type d'accusation témoigne du fait que les païens ne pouvaient pas penser le christianisme comme autre chose qu'une forme dégradée de l'hellénisme – ou bien parce qu'ils considéraient vraiment les chrétiens comme des Grecs qui avaient mal tourné[68], ou bien parce que, plus généralement, il faut, pour mettre l'erreur en évidence, lui trouver une origine. Mais même si l'accusation implique la reconnaissance d'une tradition commune, elle a avant tout pour but, dans l'optique grecque, d'en *exclure* les chrétiens. Dans l'utilisation chrétienne de l'argument, au contraire, la perspective est exactement l'inverse. Certes, l'accusation permet de montrer combien les Grecs se sont trompés et combien ils ont manqué de la grâce qui permet de comprendre les Écritures. Mais l'enjeu essentiel est cette fois la mise en évidence d'une tradition commune, parce que les chrétiens cherchent à montrer aux Grecs que leurs doctrines ne sont pas fondamentalement différentes des leurs. La finalité de l'accusation, chez les chrétiens, est d'*intégrer* l'hellénisme à la tradition biblique. Les Grecs cherchent à montrer comment, de la vérité, est née l'erreur. Les chrétiens, au contraire, s'efforcent de remonter de l'erreur à la vérité.

---

68 Andresen (1955), 146, parle à ce propos d'un « entlehntes und entartetes Griechentum ».

Dans un article mémorable, Pierre Hadot a montré jadis la place centrale et la fécondité du contresens dans la tradition philosophique grecque[69]. Le dossier réuni ici montre qu'il existe aussi, dès l'Antiquité, une *réflexion* sur le contresens, même si ceux que croient déceler les Anciens ne sont pas toujours – et ne sont pas, en général – ceux que nous identifions.

---

69 Hadot (1968), 333-339 (repris dans *Études de philosophie ancienne*, Paris (2010), 3-11).

ROBBERT M. VAN DEN BERG

Plato's Violent Readers*

Pagan Neoplatonists against Christian Appropriations of Plato's Timaeus

> When it has once been written down, every discourse roams about everywhere, reaching indiscriminately those with understanding no less than those who have no business with it, and it doesn't know to whom it should speak and to whom it should not. And when it is faulted and attacked unfairly, it always needs its father's support; alone it can neither defend itself nor come to its own support. (Plato *Phaedrus* 275d9–e5; tr. Nehamas & Woodruff)[1]

Dealing with disagreement in and outside the Platonic tradition

According to the well-known passage from the *Phaedrus* quoted above, a text is always in danger of being misunderstood and – even worse – to be violated by its readers.[2] This holds especially true in the case of Plato, who, hiding behind the characters of his dialogues, refrains from providing a clear exposition of his own views. If, as is often suggested, Plato's reason for doing so was to stimulate philosophical discourse, he certainly succeeded. From the days of the Old Academy

---

* Previous versions of this chapter were read at the FRIAS colloquium from which this volume originates and at the CRASIS Ancient World Seminar at the University of Groningen (November 2015). I am thankful to the audiences on both occasions for their helpful comments and suggestions, as well as to the anonymous reader of the press.
1 ὅταν δὲ ἅπαξ γραφῇ, κυλινδεῖται μὲν πανταχοῦ πᾶς λόγος ὁμοίως παρὰ τοῖς ἐπαΐουσιν, ὡς δ' αὕτως παρ' οἷς οὐδὲν προσήκει, καὶ οὐκ ἐπίσταται λέγειν οἷς δεῖ γε καὶ μή. πλημμελούμενος δὲ καὶ οὐκ ἐν δίκῃ λοιδορηθεὶς τοῦ πατρὸς ἀεὶ δεῖται βοηθοῦ· αὐτὸς γὰρ οὔτ' ἀμύνασθαι οὔτε βοηθῆσαι δυνατὸς αὑτῷ.
2 I borrow the concept of violent interpretation from Sluiter (2013), 203–207, who discusses the above-quoted passage from the *Phaedrus* on 205.

Dealing with Disagreement, ed. by Albert Joosse and Angela Ulacco, Monothéismes et Philosophie, 33 (Turnhout: Brepols, 2022), pp. 111–124

onward, there has always been much discussion among Plato's readers about the correct interpretation of his works and hence of his philosophy. In such debates, emotions could run high. Numenius and Atticus in particular used the trope of violent misinterpretation to discredit their opponents.[3] A good illustration is provided by Numenius' treatise *On the Dissension of the Academics from Plato*. While his main target is the skeptical interpretation of Plato that had been championed by Arcesilaus and others, he even accuses Plato's immediate successors, and in particular Xenocrates, of having 'thrown out some elements of Plato's heritage and perverted others' not just out of ignorance, but motivated by ambition to make a name for themselves.[4]

Later Neoplatonists appear to have dealt with alternative interpretations of Plato by other Platonists in a more relaxed way. At the beginning of his *Platonic Theology*, for example, Proclus presents his readers with an overview of

> [t]hose exegetes of the Platonic mysteries who have revealed for us the most sacred interpretations concerning the divine and who have received a nature nearly equal to that of their own leader (sc. Plato) (Proclus, *Platonic Theology* I.1, 6.16–18).[5]

This list of venerated Neoplatonic teachers starts with Plotinus, with whom Proclus disagreed about the (to them) crucial matter of the (un)descended soul, and includes, among others, Porphyry, whose interpretation of the *Timaeus* attracts a considerable amount of flak in Proclus' commentary on that dialogue, and Theodore of Asine, whose interpretation of the myth of the winged charioteer from the *Phaedrus* Proclus will reject in *Platonic Theology* IV.23 (69.5–70.17). I assume that Proclus' mild attitude toward fellow Platonists whose interpretations he rejected was in part motivated by the urge that he and others felt to present pagan Platonism as a unified front against Christianity.

In dealing with such competing readings of Plato originating from outside their own circle, the pagan Neoplatonists were far less tolerant. As is widely known, many Christian intellectuals had taken a serious interest in Plato's works. The difference between the Neoplatonists and the Christian readers of Plato is, obviously, that for the latter Plato was not 'their own leader', i.e. they did not accept Plato's authority. As Dirk Baltzly observes in regard to the passage just quoted, this authority was 'not merely epistemic, but moral', i.e. the Neoplatonists claimed that Plato's texts offered a path to salvation and divinization.[6] Hence, authority in Neoplatonic circles – or textual communities, as Baltzly calls them – was 'not so much a matter of doctrine as an attitude towards the text of Plato'.[7] It is

---

3 As the anonymous reader kindly pointed out to me.
4 Numenius frg. 24.10–14.
5 Τούτους δὴ τοὺς τῆς Πλατωνικῆς ἐποπτείας ἐξηγητὰς καὶ τὰς παναγεστάτας ἡμῖν περὶ τῶν θείων ὑφηγήσεις ἀναπλώσαντας καὶ τῷ σφετέρῳ καθηγεμόνι παραπλησίαν τὴν φύσιν λαχόντας [...].
6 Baltzly (2014), 793.
7 Baltzly (2014), 797.

in this context of anti-Christian polemics that the pagan Neoplatonists reverted to the trope of violent misinterpretation. The Neoplatonists explained such misinterpretations by pointing to the inherently immoral character of Christianity. As they saw things, Christians violently rejected both the authority of Plato in the double sense just described and the whole of pagan Greek culture, precisely because they were immoral persons. They approached Plato's texts with the wrong attitude and hence their interpretations of Plato were bound to be no good. To put it in the words of the passage from the *Phaedrus*, Christians were people who had 'no business' with the texts of Plato, whom they 'attacked unfairly'. In the first part of this chapter, I shall discuss the way in which Plotinus and Proclus deal with Christian readings of Plato, and in particular of the *Timaeus*, along these lines. In the second part, we shall look at a Christian response, that by John Philoponus, who in his polemic against Proclus' interpretation of the *Timaeus* turns the tables on his pagan adversary.[8]

Immorality as a cause of violent interpretation: Plotinus against Gnostic readings of the *Timaeus*

According to Porphyry (*Life of Plotinus* c. 16.1–9), '[t]here were in his (i.e. Plotinus') time apart from many other Christians also certain sectarian ones who based their teachings on the ancient philosophy'.[9] These sectarian groups, listed subsequently by Porphyry, are Gnostics. A modern scholar of Gnosticism might balk at Porphyry's suggestion that these Gnostics were Christians. Even though there were indeed Christian Gnostics around in Porphyry's time, Plotinus and his school seem in particular to have taken issue with the so-called Platonizing Sethian treatises, such as *Zostrianus*, which is mentioned by Porphyry in the passage under discussion (*Life of Plotinus* c. 16.6) and quoted from by Plotinus in his

---

8 The fact that the three cases of contested interpretations that I discuss in this chapter all concern the *Timaeus* is hardly coincidental. As Maren Niehoff (2007) has recently argued, pagan Greek philosophers from the 2nd century CE onward sought to distinguish themselves from Christians on the basis of the alleged superiority of their interpretations of the *Timaeus*, a text that enjoyed great authority among both pagans and Christians.

9 Γεγόνασι δὲ κατ' αὐτὸν τῶν Χριστιανῶν πολλοὶ μὲν καὶ ἄλλοι, αἱρετικοὶ δὲ ἐκ τῆς παλαιᾶς φιλοσοφίας ἀνηγμένοι [...]. The precise meaning of this phrase is debated. I here follow the interpretation of Igal (1981), 138–139; for another reading of the phrase, see M. Tardieu in Brisson et al. (1992), 509–517. I have translated αἱρετικοί here as 'sectarians', rather than 'heretics' as, e.g., Mark Edwards (2000), 28 renders the word. As Edwards (2000), 28 n. 155, observes, the word αἱρετικός 'had been in common use among Christians in the sense of "heretic" since Irenaeus (fl. 170), though among pagans it still denoted merely a "choice" (*hairesis*) of philosophical alliance'. While Porphyry may have known of this specific Christian use of the word, for him as a prominent pagan all forms of Christianity were equally misguided, so it would make little sense for him to take sides in inner-Christian discussions about orthodoxy and brand some Christian schools as 'heretic'.

Treatise against the Gnostics (*Enn.* II.9 [33], 10.19–33). These treatises 'represent a form of Gnosticism virtually devoid of Christian influences'.[10] Be that as it may, these sectarians, according to Porphyry, had 'claimed that Plato had not reached the depths of intelligible being'. This situation, Porphyry continues, triggered a flow of polemical works by members of Plotinus' school, including Plotinus' own lengthy *Treatise against the Gnostics*. Porphyry ascribes to the Gnostics a somewhat ambiguous attitude toward Plato.[11] On the one hand, they accused him of having failed to penetrate the secrets of the intelligible realm, on the other they partly derived their doctrines from so-called 'ancient philosophy', which included notably that of Plato. As modern scholarship has clearly shown, the Gnostics were not just avid readers of Plato's dialogues, but were equally well acquainted with the contemporary Platonic commentaries on them.[12] Some Platonists took the Gnostics seriously, as is clear from the afore-mentioned *Treatise against the Gnostics*, which addresses not so much hard-core Gnostics, but rather Platonists who thought that Platonism and Gnosticism could somehow be squared.

From the fact that the Gnostics borrowed from Plato, one could have concluded that Gnosticism is part of the Greek philosophical tradition. In fact, some modern scholars working on Gnosticism have made precisely this claim.[13] Plotinus, though, insists that the Gnostics are beyond the pale. Admittedly, there is much Platonism in Gnostic texts, yet the Gnostics try to pass their ill-understood version of Plato off as something altogether new.[14] They try to conceal their plagiarism by

> inventing a new jargon to recommend their own school. They contrive this meretricious language as if they had no connection with the ancient Hellenic school, though the Hellenes knew all this and spoke **clearly without pomposity** (*atuphôs*) of ascents from the cave and advancing gradually closer

---

10 Thus Moore & Turner (2000), 182, who offer a helpful overview of various types of Christian and non-Christian Gnosticism.
11 On the ambiguous relation of the Gnostics with this 'ancient philosophy', see further Igal (1981).
12 For the case of the *Parmenides*, see, e.g., Turner (2011).
13 See, e.g., Turner (2012), 153: 'While I would not wish to assert *tout court* that Gnosticism is a form of Greek philosophy, I do not agree that Gnosticism can be called "unphilosophical" (Dillon), or that Greek philosophy's influence was "extraneous and for the most part superficial" (Armstrong)'. Elsewhere, I have expressed my reservations about the philosophical nature of Gnosticism (van den Berg (2013b)), yet Turner is obviously right about the strong Platonic influence on Gnosticism.
14 Ironically, in his discussion of the Gnostic material, Plotinus commits the very offences of which he accuses the Gnostics: 'Plotinus is overly eager to trace back the Gnostic doctrines to Plato, and this remarkable feat he achieves by the curious procedure of drastic simplification and reinterpretation' (Igal (1981), 141).

and closer to a truer vision. (Plotinus, *Enn.* II.9 [33], 6.5–10; trans. Armstrong LCL adapted)[15]

Especially relevant for my present purpose is the characterization of Hellene, i.e. traditional Greek, philosophical writings as 'clear' and 'without pomposity'. The idea that a philosopher ought to express himself clearly goes back to Aristotle (*Rhet.* III.2, 1404b1–4), who had argued that, since the function of language is communication, the one virtue of language is clarity (*saphêneia*). This idea was subsequently embraced by almost all Greek philosophical schools, including Stoicism, Epicureanism, and Neoplatonism, hence Plotinus' remark that Greek philosophers express themselves clearly.[16] Plotinus next suggests that the Gnostics' lack of clarity – their main stylistic failure – is due to the very moral failure that made them break away from the Greek tradition in the first place: Plotinus describes the style of the old Greek philosophers as *atyphos* ('without pomposity'). The word, of course, recalls the beginning of the *Phaedrus*. There Socrates declares that he is not interested in rationalizing local mythology, such as the story of how Boreas abducted a girl on the spot where the dialogue is said to take place. He has no time for such things, since, he says, 'I am still unable, as the Delphic inscription orders, to know myself'. Rather than speculating about mythological accounts of violent winds, Socrates says, he does not

> look into them, but into my own self. Am I a beast more complicated and savage than **Typhon**, or am I a tamer, simpler animal with a share in a divine and ***atyphos*** nature? (Plato, *Phdr.* 230a3–6; trans. Nehamas-Woodruff adapted)[17]

The word *atyphos* is difficult to render into English. *Typhos* is associated with the verb *epityphô*, 'to puff up'. It implies that a philosopher who cultivates the divine element in himself should be free from vanity and the sort of violent behaviour that goes with it. The Stoics, who had adopted Socrates as their role model, make being *atyphos* one of the qualities of their sage, as do the Cynics.[18] Likewise, Plotinus here uses the word to contrast the true, i.e. Greek, philosophers to the puffed up Gnostics, whose eagerness for renown motivates their plagiarism of Plato. Thus, when Neoplatonists use the term 'typhonic' to refer to Christians, as

---

15 καινολογούντων ἐστὶν εἰς σύστασιν τῆς ἰδίας αἱρέσεως· ὡς γὰρ τῆς ἀρχαίας Ἑλληνικῆς οὐχ ἁπτόμενοι ταῦτα σκευωροῦνται εἰδότων καὶ **σαφῶς** τῶν Ἑλλήνων **ἀτύφως** λεγόντων ἀναβάσεις ἐκ τοῦ σπηλαίου καὶ κατὰ βραχὺ εἰς θέαν ἀληθεστέραν μᾶλλον καὶ μᾶλλον προιούσας.

16 On the adoption of Aristotle's principle of clarity by later Greek philosophers such as the Epicureans and Stoics, see van den Berg (2008), 57–58. The Neoplatonic commentators on Aristotle frequently discuss Aristotle's own lack of clarity (cf. Mansfeld (1994), 22–26).

17 σκοπῶ οὐ ταῦτα ἀλλ' ἐμαυτόν, εἴτε τι θηρίον ὂν τυγχάνω **Τυφῶνος** πολυπλοκώτερον καὶ μᾶλλον ἐπιτεθυμμένον, εἴτε ἡμερώτερόν τε καὶ ἁπλούστερον ζῷον, θείας τινὸς καὶ **ἀτύφου** μοίρας φύσει μετέχον.

18 On the Stoic sage as *atyphos* and its relation to the *Phaedrus* passage, see Brouwer (2013), 149–163; on the Cynics, see Long (2006), 80–81.

they do here and elsewhere, it disqualifies them both as Greeks because of their inadequate style and as philosophers because of their vanity.[19]

Their typhonic nature makes Christians violent interpreters of ancient texts, i.e. they distort the obvious meanings of those texts. This point is explicitly made by Porphyry when he criticizes Christian interpretations of the writings of Moses, whom many pagan authors were ready to accept as a decent philosopher:[20]

> They boast that things said **clearly** by Moses are riddles and treat these with religious reverence as if they were divine oracles full of hidden mysteries. Having thus cast a spell of pomposity (***typhos***) over the critical faculties of the soul, **they impose their exegesis**. (Porphyry, *Against the Christians* Fr. 39 Harnack = Eusebius, *Ecclesiastical History* VI.19.4)[21]

In his new German edition of the remains of Porphyrius' *Against the Christians*, Matthias Becker identifies *typhos* as a *Signalwort* that characterizes the Christians as sophists who practice some sort of verbal witchcraft.[22] In a similar vein, Porphyry rejects accusations that Plotinus had plagiarized Numenius on the grounds that Plotinus' detractors despised the latter, 'because they do not understand what he says and because he is entirely free of sophistic deceit and pomposity'.[23] Furthermore, another recent, Italian edition of *Against the Christians* makes the interesting suggestion that the Greek expression that I have rendered above as 'to impose their exegesis' (*epagousin exêgêseis*) is polemical: an exegesis (*exêgêsis*) is supposed to derive from (*ex-*) the text, yet the Christians impose theirs upon (*epi-*) it.[24] All of this fits nicely with Plotinus' own accusation that the pompous Gnostics had invented a new jargon to hide the fact that their philosophy was nothing but a travesty of Plato's.

Plotinus elaborates on the Gnostics' misguided interpretation of Plato in the next passage, which deals with their misunderstanding of the *Timaeus* and particularly of the Demiurge:

> And the idea to construct a plurality in the intelligible world – Being, and Intellect, and the Demiurge (as different from Intellect), and Soul –

---

19 For an example of 'typhonic winds' as a cryptic reference to ('code phrase' for) Christians, see Marinus, *Proclus* c. 15, 16 together with the instructive comments by the editors Saffrey & Segonds (2001), 117 n. 3 to 18.
20 Cf., e.g., Numenius' famous rhetorical question 'What is Plato, but Moses speaking in Attic Greek?' (frg. 8.9–13).
21 αἰνίγματα γὰρ τὰ **φανερῶς** παρὰ Μωυσεῖ λεγόμενα εἶναι κομπάσαντες καὶ ἐπιθειάσαντες ὡς θεσπίσματα πλήρη κρυφίων μυστηρίων διά τε **τοῦ τύφου** τὸ κριτικὸν τῆς ψυχῆς καταγοητεύσαντες, **ἐπάγουσιν ἐξηγήσεις**.
22 Becker (2016), 148–149.
23 Porphyry, *Life of Plotinus* c. 18.4–6: κατεφρόνουν τῷ μὴ νοεῖν ἃ λέγει καὶ τῷ πάσης σοφιστικῆς αὐτὸν σκηνῆς καθαρεύειν καὶ **τύφου**.
24 Muscolino and Girgenti (2009): 'sovrappongono le (loro) interpretazioni'; cf. their note 164 on 478.

is taken from the words in the *Timaeus*: for Plato says, 'The maker of this universe thought that it should contain all the forms that intelligence discerns contained in the Living Being that truly is' (*Tim.* 39e7–9). **But they did not understand**, and took it to mean that there is one intellect (*nous*) which contains in it in repose all realities, and another intellect different from it which contemplates them, and another which plans – but often they have soul as the Demiurge instead of the planning intellect – and **they think that this is the Demiurge according to Plato, being a long way from knowing who the Demiurge is**. And in general they give a false account of him both concerning the manner of demiurgy and concerning many other topics, and **they drag the great man's teachings towards the worse** as if they had understood the intelligible nature, but he and the other blessed philosophers had not. (Plotinus, *Enn.* II.9 [33], 6.14–24; trans. Armstrong LCL adapted)[25]

Once again, Plotinus here presses the charge of plagiarism against the Gnostics. They borrow the figure of the Demiurge, whom Plotinus identifies with the divine Intellect, from Plato. Yet, the Gnostics fail to grasp the unity that characterizes the divine Intellect, coming as it does directly after the One, by distinguishing between various forms of Intellect and by conflating Intellect with Soul. Such is, of course, only to be expected in the case of *typhonic* souls that are characterized by plurality rather than simplicity and that are out of touch with the Intellect. They thus 'drag (*helkô*) the teachings of Plato towards the worse'. The verb 'to drag' (*helkô*) suggests that the Gnostics do a fair amount of violence to Plato's text.[26] According to Plotinus, the Gnostics' violent treatment of Plato is part of a bigger pattern. Out of vanity, in order to appear original, the Gnostics seek to violate Greek intellectual authorities: they 'tear to pieces and insult (*hybrizein*) the Hellenes'. In doing so, they show themselves to be the opposite of a real philosopher, who always treats the views of his opponents 'courteously' (*eumenôs*) and 'fairly' (*dikaiôs*).[27]

---

25 Καὶ ἐπὶ τῶν νοητῶν δὲ πλῆθος ποιῆσαι, τὸ ὂν καὶ τὸν νοῦν καὶ τὸν δημιουργὸν ἄλλον καὶ τὴν ψυχήν, ἐκ τῶν ἐν τῷ Τιμαίῳ λεχθέντων εἴληπται· εἰπόντος γὰρ αὐτοῦ «ᾗπερ οὖν νοῦς ἐνούσας ἰδέας ἐν τῷ ὅ ἐστι ζῷον καθορᾷ, τοσαύτας καὶ ὁ τόδε ποιῶν τὸ πᾶν διενοήθη σχεῖν». Οἱ δὲ **οὐ συνέντες** τὸν μὲν ἔλαβον ἐν ἡσυχίᾳ ἔχοντα ἐν αὐτῷ πάντα τὰ ὄντα, τὸν δὲ νοῦν ἕτερον παρ' αὐτὸν θεωροῦντα, τὸν δὲ διανοούμενον – πολλάκις δὲ αὐτοῖς ἀντὶ τοῦ διανοουμένου ψυχή ἐστιν ἡ δημιουργοῦσα – **καὶ κατὰ Πλάτωνα τοῦτον οἴονται εἶναι τὸν δημιουργὸν ἀφεστηκότες τοῦ εἰδέναι τίς ὁ δημιουργός**. Καὶ ὅλως τὸν τρόπον τῆς δημιουργίας καὶ ἄλλα πολλὰ καταψεύδονται αὐτοῦ καὶ **πρὸς τὸ χεῖρον ἕλκουσι τὰς δόξας τοῦ ἀνδρὸς** ὡς αὐτοὶ μὲν τὴν νοητὴν φύσιν κατανενοηκότες, ἐκείνου δὲ καὶ τῶν ἄλλων τῶν μακαρίων ἀνδρῶν μή.
26 Cf. Sleeman and Pollet, *Lexicon Plotinianum s.v.* ἕλκειν: 'drag about with violence'.
27 Cf. Plotinus, *Enn.* II.9 [33], 6.43–52.

Proclus on interpreting the *Timaeus* correctly, immorality, and speaking Greek (*hellēnizein*)

About two centuries after Plotinus' attack on the Gnostic appropriation of the *Timaeus*, Proclus, in part inspired by Plotinus' treatise, elaborated on the relation between immorality and misinterpretation when criticizing Christian readings of the *Timaeus*. In *Tim.* 29e4–30a2 we are told that if one receives (*apodechomenos*) the words of 'the wise men' (*andres phronimoi*) correctly (*orthotata*), one will find that they say that God's goodness is the 'most sovereign principle' (*kuriōtata aitia*) for the coming to be of the world. Proclus insists that Plato here does not have the goodness of the Demiurge in mind but the Good that is the ultimate principle of Neoplatonic metaphysics. This prompts Proclus to reflect on the intellectual qualities required to read Plato successfully:

> And since in [teachings of] doctrines about the very highest causes there is need both of a speaker with intellectual capacity and of wise (*emphrōn*) judgement on the part of the listeners, and especially so in accounts of the Good – for Intellect (*Nous*) can reach up towards the Good, both the universal [Intellect] towards the absolute Good and the intellect in us towards [the good] in us – for this reason he believes that those who say anything about the 'most sovereign principle' should be 'wise' (*phronimos*) and that those who listen should 'receive' these words 'correctly'. (Proclus, *Commentary on the Timaeus* I.369.12–19; trans. Runia & Share (2008), 232 adapted)[28]

Proclus next imagines the following objection:

> What then? Couldn't also any chance person say something about God and the final cause? Furthermore, couldn't one every day hear the many say 'God is good?'. But this 'God' is a mere name when it is said without virtue, as Plotinus says,[29] and used by the many without wisdom (*ou kata phronēsin*), but in an arbitrary manner. (Proclus, *Commentary on the Timaeus* I, 369.19–25)[30]

Proclus here is probably referring to the following passage from Plotinus' *Treatise against the Gnostics*:

---

28 ἐπεὶ δὲ ἐν τοῖς περὶ αὐτῶν τῶν ἀκροτάτων αἰτίων δόγμασι τοῦ τε λέγοντος δεῖ νοερὰν ἔχοντος ἕξιν καὶ τῆς ἔμφρονος τῶν ἀκουόντων κρίσεως καὶ μάλιστα ἐν τοῖς περὶ τἀγαθοῦ λόγοις – νοῦς γὰρ ἐπὶ τἀγαθὸν ἀνατείνεσθαι δύναται, ὅ τε ὅλος ἐπὶ τὸ ἁπλῶς ἀγαθὸν καὶ ὁ ἐν ἡμῖν νοῦς ἐπὶ τὸ ἐν ἡμῖν – διὰ δὴ τοῦτο καὶ τοὺς λέγοντάς τι περὶ τῆς κυριωτάτης ἀρχῆς φρονίμους οἴεται δεῖν εἶναι καὶ τοὺς ἀκούοντας ὀρθότατα ἀποδέχεσθαι τοὺς λόγους.

29 Runia and Share (2008), 232 n. 116 rightly assume that Proclus is here referring to Plotinus, *Enn.* II.9 [33], 15 (i.e. the passage discussed below), not to *Enn.* I.2 [19], 1 (*pace* Diehl); their translation – 'Yes, but the word "God" is, as Plotinus says, "a different thing from (*chōris*) virtue"' – however, seems to miss the point that both Plotinus and Proclus wish to make.

30 τί οὖν; οὐχὶ καὶ ὁ ἐπιτυχὼν εἴπειεν <ἄν> τι περὶ θεοῦ καὶ τῆς τελικῆς αἰτίας; τί δέ; οὐ καθ᾽ ἑκάστην ἡμέραν πολλῶν ἔστιν ἀκούειν λεγόντων· ὁ θεὸς ἀγαθός; ἀλλὰ τὸ θεὸς ὄνομά ἐστι χωρὶς ἀρετῆς, ὥς φησι Πλωτῖνος, καὶ οὐ κατὰ φρόνησιν, ἀλλὰ κατ᾽ ἐπιτυχίαν λέγεται παρὰ τῶν πολλῶν.

For it does no good at all to say 'Look to God', unless one teaches how one should look. For one could say, 'What prevents me from looking and refraining from no pleasure, or from having no control over my emotions (*akratê thymou*) and from remembering the name "God" and at the same time being in the grip of all the passions and making no attempt to get rid of any of them?'. In reality it is virtue which goes before us to the goal and, when it comes to exist in the soul along with wisdom (*meta phronêseôs*), shows God; but God, if you talk about him without true virtue, is only a name. (Plotinus, *Enn.* II.9 [33], 15.32–40; trans. Armstrong LCL adapted)[31]

Both passages take their inspiration from the well-known digression in the *Theaetetus*. There, becoming God is described in terms of moral virtue: 'a man becomes like God when he becomes just and pious, with wisdom (*meta phronêseôs*)' (Plato, *Theaetetus* 176b; trans. Levett adapted). As Dirk Baltzly rightly stresses, this famous phrase already suggests a close connection between becoming a better person and an understanding of divine nature in the Platonic tradition.[32] Let us now briefly examine how Plotinus envisages this connection in the case of the Gnostics. Why exactly does he believe that the akratic state of the Gnostics prevents them from attaining knowledge about God, who is only a name to them? Already Aristotle, when discussing *akrasia* in the *Nicomachean Ethics*, had compared the akratic person to a drunk who recites mathematical proofs or Empedocles' verses without understanding what he is saying.[33] Such a person does not actualize his passive knowledge of mathematics or Empedocles. Plotinus (*Enn.* III.6 [26], 2.20–32) arrives at a somewhat similar analysis. According to him, virtue consists in listening to *logos*, reason. This applies primarily to the rational part of the human soul, which receives its *logos* directly from *Nous* (the divine Intellect). This virtue of the rational part of the soul amounts to knowledge of the intelligible in a manner that befits the discursive thought of the rational soul, i.e. the wisdom (*phronêsis*) that Plotinus mentions in the passage against the Gnostics quoted above. The rational soul passes *logos* on to its inferior parts, including the desiring part. It thus controls the desiring part, which otherwise would be 'unrestrainedly lustful'. Virtuous behaviour, then, is the result of reason (*logos*), which the rational human soul derives from the divine Intellect (*Nous*).[34] Thus, a Gnostic who gives in to his irrational lusts is clearly not tuned in to the divine Intellect. To put it in Aristotelian terms, he has not actualized his passive knowledge of the divine. However, texts are the expression of their authors' *nous*

---

31 Οὐ γὰρ δὴ τὸ εἰπεῖν 'βλέπε πρὸς θεόν' προὔργου τι ἐργάζεται, ἐὰν μὴ πῶς καὶ βλέψῃ διδάξῃ. Τί γὰρ κωλύει, εἴποι τις ἄν, βλέπειν καὶ μηδεμιᾶς ἀπέχεσθαι ἡδονῆς, ἢ ἀκρατῆ θυμοῦ εἶναι μεμνημένον μὲν ὀνόματος τοῦ 'θεός', συνεχόμενον δὲ ἅπασι πάθεσι, μηδὲν δὲ αὐτῶν πειρώμενον ἐξαιρεῖν; Ἀρετὴ μὲν οὖν εἰς τέλος προιοῦσα καὶ ἐν ψυχῇ ἐγγενομένη μετὰ φρονήσεως θεὸν δείκνυσιν· ἄνευ δὲ ἀρετῆς ἀληθινῆς θεὸς λεγόμενος ὄνομά ἐστιν.
32 Baltzly (2014), 803.
33 Cf. Aristotle, *Nicomachean Ethics* VII.3, 1147a17–22.
34 I discuss this passage in van den Berg (2013a), 225–226.

and may only be understood by a reader who has activated his own *nous*. For example, when celebrating Plotinus' qualities as a philosopher and an exegete, Porphyry mentions that Plotinus' *nous* would at times 'visibly light up his face' and that he would 'quickly absorb what was read, and would give the sense (*nous*) of some profound subject of study in a few words'.[35]

In short, then, for both Plato and Proclus to receive the words of the *Timaeus* 'correctly' requires that one adopt a virtuous, i.e. Platonic, lifestyle. In their recent translation of this text, David Runia and Michael Share – rightly, I believe – suggest that Proclus' remark that the many fail to do so constitutes a veiled attack on the Christians.[36] The latter, after all, identify the Demiurge with God, an identification that Proclus also criticizes elsewhere.[37] Of special interest for our present concern regarding the accusation of misinterpreting Plato because of moral badness is Proclus' remark that Christians use the word 'God' 'in an arbitrary manner'. This should be understood against the background of a discussion of the meaning of *hellênizein*, speaking Greek, in Proclus' *Commentary on the Alcibiades* (258.15– 259.21).[38] In that dialogue, Socrates and Alcibiades discuss the question whether one can learn something from the many, for example to speak Greek (*hellênizein*). Proclus comments that *hellênizein* is used in three senses. The first sense is that of sticking to the conventions of the Greek language: for example, knowing that Greek speakers use the name *hippos* to refer to a certain type of animal. This is the sort of *hellênizein* that one may learn from the many. It is different from what one may learn from a grammarian, who teaches one to speak Greek correctly, i.e. according to grammatical rules. The third way of speaking Greek is the privilege of the philosopher. The latter knows how to assign names to things in such way as to fit their nature. When describing this third sense of *hêllenizein*, Proclus has Plato's *Cratylus* in mind, in which the question is examined whether naming things is a matter of convention and thus arbitrary or not. In the *Cratylus* it is concluded that name-giving requires a profound understanding of the nature of things and thus is the job for the Platonic dialectician, not of any chance person. Proclus' point, both in the *Commentary on the Alcibiades* and in that on the *Timaeus*, is that the many understand what today we would call the rules of the language-game, i.e. they know when to use certain names – for example, when to use the Greek word *hippos* – without being able to produce a clear definition of the entities

---

35 For the visible expression of Plotinus' *nous*, see Porphyry, *Life of Plotinus* c. 13.5–10, for Plotinus easily grasping the *nous* of a text, see Porphyry, *Life of Plotinus* c. 14.14–16; translations taken from Armstrong LCL.
36 Cf. Runia and Share (2008), 232 n. 117.
37 Cf. Proclus, *Platonic Theology* II.11, 65.5–7: 'And let us celebrate him (God) as if singing a hymn, but without saying that he made earth and heaven nor that he made the souls and all sorts of living beings'. As Saffrey and Westerink (1974), 123 n. 7 to 65 observe, that is almost certainly an allusion to the Christian creed.
38 I have discussed this passage in greater detail as part of my study of Neoplatonic ideas about language in van den Berg (2008), 89–91.

which those names indicate. By naming a horse '*hippos*', they follow linguistic conventions that are seemingly arbitrary. What they fail to realize is that these names, which are after all the products of a Platonic dialectician, are not arbitrary at all. A philosopher, when he uses that name, realizes this: he is able both to describe the essence of a horse and to explain why the Greek name *hippos* is an appropriate expression of that essence. Thus he uses the Greek name '*hippos*' with understanding (*kata phronêsin*), not arbitrarily. Succinctly put, Christians cannot hope to interpret the *Timaeus* correctly by identifying, as they do, the Demiurge with the first God, since they do not really grasp the meaning of the word 'God'.

Philoponus *Against Proclus' 'On the Eternity of the World'*

Pagan Platonists and Platonizing Christians shared a common intellectual upbringing. It comes as no surprise, then, that Christian readers of Plato criticize the pagan readings of Plato in much the same way as the pagans criticized theirs. John Philoponus provides a good illustration of this in his work *Against Proclus' 'On the Eternity of the World'*. In his treatise *On the Eternity of the World*, Proclus had taken on one of the most controversial issues in the ancient interpretation of Plato, i.e. the question whether the material cosmos had a beginning in time, as a literal reading of the *Timaeus* suggests, or not. Proclus rejects such a literal interpretation and argues that Plato rightly holds that the material world is eternal, i.e. that it has no beginning in time. Christian readers of the *Timaeus*, however, tended to favor a literal reading of the text, since in this way they can align Plato with the Christian account of creation. For this reason, it has sometimes been suggested that Proclus' treatise is directed against such a Christian reading of the *Timaeus*. The present consensus, however, is that Proclus is here addressing fellow pagan Neoplatonists as part of an internal debate about the interpretation of the *Timaeus*. As for Philoponus' reply, opinions diverge. The recent translators of Proclus' treatise, Helen S. Lang and A. D. Macro have argued that in the present context Philoponus' Christian identity does not play any role. According to them, it is a debate between two philosophers, whose religious affiliations are irrelevant. The recent translator of Philoponus' reply, Michael Share, disagrees. According to him, Philoponus consciously presents himself as a Christian who criticizes Proclus' pagan reading of the *Timaeus*.[39]

I concur with Share. The way in which Philoponus addresses Proclus recalls the arguments with which Plotinus and Proclus had sought to disqualify Christian interpretations of Plato. According to Philoponus, Plato's position is crystal clear and can hardly be missed: 'he everywhere **with a clear voice** calls out that the

---

39 See Lang and Macro (2001), 3–16 and Share (2005a), 1–6.

cosmos has come into being and is generated'.[40] The pagan interpreters of Plato, however, who

> always prefer what is plausible over what is true and who are **too much in love** (*erôtikôs agan*) with the eternity of the cosmos turn everything upside down when they **drag** (*helkô*) Plato's opinions towards their own. However, to those who have a brain it will be immediately clear from the subtlety and versatility of their words that they **violate** (*ekbiazontai*) Plato's ideas. (Philoponus, *On the Eternity of the World* 125.13–19)[41]

The first point to observe is that Philoponus shares Plotinus' claim that ancient authors, including Plato, have expressed themselves clearly ('with a clear voice'), but that later interpreters have muddled things. Philoponus ascribes the pagan Neoplatonists' failure to interpret Plato correctly to some sort of mental disorder (in this case excessive erotic feelings), just as Plotinus and Proclus assume that Christians get Plato wrong because of their 'typhonic' and akratic state of mind. Like the Neoplatonists, Philoponus condemns alternative interpretations of the text as violent interpretations. According to Philoponus, the pagan Neoplatonists 'drag' around – *helkô*, the same verb that we found in Plotinus – Plato's opinions and 'violate' (*ekbiazomai*) his text.

The accusation of violent interpretation is aired again in the following passage in which Philoponus attacks Proclus' attempts to understand the words *archê* and 'generated' in a special sense that is different from its ordinary usage.

> For if, as Porphyry rightly holds, no one is so devoid of wit as to claim that Plato uses invalid premises, then anyone who believed that Plato makes hypotheses that lead to innumerable conclusions that are either worthy of **ridicule** or are **absurdities of the grossest kind** and who claimed that he employs incorrect words and uses ambiguous terms without distinguishing their proper senses and that he is **careless of the normal meanings of words** and uses words in a novel sense **unknown to the Hellenes**, would, I presume, be even more bereft of wits. (Philoponus, *On the Eternity of the World* 161.17–28; trans. Share (2005b))[42]

---

40 Philoponus, *Aet. Mundi* 125.7–10: Οὐδαμοῦ τοῦ Πλάτωνος κατ' οὐδένα τρόπον ἀγένητον εἶναι τὸν κόσμον ἀποφηναμένου, τοὐναντίον δὲ πανταχοῦ **λαμπρᾷ τῇ φωνῇ** γεγονέναι τε καὶ γενητὸν εἶναι βοῶντος [...].

41 οἱ τὸ πιθανὸν ἀεὶ τῆς ἀληθείας προκρίνοντες καὶ **ἐρωτικῶς ἄγαν** τῆς τοῦ κόσμου ἀϊδιότητος ἔχοντες πάντα ἄνω καὶ κάτω κυκῶσι πρὸς τὸ ἑαυτοῖς δοκοῦν τὰ τοῦ Πλάτωνος **ἕλκοντες**. καίτοι δι' αὐτῆς εὐθὺς τῆς τῶν λόγων κομψείας τε καὶ ποικιλίας κατάφωροι τοῖς νοῦν ἔχουσιν γίνονται, ὡς **ἐκβιάζονται** τὰ τοῦ Πλάτωνος.

42 εἰ γάρ, ὡς τῷ Πορφυρίῳ καλῶς ἔδοξεν, μηδεὶς τοσοῦτον τῶν φρενῶν ἐξέστηκεν, ὡς λέγειν ἀσυλλογίστοις λήμμασιν κεχρῆσθαι τὸν Πλάτωνα, πολλῷ δήπου μᾶλλον κενὸς ἂν εἴη φρενῶν ὁ τοιαύτας ὑποθέσεις λαμβάνειν οἰόμενος Πλάτωνα, ὡς μυρία αὐταῖς πῇ μὲν **γέλωτος** ἄξια ἕπεσθαι πῇ δὲ **ἀτοπώτερα πάσης ἀτοπίας**, ἀκύροις τε λέξεσιν λέγων κεχρῆσθαι καὶ ὁμωνύμοις ἄνευ τῆς

When Philoponus rejects the pagan interpretation of Plato as ridiculous and absurd, he uses the same vocabulary as we find, e.g., in scholia to reject a certain interpretation as forced.[43] Moreover, he accuses Proclus of committing an offense against the ideal of *hellênizein*. As Philoponus puts it in the summary of the argument, Proclus uses the word *archê* in a sense that is 'unusual both among the Hellenes and in common usage'.[44] 'Hellenes' here probably refers to pagan Greek philosophers.[45] In other words, when we call to mind the three senses that Proclus distinguishes of *hêllenizein*, Proclus not just fails to speak Greek with understanding as a philosopher does, he does not even manage to speak Greek by simply sticking to linguistic conventions. In short, Philoponus gives the pagan interpreters of Plato a taste of their own medicine. There is one important difference, though. Unlike the pagan Neoplatonists, Philoponus finds it necessary to refute his opponent in minute detail, thus, ironically, underscoring the importance of Proclus as a reader of Plato.

τούτων εἰς τὰ σημαινόμενα τὰ οἰκεῖα διαιρέσεως καὶ **τῆς μὲν συνήθους σημασίας τῶν λέξεων ἀμελεῖν**, κατ' ἄλλων δὲ σημαινομένων φέρειν τὰς λέξεις **μὴ ἐγνωσμένων τοῖς Ἕλλησιν**.

43 For an overview of Greek terms related to forced interpretation, see Sluiter (2013), 208–212.
44 Ὅτι ἀσύνηθες καὶ τοῖς Ἕλλησι καὶ τῇ κοινῇ χρήσει τὸ προκείμενον τοῦ γενητοῦ σημαινόμενον. (Philoponus, Aet. Mundi 122.3–4).
45 As Share (2005b), 130 n. 19 observes.

HELMUT SENG

Mythenkritik und Kultpolemik bei Firmicus Maternus

Einleitung

Iulius Firmicus Maternus genießt bei seinen modernen Lesern nicht den besten Ruf.[1] Oppressiv gesinnte Intoleranz, oberflächliche Kenntnis der zeitgenössischen Philosophie und der christlichen Theologie sowie schließlich ungenierter Opportunismus lauten die Vorwürfe gegen den Autor der Schrift *De errore profanarum religionum*, die sich an Constantius II und Constans richtet, die Söhne des Constantin, die als seine Nachfolger ab 337[2] eine antipagan ausgerichtete Politik verfolgten. In den Schlusskapiteln fordert Firmicus die Herrscher gar zu Zwangsbekehrungen, Tempelzerstörungen und Verfolgung der Heiden auf.

Eine persekutorisch ausgerichtete Intoleranz[3] ist insofern nicht zu übersehen, so unklar der Unterschied zwischen exzessiver Rhetorik[4] und konkreter Politikempfehlung bleibt.[5] Jedenfalls verlässt Firmicus hier die Bahnen der christlichen

---

1 Antike Rezeptionszeugnisse fehlen, cf. Wlosok (1997), 93 und siehe unten Anm. 5 und Anm. 178.
2 Der zunächst mitregierende Bruder Constantin II starb bereits 340 und wird bei Firmicus nicht erwähnt.
3 Ganz in den Vordergrund gerückt bei Annecchino (2011); Problematisierung des Toleranzbegriffs bei Kahlos (2009a), 6–8 und (2009b).
4 Cf. Ziegler (1953a), 13 „hemmungslose, überhitzte Rhetorik"; dazu gehören auch Elemente des Diatribenstils, cf. Wlosok (1997), 92. Eine starke Tendenz gereizter Expressivität findet sich in christlicher Polemik häufig, cf. etwa Männlein-Robert (2014), 130–132 zur Verunglimpfung des Porphyrios; Aufbereitung reichen Materials bei Opelt (1980), die Firmicus selbständig in Opelt (1974) behandelt, und Wischmeyer/Scornaienchi (ed.) (2011); cf. auch Kahlos (2009a), 67 und (2011), 171–184.
5 Insbesondere wird diskutiert, ob die Formulierung *gladius vindex* im Gesetz zum Opferverbot Cod. Theod. 6.10.4 auf Firm., err. 29.2 (cf. auch 6.9) rekurriert oder umgekehrt, cf. Wlosok (1997), 90 mit Literaturangaben. Oft – etwa bei Kahlos (2009a) 72 – wird nicht beachtet, dass die Appelle zur Verfolgung zwar mit alttestamentlichen Weisungen zur Ausrottung der Götzendiener untermauert werden, ohne dass aber zur Durchführung solcher Greuel direkt und konkret aufgefordert wird.

Dealing with Disagreement, ed. by Albert Joosse and Angela Ulacco, Monothéismes et Philosophie, 33 (Turnhout: Brepols, 2022), pp. 125–150
BREPOLS PUBLISHERS   10.1484/M.MON-EB.5.132751
This is an open access article made available under a CC BY-NC 4.0 International License.

Apologetik mit Vertretern wie noch Arnobius und Lactanz, die auf Toleranz der Herrschenden gegenüber dem Christentum zielt;[6] diese ist nicht nur für den Augenblick erreicht,[7] sondern die aktuelle Politik begünstigt die Christen sogar und setzt die Heiden unter Druck.[8] Vielmehr tritt Firmicus in die Fußstapfen der philosophischen Christengegner und Propagandisten der Christenverfolgung unter Diocletian.[9] So war etwa Sossianus Hierocles, Verfasser der antichristlichen Schrift Φιλαληθής, laut Lactanz *auctor et consiliarius ad faciendam persecutionem*.[10] Kontrovers diskutiert wird die Rolle des Porphyrios;[11] von Bedeutung ist dabei nicht zuletzt der bei Eusebios, PE 1.2.3 überlieferte Text mit den rhetorisch als Frage gestalteten Aufforderungen zur Christenverfolgung.[12] Mag dessen Zuschreibung an Porphyrios auch äußerst ungewiss bleiben,[13] so ist jedoch kaum zu bezweifeln, dass der Philosoph die „große Christenverfolgung in den Jahren ab 303 n. Chr. zumindest atmosphärisch und argumentativ vorbereitet".[14]

Die mäßige Kenntnis christlicher Theologie[15] ist hier nicht weiter zu verfolgen. Hierin ist Firmicus den genannten Apologeten Arnobius und Lactanz nicht

---

6 Vergleichender Überblick zu Arnobius, Lactanz und Firmicus bei Wlosok (1989c); cf. auch Gassman (2020), 73–75.
7 Dass die Situation prekär bleibt, ist angesichts der paganen Reaktion mit dem Alleinherrscher Iulianus an der Spitze schon wenige Jahre später zu betonen. Keineswegs unberechtigt scheint die Überlegung bei Simmons (2000), 861: „One can only imagine what Julian would have done if his Persian campaign had been successful".
8 Zur Politik cf. Wlosok (1997), 89–90, Noethlichs (1991), 1155–1157 und Massa (2013), 493–494 mit weiteren Hinweisen; Einschränkungen zur praktischen Durchführung bei Barnard (1990), 512–513 mit Anm. 30.
9 Cf. allgemein Frend (1987) sowie Simmons (2000), dessen Belege allerdings nicht immer treffend sind. Kelsos bei Origenes, CC 8.56 ist vielleicht böswillig verdreht.
10 *De mortibus persecutorum* 16.4; die Kommentare setzen ihn mit dem bei Lact. *inst.* 5.2.12 genannten Autor gleich: Monat (1973), 44; Creed (1984), xxvi Anm. 68. Zu Sossianus Hierocles cf. auch Simmons (2000), 848–849.
11 Cf. Chiaradonna (2014), 39 Anm. 4: „Il dibattito sul ruolo di Porfirio nella Grande Persecuzione è particolarmente ricco e tutt'ora in evoluzione" (mit Literaturangaben). Versuche, ihn mit dem bei Lact. *Inst.* 5.2.3 genannten „antistes philosophiae" gleichzusetzen, der drei Bücher gegen die Christen absonderte, überzeugen nicht; cf. Seng (2009), 152–153, dazu auch die Angaben bei Männlein-Robert (2014), 125 mit Anm. 25 und 28.
12 *Contra Christianos* fr. 1 v. Harnack = 88D. Becker: ποίας δὲ καταξιωθήσεσθαι συγγνώμης ... ποίαις δ᾽ οὐκ ἂν ἐνδίκως ὑποβληθεῖεν τιμωρίαις.
13 Cf. Becker (2016), 458–459, 465, der zu dem Schluss kommt, es sei „der vorliegende Text im Wesentlichen als eine eusebianische Collage verschiedener pagan-philosophischer Kritikpunkte anzusehen, die Zeichen von Eusebios' eigenem literarischen Stil trägt" (459). Cf. auch die umfangreiche Einleitung bei Becker (2016), 1–112.
14 Männlein-Robert (2014), 125. Cf. auch Frend (1987), 10: „Diocletian and Galerius' consultation with the Oracle of Apollo at Didyma, in the winter of 302–303, and Diocletian's choice of the Feast of Terminalia (23 February) are actions in tune with Porphyry's *Philosophy from Oracles*." Cf. jetzt auch Greenwood (2016).
15 Cf. Ziegler (1953a), 19: „Was die christlich-theologische Bildung des Firmicus angeht, so fehlt ihm jede persönliche Note"; Ziegler (1969), 958: „recht dürftige christlich-theologische

unähnlich.[16] Die Frage hat allerdings auch nur begrenzte Relevanz; denn die Absicht des Firmicus ist nicht sosehr die Belehrung in christlichen Glaubensfragen als vielmehr Kritik und Polemik gegen die heidnischen Religionen, die im Dienste christlicher Selbstdefinition zu verstehen sind;[17] die Frage philosophischer Kenntnisse[18] wird im Folgenden noch zu präzisieren sein.

Der Verdacht des Opportunismus schließlich beruht auf dem Zeitpunkt der Konversion zum Christentum.[19] Das astrologische Handbuch *Matheseos octo libri*, das Firmicus als Heiden und Anhänger des Porphyrios zeigt, ist kurz vor dem Tod des Constantin zu datieren;[20] *De errore profanarum religionum* ist dann seinen antipagan eingestellten Nachfolgern gewidmet.[21] Allerdings fehlen auch bei Constantin selbst heidenfeindliche Maßnahmen nicht;[22] zudem dürfen bei Firmicus die Kenntnis der heidnischen Mythen und Mysterien samt ihren philosophischen

---

Bildung"; Turcan (1982), 22: „Sa théologie chrétienne est plutôt sommaire"; dazu Barnard (1990), 514 und Sanzi (2006), 20–21; relativierend Gassmann (2020), 58–59. Ausführlicher ist Hoheisel (1972), 253–286; siehe ferner unten Anm. 162 – auch zur Vermutung bei Vermander (1980), Firmicus sei Arianer gewesen.

16 Cf. Wlosok (1989a), 368 und Wlosok (1989b), 381–382 mit Literaturhinweisen.

17 Nicht Apologetik, sondern „Kategorik" nach Fiedrowicz (2005), 97 und Kahlos (2009b), 79. Trotz der diatribenmäßigen Ansprache der Gegner – cf. Hoheisel (1972), 46–47 – dürfen christliche Leser als eigentliches Zielpublikum gelten, dessen Grundansichten bekräftigt werden: cf. Hoheisel (1972), 45–46 – auf die angeredeten Kaiser beschränkt – und 249 sowie Ahmed (2017), 176–181, 193–200; Opelt (1974), 119–122; Sanzi (2006), 39 und Gassmann (2020), 65–67 hingegen schreiben Firmicus die Absicht zu, Heiden zu bekehren. Zur Bedeutung von Feindbildern, „um zu einer Selbstvergewisserung der eigenen Identität zu gelangen" – laut Reichardt (2002), 251 – cf. auch die Fallstudie zu Porphyrios von Männlein-Robert (2014) mit Auswertung der modernen Feindbildforschung; dazu 133: „Auch die christlichen Apologeten und Kirchenväter, die sich polemisch mit Porphyrios auseinandersetzen, bewirken eine innere Stabilisierung ihrer Gruppe." Freilich mag diese Funktion auch schon für die früheren Apologeten gelten, cf. die Angaben bei Roselaar (2014), 189 Anm. 11 bzw. allgemeiner Cameron (2002), 224 zur „self-definition"; zur späteren Zeit cf. Kahlos (2007).

18 Cf. Ziegler (1953a), 11: „seine ... sich nicht über ein dürftiges Mittelmaß erhebenden philosophischen Kenntnisse"; Ziegler (1969), 951: „seine dürftigen philosophischen Kenntnisse". Siehe aber unten Anm. 94.

19 Cf. insbesondere Turcan (1982), 19–24 und Drake (1998); differenzierend Ahmed (2017), 195–196.

20 Zur Datierung cf. Turcan (1982), 9–10.

21 Datierung auf die Zeit zwischen 343 und 350 (vermutlich nach 346) bei Turcan (1982), 24–27 und Wlosok (1997), 90. Damit ergibt sich ein Abstand von mindestens 6 bis zu 13 Jahren zum Regierungswechsel.

22 Cf. Noethlichs (1991), 1151–1155; Gassman (2020), 48–54; wichtig die Differenzierungen bei Wallraff (2011).

Deutungen und ihre sicher zielende Widerlegung[23] als plausible Argumente für seine echte Überzeugung gelten,[24] ohne dass ein Beweis zu führen wäre.[25]

Diese Auseinandersetzung mit der heidnischen Götterverehrung und Mythologie[26] sowie der Frage ihrer philosophischen oder allgemeiner allegorischen Deutung[27] ist nunmehr in den Blick zu nehmen.[28] Ihr gilt der erste Hauptteil des Buches,[29] während der zweite sich mit den Mysterien und ihren Heilsverheißungen auseinandersetzt.[30] Die zweigeteilte Struktur wird auch in den folgenden Ausführungen aufgegriffen, wobei die Kultkritik jedoch nur ganz kurz im Sinne eines Ausblicks betrachtet werden kann.

Mythenkritik

Mit dem Ziel, das wahre Wesen der heidnischen Götter zu erweisen, verfolgt Firmicus vier Ansätze: Gegenstand der Verehrung sind demnach die Elemente, verstorbene Personen, Gestirne und abstrahierte Gestalten. Damit ist zugleich die Gliederung des ersten Teiles von *De errore* gegeben, wenngleich in der Ausführung die unterschiedlichen Aspekte auch miteinander verbunden sein können. Im Folgenden ist diese Einteilung insofern aufgenommen, als zunächst die **Elemente** betrachtet werden; die mit ihnen verbundenen Götter werden als verstorbene Menschen einer weit zurückliegenden Vergangenheit interpretiert. Sodann werden **Liber und Libera** als spezifische Gottheiten behandelt, für die als verherrlichte Kulturbringer dies ebenso gilt; durch die Verbindung von Dionysos und Sonne wird das Thema der Gestirne einbezogen. Drittens folgt ein Abschnitt

---

23 Siehe freilich unten Anm. 170.
24 Hoheisel (1972), 29–30 sieht bereits in der *Mathesis* eine distanzierte Haltung des Firmicus zum Götterkult.
25 Kinzig (2000) versteht die Schriften Πρὸς Ἕλληνας / *Ad nationes* als Selbstbeglaubigungsschriften von Vertretern des pagan geprägten Bildungsbetriebs anlässlich ihrer Konversion; das könnte ähnlich für *De errore profanarum religionum* zutreffen, cf. Sanzi (2006), 41, Kahlos (2007), 86 mit Anm. 117 und (2009), 69 mit 180–181, Anm. 109. Jedenfalls wird man Firmicus kaum den *incerti* (siehe unten Anm. 167) zurechnen, bei denen – unterschiedlich stark ausgeprägten – Opportunismus zu vermuten weit näher liegt; cf. Kahlos (2007), 42–45.
26 Konzis zur Kritik der christlichen Apologeten am paganen Mythos Graf (2011), 323–327.
27 Als grundlegenden Überblick zur Allegorese cf. Pépin (1976).
28 Vorab sei verwiesen auf die Kommentierungen von Heuten (1938), Ziegler (1953b), Pastorino (1956) und Turcan (1982).
29 Kap. 1 bis 17; verloren ist der Anfang.
30 Kap. 18 bis 27. Die abschließende Polemik gegen die Götzenbilder mündet in die Aufforderung an die Kaiser zu ihrer Zerstörung und zur Zwangskonversion ihrer Verehrer (Kap. 28–29). Mit dem Motiv der Materialität der heidnischen „Götter" – und wohl auch der intensiven Anrede an die Kaiser, die daneben immer wieder kurz angeredet werden; cf. Hoheisel (1972), 44 und die Aufstellung bei Wlosok (1997), 90 – ergibt sich eine Form der Ringkomposition.

über weitere Götter, deren **Schandtaten** breit durchgenommen werden, bevor schließlich **Etymologien** in Auge gefasst werden, die Firmicus anführt, um die Nichtigkeit bestimmter Götter als abstrakte Hypostasierungen zu erweisen.

Elemente

Dass die Heiden keine wirklichen Götter, sondern materielle Artefakte und somit die Materie anbeten, gehört zu den Topoi nicht nur der alttestamentlichen Götzenpolemik,[31] sondern auch der philosophischen Religionskritik und der christlichen Apologetik.[32] In diesem Kontext ist auch der Angriff gegen die Verehrung der Elemente zu sehen, die Firmicus an den Anfang stellt (Kap. 1–5).[33] Mit ihrer Definition als geschaffene Größen gegenüber dem Schöpfergott nimmt er einen grundlegenden Ansatz christlicher Theologie auf, kommt aber auch der typischen Dichotomie zwischen dem Geistig-Göttlichen und dem Materiellen, wie sie für die platonische Tradition charakteristisch ist, zumindest nahe; der Materie kommt der niederste Rang im ontologischen System zu und damit zugleich die von Gott am weitesten entfernte Position.[34] Im Neuplatonismus gilt die Materie als abgeleitet aus der Gottheit und entspricht insofern bis zu gewissem Grade einem Geschöpf nach christlichem Ansatz.[35]

Auch die systematische Ordnung der Elemente, die auf Komplementarität angelegt ist, entspricht philosophischem Standard.[36] Dazu gehört, wie Firmicus herausstellt, dass nicht eines der Elemente gegenüber den anderen eine Vorrangstellung etwa als eine Art Urmaterie einnimmt.[37] Die besondere Verehrung bestimmter Elemente durch bestimmte Völker,[38] die Firmicus behauptet und in diesem Sinne interpretiert, ist insofern mit dem Stand der zeitgenössischen Wissenschaft nicht kompatibel und soll dadurch diskreditiert werden.

---

31 Cf. Funke (1981), 765–768, 786–789; und Fredouille (1981), 855–860.
32 Cf. Tornau (2006), 348 und Fiedrowicz (2005), 236–238, jeweils mit weiteren Angaben; ferner Turcan (1982), 50 speziell zu den Elementen – dazu auch Ambrosiaster, *Quaestiones Veteris et Novi Testamenti* 114.2 (PL 35, 2342); allgemeiner 114.29 (PL 35, 2346).
33 Möglicherweise enthielt der verlorene Anfang einen Bezug auf die neutestamentlichen Stellen, die sich gegen eine Verehrung der στοιχεῖα τοῦ κόσμου wenden (*Gal.* 4.3, 9; *Kol.* 2.8, 20); die Bedeutung des Ausdrucks ist in den neutestamentlichen Forschung umstritten – cf. etwa Mußner (1988), 293–304 und Wolter (1993), 122–124, jeweils mit weiteren Angaben – doch scheinen nicht die klassischen vier Elemente gemeint zu sein.
34 Cf. Tornau (2006), 347–349.
35 Cf. Tornau (2006), 361–367.
36 Cf. etwa die Belege bei Turcan (1982), 167, dazu Turcan (1982), 36.
37 Vorstellungen dieser Art sind vielmehr bezeichnend für manche Vorsokratiker, cf. etwa Turcan (1982), 167 oder Lumpe (1959), 1077–1078.
38 Cf. die allgemeineren Belege bei Turcan (1982), 167–168 sowie im Einzelnen 171 (Wasser); 188–189 (Erde); 197 (Himmelsgöttinnen als Ersatz für Luft); 204–295 (Feuer).

Im Rahmen einer kosmisch geprägten Religiosität hat auch der göttliche Status der Elemente seinen Platz.[39] Doch bezieht sich Firmicus vielmehr auf die naturphilosophische Ausdeutung der Göttermythen, wie sie vor allem aus der Stoa[40] und dem Platonismus[41] bekannt sind. Gerade Mythen, die als anstößig empfunden werden könnten,[42] weil sie ein moralisch bedenkliches Handeln der göttlichen Akteure beinhalten, werden durch eine Exegese akzeptabel, die in ihnen Naturvorgänge oder kosmologische Strukturen bildhaft ausgedrückt sieht.[43] Ethische Kategorien sind damit nicht anwendbar – freilich um den Preis, dass die Götter und ihr Handeln zu bloßen Metaphern werden. Indem Firmicus in einem ersten Schritt seiner Polemik solche Allegoresen als substantielle Gleichsetzung der Götter mit den Elementen behandelt,[44] kann er die Verehrung des Materiellen bei den einzelnen Völkern behaupten, die er sodann im Einzelnen durchgeht.

Weitgehend unbeachtet[45] sind bei Firmicus Formen allegorischer Mythendeutung, welche die selbständige Existenz der Götter als eigene Wesen wahren, die den Naturgrößen zu- und übergeordnet sind;[46] so zum Beispiel Salustios 2.2:

Οὐδὲ ἐκ σωμάτων εἰσί· καὶ γὰρ τῶν σωμάτων αἱ δυνάμεις ἀσώματοι.

Sie stammen auch nicht aus Körpern, denn die Kräfte der Körper sind unkörperlich.

Die mythische Handlung bleibt dabei reine Allegorie.[47] Damit ist zwar wiederum das moralische Problem entschärft;[48] die Götter indessen sind dadurch bis zur Unkenntlichkeit transformiert. Ein instruktives Beispiel bietet etwa, im Kontrast

---

39 Cf. Lumpe (1959), 1080–1083. Cf. auch Turcan (1982), 56–59 zur Frage möglicher Vorbilder für Firmicus.
40 Cf. Cic., nat. deor. 2.63–71 und insbesondere Cornutus. Weniger klar ist die philosophische Einordnung des Herakleitos (Herakleides Pontikos), cf. Russell/Konstan (2005), xxiv mit weiteren Angaben.
41 Etwa Plutarch, De Iside et Osiride; cf. auch Bernard (1990), 183–275 und Timotin (2012), 179–190.
42 Cf. auch Porph., Ad Anebo fr. 13; 13a; 64, 10 Saffrey/Segonds zur Obszönität.
43 Gegebenenfalls können Mythen aber auch als poetische Lügen disqualifiziert werden, cf. Platon, Politeia II.377d5–378e3.
44 Dies entspräche etwa der „substitutiven Allegorese" nach Bernard (1990), 11–21, allerdings gerade unter Ausblendung des Bildhaften, auf das die Götter bei einer solchen Exegese reduziert werden.
45 Bzw. polemisch verdreht im Falle der Göttermutter, Firm., err. 3.5.
46 Cf. Bernard (1990), 22–69 zur „dihairetischen Allegorese".
47 Im Gegenzug kann ein ontologisch hierarchisierter Wirk- oder Substanzzusammenhang vorgestellt werden, cf. Bernard (1990), 22–69.
48 Cf. auch Salustios 3.4 sowie Clarke (1998), 341 mit Hinweis auf Jul., Or. V.170AB; VII.217C; 219A; 222CD; Pépin (1966), 254, 259–266; zu Iulianus auch De Vita (2011), 109–116. Ausgreifend zur ἀτοπία-Hermeneutik Schäfer (2015).

zur Darstellung bei Firmicus,[49] die Deutung des Attis-Mythos bei Salustios 4.7–9.[50]

Die Elementardeutung durch Firmicus stößt allerdings schnell an ihre Grenzen. Denn die kritisierten Mythen stehen mit den jeweiligen Elementen selbst zum Teil gar nicht in Verbindung; diese wird dann höchstens mithilfe der Zuordnung an bestimmte Völker erreicht, denen wiederum die besondere Verehrung eines Elements zugeschrieben wird. Ägypten wird einerseits mit der Verehrung des Wassers, andererseits dem Mythos von Osiris, Isis und Typhos in Verbindung gebracht. Die naturphilosophische Allegorese lautet (2.6):[51]

Defensores eorum volunt addere physicam rationem, frugum semina Osyrim dicentes esse, Isim terram, Tyfonem calorem.

Ihre Verteidiger wollen eine natürliche Erklärung beibringen, indem sie sagen, die Samen der Früchte seien Osyris, Isis die Erde, Tyfon die Wärme.

Dabei kommt das Wasser gar nicht vor, das in der Regel auf Osiris bezogen wird.[52] Im Argumentationszusammenhang wirkt das einigermaßen überraschend; nahe kommt immerhin Porphyrios, fr. 360F 33–36 Smith:

ὁ δὲ Ὄσιρις παρὰ Αἰγυπτίοις τὴν κάρπιμον παρίστησι δύναμιν, ἣν θρήνοις ἀπομειλίσσονται εἰς γῆν ἀφανιζομένην ἐν τῷ σπόρῳ καὶ ὑφ᾽ ἡμῶν καταναλισκομένην εἰς τροφάς.

Osiris stellt bei den Ägyptern die fruchtbringende Kraft dar, die sie mit Klageliedern besänftigen, wenn sie beim Säen in der Erde verborgen und von uns zur Ernährung verbraucht wird.

Im Falle der Göttermutter hingegen, die von den Phrygern verehrt wird, ist ihre explizite Gleichsetzung mit der Erde immerhin zu konstatieren (3.2):

Amare terram volunt fruges, Attin vero hoc ipsum volunt esse quod ex frugibus nascitur, poenam autem quam sustinuit hoc volunt esse quod falce messor maturis frugibus facit. Mortem ipsius dicunt quod semina collecta conduntur, vitam rursus quod iacta semina annuis vicibus reconduntur.

---

49 Firm., *err.* 3.2; siehe unten S. 131–132.
50 Zu beachten ist, das sich „substitutiv" und „dihairetisch" nach der Terminologie von Bernard (1990) nicht völlig sauber trennen lassen; die Gleichsetzung des Flusses Gallos und der Milchstraße wäre ein „substitutives" Element im „dihairetischen" Gesamtduktus.
51 Zitate aus Firmicus Maternus nach Turcan (1982), Übersetzungen nach Ziegler (1953b) mit gelegentlichen Abweichungen.
52 In der Regel wird Osiris mit dem die Erde befruchtenden Nilwasser (bzw. der Feuchtigkeit) gleichgesetzt, cf. etwa Plutarch, *De Iside et Osiride* 364A (sowie 364AB zu Typhon als trocknend und feurig und 366A zu Isis als vom Nilwasser befruchteter Erde) oder Salustios 4.3 (siehe unten S. 137).

> Sie meinen, die Erde liebe die Früchte, Attis aber, meinen sie, sei eben das, was aus den Früchten hervorgeht, die Strafe jedoch, die er erduldet hat, sei dasjenige, so meinen sie, was der Schnitter mit der Sichel an den reifen Früchten tut. Seinen Tod nennen sie es, wenn die Saat gesammelt und eingebracht wird, sein Wiederaufleben, wenn im jährlichen Wechsel der Same ausgestreut wird und wieder hervorkeimt.

Es liegt jedoch eine semantische Verschiebung vor. Denn das Element Erde ist nicht einfach mit der Erde des Ackers identisch, aus dem die Feldfrüchte hervorwachsen. Gegenüber der kosmischen Allegorie bei Salustios[53] bietet Firmicus eine bodenständigere Deutung, die Porphyrios näher kommt (fr. 358F22–29 Smith):[54]

> Ἄττις δὲ καὶ Ἄδωνις τῇ τῶν καρπῶν εἰσιν ἀναλογίᾳ προσήκοντες. Ἀλλ' ὁ μὲν Ἄττις τῶν κατὰ τὸ ἔαρ προφαινομένων ἀνθέων καὶ πρὶν τελεσιογονῆσαι διαρρεόντων (ὅθεν καὶ τὴν τῶν αἰδοίων ἀποκοπὴν αὐτῷ προσανέθεσαν, μὴ φθασάντων ἐλθεῖν τῶν καρπῶν εἰς τὴν σπερματικὴν τελείωσιν), ὁ δὲ Ἄδωνις τῆς τῶν τελείων καρπῶν ἐκτομῆς σύμβολον.

> Attis und Adonis passen zur Entsprechung mit den Früchten. Attis aber ist ein Symbol für die Pflanzen, die im Frühjahr erscheinen und vor der Reife verwelken (weshalb sie mit ihm auch das Wegschneiden der Schamteile verbinden, da die Früchte nicht schon vorher die völlige Ausbildung der Samen erreicht haben), Adonis hingegen für das Abschneiden der reifen Früchte.

Die Zuordnung der Luft zu Hera bzw. Iuno findet sich seit Empedokles und insbesondere bei den Stoikern,[55] während die Ergänzung durch Aphrodite bzw. Venus eine Erfindung des Firmicus sein könnte.[56] Die Mythenkritik freilich erschöpft sich in der inzestuösen Ehe von Iuppiter und Iuno, deren Bezug zur Deutung Iunos als Luft offen bleibt, sowie einer Seitenbemerkung zum Kult der jungfräulichen Venus (4.1):[57]

> *si tamen Veneri placuit aliquando virginitas!*

> wenn wirklich einmal Venus an der Jungfräulichkeit Geschmack gefunden hat!

---

53 Cf. auch die ähnliche Entwicklung des Themas bei Iulianus, dazu Turcan (1996), der Salustios nur praeteritorisch behandelt (401), sowie Thome (2004), 46–63, 73–79; Opsomer (2008), 150–156 und Stenger (2009), 343–344 (dazu ein kurzer Überblick zur Schrift des Salustios 320–333).
54 Von Turcan (1996), 390–391 als Bindeglied zwischen älterer Tradition (Valerius Messala) und Iulianus erachtet. Zu Diskussion und Polemik um den Kybele-Kult cf. auch Rauhala (2011), insbesondere 59–82.
55 Nachweise bei Turcan (1982), 197. Cf. auch Porph. fr. 355F Smith mit den bei Smith angegebenen Parallelen sowie Murrin (1980), 3–25.
56 Beruhend auf der Qualifizierung der Venus als *Caelestis*, cf. Turcan (1982), 197–198.
57 Hierzu Turcan (1982), 198.

Im Falle des Feuers wiederum ist es die Korrelation von Element und Volk, nämlich Persae et Magi,[58] auf der einen Seite und die Verehrung bestimmter Götter durch diese Völker auf der anderen Seite, die eine Verbindung herstellt.[59] Die Mythen und allegorischen Auslegungen werden dann separat davon angegriffen, soweit der hier lückenhafte Text erkennen lässt;[60] eine Besonderheit ist dabei die Aufspaltung des Feuers in eine männliche und eine weibliche Gottheit.[61] Die männliche Gottheit ist Mithras;[62] seine Charakterisierung als Rinderdieb ist in Mythos und Kult des Stiertöters verankert[63] – wenngleich der Ausdruck βουκλόπος θεός allein bei Porphyrios belegt ist[64] und somit auf diesen als Quelle weist – und lässt sich moralisch leicht attackieren.[65] Die Beschreibung der anderen Gottheit entspricht der zum Mithraismus gehörenden Anahita ebenso wie Hekate; der Name ist im erhaltenen Text nicht genannt (Firm., *err.* 5.1):[66]

> *Et mulierem quidem triformi vultu constituunt, monstruosis eam serpentibus inligantes.*
>
> Und zwar stellen sie das Weib mit dreifachem Gesicht dar und umwinden es mit ungeheuerlichen Schlangen.

Da Mithras auch als demiurgische Gottheit gedeutet und der zugehörige Mythos in diesem Sinne ausgelegt wird,[67] ließe sich vielleicht eine Verbindung zum schöpferischen Feuer der Stoa herstellen;[68] aber auch die Prominenz des Feuers als Chiffre des Göttlichen in den theologischen Orakeln der Zeit kommt in den Sinn.[69] Hekate ist allegorisch als Seele verstanden; eine solche Exegese könnte

---

58 Firm., *err.* 5.1.
59 Cf. auch die Kommentierung bei Blomart (2010), 245–247 mit Anm. 56–63.
60 Zum Text cf. Turcan (1982), 64–65, 210–211.
61 Firm., *err.* 5.1, zu beziehen auf Mithras und Anahita; cf. dazu Turcan (1975), 90–104.
62 Zur Auseinandersetzung christlicher Autoren mit dem Mithraskult cf. Roselaar (2014), die zwei Gruppen von Autoren mit unterschiedlichen Zugriffen unterscheidet (2./3. und 4./5. Jahrhundert); Firmicus kommt eine Mittelstellung zu, da er beide Formen der Auseinandersetzung vereint; cf. Roselaar (2014), 199–201, 208.
63 Firm., *err.* 5.2; cf. Porph. *De antr.* 18, 69.16 Nauck, dazu Turcan (1975), 62–89, insbesondere 75–77.
64 Cf. auch Turcan (1982), 207.
65 So auch Commodian, I.13.
66 Cf. Turcan (1975), 102 zu Anahita. Zur Dreigestalt Hekates cf. Roscher (1890), 1903–1909; Kehl (1988), 327–329; Werth (2006), 35–146; zahlreiche Varianten einer „triple Hécate" bei Sarian (1992) (zusammenfassend 1014–1016); zum Motiv der Schlangen cf. die Belege bei Lewy (1956) 90–92 (siehe auch unten Anm. 70), *PGM* IV.2861–2864 und Werth (2006), 201–203 sowie 284 mit Abb. 10.
67 Cf. etwa Turcan (1975), 77–80; auch hier weist die Quellenlage auf Porphyrios als Vorlage für Firmicus.
68 Cf. etwa Steinmetz (1994), 538–539.
69 Cf. etwa Busine (2005), 207 mit Anm. 225.

in das Umfeld der *Chaldaeischen Orakel* gehören,[70] desgleichen die Vorstellung von Hekate als Feuer oder vielleicht auch Aether, der für Feuer stehen kann.[71] Aber die Textlücke lässt sich mit solchen Überlegungen nur *exempli gratia* füllen. Kritisiert ist bei Firmicus die dreigeteilte Seele nach der platonischen Tradition;[72] dies lässt sich auf die Dreigestalt der Göttin beziehen, wie bei Porphyrios belegt,[73] der wiederum die Vorlage zu bieten scheint, ohne dass es einer Mythenerzählung bedarf. Tatsächlich ist die Dreiteilung der Seele mit dem Problem verbunden, dass zu den „Beweisen" für die Unsterblichkeit der Seele auch der Erweis ihrer Unvergänglichkeit aufgrund ihrer Unteilbarkeit gehört.[74] Indem Firmicus die Dreiteilung mit der Sterblichkeit der Seele verbindet,[75] kann er ihre Symbolisierung in der dreigestaltigen Gottheit als philosophisch unhaltbar erweisen; das Axiom von der Unsterblichkeit der Seele wird dabei für Christen und heidnische Philosophen bzw. Platoniker als unstrittig vorausgesetzt. Firmicus bewegt sich damit durchaus im Umfeld neuplatonischen Nachdenkens über die Seele. Denn zu den Fragen, die diskutiert werden, gehört auch die nach der Unsterblichkeit der ganzen Seele oder nur ihres rationalen Anteils bei Sterblichkeit des irrationalen.[76]

Der Durchgang durch die Elemente ist damit beendet. Der Zusammenhang zwischen ihnen und den Göttermythen bleibt eher schwach begründet. Doch die Zuordnung bestimmter Götter zu bestimmten Elementen ist nicht einfach aus der Luft gegriffen; sie stellt vielmehr ein Problem dar, das Porphyrios im *Brief an Anebo* benennt und Iamblichos in seiner *Antwort* wegerklärt.[77] Wenngleich nicht direkt, scheint sich Firmicus doch auf den zeitgenössischen Diskurs zu beziehen, und zwar gerade einen kontroversen Aspekt. Allerdings ist das eigentliche Herzstück seiner Ausführungen die im Wesentlichen moralisch begründete Kritik an den Mythen selbst;[78] sie umfasst zwei Aspekte. Zum einen bestreitet Firmicus,

---

70 Dort ist Hekate Ursprung der (Welt-)Seele (*OC* 51–52 mit Psellos, *Opusc. phil.* II.40, 149.19–22 O'M), allerdings gerade nicht mit dieser identisch, wie in der Forschung häufig angenommen – so etwa Lewy (1956), 83–93; des Places (1971), 13–14; Majercik (1989), 163.

71 Anaxagoras bei Aristoteles, *De caelo* 270b24–25 (cf. Anaxagoras 59 [46] A 73 Diels/Kranz) und anonym *Meteorologica* I.339b21–23; *Stoicorum Veterum Fragmenta* II 580, 1067; cf. auch Waszink (1950), 151–154.

72 Cf. *Politeia* IV.436a8–b3; IX.580d3–581a1; aber auch Salustios 10.

73 Cf. Porph. fr. 308F Smith (unsicher die Abgrenzung von den Äußerungen des zitierenden Eusebios). Die Ähnlichkeiten mit Proklos, *In Crat.* 94.16–95.23 Pasquali lassen Pastorino (1956), 68 an Porphyrios als gemeinsames Vorbild denken, bestritten von Turcan (1982), 211, der die Unterschiede betont.

74 *Phaidon* 78b4–80c1.

75 Firm., *err.* 5.4. Cf. auch Turcan (1982), 40–41.

76 Cf. den doxographischen Überblick von Albinos bis Iamblichos bei Proklos, *In Tim.* III.234.8–235.9 Diehl, gefolgt von der Darlegung seiner eigenen Position im Anschluss an Syrianos (III.235.9–238.26 Diehl); ferner Proklos, *In remp.* I.90.19–91.6 Kroll.

77 Porph., *Ad Anebo* fr. 11 Saffrey/Segonds; Iambl. *De myst.* I.9, 22.17–25.17 Saffrey/Segonds/Lecerf.

78 Damit steht Firmicus in der Nachfolge der Apologeten, cf. etwa Graf (2011), 323 und 336 Anm. 13–14.

dass die unmoralischen Handlungen mit Inzest, Ehebruch und Tötung ihren eigentlichen Sinn darin tragen, relativ einfache Naturphänomene wie Saat und Ernte zu beschreiben; dazu sind sie unnötig inhaltsreich und unnötig schändlich.[79] Zum anderen bietet er seinerseits eine Art oder Abart euhemeristischer Deutung,[80] die den Mythos freilich nicht auf uralte Wohltäter der Menschheit zurückführt, sondern auf verworfene Menschen, die sich im eigentlichen Sinne anstößig verhalten,[81] so im Falle von Isis, Osiris und Typhon[82] oder dem der Göttermutter und des Attis.[83] Zu Iuno und Venus als Luftgottheiten fehlen ausführliche Mythenerzählung und allegorische Deutung ebenso wie die paraeuhemeristische Deutung, zu Mithras und Hekate ist der Text lückenhaft. Allerdings wird das Ergebnis der allegorischen Auslegung deutlich und auch dieses selbst zurückgewiesen.

Zur Kritik an den Mythen und dem Ergebnis der Allegorese tritt die an den Anhängern der jeweiligen Kulte. Im Falle von Isis, Osiris und Typhon sind es demnach Menschen, die sich in ihren eigenen Schandtaten durch das göttliche Vorbild bekräftigen lassen.[84] Beim Attiskult sind es zunächst beflissene Untertanen, die mit ihrer Königin trauern, ihr zum Trost einen Totenkult um Attis einrichten und die Mär von seiner Auferstehung erfinden.[85] Zum Kult der Luftgottheiten Iuno und Venus gehört effeminiertes Gebaren der männlichen Priester; ein Bezug zum Mythos fehlt.[86] Die Anhänger des Mithras nutzen unterirdische Kultstätten, was als Hinweis darauf gesehen wird, sie hätten etwas zu verbergen;[87] die Textlücke mag Weiteres enthalten haben. Die Art der Verdächtigung gleicht Unterstellungen gegen die Christen, wie sie etwa bei Minucius Felix belegt sind:[88]

certe occultis ac nocturnis sacris adposita suspicio!

---

79 Cf. Firm., *err.* 2.7; 3.3; analog Eusebios *PE* III.13, 22 (zu Porph. fr. 353F Smith).
80 Komplementär dazu kritisiert Salustios 18.3 den Euhemerismus.
81 Von „negative Euhemerism (or *euhemerismus inversus*)" spricht Winiarczyk (2013), 150 im Zusammenhang mit christlichen Autoren, darunter Firmicus. Insofern sieht Ziegler (1953a), 12, Firmicus kaum mit Recht als Quelle für Euhemeros. Die Ausgabe von Winiarczyk (1991) führt unter den *dubia* Firm., *err.* 10.1 (T 91) und 7.1–6 (T 93) an, als *falsum* 7 Firm., *err.* 6.1–5 und 6.6–8, jeweils mit Angabe der Zuschreibungen in der Forschungsgeschichte.
82 Firm., *err.* 2.1–3.
83 Firm., *err.* 3.1.
84 Firm., *err.* 2.7; cf. auch Ahmed (2017), 175–176 (auch zum Folgenden). Vergleichbar ist Commodian, *instr.* 1.7; zur christlichen Tradition cf. wiederum Graf (2011), 323 und 336 Anm. 14. Eine analoge Problematik bietet Porph., *Ad Anebo*, fr. 64; 65 n.; 67; 68 Saffrey/Segonds (Mitwirkung der Götter bei Schandtaten der Theurgen).
85 Firm., *err.* 3.1.
86 Firm., *err.* 4.1–3.
87 Firm., *err.* 5.2; cf. Ambrosiaster, *Quaestiones Veteris et Novi Testamenti* 114.6.11–12.26 (PL 35, 2342–2343; 2346).
88 *Octavius* 9.2–10.2, hier 9.4; prägnant in der Formulierung des Athenagoras (*Legatio* 3.1.1–2): Θυέστεια δεῖπνα, Οἰδιποδείους μίξεις. Cf. auch Schubert (2014), 219–238 sowie McGowan (1994), Adamik (2001) und Leveils (2007), 291–310, jeweils auch zur Topik der Vorwürfe.

jedenfalls ist mir verdächtig, was sie nächtlichen Geheimritualen zuordnen!

Die Retorsion solcher Vorwürfe seitens des heidnischen Dialogsprechers Caecilius hatte Minucius Felix in der Erwiderung durch Octavius breit ausgeführt.[89]

Zu den Besonderheiten an der Kritik des Firmicus nach Elementen gehört die Zuordnung zu verschiedenen Völkern.[90] Firmicus nimmt dadurch den philosophischen Topos von der Weisheit der Barbaren auf[91] und dekonstruiert ihn.[92] Meist gelten als solche weisen Völker die Ägypter, sodann die Chaldaeer bzw. Assyrer, mit denen sie oft gleichgesetzt werden,[93] und die μάγοι, die entweder den Persern oder Chaldaeern nahe stehen. Aber auch Lyder und Phoiniker werden genannt; daneben nicht selten die Hebräer. Ein prägnanter Beleg ist das von Porphyrios zitierte Apollonorakel in *De philosophia ex oraculis haurienda*, fr. 323.8–14 Smith:[94]

> Αἰπεινὴ μὲν ὁδὸς μακάρων τρηχεῖά τε πολλόν,
> χαλκοδέτοις τὰ πρῶτα διοιγομένη πυλεῶσιν.
> ἀτραπιτοὶ δὲ ἔασιν ἀθέσφατοι ἐγγεγαυῖαι,
> ἃς πρῶτοι μερόπων ἐπ' ἀπείρονα πρῆξιν ἔφηναν
> οἱ τὸ καλὸν πίνοντες ὕδωρ Νειλώτιδος αἴης·
> πολλὰς καὶ Φοίνικες ὁδοὺς μακάρων ἐδάησαν,
> Ἀσσύριοι Λυδοί τε καὶ Ἑβραίων γένος ἀνδρῶν.

> Steil ist der Weg zu den Göttern und sehr rau,
> er öffnet sich zuerst durch in Erz gefasste Tore.
> Unaussprechlich weite Pfade gibt es darinnen,
> welche als erste zu der Sterblichen unbegrenztem Gebrauch aufzeigten,
> die das schöne Wasser des Landes am Nil trinken.
> Viele Wege zu den Göttern erfuhren auch die Phoiniker,
> Assyrer und Lyder und das Geschlecht der hebräischen Männer.

Die Hebräer sind bei Firmicus zwar nicht explizit erwähnt und können als Träger der alttestamentlichen Überlieferung im Kontext auch nicht negativ gezeichnet werden wie die anderen Völker. Doch lässt sich inhaltlich sehr gut der Grundgedanke auf sie rückbeziehen, der den Abschnitt einleitet (Firm., *err.* 1). Wer die Elemente verehrt, dessen Kult gilt Geschöpfen und nicht dem Schöpfer. Im Alten Testament ist das als Kritik an den Götzen mehrfach ausgeführt, die als rein materielle Geschöpfe aus menschlicher Herstellung dem Schöpfergott

---

89 *Octavius* 30.1–31.4; cf. auch Tertullian, *Apologeticum* 9 und Athenagoras, *Legatio* 32.1.
90 Busine (2009), 414–415 weist auf die übereinstimmende Vierteilung bei Cumont.
91 Cf. jetzt den Sammelband *Les Sagesses barbares* – Aufrère/Möri (ed.) (2016) – mit reicher Dokumentation.
92 Dabei kann er auch auf antibarbarische Ressentiments zählen, cf. Hoheisel (1972), 36.
93 Cf. Porph., fr. 324F.8–9 Smith.
94 Angeführt auch bei Busine (2009), 422, die hierin einen Hinweis sieht, Firmicus könne sich in der Anlage seiner Schrift (teilweise) auf Porphyrios beziehen (422–426).

gegenübergestellt werden.⁹⁵ Auch für die Zielrichtung gegen ein philosophisches Heidentum ist die Materialität der Elemente von Bedeutung, wie bereits erwähnt. Allerdings hat Firmicus mit polemischem Geschick gerade die Variante der Mythenallegorese⁹⁶ ausgewählt und an den Anfang seiner Kritik gestellt, die auch von philosophischer Seite wenig Beifall findet; einen Beleg bietet etwa Salustios, der eine Deutung anführt, die zwar nicht in den Einzelheiten, aber im Ansatz der von Firmicus angegriffenen entspricht (4.3):⁹⁷

> Ὑλικὸς δέ ἐστι καὶ ἔσχατος, ᾧ μάλιστα Αἰγύπτιοι δι' ἀπαιδευσίαν ἐχρήσαντο, αὐτὰ τὰ σώματα Θεοὺς νομίσαντες καὶ καλέσαντες [καὶ] Ἶσιν μὲν τὴν γῆν, Ὄσιριν δὲ τὸ ὑγρόν, Τυφῶνα δὲ τὴν θερμότητα, ἢ Κρόνον μὲν ὕδωρ, Ἄδωνιν δὲ καρπούς, Διόνυσον δὲ οἶνον. Ταῦτα δὲ ἀνακεῖσθαι μὲν Θεοῖς λέγειν ὥσπερ καὶ βοτάνας καὶ λίθους καὶ ζῷα σωφρονούντων ἐστὶν ἀνθρώπων, Θεοὺς δὲ καλεῖν μαινομένων· εἰ μὴ ἄρα ὥσπερ τοῦ ἡλίου τὴν σφαῖραν καὶ τὴν ἀπὸ τῆς σφαίρας ἀκτῖνα Ἥλιον ἐν συνηθείᾳ καλοῦμεν.

> Materiell und letztrangig ist die Erklärung, derer sich vor allem die Ägypter aus Mangel an Bildung bedienten: Sie hielten die Körper selbst für Götter und bezeichnen als Isis die Erde, als Osiris das Feuchte, als Typhon die Wärme, oder als Kronos das Wasser, als Adonis die Früchte, als Dionysos den Wein. Die Behauptung, dass den Göttern diese Dinge geheiligt sind, wie auch Pflanzen und Steine und Tiere, passt für verständige Menschen; sie als Götter zu bezeichnen, für Wahnsinnige – es sei denn, wie wir das Rund der Sonne und den von dem Rund ausgehenden Strahl gewohnheitsmäßig „Sonne" nennen.

Die geographischen bzw. ethnischen Zuordnungen hat Firmicus weitgehend treffend gewählt.⁹⁸ Der Isis- und Osiris-Kult gehört nach Ägypten, die Göttermutter und mit ihr verbunden Attis stammen aus Phrygien, der Mithraskult aus Persien; Hekate als Göttin der Magie⁹⁹ lässt sich mit den Magi verbinden. Lediglich die Zuordnung der als Luftgottheiten gedeuteten Iuno und Venus an Assyrer und Afrikaner, die hier die Phoiniker in beiden Regionen zu vertreten scheinen (Assyrien als Syrien verstanden), ist angesichts der Zugehörigkeit dieser Göttinnen zu den Olympiern weniger zwingend, wenn sie sich auch durch die besondere Bedeutung Iunos in Karthago und den Kult der Aphrodite-Astarte als Himmelsgottheit¹⁰⁰ rechtfertigen lassen.

---

95 Cf. etwa die Belege in Firm., err. 28.2–5; dazu Funke (1981), 765–768 und Fredouille (1981), 855–860.
96 Salustios 4.1–3 unterscheidet θεολογικός, φυσικός, ψυχικός und ὑλικός; cf. auch Bernard (1990), 59–69, insbesondere 62–68.
97 Sein Gegenvorschlag entspricht der im Neuplatonismus verbreiteten Vorstellung der σειρά; cf. das einschlägige Standardwerk von Lévêque (1959) sowie Bernard (1990), 165–178.
98 Siehe oben Anm. 38.
99 Cf. Roscher (1890), 1893–1895; Kehl (1988), 320–321.
100 Cf. Turcan (1982), 197–198.

Die spezifische Zuordnung bestimmter Götter zu bestimmten Völkern entspricht nicht nur beobachtbaren Tatsachen, sondern nimmt zugleich die religionsphilosophische Theorie der ethnischen Partikulargötter auf. Demnach sind bestimmte Götter sekundären oder noch niederen Ranges einzelnen Völkern und Weltgegenden zugeordnet, während die oberste Gottheit für alle gleichermaßen, aber weniger unmittelbar zuständig ist. Für die neuplatonische Theologie ist diese Stufung wesentlich. Indem die Angriffe des Firmicus ganz auf der Ebene partikularer Götter verbleiben, dabei aber einen jeweiligen Vorrang behaupten, suggerieren sie eine systematische Schwäche, wie sie die Angreifer des Christentums bei Juden und Christen sehen: Ein partikularer Gott, der für die Juden zuständig sei, werde fehlerhaft als universal angesehen.[101]

Methodisch lässt sich feststellen, dass Firmicus nicht nur mit den Mythen und Kulten vertraut ist, die er angreift, sondern auch mit Formen ihrer Allegorese auf der einen Seite und Formen der Kritik auf der anderen Seite, sowohl an den Mythen selbst als auch an ihrer Exegese. Dabei folgt er nicht nur genuin christlichen Traditionen. So geht der Kritik an paganer Allegorese bei Firmicus etwa die Kritik des Kelsos an der Genesisallegorese durch die Christen voraus.[102] Mit dem freilich ins Gegenteil verkehrten Euhemerismus greift Firmicus einerseits ein wohlbekanntes Erklärungsmuster auf.[103] Andererseits aber rekurriert er auf heidnisch-philosophische Kritik an der Verehrung des Menschen Jesus als Gott,[104] so Kelsos (bei Origenes, CC 7.68):[105]

> ὅτι μὲν οὖν αὐτοὶ διελέγχονται σαφῶς οὐ θεὸν ἀλλ' οὐδὲ δαίμονα, ἀλλὰ νεκρὸν σέβοντες.
>
> dass sie sich nun selbst ganz klar überführen: Sie verehren keinen Gott, aber auch keinen Dämon, sondern einen Toten.

Dabei kann Jesus als vorbildlicher Mensch gesehen werden, dessen Anhänger jedoch das rechte Maß der Verehrung überschreiten, indem sie ihn als Gott ansehen; so etwa Porphyrios, fr. 345F und 345aF Smith.[106] Auch die mit Irrglauben

---

101 Cf. etwa Iulianus, *Contra Galilaeos* 141C–143B (fr. 25 Masaracchia) und Kelsos bei Origenes, CC 5.25; ferner Schott (2005) 279–281, 303–309.
102 Nach Origenes, CC 1.17.20; 4.38, etc.; cf. Simmons (2000), 846.
103 Cf. dazu das Kapitel „Euhemerism in the ancient world" sowie die Listen „Homines pro diis culti" und „Deos homines fuisse" bei Winiarczyk (2013), 167–175; ferner Thraede (1966), dort 883–890 zu christlichen Autoren, und Fiedrowicz (2005), 236 mit Anm. 31–33.
104 Treffend verweist Gamble (1979), 15 auf die umgekehrte christliche Perspektive: „here was no man become a god, but God manifested as man"; ebenso Fiedrowicz (2005), 236. Cf. ferner Gamble (1979), 15–22 zu Kelsos bei Origenes, CC 3.22–43 und Gamble (1979), 22–29 zur Replik des letzteren.
105 Spezifischer ist die Behauptung, das Palladium bestehe aus den Knochen des Pelops (15.1–2). Hier scheinen eher Vorwürfe gegen die Verehrung christlicher Märtyrer und ihrer Reliquien gespiegelt; cf. auch Torres (2009), insbesondere mit Bezug auf die Unreinheit von Leichen.
106 Cf. Walter (2016), 212–214 mit Literaturhinweisen.

verbundene Klage über den toten Gott als abergläubische Ritualpraxis, wie bei Firmicus im Falle des Osiris- und des Attiskultes, schreibt Porphyrios den Christen zu (343 F Smith):[107]

> *Forte magis poteris in aqua inpressis litteris scribere aut adinflans leues pinnas per aera auis uolare, quam pollutae reuoces impiae uxoris sensum. Pergat quo modo uult inanibus fallaciis † perseuerans et lamentari fallaciis mortuum Deum cantans, quem iudicibus recta sentientibus perditum pessima in speciosis ferro uincta mors interfecit.*

> Vielleicht wirst du eher mit Buchstaben schreiben können, die du ins Wasser eindrückst, oder als Vogel durch die Luft fliegen, indem du leichte Federn aufplusterst, als dass du den Verstand deiner frevelbeschmutzten Ehefrau wieder herbeirufst. Soll sie weiter, wie sie will, verharren in leeren Täuschungen und jammern, indem sie einen toten Gott besingt, den bei den Richtern von rechter Gesinnung verworfen der elendigste Tod, mit Eisen festgenagelt, in der Blüte seiner Jahre vernichtet hat.

Darüberhinaus wird hier das Todesurteil gegen Jesus für rechtens erklärt.[108] Diese unterschiedlichen Bewertungen sind auch kontextbedingt, da sie aus Orakeln unterschiedlicher Provenienz stammen, die Porphyrios in *De philosophia ex oraculis haurienda* gesammelt vorlegt. Daneben stehen Alternativerzählungen und Verdrehungen (Jesus sei nicht der Sohn Gottes gewesen, sondern das außereheliche Kind eines römischen Legionärs;[109] Jesus sei ein Straßenräuber gewesen;[110] etc.), außerdem der Vorwurf, Jesus selbst sei ein Scharlatan und Schandbube,[111] und seine Zuwendung zu den Sündern disqualifiziere nicht nur ihn selbst moralisch, sondern zugleich alle diejenigen, die ihm – angeblich – mit der Absicht anhängen, ihr schändliches Treiben mit Bezug darauf zu rechtfertigen; so Kelsos bei Origenes, CC 3.65.[112] Den Ansatz dieser zweiten Variante verfolgt Firmicus umgekehrt gegen die Anhänger der heidnischen Götter (etwa 12.5):[113]

> *Semina paene omnium scelerum a diis suis peccantium turba collegit et, ut perditus animus impune facinus posset admittere, ex praecedentibus facinorum exemplis maiore se auctoritate defendit.*

---

107 Cf. Walter (2016), 206–212; allgemeinere Kritik an der Verehrung Jesu als eines Toten und Bestreitung der Auferstehung bei Kelsos (nach Origenes, CC 7.36).
108 Cf. auch Kelsos bei Origenes, CC 2.5.10.
109 Kelsos bei Origenes, CC 1.32 (cf. auch 1.28).
110 Hierokles Sossianus (zur Identifizierung siehe oben Anm. 10) bei Lact., *inst.* 5.3.4.
111 CC 1.62; 1.71; 7.56, cf. Simmons (2000), 852–853.
112 Cf. Simmons (2000), 859, auch allgemein zum üblen Charakter sowie der niedrigen sozialen Stellung als Vorwurf gegen die Christen (nach Kelsos bei Origenes, CC 1.62; 2.46). Origenes bestreitet seinerseits die Apotheosen von Herakles, Asklepios und anderen „Wohltätern" mit dem Argument, dass allein Christus ein wahrer Wohltäter sei, da nur er die Menschen moralisch bessere; cf. Gamble (1979), 23–24.
113 Cf. den ganzen Abschnitt Firm., *err.* 12.1–7, ferner Gassmann (2020), 64–65.

> Die Aussaat für fast alle Verbrechen hat die Schar der Sünder von ihren Göttern geliefert bekommen, und damit der verderbte Sinn ungestraft seine Untaten begehen kann, verteidigt er sich mit den Präzedenzfällen solcher Untaten mit größerer Autorität.

Selbst der Bezug auf den Teufel als Urheber der Lüge[114] ist nicht ohne Pendant innerhalb des philosophischen Diskurses, der ebenfalls Lügengeister kennt, nicht nur als störende Kräfte beim theurgischen Ritual,[115] sondern auch als böse Dämonen, die Menschen zum Glauben an Christus verleiten.[116] In dieser Form der Polemik stehen die verfeindeten Lager einander um nichts nach.

Liber und Libera

Nach dem Abschnitt zu den Elementen geht Firmicus zu Liber und Libera über, Dionysos-Bacchus und Demeter-Ceres, deren Mythen ausführlich erzählt werden (Kap. 6–8). Zu Libera als Ceres gehört eine ländliche Travestie der Mythenerzählung vom Raub der Persephone bzw. Proserpina, wie sie im homerischen Demeterhymnus vorliegt;[117] Firmicus verwendet dabei sogar das euhemeristische Wohltätermotiv. Der Bezug von Demeter bzw. Ceres auf den Mond bleibt im Zusammenhang willkürlich.[118] Zu Dionysos gehören zwei Mythen, die auf zwei homonyme Götter verteilt sind: der orphische Mythos vom zerrissenen Dionysos und der vor allem aus den Bakchen des Euripides bekannte Mythos von der Vertreibung des Dionysos aus Theben; allerdings kommt bei Firmicus nicht der König ums Leben, der sich dem Gott widersetzt, sondern der falsche Gott selbst.[119] Solche Verdrehungen sind Teil der Polemik, und das aus dem Zusammenhang gerissene Homerzitat ist geschickt zur Beglaubigung eingesetzt (*Ilias* 6.135–137):[120]

> ——Διώνυσος δὲ φοβηθεὶς
> δῦσεν ἁλὸς κατὰ κῦμα. Θέτις δ᾽ ὑπεδέξατο κόλπῳ
> δειδιότα· κρατερὸς γὰρ ἔχεν τρόμος ἀνδρὸς ὁμοκλῇ.

> ——Dionysos aber, flüchtend,
> Tauchte in die Woge des Meers, und Thetis nahm ihn auf in ihrem Bausch,
> Den erschrockenen, denn ein starkes Zittern ergriff ihn vor dem Drohen
> Des Mannes.

---

114 Cf. auch Ahmed (2017), 170–171 und Gassman (2020), 60–61; 73–75.
115 Cf. etwa *OC* 90.
116 Iul., *ep.* 89b [Bidez], 288B.
117 Cf. Kledt (1999).
118 Firm., *err.* 7.7.
119 Cf. insgesamt auch Weaver (2011).
120 Text nach dem Zitat bei Firm., *err.* 6.8; Übersetzung nach Schadewaldt (1975).

Zur antichristlichen Polemik gehört die entsprechende Bearbeitung der Geschichte Jesu bzw. der Heilsgeschichte bei paganen Autoren; auf die Behauptung, Jesus sei das uneheliche Kind eines Legionärs und selbst ein Straßenräuber wurde bereits hingewiesen.

In der para-euhemeristischen Deutung des Mythos vom zerrissenen Dionysos fällt die Vorstellung auf, das unversehrte Herz des zerstückelten Gottes sei in eine Statue eingesetzt worden;[121] das erinnert an telestische Praktiken der Statuenbelebung in der zeitgenössischen Theurgie[122] – nur dass bei Firmicus die Dionysos-Statue natürlich ebenso tot bleibt wie das Herz der Leiche. Weiterhin gehört die Differenzierung von Gottheiten durch Homonymie zu den Praktiken neuplatonischer Systematik, auch wenn diese anders erfolgt als hier bei Firmicus.[123] Die Deutung des zerrissenen Leibes und des unzerteilten Herzens als unzerteilter und geteilter Intellekt, τὸν ἀμέριστον καὶ τὸν μεμερισμένον νοῦν, wie Firmicus auf Griechisch zitiert,[124] ähnelt der allegorischen Exegese, wie sie Kaiser Iulianus etwa 20 Jahre später in seiner hymnischen *Rede auf Helios den König* aufnimmt, mit Bezug auf Apollon und Dionysos als differenziert und unmittelbar der Sonne zugeordnet.[125] Firmicus stellt dem die biblische Auffassung entgegen, dass die Sonne nur ein Geschöpf ist;[126] ein Geschöpf freilich, dass sich durch die dionysischen Mythen und ihre Allegoresen nur beleidigt fühlen kann, wie in einem ausführlichen *ethopoeiacus sermo* dargelegt,[127] der ausdrücklich als solcher benannt ist,[128] wodurch zusätzlich betont wird, dass es sich bei der Sonne nicht um ein göttliches Wesen handelt. Der breiten Ausführung entspricht, dass nicht nur die Vorstellung von der Göttlichkeit der Gestirne allgemein und vor allem in astrologischem Kontext geläufig ist und unter Neuplatonikern kontrovers diskutiert wird,[129] sondern gerade die Sonne dabei eine herausragende Stellung einnimmt, wie nicht zuletzt Firmicus selbst in *Mathesis* 1.10.14 bezeugt.[130] Eine Art neuplatonisch geprägter Sonnentheologie lässt sich freilich erst ab Iulianus belegen;[131] als prominentestes Zeugnis darf der zitierte Prosahymnus auf Ἥλιος βασιλεύς gelten.

---

121 Firm., *err.* 6.4.
122 Cf. Porph., *Ad Anebo* fr. 59; 62 Saffrey/Segonds sowie Johnston (2008).
123 Cf. Lecerf/Saudelli (2016).
124 Firm., *err.* 7.8.
125 144AB. Cf. auch Turcan (1982), 239–240.
126 Firm., *err.* 8.3.
127 Firm., *err.* 8.1–3; cf. Ambrosiaster, *Quaestiones Veteris et Novi Testamenti* 114.3 (PL 35, 2342). Zur möglichen Bezugnahme des Abschnitts auf Porphyrios cf. Turcan (1982), 242–243; allerdings ist die Existenz einer porphyrischen Schrift *Sol* zweifelhaft, cf. Porph., fr. 477–478F Smith mit den Angaben im Apparat.
128 Firm., *err.* 8.4.
129 Cf. etwa Clarke (1998), 331 mit weiteren Angaben.
130 „Sol optime maxime", etc. Zur *Mathesis* cf. Hübner (1997).
131 Cf. Stöcklin-Kaldewey (2014), 96–100 mit weiteren Angaben.

Schandtaten der Götter

Mit den ersten beiden Abschnitten ist die Behandlung der Göttermythen abgeschlossen, die zu den wichtigsten Mysterienkulten der Spätantike gehören;[132] ihre Deutung als tatsächliche Erzählungen vom schändlichen Treiben verworfener Menschen ist dabei in größere Zusammenhänge polemischer Interpretation eingebunden. Der nunmehr folgende Teil beschränkt sich weitgehend auf diese Form der Mythenkritik, doch treten ergänzend Leiden und Leidenschaften der nach einem philosophischen Gottesbegriff doch davon freien Götter[133] hinzu (Kap. 9–16):[134] Das braucht hier nicht im Einzelnen dargelegt zu werden. Aber zwei methodische Bemerkungen sollen nicht fehlen. Zum einen ist festzuhalten, dass Firmicus hier ein grundsätzliches Problem aufgreift, das die Schandtaten der Göttermythen für eine philosophische Religiosität darstellen.[135] Die Kritik ist bei heidnischen Philosophen von den Vorsokratikern an präsent und wird durch die oft äußerst phantasievolle, wenn nicht gewaltsame Allegorese der zeitgenössischen Philosophen, die sie weniger widerlegt als umgeht, nur bestätigt. Das Problem ist und bleibt somit virulent. Die christliche Polemik kann diese Kritik folglich seit jeher aufgreifen und ausbauen;[136] das Verfahren ist zwar traditionell, wird aber nicht obsolet, wie etwa die Fortführung bei Augustinus rund 70 Jahre später belegt.[137]

Zum anderen ist der Bezug auf die Götterverehrer selbst rhetorisch nicht ungeschickt. Denn der hohe moralische Anspruch der Philosophen kontrastiert allzu deutlich mit den amoralischen Göttergeschichten. Insofern sind die Betonung dieser Amoralität und entsprechende Unterstellungen gegenüber den Götterverehrern (als eine pervertierte ὁμοίωσις θεῷ) sicher polemisch, weisen aber doch auf eine Inkohärenz zumindest in der Wahrnehmung bzw. Imagination. Gesteigert ist die Polemik in dem sarkastischen Vorschlag (12.9), das schändliche Treiben der Götter im Theater darzubieten[138] und Schauspieler zu Priestern zu machen – eine Volksbelustigung,[139] die den esoterischen Anspruch philoso-

---

132 Dazu treten etwas künstlich Iuno und Venus, im Rahmen der Mysterienreligionen zwar unbedeutend, aber notwendig für das Elementarschema.
133 Cf. z. B. Salustios 14.1.
134 Entsprechend verwendet Kelsos (bei Origenes, CC 2.23) die Passion Christi als Argument gegen seine Göttlichkeit (CC 8.41 eher das Fehlen der göttlichen Rache angesichts der Passion).
135 Cf. Attridge (1976).
136 Fiedrowicz (2005), 233–234.
137 Cf. etwa civ. 2.7; 3.3.5; dazu 4.9 die Kritik an der Naturallegorese.
138 Cf. auch Firm., err. 12.7: *O infelicis imitationis cruenta meditatio! Scaenam de caelo fecistis et errantes animos per abrupta praecipitia crudeli calamitate duxistis, cum hominibus peccare cupientibus facinorum via de deorum monstratur exemplis.*
139 Treffend kontrastiert Firmicus damit die zurückliegenden Christenverfolgungen; cf. Potter (1993).

phischer Religiosität[140] ebenso wie die gesellschaftliche Ehrenstellung der heidnischen Priester[141] ins lächerliche Gegenteil verkehrt.[142]

Eine Sonderstellung nehmen die Ausführungen zu Sarapis ein (Kap. 13). Zum einen durch den positiven Ansatz der euhemeristischen Deutung: Sarapis, gedeutet als Kompositum aus Σάρρας und παῖς, bezeichnet demnach Joseph, den Urenkel der Sarah und des Abraham, dessen Verehrung aufgrund seiner Verdienste um das Land berechtigt ist – wenngleich die Vergottung unangebracht ist.[143] Zum anderen aber wird anhand des Sarapis eine Kult- und Ritualkritik durchgeführt. Die blutigen Opfer, die dargebracht werden, nähren die Dämonen (Firm., err. 13.4):

> Nihil enim operantur victimae et cruor ex assidua pecorum caede profusus nisi ut daemonum substantia qui diaboli procreatione generantur ex isto sanguine nutriatur.

> Denn nichts anderes bewirken die Opfer und das infolge des fortgesetzten Schlachtens von Tieren vergossene Blut, als daß der Bestand der vom Teufel gezeugten und hervorgebrachten Dämonen aus diesem Blute Nahrung empfängt.

Dies entspricht ganz der Darstellung des Porphyrios (*De abstinentia* 2.42.2–3):[144]

> Βούλονται γὰρ εἶναι θεοὶ καὶ ἡ προεστῶσα αὐτῶν δύναμις δοκεῖν θεὸς εἶναι ὁ μέγιστος. Οὗτοι οἱ χαίροντες „λοιβῇ τε κνίσῃ τε", δι' ὧν αὐτῶν τὸ πνευματικὸν <καὶ σωματικὸν> πιαίνεται. Ζῇ γὰρ τοῦτο ἀτμοῖς καὶ ἀναθυμιάσεσι ποικίλως διὰ τῶν ποικίλων, καὶ δυναμοῦται ταῖς ἐκ τῶν αἱμάτων καὶ σαρκῶν κνίσαις.

> Sie wollen nämlich Götter sein, und die Macht an ihrer Spitze der größte Gott scheinen. Diese sind es, die sich an „Trankopfer und Opferduft" freuen: genau das, woran das Gespensthafte und Körperliche sich mästet. Denn es lebt durch Dämpfe und Ausdünstungen, in mannigfaltiger Weise durch mannigfaltige Dinge, und gewinnt Kraft aus den Opferdüften von Blut und Fleisch.

Als Herr der Dämonen ist Sarapis bei Porphyrios, *De philosophia ex oraculis haurienda* fr. 327F Smith gezeichnet. Laut Firmicus werden sie in menschliche

---

140 Cf. Iul,. *Or* VII.221D: οὐκ ἐθέλοντι τὸν κρύφιον ἅμα καὶ φανερὸν θεὸν ὥσπερ ἐν θεάτρῳ προβάλλειν ἀκοαῖς ἀνεξετάστοις.
141 Cf. auch Firm., *err.* 18.6.
142 Cf. auch die gänzlich gegensätzlichen Vorschriften zum Verhalten der Priester gegenüber Theater und Schauspielern bei Iulianus, ep. 89a [Bidez] 304B–D.
143 Wie die Verehrung Christi als Gott in der Kritik bei Porphyrios, siehe oben S. 138–139 mit Anm. 106–107.
144 Cf. auch Porph., *Ad Anebo* fr. 62; 65; 65b; 65e; 65j; 65o; 69 Saffrey/Segonds.

Medien gerufen, dort festgehalten und zum Reden gezwungen (13.4 = fr. 306F Smith):[145]

> *Serapis vocatus et intra corpus hominis conlatus talia respondit ...*
>
> Serapis, gerufen und in den Leib eines Menschen versetzt, gab folgende Antwort ...

Firmicus beschreibt hier das Phänomen des Götterzwangs,[146] wie er nicht nur aus den ägyptischen Zauberpapyri bekannt ist (insofern eignet sich Alexandria besonders als Ort der Anbindung),[147] sondern auch als methodisches Grundlagenproblem der Theurgie zwischen Porphyrios und Iamblichos diskutiert wurde;[148] auch Augustinus wird Porphyrios (der die stärker problematisierende Position vertritt) in *De civitate dei* angreifen.[149] Wiederum zeigt sich, dass Firmicus mit den Problemen und den Diskussionen pagan-philosophischer Religiosität und Kultpraxis vertraut ist und die Schwierigkeiten als treffenden Einwand ins Feld führen kann. Auch die Polemik gegen Statuen bzw. Götterbilder im Gefolge alttestamentlicher Götzenkritik (Kap. 28) und der älteren christlichen Tradition[150] gehört zu der Art von Einwänden, gegen die sich etwa Kelsos, Porphyrios oder Iulianus[151] wenden.

Etymologien

Auch der Versuch, Götternamen etymologisch zu erklären (Kap. 17), hat eine lange philosophische Tradition, deren Höhepunkte durch den platonischen Kratylos und seine Auslegung durch Proklos sowie durch die *Epidrome* des Cornutus markiert sind; auf lateinischer Seite ist etwa Cicero, *De natura deorum* 2, 63–71 zu nennen. Firmicus greift diese Interpretationsmethode auf, doch sind die Auflösungen eher banal, was sich im Duktus der Schrift immerhin als gelinde Form der Polemik verstehen lässt. Vor allem aber hat diese Weise der Erklärung die Funktion, zum Fazit überzuleiten (17.4).

> *Videtis ut <istos> commenticios et fictos deos turbulentus error excogitet, ut superstitionibus anilibus et formae nobis deorum generentur et nomina. Sed haec*

---

145 Cf. auch Tanaseanu-Döbler (2016), 181–182; ferner Porph., fr. 308F; 347F; 350F Smith.
146 Cf. Graf (1996), 198–201; Tanaseanu-Döbler (2013), 67–70.
147 Cf. auch Porph., *Ad Anebo* fr. 13; 64; 65m; 65q–s; 66; 73; 75 Saffrey/Segonds (nicht alle Belege zu Ägypten). Hinzuweisen ist auch auf Chairemon und die ägyptische Scharade zwischen Porphyrios (*Ad Anebo*) und Iamblichos (*Antwort des Abamon*); andere Überlegungen dazu bei Saffrey/Segonds (2012) XIX–XXXVIII und Saffrey/Segonds/Lecerf (2013), LXI–LXXI.
148 Cf. Porph., *Ad Anebo* fr. 13; 64; 65m; 65q–s; 66; 73; 75 Saffrey/Segonds.
149 Cf. *civ.* 10.9.
150 Siehe oben Anm. 95.
151 Cf. etwa Kelsos bei Origenes, *CC* 1.5; Porphyrios, Περὶ ἀγαλμάτων, fr. 351F 14–24 Smith; Iulianus, *ep.* 89a [Bidez] 294BC–296D.

omnia ueritas detexit et ratio sanae mentis inuenit ut inuestigatis omnibus atque detectis, quae sacrilegus error absconderat, ueritas renata luceret. Haec enim omnia cum essent male composita terrori primum fuere mortalibus, dehinc consumpta nouitate quasi ex longa aegritudine conualescentibus hominibus natus est quidam ex admiratione contemptus. Sic paulatim quod stupebat animus ausus est diligenter inquirere et statim in arcana fictarum ac uanarum superstitionum sagax misit ingenium. Tunc ex assiduis tractatibus latentium ratione collecta peruenit ad causas, ut profanarum religionum miseranda commenta humanum genus primum disceret, deinde contempneret, tertio recusaret.

> Ihr seht, wie diese erfundenen und erdichteten Götter verworrener Irrwahn sich ausdenkt, wie in altweibermäßigem Aberglauben uns Gestalten und Namen von Göttern zurechtgemodelt werden. Aber alles dies hat die Wahrheit aufgedeckt und das Denken eines gesunden Verstandes herausgefunden, damit nach Erforschung und Aufdeckung alles dessen, was gottloser Irrwahn verborgen hatte, die Wahrheit neu geboren leuchte. Denn nachdem dies alles auf üble Weise erdichtet worden war, erregte es zuerst Schrecken bei den Sterblichen, danach, als die Neuheit sich verflüchtigt hatte, entstand bei den gleichsam von langer Krankheit genesenden Menschen aus der Bewunderung eine Art von Geringschätzung. So wagte der Geist allmählich, was er bestaunte, sorgfältig zu untersuchen und entsandte alsbald in die Geheimnisse erdichteter und nichtiger Wahnideen seinen scharfen Forschergeist. Nachdem er dann auf Grund ständiger Beschäftigung den Sinn des Verborgenen aufgespürt hatte, gelangte er zu den Ursachen, so daß das Menschengeschlecht die erbärmlichen Erdichtungen der heidnischen Religionen zuerst durchschaute, dann verachtete und drittens von sich wies.

Auch hier ist die methodische Übereinstimmung mit der paganen Religionsphilosophie zu betonen: Mythen und Wesen der Götter sind erklärungsbedürftig und verbergen einen tieferen Sinn, der freilich auch banal ausfallen kann.[152] Während jedoch die Neuplatoniker versuchen, durch ihre Exegesen die religiöse Tradition in ihre philosophische Vorstellungswelt zu integrieren, gibt Firmicus konkurrierende Deutungen, um Mythen, Exegese und Kulte der Heiden zurückzuweisen.[153] Das erinnert einerseits an die Religionskritik bei Lucrez;[154] dass

---

152 Der Gedanke, die Namen der Götter als Metonymie zu verstehen, findet sich bereits bei Prodikos 84 [77], B5 Diels/Kranz.
153 Wobei auch die heidnisch-philosophischen Exegeten immer wieder konkurrierende Deutungen vorlegen, cf. etwa Bernard (1990), 70–90 (insbesondere 79–81 zwei Varianten einer „dihaireteischen Allegorese") oder Proklos, *In Tim* I.152.10–155.2 Diehl (Porphyrios, Iamblichos, Syrianos).
154 Cf. neben dem gerade zitierten Text aus Firmicus insbesondere Lucrez 1.62–71; dazu auch Hoheisel (1972), 334–336. Cf. auch Turcan (1982), 43: „théorie évolutionniste".

andererseits diese Methode der Umkehrung auf pagane Vorbilder zurückgreifen kann, die ihrerseits christliche Überlieferungen umdeuten, wurde bereits erwähnt.[155]

Kultpolemik: Symbola

Der erste Teil der Schrift, der auf die Götter und ihre Mythen selbst zielt, ist damit abgeschlossen. Der zweite stellt rituellen Sprüchen und Symbolen heidnischer Erlösungskulte jeweils eine Vielzahl von Bibelzitaten entgegen, die Firmicus weitgehend aus vorliegenden Kompendien übernehmen kann.[156] Das gleiche gilt für die abschließende Polemik gegen die Götzen und ihre Verehrer.[157] Auch die Theorie vom Teufel als vorab wissendem Urheber heidnischer Riten, die christlicher Praxis und Symbolik im Modus der Perversion nahekommen, ist in der christlichen Literatur vor und nach Firmicus geläufig[158] und lässt sich den paganen Diskussionen um das Vorherwissen der Götter und Dämonen[159] sowie die Rolle betrügerischer und böser Dämonen im Kult an die Seite stellen.[160] Firmicus zeigt sich also wohl informiert, und wenn die Feststellung geringer Originalität in dieser Hinsicht nicht zu bestreiten ist,[161] darf die treffende Aufnahme vorliegenden Materials und geläufiger Argumente als Ausweis seiner Kompetenz gelten.[162] Zu den panegyrischen Elementen schließlich, die in den Schlussteil eingearbeitet sind, zählt die Manifestation des göttlichen Beistands für die christlichen Kaiser; Firmicus widerlegt damit durch Umkehrung,[163] aber ohne direkte Bezugnahme die Annahme, das Gedeihen des Reiches hänge an der Verehrung der alten Götter – ein nicht nur bei der diocletianischen wie früheren Christenverfolgung

---

155 Siehe oben S. 139 mit Anm. 108–110.
156 Cf. Vermander (1980), 6. Turcan (1982), 50–51 stellt fest, dass sich in der älteren Literatur nichts Vergleichbares zur Gegenüberstellung heidnischer und christlicher Symbola findet.
157 Cf. Wlosok (1997), 91–92; siehe ferner oben Anm. 95.
158 Fiedrowicz (2005), 238–239; cf. auch Gassman (2020), 67–73 und, weiter ausgreifend, Massa (2013), vor allem 503–508.
159 Cf. etwa die Auseinandersetzung mit Porphyrios (*Ad Anebo* fr. 44 Saffrey/Segonds) bei Iamblichos, De myst. III.17, 104.11–107.18 Saffrey/Segonds/Lecerf.
160 Siehe oben mit Anm. 123, dazu die Auseinandersetzung mit Porphyrios (*Ad Anebo* fr. 63 und 63a Saffrey/Segonds) bei Iamblichos, De myst. III.31. Bemerkenswert der Bezug auf die Christen (Μάτην οὖν ἐπεισάγεις τὴν ἀπὸ τῶν ἀθέων δόξαν, 134.20 Saffrey/Segonds/Lecerf) als Element der Polemik, cf. Saffrey/Segonds/Lecerf (2013), 300.
161 Siehe oben Anm. 15.
162 Cf. Turcan (1982), 49–54. Zu nennen ist insbesondere die Übernahme von Bibelstellen aus den Zusammenstellungen bei Cyprian; tabellarisch dazu Vermander (1980). Die jeweiligen Textfassungen weichen öfters voneinander ab; im abweichenden Zuschnitt sieht Vermander einen Hinweis darauf, Firmicus sei Arianer gewesen, doch bleibt die Argumentation schwach. Die Unterschiede im Wortlaut gehen darüber hinaus und wären insofern eigens zu untersuchen. Allgemein zur biblischen Hermeneutik Hoheisel (1972), 307–315.
163 Cf. auch Turcan (1982), 48–49.

maßgeblicher,[164] sondern auch lang fortdauernder Gedanke, gegen den sich wiederum Augustinus nach der Eroberung Roms durch die Westgoten im Jahr 410 wenden wird.[165]

Schluss

Abschließend und in aller Kürze ist die Mythen- und Kultkritik des Firmicus Maternus im Religionsdiskurs der Spätantike einzuordnen. Seine Schrift *De errore profanarum religionum* gehört zu einer Strömung, die nach dem Ende der diocletianischen Verfolgung gegenüber den Heiden immer intoleranter wird, bis zur Einführung des Christentums als Staatsreligion unter Theodosius I oder der Schließung der platonischen Akademie durch Justinian.[166] An Stelle der apologetischen Ausrichtung bei früheren Autoren ist die Polemik der Offensive getreten.[167] Die Angriffe der paganen Autoren werden durch gleichartige Vorwürfe pariert:[168] so die Annahme vom Dämonentrug, Verdrehungen und Umdeutungen der Überlieferung, Ablehnung der Allegoresen (einschließlich der Umkehrung wenigstens der Intention der Sprachspiele im Kratylos), moralische Vorwürfe. Für

---

164 Cf. etwa Fiedrowicz (2005), 194–196 oder die Belege bei Levieils (2007), 368–380; dazu die Konkretisierungen bei Lactanz, *De mortibus persecutorum* 10. Hoheisel (1972), 39 mit Anm. 1 führt als prägnanten Beleg der zugrunde liegenden Ideologie eine Formulierung an, die freilich nicht primär auf die Kultausübung, sondern auf die Ehe als religiös sanktionierte Institution zielt (*Mosaicarum et Romanorum legum collatio* 6.4, 1.157.18–23 Mommsen): *ita enim et ipsos immortales deos Romano nomini, ut semper fuerunt, faventes atque placatos futuros esse non dubium est, si cunctos sub imperio nostro agentes piam religiosamque et quietam et castam in omnibus more <maiorum> colere perspexerimus vitam* [*more <maiorum>* Cuiacius; *more* codd., *mere* Mommsen].
165 Insbesondere in *De civitate dei*, cf. Fiedrowicz (2005), 138–141 mit weiterführenden Angaben; dazu Hoheisel (1972), 27–28 zum „Staatskult".
166 Zur historischen Kontextualisierung cf. Hoheisel (1972), 343–404 („Das Programm zur Ausrottung der nichtchristlichen Religionen") sowie umfassend Noethlichs (1991). Kahlos (2009a), 72 stellt Firmicus insbesondere Eusebios von Caesarea und Athanasios von Alexandria als „loud lobbyists" zur Seite.
167 Cf. auch Fiedrowicz (2005), 99: „Die religiöse Intransigenz eines Firmicus Maternus war nur die letzte Konsequenz solcher triumphalistischen Apologetik, die der Geschichte eine neue Sakralität verliehen hatte," dazu Roselaar (2014), 206: „Sometimes, especially in the fourth century, the rhetoric of dominance may have been born by a sense of attack being the best defence against pagans, which was in fact still strong; but that this language could be used at all shows the great leap forward that Christianity had made." Dass sich polemische Angriffe auch schon eingebettet in die Apologien früherer Autoren finden, versteht sich von selbst; doch mag die neue Intensität gerade auf den äußeren Erfolg des Christentums reagieren, in dessen Folge synkretistische *incerti* – cf. Kahlos (2004) und (2007) – eine so große Gefahr für die christliche Identität darstellen, dass in der modernen Forschung vermehrt die Frage gestellt wird, wo in der religiösen Praxis eine klare Unterscheidungslinie zwischen Christen und Heiden verläuft.
168 Wie der Aufruf zur Verfolgung der Heiden die tatsächlichen Christenverfolgungen erwidert.

seine Zwecke muss Firmicus natürlich keine kohärente Religionstheorie bieten,[169] sondern er braucht nur zu widerlegen (bzw. zu widersprechen).[170] Dabei kann er sich traditioneller Themen und Topoi bedienen; vieles gehört zum Standardrepertoire bereits paganer und dann christlicher Kritik an der heidnischen Religion.[171] Interessant sind bestimmte Schwerpunkte: Attis und die Magna Mater lassen schon an Salustios und Kaiser Iulianus denken, an diesen auch die Prosopopoeie der Sonne; die Torheit der barbarischen Elementenverehrung wendet den Topos von der Weisheit der Barbaren ins Gegenteil. Auch der Angriff gerade auf die blühenden Mysterienreligionen[172] und Phänomene der Theurgie entspricht der zeitgenössischen religiösen Praxis. Immer wieder sind Probleme und kontroverse Themen der aktuellen Philosophie aufgenommen; namentlich erwähnt wird Porphyrios,[173] anderes weist wiederum auf Iulianus oder Salustios voraus. Insofern zeigt sich Firmicus wohlinformiert[174] und führt die Auseinandersetzung ganz auf der Höhe seiner Zeit.[175]

Mythenkritik und Kultpolemik bleiben auch in der Folgezeit Themen christlicher Apologetik, die sich immer mehr zur Kategorik entwickelt. Firmicus hat seinen Platz in dieser Tradition;[176] ob und in welchem Maße seine Schrift jedoch

---

169 Deren Fehlen vermerkt Baudy (1998); cf. auch Hoheisel (1972), 318: Firmicus bleibe „eine souveräne, fruchtbare Götterkritik schuldig", dazu Hoheisel (1972), 333–342. Cf. auch Turcan (1982), 34: „Dans le détail, cet ancien avocat nous apparaît souvent comme un rhéteur assez brouillon"; zustimmend Sanzi (2006), 43. Treffender Turcan (1982), 38: „Le polémiste change de stratégie suivant le cas".
170 Dabei gilt im Wesentlichen, was Aland (2005), 46 zu den frühen Auseinandersetzungen zwischen Christen, Heiden und Häretikern konstatiert: „Bei allen verhandelten Konfliktfeldern verstehen sich die Gesprächspartner nicht und wollen sich nicht verstehen. Sie argumentieren unfair, unverständig, obwohl sie es hätten besser wissen können, und scharf. Sie zeigen keine Neigung, dem anderen zuzuhören, ja, mehr noch, sie verzerren seinen Argumentationsansatz". Analog attestiert Blomart (2010), 258 der christlichen Polemik gegen Mithras: „une logique volontairement inadéquate pour interpréter la pensée de l'interlocuteur". Cf. auch Cameron (2002), 223.
171 Cf. etwa Attridge (1976) oder Fiedrowicz (2005), 228–230 mit weiteren Angaben.
172 Siehe auch oben S. 142 mit Anm. 132. Turcan (1982), 46 spricht von „un effort d'adaptation en fonction de l'actualité païenne"; cf. auch Massa (2013), 501–503 und Gassman (2020), 62–64.
173 Firm., err. 13.3: *Porphyrius, defensor sacrorum, hostis dei, veritatis inimicus, sceleratarum artium magister* mit Bezug auf die *Philosophia ex oraculis haurienda*; (fr. 306F.6–7 Smith); in *Mathesis* 7.1.1 hieß es noch *noster Porphyrius* (fr. 488F.1 Smith).
174 Cf. auch Barnard (1990), 513: „La conoscenza che Firmico aveva del tardo paganesimo del quarto secolo era profonda e, a parte Sallustio, non ha rivali".
175 Cf. Wlosok (1989c) 148 [= 231–232] und Gassman (2020), 59–60; 65–66; zur Auseinandersetzung mit dem Mithraskult siehe oben Anm. 62.
176 Siehe auch oben Anm. 62.

auf diese eingewirkt hat, ist nicht zu ersehen. Erwähnt wird sie in der Antike an keiner Stelle; auch die Überlieferung in nur einer Handschrift[177] ließe sich als Indiz für ihre geringe Bekanntheit deuten, wenn auch nicht als Beweis. Rezeptionsspuren sind nicht nachzuweisen.[178]

---

177 Cf. Wlosok (1997), 93.
178 Cf. Wlosok (1997), 93, möglicherweise mit Ausnahme der bei Heuten (1938), 191–193 zusammengestellten Parallelen aus Ambrosiaster, *Quaestiones Veteris et Novi Testamenti* 82, 114.1–16 (PL 35, 2275, 2341–2344); näher liegt aber vielleicht die Annahme gemeinsamer Vorlagentexte, wie Pépin (1982), 257–261 für Firm., *err.* 18 und *Quaestio* 84 (PL 35, 2278–2279) vermutet. Cf. auch Turcan (1982), 59–63 mit weiteren Literaturangaben sowie Sanzi (2006), 60–62. Siehe auch oben Anm. 5.

ALEXANDRA MICHALEWSKI

« L'âme est le lieu des formes »[*]

Une réponse à l'argument du troisième homme à travers la symphônia de Platon et d'Aristote dans le Commentaire à la Métaphysique *d'Asclépius de Tralles*

Cet article se propose d'analyser un cas spécifique de stratégie néoplatonicienne visant à montrer l'accord de Platon et d'Aristote sur l'un des points traditionnellement les plus litigieux, la théorie des Formes intelligibles, en examinant le sens qu'Asclépius de Tralles, dans le commentaire à la *Métaphysique*, rédigé d'après le cours dispensé par son maître Ammonius, donne à une citation extraite du chapitre 4 du livre III du *De Anima*, selon laquelle « l'âme est le lieu des formes » (429a27–28). Dans le commentaire d'Asclépius, cette citation est détournée de son sens initial : loin de nourrir une réflexion sur la réceptivité de l'âme intellective à l'égard des formes issues du sensible, elle soutient l'interprétation selon laquelle Aristote ne rejette pas la conception d'un intellect divin en acte, producteur, contenant en lui les *logoi* démiurgiques. La citation de *DA* 429a27–28 apparaît à deux reprises, en *in Met.* 69.18–20 (= *Mét.* A9, 990a34–b1) et *in Met.* 167.30–31 (= *Mét.* B2, 997b3), dans le cadre d'une argumentation soutenant qu'au-delà de l'opposition apparente d'Aristote à son maître existe en réalité un accord de fond entre eux sur la question de la causalité des Formes.

Les références au traité de l'âme étaient déjà familières aux disciples d'Ammonius qui, avant d'aborder la *Métaphysique*, avaient étudié la psychologie aristotélicienne, en suivant un canon de lecture des textes fixé par Jamblique. Commenter le *DA* suppose un niveau avancé dans le cursus aristotélicien, ce traité se trouvant à mi-chemin entre la physique et la métaphysique[1]. Dans l'histoire de l'intégration

---

[*] Cet article a bénéficié des discussions menées ces dernières années avec les membres du groupe de l'IEA (Centre Léon-Robin, Paris-DWMC, KU-Leuven) portant sur le commentaire à la *Métaphysique* d'Asclépius.

[1] (Ps.-) Simplicius, *in De Anima* 3.4–18. Olympiodore (*in Meteor.* 4.5) compare ce traité à un animal amphibie, à la fois physique et théologique. L'attribution à Simplicius d'un commentaire au *DA* a suscité de longues et nombreuses polémiques. Je n'entre pas ici dans le détail de ce dossier, ouvert pour la première fois au début du XVIIe siècle par F. Piccolomini qui remarque que le style de ce commentaire est beaucoup plus laconique que celui des autres œuvres de Sim-

des commentaires d'Aristote au sein du cursus d'études philosophiques qui commence avec Porphyre, Syrianus – qui fut le maître de Proclus et d'Hermias, père d'Ammonius – marque une nouvelle étape. À ses yeux, Aristote est non seulement un maître dans les domaines de la logique, de la morale et de la physique, mais il doit également être loué pour avoir montré dans la *Métaphysique* que les réalités divines sont des causes immobiles et séparées[2]. Or dans cette enquête, si bien commencée, Aristote, qui n'a pas vu que les Formes sont les paradigmes des réalités sensibles ni que l'intellect divin est cause productrice du monde, finit par formuler contre Platon des objections dépourvues de pertinence (παρὰ θύρας)[3]. Pour Syrianus, commenter la *Métaphysique*, ce n'est donc pas tant élucider les doctrines aristotéliciennes que défendre Platon, en montrant comment aucune de ses théories ne peut être atteinte par les critiques tournant à vide d'Aristote et de son commentateur Alexandre d'Aphrodise[4]. De manière générale, Syrianus – suivi par Proclus –, a tendance à souligner qu'Aristote n'arrive pas toujours à se hisser jusqu'au sommet de la philosophie platonicienne, notamment en passant à côté de la nature réelle des Formes, qui sont des substances séparées du sensible, et de l'intellect divin, qui est une cause productrice de l'univers[5]. L'attitude d'Ammonius est sensiblement différente.

Ammonius, après avoir été le disciple de Proclus à Athènes, devient professeur à Alexandrie aux alentours de 470. À la différence de son ancien maître, Ammonius fait du premier principe péripatéticien une cause efficiente du monde, contenant les Formes, causes paradigmatiques et productrices des réalités sensibles[6]. Le commentaire à la *Métaphysique*, qu'Asclépius rédigea à partir de l'en-

---

plicius. F. Bossier et C. Steel (1972) l'attribuent à Priscien. Pour une présentation détaillée de ce débat et de ses nombreuses phases, cf. I. Hadot (2014), 182–223, qui tient que ce texte est bien de Simplicius. L'auteur de ce commentaire citant à deux reprises l'existence d'un commentaire à la *Métaphysique* qu'il aurait rédigé, la question de l'auteur du commentaire au DA est liée à celle de savoir si Simplicius fut également l'auteur d'un commentaire à la *Métaphysique*. *Contra*, M. Rashed (2016), pour qui cette attribution reste improbable. M. Perkams (2003) et (2008), spec. 19–25, argumente également en faveur de Priscien. Pour une récapitulation de ce vaste dossier, cf. la note (n. 2) de J. Finamore (2014), 290.

2 Syr., *in Met.* 80.4–7 ; H.-D. Saffrey (1987).
3 Syr., *in Met.* 80.28. Syrianus est, semble-t-il, le premier à faire usage de cette expression, qui sera largement reprise dans la tradition ultérieure. Elle apparaît cinq fois, toujours dans le commentaire aux livres M et N – notamment à l'ouverture (*in Met.* 80.28) et à la clôture (*in Met.* 195.9) pour souligner l'écart entre le niveau d'Aristote et celui des « hommes divins » auxquels il s'en prend.
4 Sur la réception par Syrianus du commentaire à la *Métaphysique* d'Alexandre d'Aphrodise, cf. L. Cardullo (1993), C. d'Ancona Costa (2000) et C. Luna (2000 ; 2001).
5 Procl., *in Tim.* I.295.20–26. Sur ce point, C. Steel (1987), 225.
6 Simpl., *in Phys.* 1363.8–12. Sur cette question, cf. R. Sorabji (1990), 182–183 ; K. Verrycken (1990), 229–231 ; L. Cardullo (2011), 42–44. *Contra* I. Hadot (2015), qui voit en Thémistius le précurseur de cette lecture concordiste, 28, 93–94.

seignement oral d'Ammonius[7], est un témoin important de cette interprétation. Ce type de commentaire relève d'un genre littéraire particulier puisqu'il expose les notes de cours du maître, accumulant parfois les répétitions ou recopiant à titre d'aide-mémoire de longs passages du commentaire d'Alexandre d'Aphrodise à la *Métaphysique*[8]. Comme le fait Syrianus, Asclépius soutient que Platon ne peut être ébranlé par les objections péripatéticiennes. Or tandis que le premier souligne qu'Aristote et Alexandre se sont égarés dans de fallacieux raisonnements lorsqu'ils critiquent la théorie des Formes, Asclépius (Ammonius) adopte une stratégie à plusieurs niveaux, parce que son rapport à Aristote n'est pas le même. Il construit une certaine lecture de la *Métaphysique*, en sélectionnant et en reformulant quelques éléments doctrinaux choisis, afin de montrer qu'Aristote ne refuse pas l'existence d'un intellect divin producteur, contenant en lui les Formes.

Avant d'examiner comment, dans l'*in Met.* d'Asclépius, les citations et les emprunts au livre III du *DA* visent à montrer l'accord d'Aristote avec Platon au sujet de l'existence des Formes, je vais commencer par proposer un aperçu des usages de la citation de *DA* 429a27–28 dans la tradition exégétique antérieure. Cela permettra d'en dégager la spécificité au sein du commentaire à la *Métaphysique* et de voir la construction de l'autorité des propos aristotéliciens qu'elle met en œuvre.

Aperçu de l'interprétation de *DA* 429a27–28 dans le néoplatonisme

Avant Ammonius

Aristote, en *DA* 429a27–28, évoque une définition selon laquelle l'âme est le « lieu des formes », définition à laquelle la tradition a massivement attribué une origine platonicienne[9] – bien que dans les textes de Platon, il ne soit jamais fait mention de l'âme comme d'un « lieu » qui recevrait ou contiendrait les formes.

> καὶ εὖ δὴ οἱ λέγοντες τὴν ψυχὴν εἶναι τόπον εἰδῶν, πλὴν ὅτι οὔτε ὅλη ἀλλ' ἡ νοητική, οὔτε ἐντελεχείᾳ ἀλλὰ δυνάμει τὰ εἴδη. (Ar., *DA* 429a27–29)

---

7 Sur l'histoire de la locution *apô phônès*, cf. M. Richard (1950) ; H. J. Blumenthal (1996), 58–59 ; L. Cardullo (2002) et (2012), 216.

8 C. Luna (2001) les a répertoriés, Appendice VI, 218–221.

9 On ne sait à qui précisément Aristote fait ici référence. G. Rodier dans la note *ad. loc.* de sa traduction y voit une allusion à Platon lui-même. Parmi les commentateurs anciens, seul (Ps.-) Philopon l'attribue explicitement à Platon (*in De Anima* 524.6). R. Polansky (2007), 441, suggère qu'il s'agit du résultat d'une association de deux passages du *Timée*, le premier situant l'âme dans l'intellect (30b) et le second autorisant l'identification du démiurge aux Formes elles-mêmes (46d), tandis que R. D. Hicks (1907), 482, y voyait un écho de *Parménide* 132b. Il est probable qu'Aristote fasse ici plus généralement allusion à des discussions internes à l'Académie.

> Et ils ont bien parlé ceux qui ont dit que l'âme est le lieu des formes, sauf qu'il ne s'agit pas de l'âme tout entière, mais de l'âme intellective, et que les formes n'y sont pas en entéléchie, mais en puissance.

Cette définition a servi de support exégétique à de nombreux développements proposés par les commentateurs péripatéticiens et néoplatoniciens[10]. La définition de l'âme comme lieu (τόπος) capable d'accueillir et de recevoir les Formes intelligibles a très tôt nourri des analyses visant à élucider l'analogie entre la réceptivité psychique et la réceptivité matérielle. Philopon rapporte la position de Xénarque[11] – qui considère que la réceptivité de l'intellect est analogue à celle de la matière – et l'objection que lui opposa Alexandre, pour qui l'intellect ne peut pas être comparé à un substrat modifié par les formes. Or Aristote lui-même qualifie, non sans ambiguïté, l'intellect en puissance d'intellect analogue à la matière dans la mesure où il peut devenir tous les intelligibles (*DA* III.5, 430a10–15). D'après lui, il en va de cet intellect comme d'une tablette sur laquelle rien n'est écrit en acte (*DA* III.4, 429b31–430a2). La réceptivité de l'âme à accueillir les formes se dit chez Aristote à travers plusieurs images, celle du lieu, de la matière, de la tablette. Selon Alexandre, l'intellect en puissance n'est pas comparable à une tablette de cire prête à recevoir l'écriture car cette comparaison évoque encore trop l'image d'un substrat : l'intellect dit « matériel » est non pas une substance, mais l'aptitude de l'âme à recevoir les formes[12]. En accueillant les formes abstraites du sensible, l'intellect n'est pas altéré comme l'est un substrat sensible[13]. Dès lors, selon Alexandre, il doit être comparé à la « non-écriture » de la tablette, et non à la tablette elle-même (*in DA* 84.25–85.5).

Or l'interprétation de la réceptivité impassible de l'âme prend, à partir de Plotin, une nouvelle dimension. Refusant de comprendre la manière dont l'âme reçoit en elle les Formes sur le modèle péripatéticien de l'abstractionnisme, il considère au contraire que l'âme reçoit les formes intelligibles du principe dont elle dérive, l'intellect divin. Le « lieu des formes », c'est, au premier chef, le *topos* intelligible dont il est question en *République* VII, 517b5 (*Enn.* I.6 [1],

---

10 C. Steel (2016) a donné des analyses détaillées de certains aspects de la réception de cette formule dans le néoplatonisme, sans toutefois aborder son traitement dans les commentaires au *DA* et à la *Métaphysique* transcrits à partir de l'enseignement d'Ammonius.
11 Philopon, *in De Anima* III.4 (15.65–69, Verbeke). Ce passage renvoie à la partie du cours d'Ammonius, dont la version originale, perdue, a été partiellement préservée (III.4–8) dans la traduction latine de G. de Moerbeke. Cette version latine est traditionnellement appelée *De intellectu*.
12 Cette interprétation, qui vide l'intellect de toute teneur substantielle, fera l'objet de la critique d'Averroès. Pour une mise en perspective de l'histoire de cette réception, cf. J.-B. Brenet (2003), 92–94.
13 Pour un examen plus détaillé des trois états de l'intellect selon Alexandre, qui correspondent respectivement aux trois degrés de la puissance et de l'acte, et sur le fait que la description de l'intellect matériel est donnée non tant en « terme de puissance, qu'à travers des concepts qui servent ailleurs à l'Exégète pour expliciter la nature de la matière », cf. G. Guyomarc'h (2015), 267–270.

9.40-41). Dans ce « lieu », que Plotin identifie à l'intellect divin, vivent les Formes transcendantes à titre premier. L'âme, image de l'intellect, contient et déploie sous le mode qui est le sien les images des Formes. Cette thèse fondamentale, selon laquelle les Formes se trouvent dans l'âme parce qu'elles existent sous une forme plus parfaite et plus unifiée dans l'intellect divin[14], son principe, va parcourir l'ensemble de la tradition néoplatonicienne. Le motif de l'écriture dans l'âme, chez Plotin, est associé à la réminiscence : les raisons innées de l'âme sont comme des lettres tracées en elle par l'intellect (*Enn.* V.3 [49], 4.1-4). Ces lettres, que l'on dit gravées en l'âme, demeurent en elle, la plupart du temps, comme dans l'obscurité, de manière inconsciente et l'opération par laquelle l'âme éclaire et découvre ce qu'elle possède en elle, est appelée « réminiscence » (*Enn.* I.2 [19], 4.17-28)[15].

Les commentateurs néoplatoniciens ne furent pas tous du même avis sur la question de savoir si les analyses du *DA* sont compatibles avec la théorie platonicienne de l'âme et de la réminiscence[16]. Pour en donner un simple exemple, Proclus rappelle, dans le prologue de l'*in Euclidem*, que la matière et l'âme sont des « lieux », mais en des sens différents. La matière est le lieu des raisons immanentes, tandis que l'âme est le lieu des Formes (τόπος μὲν γὰρ καὶ ἡ ὕλη τῶν ἐνύλων λόγων καὶ ἡ ψυχὴ τῶν εἰδῶν) – non pas des formes abstraites du sensible, mais des Formes dérivées de l'intellect. Or les péripatéticiens, qui n'admettent la présence dans l'âme que de formes abstraites de la matière, considèrent que l'âme n'est « lieu des formes » qu'en un sens second, lui conférant finalement ainsi, selon Proclus, une dignité inférieure à la matière[17]. Cette manière de voir renverse l'ordre des choses puisque les raisons psychiques précèdent la multiplicité qu'elles fondent. Selon Proclus, elles existent non pas en puissance, comme le dit Aristote, mais au sens premier de l'être en acte[18].

---

14 On trouve une seule occurrence de la citation de *DA* 429a27-28 dans les *Ennéades*, pour désigner la réceptivité impassible de la matière. Selon Plotin, la matière, qui est dépourvue de toute substantialité, n'est pas un substrat au sens hylémorphique. Définie comme un incorporel infra-sensible, elle partage avec les incorporels supra-sensibles (l'âme, l'intellect et l'Un), la caractéristique d'être parfaitement impassible. En *Enn.* III.6 [26], 13.18-20, l'expression « lieu des Formes » dénote l'impassibilité de la matière qui n'est pas altérée par les ultimes images des formes que l'âme projette sur elle.
15 Voir A. Michalewski (2021).
16 Sur cette question, cf. D. P. Taormina (1993).
17 Procl., *in Eucl.* 14.24-15.9. Dans la *Théologie Platonicienne*, il indique que la réceptivité de l'âme n'est pas comparable à celle de la matière : tandis que celle-ci, uniquement passive, ne peut que recevoir les raisons, l'âme, qui reçoit les Formes de l'intellect, possède également une puissance productrice (*Th. Plat.* IV.10.195).
18 Procl., *in Parm.* IV.892.22-28. La critique de la définition de l'âme comme d'une tablette vierge est utilisée dans l'*in Alc.* (voir particulièrement 277.20-278.1 ; 280.26-281.16) pour mettre l'accent sur le lien entre l'intériorité des *logoi* découverts par la réminiscence et la nature automotrice de l'âme rationnelle. Sur cette question, et pour une mise au point sur les passages du corpus proclien et la bibliographie pertinente, cf. Ch. Helmig (2012), 267-268 ; 303-304.

Dans une autre perspective, (Ps.-) Philopon rapporte la lecture de Plutarque d'Athènes, qui fait d'Aristote un partisan de la réminiscence et lui attribue la thèse selon laquelle l'intellect possédant toujours déjà en lui les *logoi*, l'apprentissage se confond avec la réminiscence[19]. Cette lecture est celle de Jamblique[20], qui attire l'attention sur l'objet de la comparaison aristotélicienne. Aristote en effet a comparé l'intellect de l'âme non à une feuille de papyrus vierge, mais à une tablette sur laquelle rien n'est encore écrit en acte (ὥσπερ ἐν γραμματείῳ ᾧ μηθὲν ἐνυπάρχει ἐντελεχείᾳ γεγραμμένον, *DA* III.4, 430a1–2). La précision est significative[21], puisque les tablettes de cire rendent possible une pratique pédagogique que ne permet pas le simple feuillet : le maître effectue sur elles un premier et discret tracé préalable des lettres, presque illisible, sur lequel l'élève peut repasser pour se familiariser avec la technique d'écriture. S'il est question d'une tablette ἄγραφος, il faut donner, selon Jamblique, un sens particulier à cet adjectif, la négation signifiant non pas l'absence, la faiblesse. Ainsi au lieu de signifier « non écrit », il aurait ici le sens de « mal écrit » (κακόγραφος), tout comme on dit d'un chanteur au coffre peu puissant qu'il « n'a pas de voix ». Cette comparaison autoriserait l'interprétation selon laquelle Aristote aurait lui aussi admis la préexistence des Formes dans l'âme – tout comme les lettres sont, avant que l'élève ne les écrive à son tour, non pas « non écrites », mais difficiles à lire, ayant déjà été légèrement esquissées par le maître sur la tablette. Jamblique est vraisemblablement le premier néoplatonicien[22] qui, en la modifiant légèrement, interprète la définition de *DA* 429a27–28 dans le cadre d'une analyse du « lieu » pouvant se dire aussi

---

19 (Ps.-)Philopon, in *De Anima* 519.37–520.7. L'identité de l'auteur de ce commentaire au livre III du *DA* est débattue. M. Hayduck, dans la préface de son édition de 1897, le considère comme inauthentique et propose de l'attribuer à Etienne d'Alexandrie. C'est cette piste que suit W. Charlton dans la préface de sa traduction (*in de Anima* III.1–8), en 1999, en refusant notamment la position de P. Lautner (1992) pour qui le traité révèle les théories de Philopon ou de ses disciples – cf. également D. P. Taormina (1989), 196–197. Récemment, P. Golitsis (2016b), a réouvert ce dossier en émettant l'hypothèse selon laquelle il y aurait deux éditions du livre III, une première de Philopon et une seconde, sorte de compilation ultérieure.
20 Sur l'interprétation du sens de la tablette disposée à recevoir l'écriture chez Jamblique, cf. F. A. J. de Haas (2000), 169–170, Ph. Hoffmann (2014), 291–292 et C. Steel (2016), 247–251.
21 (Ps.-)Philopon, in *De Anima* 533.25–35.
22 Concernant la tradition platonicienne antérieure, Plutarque de Chéronée, dans le *De Iside et Osiride* (374e), évoque, quoique de manière allusive, la définition de l'âme comme « lieu des formes » dans un passage indiquant que l'âme et la pensée sont comme la matière de la science et de la vertu, en recevant le perfectionnement de la raison. Dans le fr. 215d (Sandbach), Plutarque mentionne la tablette – contenant un message caché, que le Spartiate Démaratus envoya aux Athéniens pour les prévenir de l'invasion prochaine des Perses – pour signifier que certaines connaissances existent dans l'âme, tout en étant dissimulées. Sur cette question, cf. D. Scott (1995), 18.

bien des corps que des raisons : « l'âme est dite *lieu des raisons* qui se trouvent en elle, puisqu'elle leur donne la place pour demeurer et agir en elle » (*in Cat. test.* 101)[23].

Dans les commentaires d'Ammonius

Ammonius cite cette formule pour montrer qu'Aristote ne s'est pas opposé à la thèse de l'existence des Formes à l'intérieur de l'intellect divin. Ainsi, au début du premier livre du commentaire au *De Anima*, rédigé par Philopon, à partir du cours de son maître[24], la citation de *DA* 429a27–28 est mobilisée pour appuyer l'interprétation qui identifie l'intellect aristotélicien au démiurge contenant en lui les Formes. À la définition de l'âme comme « lieu des formes » est accolée une autre formule, paraphrasant *DA* 431b17, selon laquelle l'intellect en acte est identique aux réalités (πράγματα), c'est-à-dire, dans la perspective néoplatonicienne, aux Formes intelligibles[25]. Ces citations sont ensuite associées au motif de l'auto-contemplation de l'intellect divin, tiré du livre Λ de la *Métaphysique* auquel il est fait allusion : le dieu qui se pense lui-même, pense les Formes transcendantes.

> οὕτω καὶ ἡ ἐν τῷ κόσμῳ τάξις ἐκ τῆς ἐν τῷ δημιουργῷ τάξεως γέγονεν· ὥστε οἶδε καὶ τοὺς ἐξῃρημένους λόγους τῶν πραγμάτων. καὶ ἐν ταύτῃ δὲ τῇ πραγματείᾳ φησὶν 'ἔστι δὲ ὁ κατ' ἐνέργειαν νοῦς τὰ πράγματα', 'εὖ γε καὶ οἱ τὴν ψυχὴν τόπον εἰδῶν εἰρηκότες'. καὶ ἐν τῇ Μετὰ τὰ φυσικὰ πάλιν περὶ τοῦ νοῦ τοῦ θείου διαλεγόμενός φησι πάντων τὰ εἴδη ἐν αὐτῷ εἶναι. λέγει γοῦν ὅτι ἑαυτὸν ὁρῶν τὰ πράγματα ὁρᾷ, καὶ τὰ πράγματα ὁρῶν ἑαυτὸν ὁρᾷ. (Philopon, *in DA* 37.24–31)

>> et pareillement, l'ordre qui est dans l'univers provient de l'ordre qui est dans le démiurge. Par conséquent, il <Aristote> a bien connaissance aussi des raisons transcendantes des choses. Et dans le traité qui nous occupe, il dit : « l'intellect en acte est les réalités » ; « ils ont bien parlé ceux qui dont dit que l'âme est le lieu des formes ». Et dans la *Métaphysique*

---

23 Sur ce passage, cf. D. P. Taormina (1999), 151.
24 Plutôt que de voir, ainsi que le fait K. Verrycken, une rupture doctrinale dans la pensée de Philopon, P. Golitsis propose de distinguer deux projets d'écriture parallèles : les commentaires qu'on lui a confiés (ainsi qu'à Simplicius) consistant à transcrire les cours de son ancien maître et les commentaires écrits en son nom propre. Au sein des premiers, il arriva à Philopon d'insérer sa propre impression sur les théories de son maître et l'expression de son désaccord. Voir à ce sujet, et en lien avec l'étude de la réception de *DA* 429a27–28, Philopon, *in An. Post.* 242.26–243.26. Selon P. Golitsis, c'est cette prise de distance croissante avec l'interprétation d'Ammonius qui conduisit progressivement Philopon à revoir sa propre lecture d'Aristote. Cf. P. Golitsis (2016a), 401–406 et (2016b).
25 Cf. Ph. Hoffmann (2014), 300. Sur le sens de πράγματα comme désignant les Formes intelligibles, cf. A. J. Festugière (1971), 568–574. Cf. aussi, Procl., *In Alc.* 30.6 ; *In Tim.* III.107.31 ; 108.7.

> à nouveau, lorsqu'il traite de l'intellect divin, il dit que les formes de toutes choses sont en lui. En tout cas, il dit que lorsque l'intellect se contemple, il voit les réalités, et lorsqu'il voit les réalités, c'est lui-même qu'il contemple[26].

Attribuer à Platon la thèse selon laquelle l'auto-contemplation de l'intellect divin coïncide avec la pensée des Formes va de soi pour un commentateur néoplatonicien. En revanche, l'attribuer à Aristote est loin d'être aussi évident. Proclus, par exemple, reproche précisément aux péripatéticiens d'avoir manqué l'articulation de la question de l'efficience de l'Intellect à celle de la cause paradigmatique[27] : en supprimant les Formes transcendantes, modèles du monde sensible, ils ont mis à la tête de l'univers un intellect sans multiplicité (νοῦν ἀπλήθυντον) qui, de ce fait, ne peut rien produire.

> οἱ δὲ Περιπατητικοὶ χωριστὸν μὲν εἶναί τι, ποιητικὸν δὲ οὐκ εἶναι, ἀλλὰ τελικόν· διὸ καὶ τὰ παραδείγματα ἀνεῖλον καὶ νοῦν ἀπλήθυντον προεστήσαντο τῶν ὅλων. (Procl., in Tim. I.266.28–267.1)
>
> Quant aux péripatéticiens, bien qu'ils admettent l'existence d'une réalité séparée, ils ne veulent pas qu'elle soit cause efficiente, mais cause finale : aussi ont-ils supprimé les modèles et mis à la tête de l'univers un intellect non multiplié. (Trad. A. J. Festugière)

Le rejet des Idées par Aristote explique pour Proclus plusieurs erreurs de sa doctrine, comme l'impossibilité pour l'intellect d'être cause efficiente. Or dans les commentaires d'Ammonius, il est dit qu'Aristote ne rejette pas l'existence de Formes transcendantes qu'il situe dans l'intellect divin, la définition du premier Moteur fusionnant avec celle du démiurge platonicien. Pour Ammonius, l'activité de l'intellect divin aristotélicien aurait pour objet l'ensemble des Formes transcendantes.

Le procédé consistant à lier la formule selon laquelle « l'intellect en acte est les réalités » à la définition de l'âme comme « lieu des formes » se retrouve dans l'*in Met.* afin d'indiquer qu'Aristote ne refuse pas d'admettre la présence des Formes dans l'intellect divin. Cette interprétation est une caractéristique de l'enseignement d'Ammonius qui cherche à montrer qu'Aristote ne réfute que *le sens apparent* de Platon (ἀεὶ ὁ Ἀριστοτέλης κἀνταῦθα τὸ φαινόμενον ἐλέγχει, Philopon, *in DA* 116.26–27). Dans le premier extrait (**T1**), le verbe δοκεῖ est utilisé à deux reprises pour montrer ceci. Certes, Aristote semble s'opposer à Platon. Mais en réalité (κατ' ἀλήθειαν), si l'on associe entre eux certains passages tirés de ses œuvres, il apparaît qu'il va dans le sens même de son maître. La citation du *DA* est

---

26 Toutes les traductions des commentaires d'Ammonius proposées ici sont miennes.
27 Procl., *in Parm.* 788.12–28 ; 842.26–35 ; *in Tim* I.266.29–267.11. Sur cette question, C. Steel (1984), 19–27.

utilisée, dans l'*in Met.*, dans le cadre d'un raisonnement *a fortiori* visant à montrer que si l'âme est le « lieu des formes », à plus forte raison (πολλῷ μᾶλλον), celles-ci sont-elles contenues dans l'intellect divin.

L'âme comme « lieu des formes » dans *l'in Met.* d'Asclépius

Les textes

Les deux passages de l'*in Met.* où apparaît la définition de l'âme comme « lieu des formes », sont les suivants : *in Met.* 69.18–20 (= *Mét.* A9, 990a34–b1) et *in Met.* 167.30–31 (= *Mét.* B2, 997b3).

T1

<990a34–b1> οἱ δὲ τὰς ἰδέας αἰτίας τιθέμενοι πρῶτον μὲν ζητοῦντες τῶν ὄντων λαβεῖν τὰς αἰτίας

[17] Ἐντεῦθεν δοκεῖ πρὸς τὸν Πλάτωνα ἀποτείνεσθαι περὶ τῶν ἰδεῶν. εἰρήκαμεν δὲ τὸν σκοπὸν τοῦ Ἀριστοτέλους περὶ τούτου. αὐτὸς γάρ ἐστιν ὁ λέγων ἐν τῇ Περὶ ψυχῆς πραγματείᾳ 'καὶ εὖ γε οἱ τὴν ψυχὴν εἰρηκότες [20] τόπον εἰδῶν', καὶ ὅτι ὁ ἐνεργείᾳ νοῦς ἐστι τὰ πράγματα, καὶ πάλιν ὅτι ὁ μὲν δυνάμει νοῦς ἐνεργεῖ, ὁ δὲ ἐνεργείᾳ νοῦς ποιεῖ. ὥστε ἄντικρυς καὶ αὐτὸς ἐναποτίθεται ἰδέας τῷ νῷ. πῶς οὖν, εἴποι ἄν τις, καὶ αὐτὸς πρεσβεύων ἰδέας δοκεῖ τῷ Πλάτωνι μάχεσθαι ; καὶ λέγομεν ὅτι κατ' ἀλήθειαν οὐ τῷ Πλάτωνι μάχεται, ἀλλὰ τῷ ἐν ἄλλῳ καὶ ἄλλῳ ὄντι Πλάτωνι μάχε- [25] ται, τοῖς ὑποτιθεμένοις τὰς ἰδέας ταύτας αὐτὰς καθ' ἑαυτὰς ὑπαρχούσας καὶ οὔσας κεχωρισμένας τοῦ νοῦ. ὥστε φανερὰ ἡμῖν γέγονεν ἡ ὅλη ἔννοια τοῦ Ἀριστοτέλους ἡ περὶ τῶν ἰδεῶν. (Ascl., *in Met.* 69.17–28.)

T2

<997b3> ὡς μὲν οὖν λέγομεν τὰ εἴδη αἴτιά τε καὶ οὐσίας εἶναι καθ' ἑαυτὰς εἴρηται ἐν τοῖς πρώτοις λόγοις

[24] καὶ πρὸς τούτους μὲν διαμάχεται ὁ Ἀριστοτέλης, ὡς εἴρηται, πρὸς τοὺς λέγοντας εἶναι ἄνθρωπον αὐτὸν καθ' αὑτὸν ἐν ὑποστάσει, καὶ οὕτως ἐξ αὐτοῦ παράγεσθαι τὰ ἄλλα, ὁμοίως δὲ καὶ ἐπὶ τῶν ἄλλων. ὁ μέντοι γε Πλάτων, ὡς πολλάκις εἴρηται, οὐ τοῦτο ὑποτίθεται, ἀλλὰ λόγους δημιουργικοὺς εἶναι παρὰ τῷ θεῷ τοῦ ἀνθρώπου καὶ πάντων τῶν γινομένων· καὶ τοῦ οὐρανοῦ λόγος ὑγείας, εἴ γε μέλλει διατελεῖν ἀγήρως καὶ ἄνοσος, καὶ τῶν ἄλλων ἁπάντων. εἰ γὰρ ὁ ἰατρὸς ἔχει λόγους ἐν ἑαυτῷ ὑγείας, πολλῷ μᾶλλον καὶ ὁ θεὸς ἔχει λόγον ὧν παράγει ὁμοίως δὲ καὶ αἱ ψυχαὶ ἔχουσιν ἐν ἑαυταῖς τοὺς λόγους τῶν [30] πραγμάτων, εἴ γε αὐτός φησιν ὁ Ἀριστοτέλης 'εὖ γε οἱ τὴν ψυχὴν εἰρηκότες τόπον εἰδῶν', καὶ ὅτι ὁ κατ' ἐνέργειαν νοῦς τὰ πράγματα. ὥστε καὶ νοηταὶ οὐσίαι ὑπάρχουσιν οἱ λόγοι οἱ παρὰ τῷ δημιουργῷ καὶ διανοηταὶ οἱ λόγοι οἱ ἐν τῇ ψυχῇ· οὐκέτι μέντοι γε αὐτοΐππος καὶ βοῦς καὶ τὰ τοιαῦτα αὐτὰ καθ' αὑτὰ ἐν ὑποστάσει ὄντα, ὥσπερ καὶ τὰ αἰσθητά. (Ascl., *in Met.* 167.24–34.)

T1 <990a34–b1> Ceux qui posent les Idées en cherchant d'abord à saisir les causes des êtres
À partir de là, il semble s'en prendre à Platon au sujet des Idées. Nous avons déjà parlé du but d'Aristote à ce sujet. En effet, c'est bien lui, dans le traité *De l'âme*, qui dit : « ils ont bien parlé ceux qui ont dit [20] que l'âme est le lieu des formes » ; il dit également que l'intellect en acte est les réalités ; il dit encore que l'intellect en puissance agit, tandis que l'intellect en acte produit. De telle sorte que lui aussi, sans conteste, dépose les Idées au sein de l'intellect. Mais, pourrait-on dire, comment est-il possible qu'il semble polémiquer contre [25] Platon, alors que lui-même tient en si grande considération les Idées ? Or nous disons qu'en vérité, ce n'est pas Platon qu'il combat, mais le Platon que l'on trouve ici et là, chez ceux qui postulent que les Idées existent en elles-mêmes et par elles-mêmes et qu'elles sont séparées de l'intellect. De cette façon, toute la conception aristotélicienne des Idées est à présent claire à nos yeux.

T2 <997b3> En quel sens nous disons que les formes sont causes et sont des substances par soi, cela a été dit dans les premiers exposés sur ces sujets.
Et c'est contre ces gens-là que polémique Aristote, comme cela a été dit, contre ceux qui disent qu'il y a un homme en soi et par soi en subsistance[28], et que c'est ainsi que les autres [hommes] sont produits à partir de lui – et cet exemple vaut pour tous les autres cas. Quant à Platon, comme cela a souvent été dit, telle n'est pas sa [25] position, mais il pose qu'il y a, auprès du dieu, des raisons démiurgiques, celles de l'homme et de tous les êtres soumis au devenir. Et il y a une raison de la santé du ciel, s'il est bien vrai qu'il est amené à perdurer sans subir la vieillesse ni la maladie, et de toutes les autres choses. Car si le médecin possède en lui-même les raisons de la santé, bien davantage encore le dieu possède-t-il en lui-même la raison des choses qu'il produit. Semblablement, les âmes ont en elles les raisons des [30] choses, si réellement Aristote lui-même dit qu'« ils ont bien parlé ceux qui ont dit que l'âme est le lieu des formes » et aussi que l'intellect en acte est les réalités. Si bien que les raisons qui sont auprès du démiurge sont des substances intelligibles et que les raisons qui sont dans l'âme sont [des substances] dianoétiques. Donc, il n'y a plus de Cheval en soi, ni de Bœuf, ni rien de semblable, qui a une subsistance en soi et par soi, comme c'est le cas pour les sensibles.

Construire l'autorité d'Aristote

Asclépius commente deux fois *Mét.* 990a34. T1 correspond à la première explication, où le sens véritable des propos d'Aristote est délivré (λέγομεν κατ'

---

28 Sur la traduction de ce terme, cf. Ph. Hoffmann (2001), 20, note 1.

ἀλήθειαν)²⁹. La seconde, beaucoup plus brève, uniquement paraphrastique, est donnée à la page suivante (70.15-21). L'impression de répétition maladroite que ce procédé suscite provient sans doute du style *apo phônès* du commentaire d'Asclépius. En **T1** (69.17-27), l'argumentation est très serrée et son caractère elliptique pose certaines difficultés d'interprétation. Dans son ensemble, la première explication du lemme aristotélicien court de 69.17 à 70.13 et vise à désamorcer l'une des plus sévères critiques d'Aristote contre l'hypothèse des Formes, consistant à dire que celles-ci redoublent inutilement les sensibles. Ammonius, par la voix de son disciple, commence par rappeler les analyses développées auparavant à l'occasion du commentaire à *Mét.* A6. Son projet est de montrer, en s'appuyant sur un jeu de citations réelles et fabriquées, tirées du *De Anima*, que sur le fond, ce n'est pas Platon, mais l'une de ses interprétations fallacieuses, qui est mis en cause par Aristote. Derrière ce qui semble être une critique de Platon, il faut voir en réalité une critique de ses mauvais exégètes. Puis, à la fin du commentaire, il indique que l'argument du redoublement des Formes à l'égard des sensibles ne peut valoir sérieusement puisque, par ailleurs, Aristote reconnaît la distinction fondamentale entre les causes intelligibles et ce qui en dépend³⁰.

Ce résultat concordiste nécessite beaucoup d'acrobaties herméneutiques. Rappelons tout d'abord le propos d'Aristote. À l'ouverture du chapitre 9 du livre A, Aristote formule une critique d'ordre général sur la nature des Formes et leur causalité : « Ceux qui posent les Idées, en cherchant d'abord à saisir les causes des êtres d'ici, ont introduit d'autres êtres en nombre égal à ceux-là, comme si, voulant compter, on croyait ne pouvoir le faire à cause du trop petit nombre des êtres et qu'on les multiplie pour arriver à les compter » (*Mét.* 990a34-b4). Aristote ironise au sujet de ce qu'il considère comme une farce épistémologique : la démarche des partisans des Idées est comparable à celle d'individus qui veulent dénombrer les sensibles et qui, incapables d'y arriver, les multiplient en croyant se faciliter la tâche. Les Formes ne sont que d'inutiles doublons éternels de réalités périssables. Elles n'apportent rien d'un point de vue épistémologique puisqu'elles sont aussi nombreuses que les réalités dont elles sont censées être les causes[31].

À l'argument de l'égalité numérique s'ajoute un peu plus loin celui de la similarité des Formes et des sensibles. Au-dessus des sensibles existent des réalités qui ont les mêmes caractéristiques et le même nom, à cette différence près que les unes sont éternelles et les autres périssables (*Mét.* 997b5-8). C'est dans ce second point que, selon Alexandre d'Aphrodise, réside la force véritable de la critique aristotélicienne (*in Met.* 76.21-23). Celle-ci ne repose pas tant sur l'argument de l'égalité numérique entre les sensibles et leurs causes que sur la similarité qui existe entre l'homme particulier et la Forme de l'homme (ὅμοιοι γὰρ οἵ τε ἄνθρωποι καὶ αἱ ἰδέαι, *in Met.* 85.5). Si l'homme est similaire à la Forme de l'homme, on aboutit à la régression infinie et à l'une des versions de l'argument du

---

29 Cf. L. Cardullo (2012), 397.
30 Sur cette tactique faisant jouer *Aristotelem contra Aristotelem*, cf. L. Cardullo (2012), 110.
31 Cf. D. Lefebvre (2008) ; A. Jaulin (2016).

« troisième homme »[32]. L'une d'entre elles est donnée dans la quatrième aporie du chapitre 2 du livre B. Comme l'indique Alexandre, si la Forme et la réalité sensible sont similaires,

> de même qu'il y a quelque chose de commun à ceux qui en participent (ils ont en effet la même forme), il y aura aussi un prédicat commun à ceux-ci et à l'Idée qui est la leur : en effet, cette dernière aussi a la même forme que les autres. Si tel est le cas, ce qui en est prédiqué en commun sera une Idée à son tour, et il y aura ainsi une Idée d'Idée et cela ira à l'infini. Ce qu'Aristote présente ici nous l'avons expliqué dans l'exégèse du troisième homme. (Alex., in Met. 93.1–7.)[33]

Syrianus, dans son commentaire, montre que l'argument de la similarité est fallacieux et qu'en outre Alexandre se trompe dans son interprétation des sens de l'homonymie et de la synonymie[34]. Alexandre en voulant diminuer autant que possible la différence entre le particulier et la Forme platonicienne, attribue à Platon une théorie de la synonymie entre le sensible et l'intelligible. Ainsi, la mortalité est inhérente à la définition de l'homme ; or la Forme de l'homme est éternelle. Elle ne peut donc être synonyme de l'homme sensible. D'ailleurs, l'individu et la Forme spécifique ne diffèrent pas uniquement sous le rapport de l'éternité. Les Formes diffèrent en tout point des réalités sensibles, parce qu'elles en sont les causes. Selon Syrianus, ce qui est au cœur de la relation de participation, c'est une certaine forme d'homonymie, l'homonymie ἀφ' ἑνὸς καὶ πρὸς ἕν, qui fonde le rapport de dépendance de l'image envers son modèle[35], ainsi que l'asymétrie de leur ressemblance. L'image ressemble à son modèle, dont elle reçoit des qualités que lui-même ne possède pas, car il lui est supérieur et existe sur un mode plus unifié et plus parfait[36]. Les Formes ne sont pas des universels hypostasiés, mais des principes producteurs intelligibles, possédant une nature différente de celle de leurs dérivés.

Pour Syrianus, l'erreur des péripatéticiens vient de ce qu'ils partent des images pour remonter ensuite à leurs causes. Au lieu de se placer depuis l'unité propre des intelligibles, ils prennent le sensible comme point de départ et en déduisent à tort que les Formes ressemblent à ce dont elles sont les causes. Les choses sensibles ne possèdent que de manière dérivée des propriétés que la Forme contient de manière éminente. Donc les qualités sensibles n'ont pas de correspondant terme à terme dans l'intelligible. Alexandre, qui méconnaît ce principe de différence, établit une fausse similarité entre l'homme sensible et la Forme de l'homme.

---

32 Une abondante littérature secondaire est consacrée à l'étude de cet argument, qui doit son appellation à Aristote (*Réfutations sophistiques* 22, 178b36). Pour un *status quaestionis*, cf. L. Gazziero (2008).
33 Trad. L. Gazziero (2008), 223–224 (n. 3).
34 J. Opsomer (2004).
35 M. Narcy (1981).
36 Syrianus, *in Met.* 114.35–115.1. Sur cette question, cf. P. d'Hoine (2016).

Syrianus conclut en notant que sur ce point, Aristote ne diffère pas beaucoup d'Alexandre, aucun des deux ne parvenant à atteindre « les vues divines de Platon, tout comme les Thraces n'atteignent pas les cieux éthérés »[37].

Asclépius (Ammonius) déplace la perspective. Pour lui, Alexandre est un guide valable pour lire Aristote, et l'argument de la similarité sur lequel il s'appuie vaut comme une sorte de mise en garde contre une interprétation superficielle de Platon. Il s'agit d'une stratégie typique d'Ammonius, que l'on retrouvera encore par exemple dans le commentaire à la *Physique*[38] de Simplicius, consistant à dire qu'Aristote ne s'oppose pas à Platon, mais à celle de ses interprétations qui estime que de toutes les réalités d'ici-bas, « il y a des Idées, » et qui pense « que la similitude de celles d'ici par rapport à celles-là ne se comprend pas sur le mode des images aux modèles, mais sur le mode de l'identité » (*in Phys.* 295.15–18)[39]. En *in Met.* 75.21–33, il et dit que l'argument du « troisième homme » se produit lorsqu'on pose une similarité entre les Idées et les réalités perceptibles. La similarité ne peut exister qu'entre deux entités appartenant au même niveau ontologique, par exemple entre deux hommes sensibles.

Or c'est précisément ce qui arrive, selon Ammonius, si l'on sépare les Formes du démiurge. Dans ce cas, on perd la spécificité de la nature intellectuelle des Formes. C'est pourquoi ceux qui situent les Formes en dehors de l'intellect aboutissent à l'argument du « troisième homme » et tombent sous le coup de critiques péripatéticiennes. Pour lui, c'est donc contre cette séparation des Formes et de l'intellect, et non contre Platon, que polémique Aristote. Elle est liée à une certaine interprétation de la théorie des Formes qui réifie les intelligibles, transposant indûment les qualités sensibles dans l'intelligible. Selon Asclépius (Ammonius), cette intériorité, que Platon a défendue, Aristote lui aussi l'a reconnue puisqu'il admet que l'âme est le « lieu des formes ». Aussi, derrière ce qui, en *Mét.* A9 et B2, se présente comme une opposition d'Aristote à la théorie des Formes, il faut en réalité comprendre autre chose : les critiques aristotéliciennes et l'argument du « troisième homme » ne portent que si l'on pose que les Formes sont séparées de l'intellect divin[40]. En revanche, défendre l'existence des Formes à l'intérieur de l'intellect divin permet de justifier la différence homonymique du sensible et de l'intelligible qui en est la cause, et par là de défendre la nature paradigmatique des Formes ainsi que leur puissance de production et d'unification des sensibles (Ascl., *in Met.* 71.10–24). Sur ce point, Ammonius est sur la même ligne que Syrianus. Mais, tandis que Syrianus reproche à Aristote de n'avoir pas saisi la dynamique de production du sensible par l'intelligible, en vertu de leur différence homonymique, Ammonius indique que les critiques d'Aristote portent sur une mauvaise lecture de Platon. Si l'on compare la manière

---

37 Cf. L. Cardullo (2003).
38 Pour une étude de cette conciliation chez Simplicius dans le commentaire à la *Physique*, cf. M.-A. Gavray (2011).
39 Trad. M.-A. Gavray (2011), 149.
40 Cf. aussi par exemple, Ascl., *in Met.* 75.28 ; 76.34.

que les deux commentateurs ont d'interpréter *Met.* B2, 997b3–4[41], il apparaît que, pour Ammonius, les objections d'Aristote ne portent pas tant sur l'existence des Formes que sur une certaine conception de celles-ci. Cette perspective lui permet de dire que ce n'est pas Platon qui est visé par les critiques d'Aristote, mais ceux qui ont séparé les Formes de l'intellect divin[42].

Pour développer ce point, Ammonius remarque qu'Aristote a admis que l'âme est le « lieu des formes ». Cette citation se retrouve dans le commentaire à *Mét.* A9, 990a34–b1 (**T1**) et B2, 997b3–4 (**T2**). En *Mét.* B2, 997b3–4, Aristote examine la genèse de l'hypothèse des Formes platoniciennes qui s'inscrit dans le cadre plus général de l'examen des universaux mathématiques[43]. Le passage, d'où **T2** est extrait, rappelle que les réalités mathématiques ont une existence en tant qu'universels dans notre âme. Ce sont des substances dianoétiques (διανοηταὶ οὐσίαι, Ascl., *in Met.* 165.26–27), dont l'existence est garantie par la présence des substances intellectives (νοηταὶ οὐσίαι) au sein du démiurge (*in Met.* 165.35–37). Dans ce passage, à la citation de *DA* 429a27–28, est associée une autre formule, inspirée de *DA* 431b17 selon laquelle l'intellect en acte est identique aux formes. L'association de ces deux formules vise à montrer que si l'âme peut être dite le « lieu des formes », c'est parce que les raisons psychiques dérivent des Formes qui existent au sein de l'intellect et sont identiques à lui. Les raisons sont des substances véritables qui existent dans l'âme, tout comme, en dieu, existent les Formes transcendantes et les nombres intelligibles. Il existe donc une intériorité des raisons dans l'âme et une intériorité des Formes dans l'intellect. C'est cette intériorité qui rend les Formes productives et l'intellect producteur.

Dans le **T1**, on trouve, jointe à ces deux formules, une troisième expression attribuée à Aristote. Immédiatement après avoir cité *DA* 429a27–28, Asclépius (*in Met.* 69.19–21) juxtapose ce qu'il présente comme étant deux autres citations, mais qui sont en réalité des formules qu'il compose à partir de différents éléments doctrinaux tirés de *DA* III[44].

(1) En effet, c'est bien lui, dans le traité *De l'âme*, qui dit : « ils ont bien parlé ceux qui ont dit que l'âme est le lieu des formes » ; (2) il dit également que l'intellect en acte est identique à ses objets ; (3) il dit enfin que l'intellect en puissance agit, tandis que l'intellect en acte produit.

Chacune de ces trois formules a un statut différent : la première est une citation littérale d'Aristote, la seconde est une paraphrase, et la troisième est une

---

41 C. d'Ancona (2005), 35–37.
42 Pour une comparaison plus détaillée de ces deux attitudes exégétiques, et un examen des mauvais exégètes platoniciens visés par Ammonius, cf. A. Michalewski (à paraître).
43 Pour une analyse de cette question dans les commentaires de Syrianus et d'Asclépius, cf. A. Madigan (1986).
44 Sauf erreur de ma part, il me semble que ce processus rhétorique n'a pas été remarqué par les spécialistes qui semblent mettre les trois formules sur le même plan. Cf. par exemple K. Verrycken (1990), 220 ; E. Tempelis (1998), 79 ; L. Cardullo (2012), 396.

construction d'Asclépius. Comme dans le **T2**, par cette accumulation de formules qui s'éloignent *crescendo* de la lettre du texte du *De Anima*, Asclépius réussit à faire tenir à Aristote des propos censés corroborer la théorie selon laquelle les Formes transcendantes existent dans l'intellect divin. Le caractère elliptique et paratactique de la phrase – qu'il faut peut-être attribuer au style oral du commentaire – autorise un tel glissement. Cette succession peut être lue comme l'indication des différentes étapes d'une remontée vers les niveaux supérieurs – de l'âme à l'intellect, de l'intellect humain pensant à l'intellect divin producteur – Asclépius indiquant par là que ce qui vaut pour l'âme individuelle, qui contient en elle les Formes, vaut *a fortiori* pour l'intellect divin. Ce passage est facilité par l'emploi, au sein du commentaire, d'un même terme, *logoi*, désignant les Formes contenues dans la nature, dans l'âme humaine et dans l'intellect divin. Les Formes existent à trois niveaux et, selon leur situation dans la hiérarchie ontologique, n'exercent pas la même activité. Dans l'intellect divin, elles sont cognitives et productives, dans la nature, seulement productives, et dans l'âme humaine, seulement cognitives[45]. Au niveau de l'intellect démiurgique, les Formes sont en lui ou, selon une autre formule, « auprès de lui »[46]. C'est pour autant que le démiurge porte les Formes en lui qu'il peut être producteur. De manière générale, pour produire, il faut porter des raisons en soi, quel que soit le niveau ontologique considéré[47].

Pour résumer les choses, dans le **T1**, Asclépius procède de la sorte : (1) Après avoir évoqué une citation où il est question de la présence des Formes dans l'âme humaine, il utilise une formule qui, dans la tradition néoplatonicienne, évoque l'identité de nature entre les Formes et l'intellect divin.

(2) Dire que l'intellect est <identique à> ses objets (ὁ ἐνεργείᾳ νοῦς ἐστι τὰ πράγματα) est une reprise à peine modifiée de *DA* 431b17 (ὅλως δὲ ὁ νοῦς ἐστιν, ὁ κατ' ἐνέργειαν, τὰ πράγματα). C'est un motif classique du néoplatonisme développé pour la première fois par Plotin à partir de sa lecture d'Alexandre d'Aphrodise qui associe l'interprétation du livre III du *De Anima* avec les analyses qu'Aristote donne de l'intellect divin en *Métaphysique* Λ 9. Si l'intellect est bien identique aux Formes intelligibles, en les pensant, le démiurge se pense lui-même et, par là même, produit (παράγει) éternellement, par le seul effet de sa bonté immobile (Ascl., *in Met.* 28.6)[48].

(3) Après avoir rappelé que, selon Aristote, l'âme est le « lieu des formes » et que l'intellect en acte est identique aux réalités, Asclépius ajoute une dernière formule. Cette troisième citation supposée est un hapax dans le commentaire. Son caractère oxymorique pose problème : « l'intellect en puissance agit (ὁ μὲν δυνάμει νοῦς ἐνεργεῖ), l'intellect en acte, produit ». Com-

---

45 Ascl., *in Met.* 81.1–4 ; L. Cardullo (2012), 424.
46 Cf. par exemple, Ascl., *in Met.* 70.3 ; 80.30.
47 Ascl., *In Met.* 91.23–26. Cf. aussi 82.22–24 ; 85.26–28 ; 87.30–32.
48 Concernant la traduction et la signification du verbe παράγει, cf. L. Cardullo (2012), 318 ; 359.

ment comprendre que « l'intellect en puissance agit »[49] ? Sans doute y a-t-il dans le caractère extrêmement ramassé de cette formule quelque chose du raccourci de la note de cours. Elle repose sur une distinction classique, issue du chapitre 5 du livre III du *DA*, et longuement développée dans la tradition néoplatonicienne entre l'intellect analogue à la matière et l'intellect agent. Ici l'intellect agent est interprété comme l'intellect divin, Asclépius jouant peut-être sur plusieurs sens possibles du verbe ποιεῖν – *produire l'intelligibilité* dans un autre intellect ou *produire les réalités* dérivées. Le contraste qu'il s'agit d'établir est le suivant : lorsque l'intellect humain passe de la puissance à l'acte, il connaît, tandis que l'intellect divin, toujours déjà en acte, est également éternellement producteur. Quelques pages plus loin dans le commentaire, une opposition similaire est développée, entre l'âme humaine, qui reçoit les formes du dieu, et le dieu qui les possède toujours (Ascl., *in Met*. 80.30-33).

Citant, paraphrasant, reformulant certaines formules du *DA*, isolées de leurs contexte, Asclépius (Ammonius) utilise Aristote comme allié pour combattre une position jugée comme étant non-platonicienne, celle qui sépare l'intellect divin des intelligibles et considère les Formes comme des paradigmes dépourvus de toute efficience[50]. Il parvient ainsi à montrer que le texte d'Aristote porte en lui des indications permettant de voir que celui-ci n'est pas si éloigné de son maître qu'il le paraît. Si Aristote reconnaît que l'âme est le « lieu des formes », alors, il doit admettre que les Formes existent à titre premier comme des principes producteurs dans l'intellect en acte, qui est la cause efficiente du monde. Promouvoir l'accord de Platon et d'Aristote sur la question de la nature et de la causalité des Formes intelligibles est une spécificité de l'exégèse d'Ammonius, dont on trouve la trace dans différents commentaires transcrits par Philopon et dans le commentaire à la *Métaphysique* d'Asclépius. Le procédé consistant à isoler et à reformuler des citations ou des points de doctrine du *DA* permet à Asclépius (Ammonius) d'opérer une torsion des thèses aristotéliciennes au service de sa lecture concordiste. Dans les deux passages de l'*in Met.* l'argumentation est elliptique. La juxtaposition paratactique de formules tirées ou inspirées des chapitres 4 et 5 du livre III du *DA* vise à indiquer qu'un Platon bien compris échappe aux critiques péripatéticiennes et qu'Aristote n'est pas hostile à la théorie des Formes puisqu'il considère l'intellect divin comme une cause productrice qui contient les raisons démiurgiques.

Dans cette perspective, commenter la *Métaphysique* est un exercice destiné à mettre Aristote en cohérence avec lui-même : s'il prétend que l'âme est le « lieu des formes », il reconnaît qu'*a fortiori* l'intellect divin contient en lui les intelligibles, ce qui fait de lui la cause productrice du monde. Commenter consiste donc à révéler, par-delà les désaccords apparents, qu'il n'y a pas d'opposition

---

49 Il est sans doute possible que le verbe ἐνεργεῖ qui exprime l'activité de l'intellect humain, ait ici le sens de « s'actualise », « se met en acte », par opposition à l'autre intellect, l'intellect divin, qui est toujours déjà en acte et éternellement producteur.
50 L. Gerson (2005), 223.

foncière entre les enseignements de Platon et ceux d'Aristote. Par cette attitude, Ammonius signe sa différence par rapport à ses maître athéniens, dans la mesure où il ne s'agit plus pour lui uniquement de défendre Platon contre des critiques, mais aussi de montrer tout ce que le texte d'Aristote porte en lui de fondamentalement platonicien. Dès lors, la valeur accordée à l'exégèse d'Aristote change radicalement : étudier ses textes, ce n'est plus se livrer à un exercice propédeutique à l'étude de Platon, mais c'est lire un auteur dont l'importance philosophique n'est pas moindre que celle de son maître. Si les analyses de K. Praechter qui soulignent l'écart entre Athènes et Alexandrie tendent à occulter la continuité pédagogique réelle qui existe entre les deux écoles, il est, à mon avis, également exagéré de réduire à de simples points de détail[51] les différences qui existent entre les perspectives exégétiques de Proclus ou Syrianus d'une part et d'Ammonius de l'autre[52].

---

51 I. Hadot (2015), 153.
52 B. van den Berg (2004), 200.

MAREIKE HAUER

The Use of Stoic References in Simplicius' Discussion of Quality*

Introduction

In his commentary on chapter eight of Aristotle's *Categories*, the late Neoplatonist Simplicius investigates Aristotle's account of quality.[1] His analysis includes references to and discussions of different positions regarding qualities that were defended by philosophers belonging not only to the Platonic or Aristotelian tradition but also to the Stoic one. In the present chapter, I will deal with Simplicius' references to the Stoic conception of quality[2] and I will focus, in particular, on the nature and possible purpose of these references.

Simplicius mentions aspects of the Stoic conception of quality throughout his analysis of Aristotle's account; in other words, Simplicius does not present the Stoic position on quality as a whole, but rather discusses certain aspects of this position at different points in the text. This leads to a juxtaposition of elements of the Aristotelian, the Neoplatonic and the Stoic theoretical frameworks; and although these theoretical frameworks and their technical terminology remain conceptually distinguished, they converge on an explanatory level. As one would expect, Simplicius is generally critical towards the Stoics and raises several objections against their conception of quality. However, he does not cease to refer to this conception – there are more than 15 explicit references to the Stoics in his

---

* This contribution was completed during my affiliation with the project 'Not another history of Platonism', which has received funding from the European Research Council (ERC) under the European Union's Horizon 2020 research and innovation programme (grant agreement No. 885273).
1 Greek ed.: Kalbfleisch (1907). English transl.: Fleet (2002).
2 I am aware that by speaking of 'the Stoic conception, or position, of quality' or 'the Stoic categorial scheme' I am simplifying matters. These topics were subject to debate among Stoic philosophers and there were, of course, differences between their views. I remain general to avoid the implication that Simplicius knew about these differences and had particular Stoic philosophers in mind when discussing Stoic views.

Dealing with Disagreement, ed. by Albert Joosse and Angela Ulacco, Monothéismes et Philosophie, 33 (Turnhout: Brepols, 2022), pp. 169–184
BREPOLS ❧ PUBLISHERS   10.1484/M.MON-EB.5.132753
This is an open access article made available under a CC BY-NC 4.0 International License.

commentary on chapter eight.[3] References to and criticism of Stoic positions can be found in Neoplatonic texts going as far back as Plotinus, which may not be very surprising given the fact that Stoicism once represented an influential rival philosophical school to Platonism. However, there are at least two points that are worth noting with regard to Simplicius' discussion of the Stoics: 1. In Simplicius' day, in the 6th century CE, the Stoic school had long passed its peak and practically did not exist anymore. Hence, it was no longer the influential rival school that it had once been. 2. Although Simplicius often rejects Stoic views, he equally often discusses them in a constructive manner; in other words, he does not simply dismiss the Stoic position altogether, but instead critically engages with it. Moreover, there are certain aspects that Simplicius does not criticize at all. These points indicate that Simplicius' recurrent criticism of the Stoic conception of quality is not merely polemical. Both the high number of references and his critical engagement rather suggest that Simplicius acknowledges the Stoic position as an established one within the Greek philosophical tradition. As Simplicius often remarks, the Stoics do not only deal with similar questions, but their position also includes some theoretical elements that are appealing to or compatible with Simplicius' interpretation of Aristotle's account. However, when juxtaposed with the Aristotelian view, the Stoic one also appears to serve as a means for Simplicius to show the explanatory superiority of Aristotle's account.

Before taking a closer look at some of Simplicius' discussions of Stoic views on quality, a few words should be said about the question of the origin of Simplicius' references to the Stoics. At the beginning of his *Commentary on Aristotle's Categories*, Simplicius presents himself and his commentary in a rather modest way.[4] He states that he closely follows Iamblichus in his interpretation of the *Categories* (which also includes literal borrowings) (*In Cat.* 3.2–4). Moreover, he informs us that Iamblichus' main source for his own commentary was Porphyry's long commentary on the *Categories* (*In Cat.* 2.9–25). Eventually, Simplicius praises both Porphyry and Iamblichus for their work and refers the reader to their

---

3 See Simpl., *In Cat.* 209.1–3; 209.10–29; 212.12–213.1; 214.24–215.18; 217.32–218.4; 222.30–223.11; 224.22–33; 237.25–238.32; 242.12–15; 264.33–36; 269.14–16; 271.20–23; 276.30–32; 284.32–285.1; 286.36–287.11; 287.31–33. In all these passages, Simplicius refers to 'the Stoics', except for *In Cat.* 209.10–29, where he refers to 'the Stoics' and to 'Antipater'.

4 Simplicius specifies that his aim in writing a commentary on Aristotle's *Categories* is threefold. He wants to 1. obtain a better understanding of Aristotle's text, 2. clarify Iamblichus' interpretation and 3. provide a text that synthesizes important and compatible elements of previous interpretations (see Simpl., *In Cat.* 3.4–10). Regarding the previous tradition of commentaries on and discussions of the *Categories*, Simplicius even says: 'I should straight away appear ridiculous for having dared to have written something myself as well (καταγέλαστος εὐθὺς ἀπ' ἀρχῆς ἂν δόξαιμι γράψαι τι καὶ αὐτὸς τολμήσας [...])', Simpl., *In Cat.* 2.31–3.1 (transl.: Chase). Although Simplicius repeatedly stresses the interpretative authority of his predecessors, especially Porphyry and Iamblichus, it is worth noting that he alludes to the fact that he might have added something to the interpretation of Aristotle's *Categories* (see Simpl., *In Cat.* 3.10–17).

commentaries (*In Cat.* 3.13–17). Unfortunately, Iamblichus' commentary on the *Categories* and Porphyry's long commentary on the *Categories* are no longer extant. The absence of these commentaries makes it very difficult to assess not only Simplicius' originality regarding his own interpretation of Aristotle's text but also the origin of Simplicius' references to Stoic (or other philosophical) views. Regarding Simplicius' references to the Stoics, one could thus ask whether they stem from Simplicius himself[5] or whether Simplicius found these references in his sources and adopted them. In his (selective) presentation of predecessors who had commented on Aristotle's *Categories*, Simplicius calls Porphyry the 'cause of all that is good for us' (ὁ πάντων ἡμῖν τῶν καλῶν αἴτιος […], *In Cat.* 2.5–6) and, interestingly, adds that Porphyry includes and discusses Stoic views regarding many of the topics dealt with in the *Categories* (*In Cat.* 2.8–9). It might thus be possible that all of Simplicius' references to the Stoics (and maybe also some of the discussions that often accompany these references) ultimately trace back to

---

5 The assumption that the references stem from Simplicius presupposes that he had access to Stoic texts, which seems rather unlikely or, at least, would be difficult to prove. Moreover, later in his commentary, Simplicius explicitly states that most Stoic texts were unavailable at his time (see Simpl., *In Cat.* 334.1–3: πολλὴ δὲ ἡ τῶν τοιούτων ἐξεργασία παρὰ τοῖς Στωικοῖς, ὧν ἐφ' ἡμῶν καὶ ἡ διδασκαλία καὶ τὰ πλεῖστα τῶν συγγραμμάτων ἐπιλέλοιπεν). This statement, of course, neither excludes the possibility that some (though few) texts were available nor does it indicate which Stoic texts were still available or which topics the remaining texts dealt with. It is also worth noting that, among the commentaries that Simplicius wrote, there is a commentary on the *Handbook of Epictetus*, i.e., on a Stoic text. The *Handbook* was quite a popular text and references to it or to Epictetus can also be found in other Neoplatonic authors. For more information on these references, see Hadot (1996), 157–160; Boter (1999), 116–117 and 432–433; Brittain/Brennan (2002), 4–5 and 28 n. 18. Hadot argues that the text might have been used in the (later) Neoplatonic school as preliminary ethical training for beginners prior to the study of Aristotle's and Plato's works (see Hadot (1978), 160–164 or Hadot (2003), XCII–XCVII; see also Brittain/Brennan (2002), 4–5; and cf. Simpl., *In Cat.* 5.3–6.5 for the assumption that preliminary ethical instruction would be necessary). At the beginning of his *Commentary on the Handbook of Epictetus*, Simplicius states that Arrian, who compiled the *Handbook* and the *Discourses of Epictetus*, provided information on Epictetus' life. Moreover, he informs us that Arrian described the *Handbook* as a selection of philosophically important and moving words by Epictetus. He adds that these words can also be found in the *Discourses* (see Simpl., *In Ench. praef.* lines 9–11 (ed. Hadot (1996))/lines 15–17 (ed. Hadot (2003)), but see also Hadot (1996), 152). Although scholars agree that Simplicius closely worked with the *Handbook*, it is a subject of debate whether Simplicius was well acquainted with the *Discourses* or not (see Brittain/Brennan (2002), 19; but see also Hadot (1996), 159–160). Regarding Simplicius' knowledge of Stoic views, Ch. Brittain and T. Brennan write that 'Simplicius exhibits a fairly extensive knowledge of Stoic metaphysics in his commentary on Aristotle's *Categories*' (Brittain/Brennan (2002), 19), but, regarding his *Commentary on the Handbook of Epictetus*, they state that '[s]ome of Simplicius' comments about Stoicism […], especially concerning their logic, epistemology and moral psychology, suggest a surprising lack of knowledge' (Brittain/Brennan (2002), 20; but see also Hadot (2003), CI–CXXII).

Porphyry.[6] However, even if one assumes that Simplicius adopted the references to Stoic views from his sources, one might still ask why he decided to do so.[7]

In what follows, I will first present two aspects of Simplicius' analysis of quality that are particularly interesting with regard to the Stoic notion of quality, in that they are structurally similar to aspects of the latter and could thus explain why certain aspects of the Stoic notion of quality might have been appealing to Simplicius. I will then turn to two aspects of the Stoic notion of quality that Simplicius criticizes heavily; two aspects that are indeed incompatible with his conception of quality in his *Commentary on Aristotle's Categories*. I will show that Simplicius conceives of the Stoic notion of quality, or rather of the qualified, as an alternative yet comparable conception to the Aristotelian one of quality presented in the *Categories*. I will conclude not only that Simplicius' criticism of the Stoic doctrine serves as a means to show the explanatory superiority of the Aristotelian conception, but also that the discussion on quality exemplifies Simplicius' assessment of the Stoic categorial scheme in general; in other words, although many scholars nowadays plausibly question the comparability of the Aristotelian categorial scheme and the Stoic one, Simplicius clearly conceives of the Stoic model as an alternative yet comparable model to the Aristotelian scheme.

Structural similarities in the accounts of quality by Simplicius and the Stoics

It is worth noting that there are at least two aspects of Simplicius' notion of quality and the Stoic one that are structurally similar: the function of quality

---

6 Unfortunately, Porphyry does not include as many references to the Stoics in his short commentary on the *Categories* (or at least not in his comments on the first nine chapters, which is where the text suddenly ends). There is only one explicit reference in his comments on the chapter on quality (see Porph., *In Cat.* 137.29–138.4; cf. Simpl., *In Cat.* 284.32–285.1 and also 237.25–238.32) and only three more in the rest of the commentary (see the references to 'Athenodorus and Cornutus' in Porph., *In Cat.* 59.10–14 and 86.22–24; cf. Simpl., *In Cat.* 18.26–19.1 and 62.24–30; and the reference to 'the Stoics' in Porph., *In Cat.* 119.34–37; cf. Simpl., *In Cat.* 192.30–193.2).

7 There are, of course, more questions worth investigating. If, e.g., one assumes that the references can ultimately be attributed to Porphyry, one could transfer the questions of the purpose and the nature of the references to Porphyry. Here, too, the previous exegetical tradition and the influence of intellectual authorities, e.g., his teacher Plotinus, and respected opponents, e.g., Alexander of Aphrodisias, are certainly important; see, e.g., Graeser (1972) and Gerson (2016). If one assumes that not only the references to but also (parts of) the discussions of Stoic views that we find in Simplicius trace back to Porphyry, the question of why Porphyry's discussions often represent a critical engagement rather than a polemical rejection may be even more pertinent than the question of why Porphyry refers to Stoic views.

within their respective metaphysical frameworks and the position of the qualified within their respective categorial schemes.

In his *Commentary on Aristotle's Categories*, Simplicius analyzes the Aristotelian notion of quality, as presented in the *Categories*, against the background of Neoplatonic metaphysics. One indication of this is Simplicius' reference to quality as μετεχόμενον, i.e., as that which is participated in. It is participated in by the qualified, to which Simplicius, accordingly, refers as μετέχον. I take these designations as references to a triadic theory of participation developed by Simplicius' predecessors, notably Iamblichus and Proclus.[8] It consists of the transcendent, or unparticipated (τὸ ἐξῃρημένον/τὸ ἀμέθεκτον), the participated (τὸ μετεχόμενον) and the participant (τὸ μετέχον/κατὰ μέθεξιν). A good presentation of the triad of participation can be found in Proclus' *Elements of Theology*, where Proclus describes the three items and their relation to one another as follows:[9] the unparticipated (τὸ ἀμέθεκτον) produces the participated (τὸ μετεχόμενον); yet, it is self-subsistent, outside of and independent from the participated. The participated, in turn, requires another entity in order to subsist. This entity, in which the participated subsists, is the participant (τὸ μετέχον). The description suggests that the unparticipated has a rather transcendent character while the participated has a rather immanent character. In his *Commentary on Plato's Parmenides*, Proclus draws a parallel between the unparticipated and a transcendent form, on the one hand, and between the participated and an immanent form, on the other.[10] There is little information on this association in Simplicius' *Commentary on the Categories*.[11] However, his commentary on chapter five of Aristotle's *Categories* reveals that Simplicius accepts both transcendent and immanent forms.[12] Moreover, in his commentary on chapter eight, we find the association of quality *qua* μετεχόμενον with an immanent form. In his interesting reply to Plotinus' objection

---

8 For the assumption that Proclus elaborates here on distinctions that can already be found in Iamblichus, see, e.g., Dodds (2004), xix–xxiii and Dillon (2009), esp. 33, 39, 52 and 342.
9 See, e.g., Procl., *ET* 23–24, where Proclus introduces the triad of participation. Simplicius does not explicitly reflect on the triad of participation in his *Commentary on Aristotle's Categories*, but it appears to underlie his analysis.
10 See Procl., *In Parm*. VI.1069.18–22 (ed. Steel): Πάσης γὰρ ἀρχικῆς τάξεως ἡγεῖσθαι χρὴ πρὸ τοῦ μετεχομένου πλήθους τὸ ἀμέθεκτον αὐτῶν καὶ πρωτουργὸν εἶδος [...]. οὕτω δήπου καὶ πρὸ τῶν ἐνύλων εἰδῶν ἔστι τὰ ἄϋλα [...].
11 This lack could be explained by the Neoplatonists' understanding of the *Categories* as both an instrumental text and a work for beginners (cf. Simpl., *In Cat*. 4.28–5.1). This assessment turned the *Categories* into the first book of Aristotle's corpus that pupils at the Neoplatonic school encountered. The position of the *Categories* within the Neoplatonic curriculum and the 'introductory character' that was ascribed to it might explain why Simplicius keeps silent not only with regard to the association between the triad of participation and forms but also generally when it comes to the metaphysical foundations of his statements and explanations in his *Commentary on Aristotle's Categories*. For more information on the Neoplatonic curriculum, see Hadot (1991) and Hoffmann (2006).
12 See Simpl., *In Cat*. 82.35–83.16; see also *In Cat*. 69.4–71.2.

that the explanation of quality through the qualified is not an explanation of quality according to its proper account,[13] Simplicius says:

> [...] if a quality were per se, it would be necessary to ask what a quality is [such] that it is participated in; but if it belongs to us and does not exist outside what is qualified, it is clear (a) that in its case being and being participated in are not two different things, and (b) that it is not per se in one mode, while giving being and predication to the qualified in another, but (c) that being possessed, existing and producing the qualified are viewed as the same way in the case of a quality; for a quality is the form of whatever possesses it. So the person who defines a quality by means of what is qualified shows its particular character in the strictest sense, and at the same time indicates what it is and what effect it produces in entities. (*In Cat.* 213.29–214.2.)[14]

In this passage, Simplicius refers to quality as μετεχόμενον and he clearly ascribes characteristic features of the μετεχόμενον to quality:[15] he says that quality is in the qualified, being participated in by the qualified and giving being to the qualified by its very existence. If we assume, on the one hand, that Simplicius works with a theory of participation which is similar to the one outlined above, and, on the other hand, that, though not all μετεχόμενα are qualities, all qualities are μετεχόμενα, as Simplicius' description of quality quoted above suggests, then it is possible to ascribe the structure and the characteristic features of the μετεχόμενον to quality analogously. Moreover, based on the description of the μετέχον and the relation between μετεχόμενον and μετέχον, it becomes apparent that the qualified represents the corresponding μετέχον to quality *qua* μετεχόμενον. Towards the end of the passage, Simplicius even states that 'quality is the form of whatever possesses it' (εἶδος γάρ ἐστιν ἡ ποιότης τοῦ ἔχοντος). Simplicius, here, associates quality *qua* μετεχόμενον with immanent form. This association, of course, is not to be understood in terms of identity. Although it is possible to associate the μετεχόμενον with immanent form and quality *qua* μετεχόμενον with immanent form, quality, strictly speaking, is not immanent form. However, one could draw the following analogy: quality is to substance, i.e., a matter-form compound,

---

13 See Simpl., *In Cat.* 213.8–10: Ἐρωτᾷ δὲ ὁ Πλωτῖνος, τί ἄρα οὖσα ἡ ποιότης τοὺς λεγομένους ποιοὺς παρέχεται· ὅτι μὲν γὰρ κατὰ τὴν ποιότητα οἱ ποιοὶ λέγονται, εἴρηται, τίς δέ ἐστιν αὐτὴ ἡ ποιότης κατὰ τὸν οἰκεῖον λόγον, οὐ διώρισται.
14 [...] ἔτι δὲ καλλίων ἀπολογισμὸς ὁ λέγων ὡς εἰ μὲν καθ' ἑαυτὴν ἦν ἡ ποιότης, ἔδει ζητεῖν, τίς οὖσα μετέχεται· εἰ δὲ ἐν ἡμῖν ἐστιν καὶ οὐκ ἐκτὸς τῶν ποιῶν ὑφέστηκεν, δῆλον ὡς οὐκ ἄλλο μὲν αὐτῇ τὸ εἶναι, ἄλλο δὲ τὸ μετέχεσθαι, οὐδὲ καθ' ἕτερον μὲν τρόπον ἐστὶ καθ' ἑαυτήν, κατ' ἄλλον δὲ τῷ ποιῷ παρέχει τὸ εἶναί τε καὶ λέγεσθαι, ἀλλ' ἐν τῷ αὐτῷ τό τε ἔχεσθαι καὶ τὸ εἶναι καὶ τὸ ποιὸν παρέχεσθαι ἐπὶ τῆς ποιότητος θεωρεῖται· εἶδος γάρ ἐστιν ἡ ποιότης τοῦ ἔχοντος. ὁ τοίνυν διὰ τοῦ ποιοῦ τὴν ποιότητα ἀποδιδοὺς τὴν κυριωτάτην ἰδιότητα αὐτῆς χαρακτηρίζει καὶ ὁμοῦ τίς τέ ἐστιν καὶ τίνα παρέχεται τὴν ἀπεργασίαν ἐν τοῖς οὖσι παρίστησιν. Transl.: Fleet.
15 For a more extensive discussion of this passage and of the relation between quality and the qualified in terms of μετεχόμενον and μετέχον, see Hauer (2016).

as form is to matter. Quality, therefore, is not a substantial form, but it is still formal. It becomes apparent that the understanding and the analysis of quality as μετεχόμενον has turned quality into a formally structuring and, thus, metaphysically relevant entity.

Interestingly, in Stoicism, quality represents a structuring, (meta)physical principle. Several scholars have pointed out that there is a functional similarity between the Stoic notion of quality and immanent form; more precisely, they have pointed out that quality functions analogously to immanent form.[16] In Stoic physics the basic constituents of beings are matter (ἡ ὕλη) and a rational, divine principle (ὁ λόγος). Both are bodily, indestructible and, *qua* basic constituents, mixed; more precisely, the rational principle pervades matter and gives it shape.[17] These two principles are the constituents of the four elements, which in turn constitute all sensible entities. Accounts and descriptions of sensible entities often present them as compounds, or mixtures, of matter and πνεῦμα.[18] This πνεῦμα is presented as being itself constituted by some of the elements, but it is also associated with the divine principle, especially on the explanatory level of sensible bodies.[19] Quality is associated with the πνεῦμα that together with matter forms an individual sensible entity, that is, a qualified.[20] It thus represents a formative

---

16 See, e.g., Brunschwig (1988); Graeser (1972), 87–100, esp. 95; Kupreeva (2003), esp. 299. One may extend the claim to transcendent forms, see, e.g., de Harven (2022), 221. The similarity, of course, is limited to the function, for, as it is well known, the Stoics reject both transcendent and immanent forms.
17 See, e.g., Diog. Laert. 7.134 (LS 44B), Chalcid., *In Tim.* 293 (LS 44E), Euseb., *Praep. evang.* 15.14.1 (SVF 1.98, LS 45G), Alex., *De mixt.* 225.1–3 (SVF 2.310, LS 45H).
18 On the different senses of matter (i.e., matter at the level of the ultimate, indestructible, principles of things, that is, a sort of prime matter, and matter at the level of constituents of sensible entities, that is, a sort of shaped matter) and on the different names and manifestations of the divine principle, both linked to the different explanatory levels, see, e.g., Long (1982), 37; Gourinat (2009); or, recently, de Harven (2022).
19 See, e.g., Galen, *De plac.* 5.3.8 (SVF 2.841, LS 47H), Aet. 1.7.33 (SVF 2.1027, LS 46A); Sedley (1999), 388–389; Gourinat (2009), 62. The πνεῦμα is the principle of coherence and unity in each single sensible entity. It manifests itself in different ways: in lifeless entities, it manifests itself as simple state (ἡ ἕξις; 'simple' because, in a sense, the πνεῦμα is also a state in its other manifestations); in plants, it manifests itself as nature (ἡ φύσις); and in animals and human beings, it manifests itself as soul (ἡ ψυχή), see, e.g., Plut., *De Stoic. rep.* 1053F–1054B (SVF 2.449, LS 47M), Origen, *De princ.* 3.1.2–3 (SVF 2.988, LS 53A). See Long/Sedley (1987), vol. 1, 288–289; Long (1982), 38; Sedley (1999), 389–390; or, recently, Helle (2021), esp. 178–179.
20 The assumption that πνεῦμα is, in a sense, a state in each of its manifestations facilitates Simplicius' discussion of Stoic views and their integration into his commentary on chapter eight of the *Categories*: for, in the context of chapter eight, states belong to the first kind of quality. Moreover, the πνεῦμα is presented as shaping and forming, or qualifying, the matter together with which it constitutes an individual sensible entity, that is, a qualified: see, e.g., Gourinat (2009), 57; Helle (2021), 182–200. Now one may raise the question of how πνεῦμα and quality, or qualities, relate exactly to each other. See on this question, e.g., Sedley (1999), 402, 407; de Harven (2022), 235 n. 32; Helle (2021), 182–200.

or structuring principle with respect to sensible beings. The structure of this formative principle is, of course, very different from the Platonic or Aristotelian theory insofar as, for example, the Stoics conceived of it as being corporeal. However, although they are structured differently, they function similarly. Quality, according to the Stoic conception, contributes decisively to what and how the qualified is. In this respect, quality can be set in parallel with a formative principle, such as immanent form. It is this position and function of quality in Stoic thought that might have been of interest to Simplicius; or, at least, these aspects might contribute to an explanation of why Simplicius discusses, or integrates, Stoic views in his commentary on chapter eight of the *Categories*.

Another aspect that is structurally similar in Simplicius' text and Stoic fragments is the position of the qualified within their respective categorial schemes. A recurrent element in Simplicius' discussion of quality is the strong connection between quality and the qualified. This connection also becomes apparent in the passage quoted above which, as has been said, represents a response to an objection raised by Plotinus concerning the explanation of quality through the qualified (*In Cat.* 213.8–214.2). According to Simplicius, Plotinus objects that by explaining quality through the qualified no explanation of quality according to its proper account is given. In his response, Simplicius qualifies Plotinus' objection. He acknowledges that the objection would be legitimate if quality existed separately from the qualified. Simplicius, however, argues that, in the sensible realm, quality does not exist separately from the qualified. Rather, quality consists in being participated and it causes the being and predication of the qualified by means of its very existence. Hence, the explanation of quality through the qualified represents an explanation of quality according to its proper account. This characterization of quality and its relation to the qualified is strongly related to Simplicius' association of quality and qualified with items from the triad of participation, i.e., the association of quality with the μετεχόμενον and the association of the qualified with the μετέχον. Simplicius' assumption that there is a strong connection between quality and the qualified also becomes apparent in his discussion of the title of chapter eight of Aristotle's *Categories*. According to Simplicius, the original title of the chapter was not 'Concerning Quality' alone but 'Concerning the Qualified and Quality' (περὶ ποιοῦ καὶ ποιότητος, *In Cat.* 206.3–7; see also *In Cat.* 207.27–35). The discussion includes the question whether quality and the qualified fall into one category or whether they comprise two categories. Simplicius argues for the first option: 'the category of the Qualified and Quality is none the less a single category' (*In Cat.* 208.16–17).[21]

---

21 [...] καὶ οὕτως οὐδὲν ἧττον μία ἔσται κατηγορία ἡ τοῦ ποιοῦ καὶ τῆς ποιότητος. Transl.: Fleet. Simplicius clearly denies that quality and the qualified constitute two categories. This denial appears to be chiefly motivated by his assumption that the number of categories presented by Aristotle is to be confirmed. It also appears to be related to his assumption that the qualified is a paronym of quality and that paronyms usually fall into the same category as that of which they are the paronym (see Simpl., *In Cat.* 38.7–9, see also *In Cat.* 19.13–14 and 65.2–13). However,

Interestingly, in the Stoic categorial scheme (also if we take its modifications over the years into account), it is, strictly speaking, the qualified (and not quality) that represents one of the Stoic categories. Presumably from Chrysippus onward, the Stoic categorial scheme consisted of four categories – ὑποκείμενον (substrate/substance), ποιόν (qualified), πως ἔχον (disposed) and πρός τί πως ἔχον (relatively disposed).²² The second category, the qualified, is usually conceived of as referring to qualified substances, i.e. sensible entities that have certain qualities.²³ This assumption, as well as a look at the four Stoic categories in general, suggests that the Stoic categories are concrete rather than abstract or, to use Stephen Menn's formulation, that '[the Stoic categories] are kinds of F rather than of F-ness'.²⁴ So it is the qualified 'white' rather than the quality 'whiteness' that falls into the second category. This concreteness is, among other aspects, one of the reasons why contemporary scholars have questioned whether and, if so, to what extent the Stoic categorial scheme can actually be compared to the Aristotelian categorial scheme. Already Samuel Sambursky had emphasized that the Aristotelian scheme represents a horizontal classification whereas the Stoic scheme represents a vertical classification – 'according to [this vertical classification] every object is determined by four successive steps of increasing

---

it is worth noting that 'the qualified' can refer to different groups of entities in Simplicius, such as paronyms that involve qualities, e.g., the brave and the grammarian, and to instantiations of qualities. While Simplicius' assumption that 'the qualified' falls under 'quality' is unproblematic if 'the qualified' is understood as an instantiation of quality, it appears to be problematic if 'the qualified' is understood as a qualified substance, such as the grammarian. Simplicius is aware of this problem (see Simpl., In Cat. 207.28–208.20). The reason why the latter is included in the discussion of the category of quality appears to be that it is in virtue of, or in accordance with, a quality that a thing is called qualified. It is in respect of its being qualified through its participation in a quality that the qualified entity is relevant for a discussion of quality.

22 See, e.g., Plut., De comm. not. 1083A–1084A (LS 28A), Plot., Enn. VI.1 [42], 25.1–5 (SVF 2.371), Simpl., In Cat. 66.32–37 (quoted below; SVF 2.369, LS 27F). For the assumption that the fourfold scheme presumably originates with Chrysippus, see Alesse (2008), 135; Brunschwig (2003), 228; Isnardi Parente (1986), 4–7; Long/Sedley (1987), vol. 1, 165–166; Menn (1999), 227; Reesor (1954), 44–45; Sedley (1982), 259 and n. 21. For attempts to reconstruct the development of the Stoic categorial scheme, see Alesse (2008), 134–135; Long/Sedley (1987), vol. 1, 165–166 and 172–179; Menn (1999), 227–242.

23 In presentations of the qualified, one can often find the distinction between being individually qualified (ἰδίως ποιόν) and being commonly qualified (κοινῶς ποιόν) and, correspondingly, between an individual quality (ἰδία ποιότης) and a common quality (κοινὴ ποιότης): see, e.g., Syrian., In Met. 28.18–19 (SVF 2.398, LS 28G), Dex., In Cat. 23.25–30 (SVF 2.374), Simpl., In Cat. 48.11–16 (LS 28E). For further discussion, see Menn (1999), 221–222; Rist (1969), 160–167; Reesor (1972); Long/Sedley (1987), vol. 1, 173–174; Sedley (1999), 402–406; Duhot (1991), 229–232; Graeser (1972), 87–100, esp. 94–97; de Harven (2022), 234–241. For this distinction and further analysis of both being individually qualified and being commonly qualified, see also the debate among scholars on the Stoic criterion of identity and individuation, e.g., Sedley (1982); Sedley (2018); Nawar (2017); Byers (2017); Irwin (1996); Lewis (1995).

24 Menn (1999), 217.

specification such that every category includes the preceding one'.²⁵ Moreover, contrary to the Aristotelian scheme, the four Stoic categories can be subsumed under a higher genus, i.e., the something (τί).²⁶ Besides the structural differences between the two categorial schemes, it is even contested whether the Stoic categories should be called categories at all, for there is neither any textual evidence that Stoic philosophers conceived of this fourfold distinction as a categorial distinction nor that they called the four classes 'categories'.²⁷ However, contested as the denotation and the comparability of the Stoic scheme with the Aristotelian scheme may be nowadays, there is no doubt that Simplicius did not contest either the denotation or the comparability. Simplicius does not only know about the four Stoic categories, but also thinks that they are in competition with the Aristotelian categories:

> For their part, the Stoics think that the number of primary genera should be reduced to a smaller one, and within this smaller plurality they made some substitutions. For they cut them into four: substrates, qualifieds, 'things disposed in a certain way', and 'things disposed in a certain way relative to something'. (*In Cat.* 66.32–67.2.)²⁸

As we can see, Simplicius refers to the Stoic categories as the primary, or highest, genera – as he also does with regard to the Aristotelian categories²⁹ – and by saying that the Stoics reduced the number of categories and adopted some in altered form, Simplicius clearly presents the Stoic categorial scheme as a modification

---

25 Sambursky (1959), 17. See, however, Rieth (1933), 190–191; Rist (1969), 171–172. Cf. Plut., *De comm. not.* 1083E7–8 (LS 28A6): ἐπεὶ τέσσαρά γε ποιοῦσιν ὑποκείμενα περὶ ἕκαστον, μᾶλλον δὲ τέσσαρ' ἕκαστον ἡμῶν· For the differences between the Aristotelian categorial scheme and the Stoic categorial scheme, see also, e.g., Duhot (1991) and de Harven (2022).

26 See, e.g., Alex., *In Top.* 301.19–25 (SVF 2.329, LS 27B), Sext. Emp., *Adv. math.* 10.218 (SVF 2.331, LS 27D), Sen., *Ep.* 58.13–15 (SVF 2.332, LS 27A), Plot., *Enn.* VI.1 [42] 25, 1–7 (SVF 2.371). See Brunschwig (2003), 220–227; Brunschwig (1988); Long/Sedley (1987), vol. 1, 162–164; Sambursky (1959), 17.

27 See, e.g., Brunschwig (2003), 227; Duhot (1991); Long/Sedley (1987), vol. 1, 165–166; Sandbach (1985), 40–42; Sedley (1982), 259; Sedley (1999), 406–410; de Harven (2022), 220 n. 3. But see also Menn (1999), 215; Rieth (1933), 191.

28 Οἱ δέ γε Στωικοὶ εἰς ἐλάττονα συστέλλειν ἀξιοῦσιν τὸν τῶν πρώτων γενῶν ἀριθμὸν καί τινα ἐν τοῖς ἐλάττοσιν ὑπηλλαγμένα παραλαμβάνουσιν. ποιοῦνται γὰρ τὴν τομὴν εἰς τέσσαρα, εἰς ὑποκείμενα καὶ ποιὰ καὶ πῶς ἔχοντα καὶ πρός τί πως ἔχοντα. Transl.: Chase, slightly modified.

29 See, e.g., Simpl., *In Cat.* 211.5–15. In conceiving of Aristotle's categories as the highest genera in the sensible world, Simplicius is following his Neoplatonic predecessors: see, e.g., Porph., *In Cat.* 86.10–14; *Isag.* 6.6–9; Dex., *In Cat.* 39.6–15; Amm., *In Cat.* 20.14–17; 44.8–10; 84.16–17. Within the Neoplatonic school, this understanding presumably goes back to Plot., *Enn.* VI.1 [42]–VI.3 [44]. Simplicius, however, is keen to show that this understanding is not restricted to Platonic philosophers and states that, e.g., Alexander of Aphrodisias conceived of the Aristotelian categories as the highest genera as well (see Simpl., *In Cat.* 10.8–19).

THE USE OF STOIC REFERENCES IN SIMPLICIUS' DISCUSSION OF QUALITY   179

of the Aristotelian one.[30] The assumption that the Stoic categorial scheme is an alternative yet comparable model to the Aristotelian categorial scheme is already present in texts by Simplicius' Neoplatonic predecessors and presumably goes back to Plotinus' critical discussion in the *Enneads*.[31]

Simplicius' criticism of the Stoic notion of quality

Regarding Simplicius' criticism of the Stoic notion of quality, I will, again, focus on two aspects – two aspects that will show that the Stoic conception of quality was ultimately unacceptable for Simplicius. The two aspects are the Stoic assumption that there are qualifieds without corresponding qualities, on the one hand, and the assumption that qualities are corporeal, on the other. According to Simplicius, some Stoics assume a threefold division of the qualified:

> Some of the Stoics define the qualified in three ways; they say that two of the meanings cover a wider field than quality, and that one of them, or part of one of them, matches it. For they say that according to one meaning everything that is differentiated is qualified, whether it is changing or in a condition, and whether it is hard or easy to remove. In this sense not only the prudent man and the man holding out his fist, but also the man running are qualified. There is another sense, in which they no longer included changes but only conditions, and which they also defined as that which is in a differentiated condition, for example the prudent man and the man who is on his guard. They introduced a third and most specific sense of qualified, in which they no longer included those in non-abiding conditions, and in which the man holding out his fist and the man on his guard were not qualified. Of those who are in an abiding differentiated condition, some are so in matching their expression and conception, others are not so – and these they rejected, while those matching and in abiding differentiated [conditions], they said were qualified. 'Matching the expression': they meant those that have the same range as the quality, like the grammarian or the prudent man; for each of these

---

30 Simplicius presents at length the discussions by previous philosophers concerning the correct number of categories (see Simpl., *In Cat.* 62.17–68.31). He defends Aristotle's tenfold division against several critics who assume the number to be greater or smaller, and he discusses schemes that differ from Aristotle's, e.g., the Stoic scheme. While Simplicius raises objections against their 'being disposed', he does not criticize the first two items of the Stoic scheme (see Simpl., *In Cat.* 67.2–8). Moreover, it is worth noting that towards the end of his overview of the discussions of, objections against and alternatives to Aristotle's categorial scheme, Simplicius states that the Stoic scheme appears to be more accurate than other divisions; see Simpl., *In Cat.* 67.15–18: τρίτον δὲ ἂν λέγοιμεν ὅτι καὶ πάντες οἱ ἄλλως διελόμενοι μείζοσιν ἂν ὑπάγοιντο τοῖς ἐγκλήμασιν, ὧν οἱ ἀκριβέστεροι δοκοῦντες οἱ Στωικοὶ τὴν εἰς τέσσαρα τομὴν ποιησάμενοι εἰς ὑποκείμενα καὶ ποιὰ καὶ πῶς ἔχοντα καὶ πρός τί πως ἔχοντα […].
31 See Plot., *Enn.* VI.1 [42], 25–30; see also Dex., *In Cat.* 34, 19–24.

neither covers a wider field nor covers a smaller field than the quality. (*In Cat.* 212.12–28.)[32]

Simplicius states right at the beginning that two meanings of qualified are broader than quality, which leads to the assumption that there are qualifieds without corresponding qualities. The first and broadest sense of qualified includes all differentiated entities, whether they are undergoing change or are in a certain condition and whether they are enduring or not. The second meaning of qualified is not as broad as the first in that it only includes that which is in a certain differentiated condition. The second meaning, then, does not include that which is changing. The third meaning of qualified is narrower still: in contrast to the first and second meaning, the third only includes that which is in an enduring differentiated condition. It includes neither that which is changing (like the first meaning of qualified) nor that which is not in an enduring differentiated condition (like the first and the second meaning). Finally, Simplicius further distinguishes the entities that are in an enduring differentiated condition. These entities can be in an enduring differentiated condition either in a way that corresponds to their expression and conception or in a way that does not correspond to their expression and conception. As we learn, only those entities that are in an

---

32 τῶν δὲ Στωικῶν τινες τριχῶς τὸ ποιὸν ἀφοριζόμενοι τὰ μὲν δύο σημαινόμενα ἐπὶ πλέον τῆς ποιότητος λέγουσιν, τὸ δὲ ἓν ἤτοι τοῦ ἑνὸς μέρος συναπαρτίζειν αὐτῇ φασιν. λέγουσιν γὰρ ποιὸν καθ' ἓν μὲν σημαινόμενον πᾶν τὸ κατὰ διαφοράν, εἴτε κινούμενον εἴη εἴτε ἰσχόμενον καὶ εἴτε δυσαναλύτως εἴτε εὐαναλύτως ἔχει· κατὰ τοῦτο δὲ οὐ μόνον ὁ φρόνιμος καὶ ὁ πὺξ προτείνων, ἀλλὰ καὶ ὁ τρέχων ποιοί. καθ' ἕτερον δὲ καθ' ὃ οὐκέτι τὰς κινήσεις περιελάμβανον, ἀλλὰ μόνον τὰς σχέσεις, ὃ δὴ καὶ ὡρίζοντο τὸ ἰσχόμενον κατὰ διαφοράν, οἷός ἐστιν ὁ φρόνιμος καὶ ὁ προβεβλημένος. τρίτον δὲ εἰσῆγον εἰδικώτατον ποιὸν καθ' ὅτι οὐκέτι τοὺς μὴ ἐμμόνως ἰσχομένους περιελάμβανον οὐδὲ ἦσαν ποιοὶ κατ' αὐτοὺς ὁ πὺξ προτείνων καὶ ὁ προβεβλημένος· καὶ τούτων δὲ τῶν ἐμμόνως ἰσχομένων κατὰ διαφορὰν οἱ μὲν ἀπηρτισμένως κατὰ τὴν ἐκφορὰν αὐτῶν καὶ τὴν ἐπίνοιάν εἰσι τοιοῦτοι, οἱ δὲ οὐκ ἀπηρτισμένως, καὶ τούτους μὲν παρῃτοῦντο, τοὺς δὲ ἀπαρτίζοντας καὶ ἐμμόνους ὄντας κατὰ διαφορὰν ποιοὺς ἐτίθεντο. ἀπαρτίζειν δὲ κατὰ τὴν ἐκφορὰν ἔλεγον τοὺς τῇ ποιότητι συνεξισουμένους, ὡς τὸν γραμματικὸν καὶ τὸν φρόνιμον· οὔτε γὰρ πλεονάζει οὔτε ἐλλείπει τούτων ἑκάτερος παρὰ τὴν ποιότητα· Transl.: Fleet, modified. This passage has been discussed by several scholars with different results. For example, S. Menn argues that the threefold division presented by Simplicius is not a distinction within the second Stoic category but rather a distinction between the second and the third Stoic category. Menn concludes: 'It is, therefore, the *strictest* sense of ποιόν, the one corresponding to ποιότης, that is the second category as distinguished from the third' (Menn (1999), 223 n. 12). But see also Brunschwig (1988), 113–116; Duhot (1991), 229–231; Isnardi Parente (1986), 14–15; Reesor (1957), 74–75; Rieth (1933), 22–29. These discussions primarily focus on a reconstruction of Stoic philosophy; in other words, this passage in Simplicius primarily serves as a means to understand Stoic theorems. As I rather wish to focus on Simplicius and, more precisely, on the nature and purpose of Simplicius' presentation of Stoic views, I will not go into detail regarding these discussions. For the present purposes, we only need to concern ourselves with the perhaps less controversial (and for scholars of Stoic philosophy perhaps also less interesting) fact that, according to Simplicius, some Stoics assume that there are qualifieds without corresponding qualities.

enduring differentiated condition in a way that corresponds to their expression and conception are qualified in the narrowest meaning of qualified. According to Simplicius, these Stoic philosophers conceived of the entities that are included in the narrowest meaning of qualified as those qualifieds that are commensurate with quality, i.e., that are neither broader nor narrower than the corresponding quality. After his presentation of the Stoic doctrine, Simplicius turns to his own interpretation of the relation between quality and the qualified, or rather to what he regards as being Aristotle's view of it. He says:

> But if the quality attains existence by being participated in, and the qualified by participating, and if both of them are in us because of one and the same fact (and neither both outside, nor one inside us and one outside), it is clear that they are on a par according to their being, and there is no need of any device of 'meanings' or any addition of parts in order that the third meaning of the qualified should be co-extensive with the quality (*In Cat.* 213.1–6).[33]

This statement is very similar to the description of the relation between quality and qualified in the first text quoted above. Simplicius again emphasizes the association of quality with the μετεχόμενον and the association of the qualified with the μετέχον. Furthermore, if we take into account that these associations – as Simplicius frequently states – entail a causal priority of the quality over the qualified, it is no surprise that, against the background of his own account, the assumption that there might be qualifieds without corresponding qualities is unacceptable, just as the Stoic division of meanings of the qualified is unnecessary for Simplicius.

The second aspect of the Stoic conception of quality which Simplicius criticizes several times in his *Commentary on Aristotle's Categories* is the assumption that qualities are corporeal. The Stoics generally assumed that only bodies can act or be acted upon and, consequently, that only bodies can act as causes.[34] The reasoning behind this assumption appears to be as follows: every cause affects or produces; but all affecting or producing occurs through contact, and only bodies can be in contact.[35] Since being-in-something also requires contact, and only bodies can be in contact, only bodies can be in something. The assumption that qualities are corporeal and the assumption that there are qualifieds without

---

33 ἀλλ' εἰ ἐν τῷ μετέχεσθαι ἡ ποιότης συνυφίσταται καὶ ἐν τῷ μετέχειν τὸ ποιόν, ἑνὶ δὲ καὶ τῷ αὐτῷ ταῦτά ἐστιν ἀμφότερα ἐν ἡμῖν καὶ οὔτε τὰ δύο ἐκτὸς οὔτε τὸ μὲν ἐκτός, τὸ δὲ ἐν ἡμῖν, δῆλον ὡς συνεξισάζει κατ' αὐτὴν τὴν οὐσίαν, καὶ οὐδὲν δεῖ μηχανῆς τινος σημαινομένων ἢ μορίων προσθήκης, ἵνα τὸ τρίτον σημαινόμενον τοῦ ποιοῦ συναπαρτίζηται πρὸς τὴν ποιότητα. Transl.: Fleet, slightly modified.
34 See, e.g., Cic., *Acad.* 1.39 (SVF 1.90, LS 45A), Nem., *De nat. hom.* 78.7–79.2 (SVF 1.518, LS 45C), Sext. Emp., *Adv. math.* 8.263 (SVF 2.363, LS 45B). For a discussion of this claim and related assumptions against the background of Plato's *Sophist*, see, e.g., Brunschwig (1988); Long/Sedley (1987), vol. 1, 274 and vol. 2, 269, 45h; de Harven (2022).
35 See, e.g., Kupreeva (2003), 300–306; Long/Sedley (1987), vol. 1, 272–274; Menn (1999), 219–220; Reesor (1954), 42–43.

corresponding qualities are connected. Simplicius discusses this connection as follows:

> The Stoics too according to their own assumptions would raise the same difficulty against the argument which states that all qualifieds are spoken of in terms of a quality. They say that qualities are 'havables', and allow 'havables' only in the case of things that are unified, while in the case of things that exist by contact, like a ship, or in a disjoint manner, like an army, [they say] there is not one thing that is 'havable', and that not a single [instance] of spirit is found in their case, nor anything possessing a single logos such as to achieve the existence of a single state. The qualified, however, can be seen in things which exist by contact and by being disjoint; for just as a single grammarian is abidingly differentiated as a result of a certain sort of acquisition of knowledge and exercise, so too a chorus is abidingly differentiated as a result of a certain sort of rehearsal. So they are qualified because of their arrangement and their co-operation towards a single function, but they are qualified without [possessing] a quality; for there is no state in them; for in general no quality or state is to be found in substances which are disjoint and have no connate unity with each other. But if there can be something qualified without there being a quality, these [two] things are not co-extensive, they would claim, nor is it possible to define the quality through what is qualified.
> In reply it can be said that the form, being bodiless, extends over many as one and the same, the same being present as a whole throughout. If this is so, there will be a single quality which pervades disjoint and touching qualifieds. (*In Cat.* 214.24–215.5.)[36]

---

36 καὶ οἱ Στωικοὶ δὲ κατὰ τὰς αὐτῶν ὑποθέσεις τὴν αὐτὴν ἂν ἀπορίαν προσαγάγοιεν τῷ λέγοντι λόγῳ κατὰ ποιότητα πάντα τὰ ποιὰ λέγεσθαι. τὰς γὰρ ποιότητας ἑκτὰ λέγοντες οὗτοι ἐπὶ τῶν ἡνωμένων μόνων τὰ ἑκτὰ ἀπολείπουσιν, ἐπὶ δὲ τῶν κατὰ συναφὴν οἷον νεὼς καὶ ἐπὶ τῶν κατὰ διάστασιν οἷον στρατοῦ μηδὲν εἶναι ἑκτὸν μηδὲ εὑρίσκεσθαι πνευματικόν τι ἓν ἐπ' αὐτῶν μηδὲ ἕνα λόγον ἔχον, ὥστε ἐπί τινα ὑπόστασιν ἐλθεῖν μιᾶς ἕξεως. τὸ δὲ ποιὸν καὶ ἐν τοῖς ἐκ συναπτομένων θεωρεῖται καὶ ἐν τοῖς ἐκ διεστώτων· ὡς γὰρ εἷς γραμματικὸς ἐκ ποιᾶς ἀναλήψεως καὶ συγγυμνασίας ἐμμόνως ἔχει κατὰ διαφοράν, οὕτως καὶ ὁ χορὸς ἐκ ποιᾶς μελέτης ἐμμόνως ἔχει κατὰ διαφοράν. διὸ ποιὰ μὲν ὑπάρχει διὰ τὴν κατάταξιν καὶ τὴν πρὸς ἓν ἔργον συνεργίαν, δίχα δὲ ποιότητός ἐστιν ποιά· ἕξις γὰρ ἐν τούτοις οὐκ ἔστιν· οὐδὲ γὰρ ὅλως ἐν διεστώσαις οὐσίαις καὶ μηδεμίαν ἐχούσαις συμφυῆ πρὸς ἀλλήλας ἕνωσίν ἐστιν ποιότης ἢ ἕξις. εἰ δὲ ποιοῦ ὄντος οὐκ ἔστιν ποιότης, οὐ συναπαρτίζει ταῦτα ἀλλήλοις, φαῖεν ἄν, οὐδὲ δυνατόν ἐστιν διὰ τοῦ ποιοῦ τὴν ποιότητα ἀποδίδοσθαι. πρὸς δὲ ταῦτα δυνατὸν μὲν λέγειν ὡς ἀσώματον ὂν τὸ εἶδος ἓν καὶ τὸ αὐτὸ διατείνει ἐπὶ πολλοῖς, πανταχοῦ τὸ αὐτὸ ὑπάρχον ὅλον· εἰ δὲ τοῦτο, ἔσται καὶ ποιότης μία διήκουσα διὰ τῶν [συν]διεστηκότων καὶ συναπτομένων ποιῶν. Transl.: Fleet, modified. For a discussion of unified and non-unified bodies in Stoic philosophy, see, e.g., Reesor (1954), 54–56; Long (1982), 37–39 (Long's presentation is not based on this passage from Simplicius but, among other passages, on one from Plutarch: see Plut., *Con. praec.* 142E12–F3, which includes the distinction between unified bodies, bodies with conjoined parts and bodies with separate parts, as well as the example of the ship for the second kind and the example of the army for the third one); Helle (2021). For further discussion of the notion of ἕξις, in its Stoic usage, see also Brunschwig (1988), 116–118;

Simplicius informs us that the Stoics restrict qualities to things that are unified. This assumption is not very controversial per se. Simplicius, too, restricts qualities to things that have a natural unity. However, since the Stoics conceive of qualities as corporeals that, in turn, constitute a part of the qualified, they deny the ascription of qualities to things that exist by contact, like a ship, and to things that exist in a disjoint manner, like an army or a chorus. Simplicius refers to the fundamental ontological assumptions of Stoicism when he says that the denial of quality in those cases is based on the lack of a single instance of πνεῦμα in things that exist by contact or in a disjoint manner. As has been mentioned in the first part of this chapter, the Stoics associate quality with the πνεῦμα which, together with matter, forms the qualified. Stoic πνεῦμα is an active, causal principle, and thus corporeal. However, according to Simplicius, the Stoics acknowledge that there is something qualified in things which exist by contact or in a disjoint manner, as becomes obvious from the example of the chorus. This acknowledgment, in turn, leads to the assumption that there are qualifieds without corresponding qualities. It is worth noting that, towards the end of the passage, Simplicius spells out the consequences of the assumption that there are qualifieds without corresponding qualities. If there were qualifieds without corresponding qualities, the ontological and causal link between quality and qualified would be much weaker than Simplicius thinks it is: the qualified would not be commensurate with the quality, and a recourse to the qualified would not contribute to an explanation of quality. It becomes apparent that these consequences represent a denial of two assumptions that Simplicius holds in his commentary on chapter eight of the *Categories*.[37]

At the end of the passage, Simplicius offers his solution – or the solution he ascribes to Aristotle – to the question of how to explain qualifieds that exist by contact or in a disjoint manner. If one adopts an incorporeal conception of the formal principle and, consequently, of quality, the fact that things which exist by contact or in a disjoint manner are qualified can be explained by resorting to the corresponding quality. In presenting this solution, which represents Aristotle's conception of quality as conceived of by Simplicius, and by means of which it is possible to explain something that cannot be explained through the Stoic conception of quality, Simplicius shows, or at least suggests, that his model is superior to that of the Stoics because it has greater explanatory power.

Duhot (1991), 228–232; Isnardi Parente (1986), 12–15; Long/Sedley (1987), vol. 1, 285–289; Rieth (1933), 92–133. See also notes 19 and 20 above.
37 See, especially, the first text quoted above (Simpl., *In Cat.* 213.29–214.2), in which both assumptions are stated.

Conclusion

The starting point of this small investigation was the striking frequency and the nature of references to Stoic positions in chapter eight of Simplicius' *Commentary on Aristotle's Categories*. By means of (only a few) examples, I have tried to show that the nature of these references, as well as the historical and scholarly context, suggests that those references and their discussions do not merely serve polemical purposes, but indicate that Simplicius deals with the Stoic model in a constructive manner. In following his predecessors, Simplicius conceives of the Stoic categorial scheme as an alternative yet comparable model to the Aristotelian scheme. It appears that the Stoic model included elements that were unproblematic or even appealing to Simplicius, but it also becomes clear that Simplicius ultimately regards the Stoic model as being inferior to the Aristotelian one. The importance of quality in the Stoic model and the connection between quality and the qualified may have been appealing to Simplicius as both features were also part of his own interpretation of quality. It is interesting that these two aspects receive no criticism from Simplicius throughout chapter eight; in other words, Simplicius does not criticize the Stoics for attributing a formative function to quality or for talking about the qualified rather than about quality in the context of the Stoic categorial scheme.

Simplicius' rejection of other features of the Stoic conception of quality, such as the Stoic assumptions that qualities are corporeal and that there are qualifieds without corresponding qualities, shows that the Stoic model is, after all, unacceptable for Simplicius. It is interesting that his criticism centers on a lack of explanatory power; in other words, he tries to show that the model falls short of providing a strong means of explanation. In contrasting the Stoic model with the Aristotelian one and in pointing to the strength of the latter to explain elements that the former cannot explain, Simplicius emphasizes the explanatory superiority of the Aristotelian model over the Stoic one. This, in turn, represents a powerful means for Simplicius to strengthen his overall account of quality.

Bibliography

Adamik, T. (2001), 'Flagitia Christianorum', *Wiener Studien* 114, 397–404.

Ahmed, L. (2017), *Bilder von den Anderen: Christliches Sprechen über Heiden bei den lateinischen Apologeten*, Münster: Aschendorff.

Aland, B. (2005), *Frühe direkte Auseinandersetzung zwischen Christen, Heiden und Häretikern*, Berlin–New York: De Gruyter.

Alesse, F. (2008), 'Alcuni aspetti del concetto stoico di sostanza e identità dell'individuo', *Chôra. Revue d'études anciennes et médiévales* 6, 127–142.

Alexander, L. (1994), 'Paul and the Hellenistic Schools: The Evidence of Galen', in T. Engberg-Pedersen (ed.), *Paul in his Hellenistic Context*, London–New York: T&T International, 60–83.

Ambury, J. M. and German, A. R. (eds) (2019), *Knowledge and ignorance of self in Platonic philosophy*, Cambridge: Cambridge University Press.

Andresen, C. (1955), *Nomos und Logos. Die Polemik des Kelsos wider das Christentum*, Berlin: De Gruyter.

Annas, J. (1985), 'Self-Knowledge in Early Plato', in D. J. O'Meara (ed.), *Platonic Investigations*, Washington: The Catholic University of America Press, 111–138.

Annecchino, M. (2011), 'La polemica nel *De errore profanarum religionum* di Firmico Materno', *Auctores nostri* 9, 341–358.

Aragione, G. (2007), 'Aspetti ideologici della nozione di plagio nell'Antichità classica e cristiana', in A. d'Anna and C. Zamagni (eds), *Cristianesimi nell'antichità: Fonti, istituzioni, ideologie a confronto*, Hildesheim: Olms, 1–15.

—— (2010), 'La transmission du savoir entre "tradition" et "plagiat"', in David Bouvier and Danielle van Mal-Maeder (eds), *Tradition classique: Dialogues avec l'Antiquité* (*Études de lettres* 285.1–2), Lausanne: Université de Lausanne, 117–138.

Armstrong, A. H. (1966), *Plotinus Enneads* II (LCL), Cambridge MA–London: Harvard University Press.

Arnim, H. von (1921–1924), *Stoicorum veterum fragmenta. 4 volumes*, Leipzig: Teubner (index vol. 4 by M. Adler). (= SVF)

Asmis, E. (2014), 'Galen's *De indolentia* and the Creation of a Personal Philosophy', in C. K. Rothschild and T. W. Thompson (eds), *Galen's De indolentia: Essays on a Newly Discovered Letter*, Tübingen: Mohr Siebeck, 127–142.

Attridge, H. W. (1976), 'The philosophical critique of religion under the early Empire', *ANRW* II 16.1, 45–78.

Aufrère, S. H. and Möri, F. (eds) (2016), *Alexandrie la divine. Sagesses barbares*, Genève: La Baconnière.

Baltes, M. (1976), *Die Weltentstehung des Platonischen Timaios nach den antiken Interpreten*, Bd. 1, Leiden: Brill.

―――― (1993), *Der Platonismus in der Antike. Grundlagen – System – Entwicklung*, Bd. 3: *Der Platonismus im 2. und 3. Jahrhundert nach Christus*, Stuttgart-Bad Cannstatt: frommann-holzboog.

―――― (1996), *Der Platonismus in der Antike. Grundlagen – System – Entwicklung*, Bd. 4: *Die philosophische Lehre des Platonismus. Einige grundlegende Axiome / Platonische Physik (im antiken Verständnis)* I, Stuttgart-Bad Cannstatt: frommann-holzboog.

―――― (1998), *Der Platonismus in der Antike. Grundlagen – System – Entwicklung*, Bd. 5: *Die philosophische Lehre des Platonismus. Platonische Physik (im antiken Verständnis)* II, Stuttgart-Bad Cannstatt: frommann-holzboog.

―――― (1999a), 'Zur Philosophie des Platonikers Attikos', in *ΔΙΑΝΟΗΜΑΤΑ. Kleine Schriften zu Platon und zum Platonismus*, Stuttgart-Leipzig: Teubner, 81–111.

―――― (1999b), 'Was ist antiker Platonismus?', in *ΔΙΑΝΟΗΜΑΤΑ. Kleine Schriften zu Platon und zum Platonismus*, Stuttgart-Leipzig: Teubner, 223–247.

Baltzly, D. (2014), 'Plato's Authority and the Formation of Textual Communities', *Classical Quarterly* 64.2, 793–807.

Barnard, L. W. (1990), 'L'intolleranza negli apologisti cristiani con speciale riguardo a Firmico Materno', *Cristianesimo nella Storia* 11, 505–521.

Barnes, J. (1991), 'Galen on Logic and Therapy', in F. Kudlien and R. Durling (eds), *Galen's Method of Healing. Proceedings of the 1982 Galen Symposium*, Leiden: Brill, 50–102.

―――― (1992), 'Metacommentary', *Oxford Studies in Ancient Philosophy* 10, 267–281.

―――― (2002), 'Galen, Christians, logic', in T. P. Wiseman (ed.), *Classics in Progress: Essays on ancient Greece and Rome*, Oxford: Clarendon Press, 399–417; repr. (2012) in J. Barnes, *Logical Matters. Essays in Ancient Philosophy II*, ed. M. Bonelli, Oxford: Clarendon Press, 1–21.

―――― (2003), *Porphyry: Introduction*, Translated with an Introduction and Commentary, Oxford: Oxford University Press.

Bastianini, G. and Sedley, D. (1995), *Commentarium in Platonis Theaetetum*, in AA.VV., *Corpus dei papiri filosofici greci e latini*, parte III: *Commentari*, Firenze: Olschki, 227–562.

Baudy, G. (1998), 'Ratio Physica. Von der apologetischen zur religionskritischen Allegorese', in E. Horn and M. Weinberg (eds), *Allegorie. Konfigurationen von Text, Bild und Lektüre*, Opladen/Wiesbaden: Westdeutscher Verlag, 251–260.

Bauer, J. B. (1989), 'Vidisti fratrem, vidisti dominumtuum (Agraphon 144 Resch und 126 Resch)', *Zeitschrift Für Kirchengeschichte* 100.1, 71–76.

Becker, M. (2016), *Porphyrios. 'Contra Christianos': Neue Sammlung der Fragmente, Testimonien und Dubia mit Einleitung, Übersetzung und Anmerkungen*, Berlin-Boston: De Gruyter.

Berg, B. van den (2004), 'Smoothing over the Differences: Proclus and Ammonius on Plato's *Cratylus* and Aristotle's *De Interpretatione*', in *Philosophy, Science and Exegesis in Greek, Arabic and Latin Commentaries* I (Supp. 83–81), P. Adamson et al. (eds), London: Institute for Classical Studies, 191–201.

Berg, B. van den (2008), *Proclus' Commentary on the Cratylus in Context: Ancient Theories of Language and Naming*, Leiden: Brill.

—— (2013a), 'Plotinus's Socratic Intellectualism', *Proceedings of the Boston Area Colloquium in Ancient Philosophy* 28, 217–231.

—— (2013b), Review of K. Corrigan, J. D. Turner (eds) (2012), *Religion and Philosophy in the Platonic and Neoplatonic Traditions: From Antiquity to the Early Medieval Period*, in *Bryn Mawr Classical Review* 2013.08.06.

Bernard, W. (1990), *Spätantike Dichtungstheorien. Untersuchungen zu Proklos, Herakleitos und Plutarch*, Stuttgart: Teubner.

Blank, D. (2007), 'The Life of Antiochus of Ascalon in Philodemus: History of the Academy and a Tale of Two Letters', *Zeitschrift für Papyrologie und Epigraphik* 162, 87–93.

Blomart, A. (2010), 'Les premiers chrétiens et Mithra, ou la rhétorique de l'exclusion', in C. Guittard (ed.), *Le monothéisme: Diversité, exclusivisme ou dialogue?*, Paris: Editions Non Lieu, 231–259.

Blumenthal, H. J. and Markus, R. A. (eds) (1981), *Neoplatonism and Early Christian Thought. Essays in honour of A. H. Armstrong*, London: Variorum Publications.

—— (1996), *Aristotle and Neoplatonism in Late Antiquity. Interpretations of the 'De anima'*, London: Duckworth.

Bodéüs, R. (2001), *Aristote. Catégories. Texte établi et traduit, avec introduction et notes*, Paris: Les Belles Lettres.

Bonazzi, M. (2003), *Academici e Platonici. Il dibattito antico sullo scetticismo di Platone*, Milano: Led.

—— (2012), 'Plutarch on the Difference between the Pyrrhonists and the Academics', *OSAPh* 43, 271–298.

—— (2013), 'Pythagoreanising Aristotle: Eudorus and the Systematisation of Platonism', in M. Schofield (ed.), *Aristotle, Plato, and Pythagoreanism in the First Century BC*, Cambridge: Cambridge University Press, 160–186.

—— (2015), *Il platonismo*, Torino: Einaudi.

—— and Helmig, C. (2007), *Platonic Stoicism – Stoic Platonism. The Dialogue between Platonism and Stoicism in Antiquity*, Leuven: Leuven University Press.

——, Levy, C. and Steel, C. (2007) (eds), *A Platonic Pythagoras. Platonism and Pythagoreanism in the Imperial Age*, Turnhout: Brepols.

Bonazzi, M. and Opsomer, J. (eds) (2009), *The origin of the Platonic system. Platonism of the Early Empire and their Philosophical Contexts*, Louvain–Namur–Paris. Walpole, MA: Peeters.

Borret, M. (1969), *Origène. Contre Celse. Tome IV (Livres VII et VIII). Introduction, texte critique, traduction et notes par M. Borret*, Paris: Éditions du Cerf.

Bossier, F. and Steel, C. (1972) (eds), 'Priscianus Lydus en de *In de Anima* van pseudo (?)-Simplicius', *Tijdschrift Voor Filosofie* 34.4, 761–822.

Boter, G. (1999), *The Encheiridion of Epictetus and its three Christian adaptations*, Leiden: Brill.

Boudon-Millot, V. (2012), *Galien de Pergame. Un médecin grec à Rome*, Paris: Les Belles Lettres.

―――― (2015), 'Le Moïse de Galien: une figure de l'irrationnel', in D. Aigle/F. Briquel-Chatonnet (eds), *Figures de Moïse*, Paris: Editions de Boccard, 133–144.

Boyancé, P. (1963), 'Cicéron et le Premier Alcibiade', *Revue des Études Latines* 41, 210–229.

Boys-Stones, G. (2001), *Post-Hellenistic Philosophy. A Study of its Development from the Stoics to Origen*, Oxford: Oxford University Press.

―――― (2018), *Platonist Philosophy 80 BC to AD 250. An Introduction and Collection of Sources in Translation*, Cambridge: Cambridge University Press.

Brenet, J.-B. (2003), *Transferts du sujet, la noétique d'Averroès selon Jean de Jandun*, Paris: Vrin.

Brennan, T. and Brittain, Ch., (2002), *Simplicius: On Epictetus Handbook 27–53* (Ancient Commentators on Aristotle), London: Duckworth.

Brisson, L. (1992), *Porphyre, La Vie de Plotin*, vol. II, Paris: Vrin.

Brittain, Ch. and Brennan, T. (2002), *Simplicius: On Epictetus Handbook 1–26* (Ancient Commentators on Aristotle), London: Duckworth.

Brouwer, R. (2013), *The Stoic Sage: The Early Stoics on Wisdom, Sagehood and Socrates*, Cambridge: Cambridge University Press.

―――― and Vimercati, E. (eds) (2020), *Fate, Providence and Free Will: Philosophy and Religion in Dialogue in the Early Imperial Age*, Leiden–Boston: Brill.

Brunschwig, J. (1988), 'La théorie stoïcienne du genre suprême et l'ontologie platonicienne', in J. Barnes and M. Mignucci (eds), *Matter and Metaphysics: Fourth Symposium Hellenisticum*, Naples: Bibliopolis, 19–127.

―――― (2003), 'Stoic Metaphysics', in B. Inwood (ed.), *The Cambridge Companion to the Stoics*, Cambridge: Cambridge University Press, 206–232.

Bryan, J., Wardy, R. and Warren, J. (eds) (2018), *Authors and Authorities in Ancient Philosophy*, Cambridge: Cambridge University Press.

Bouffartigue, J. and Patillon, M. (1979), *Porphyre, De l'abstinence. Vol. II, Livre II–III*, Paris: Belles Lettres

Busine, A. (2005), *Paroles d'Apollon: Pratiques et traditions oraculaires dans l'Antiquité tardive (IIe–VIe siècles)*, Leiden-Boston: Brill.

―――― (2009), 'De Porphyre à Franz Cumont: La construction des «religions orientales» de Firmicus Maternus', in C. Bonnet, V. Pirenne-Delforge and D. Praet (eds), *Les religions orientales dans le monde grec et romain: cent ans après Cumont (1906–2006): Bilan historique et historiographique. Colloque de Rome, 16–18 novembre 2006*, Brussels–Rome: Belgisch Historisch Instituut te Rome, 413–426.

Byers, S. (2017), 'Commentary on Nawar', *Proceedings of the Boston Area Colloquium in Ancient Philosophy* 32.1, 160–165.

Cain, A. (2013), 'The Greek *Historia monachorum in Aegypto* and Athanasius' *Life of Anthony*', *Vigiliae Christianae* 67, 349–363.

Cameron, A. (2002), 'Apologetics in the Roman Empire – a genre of intolerance?', in J.-M. Carrié and R. Lizzi Testa (eds), «*Humana sapit*»: *Études d'antiquité tardive offertes à Lellia Cracco Ruggini*, Turnhout: Brepols, 219–227.

Cardullo, R. L. (1993), 'Syrianus défenseur de Platon contre Aristote, selon le témoignage d'Asclépius (*Métaphysique* 433.9–436.6)', in M. Dixsaut (ed.), *Contre Platon I. Le platonisme dévoilé*, Paris: Vrin, 197–214.

——— (2002), 'Asclepio di Tralle: filosofo originale o mero redattore *apò phônês*', in M. Barbanti, G. R. Giardina, and P. Manganaro (eds), *Enôsis kai philia. Studi in onore di Francesco Romano*, Catania: CUECM, 495–514.

——— (2003), '"Come le frecce dei Traci…". Siriano contro Aristotele a proposito di due aporie di *Metafisica* B', in V. Celluprica (ed.), *Il libro B della Metafisica di Aristotele*, Naples: Bibliopolis, 159–225.

——— (2011), 'Creazionismo, eternalismo e causalità del primo principio. Platone, Aristotele e alcuni interpreti neoplatonici', *Documenti e studi della tradizione filosofica medievale* 22, 1–44.

——— (2012), *Asclepio di Tralle, Commentario al libro "Alpha meizon" (A) della "Metafisica" di Aristotele*, Rome: Bonanno.

Caston, V. (1997), 'Epiphenomenalisms, Ancient and Modern', *The Philosophical Review* 106, 309–363.

Centrone, B. (2012), 'L'esegesi del *Timeo* nell'Accademia antica', in F. Clelia and A. Ulacco (eds), *Il Timeo. Esegesi greche, arabe, latine*, Pisa: Plus, 57–80.

Chase, M. (2003), *Simplicius: On Aristotle Categories 1–4* (Ancient Commentators on Aristotle), London: Duckworth.

Chiaradonna, R. (2007), 'Platonismo e teoria della conoscenza stoica tra II e III secolo D.C.', in M. Bonazzi and Ch. Helmig (eds), *Platonic Stoicism-Stoic Platonism. The Dialogue between Platonism and Stoicism in Antiquity*, Leuven: Leuven University Press, 209–241.

——— (2009a), 'Autour d'Eudore. Les débuts de l'exégèse des *Catégories* dans le Moyen Platonisme', in M. Bonazzi and J. Opsomer (eds), *The Origin of the Platonic System: Platonisms of the Early Empire and their Philosophical Contexts*, Leuven: Peeters, 89–111.

——— (2009b), 'Le traité de Galien *Sur La Démonstration* et sa postérité tardo-antique', in R. Chiaradonna and F. Trabattoni (eds), *Physics and philosophy of nature in Greek Neoplatonism: proceedings of the European Science Foundation Exploratory Workshop (Il Ciocco, Castelvecchio Pascoli, June 22–24, 2006)*, Leiden-Boston: Brill, 43–76.

——— (2013), 'Platonist Approaches to Aristotle: From Antiochus of Ascalon to Eudorus of Alexandria (and Beyond)', in M. Schofield (ed.), *Aristotle, Plato and Pythagoreanism in the First Century BC*, Cambridge: Cambridge University Press, 28–52.

―― (2014), 'Tolleranza religiosa e neoplatonismo politico tra III e IV secolo', in A. Marcone, U. Roberto and I. Tantillo (eds), *Tolleranza religiosa in età tardoantica IV– V secolo: Atti delle giornate di studio sull'età tardoantica, Roma, 26–27 maggio 2013*, Cassino: Edizioni Università di Cassino, 37–80.

―― (2016), 'Porphyry and the Aristotelian Tradition', in Falcon (2016a), 321–340.

―― (2017), 'Théologie et époptique aristotéliciennes dans le médioplatonisme: La réception de *Métaphysique* Λ', in F. Baghdassarianm and G. Guyomarc'h (eds), *Réceptions de la théologie aristotélicienne. D'Aristote à Michel d'Ephèse*, Leuven: Peeters, 143–157.

―― (2019), 'The Pseudopythagorica and their Philosophical Background: A Discussion on Angela Ulacco, '*Pseudopythagorica Dorica*', *Mediterranea. International journal for the transfer of knowledge* 4, 221–238.

―― (2020a), 'Les mots et les choses', in Chiaradonna and Rashed (2020a), 81–119.

―― (2020b), 'La substance et la forme', in Chiaradonna and Rashed (2020a), 143–178.

―― and Rashed, M. (eds), (2020a), *Boéthos de Sidon: Exégète d'Aristote et Philosophe*, Berlin-Boston: de Gruyter.

――, (2020b), 'Introduction', in Chiaradonna and Rashed (2020a), 1–16.

Christes, J. (2006), 'Sieben Weise', in H. Cancik, H. Schneider and M. Landfester (eds), *Der Neue Pauly*, Brill Online Reference Works, <http://dx.doi.org/10.1163/1574-9347_dnp_e1112180>

Clarke, E. C. (1998), 'Communication, Human and Divine: Saloustios Reconsidered', *Phronesis* 43.4, 326-350.

Cook, J. G. (2004), *The Interpretation of the Old Testament in Greco-Roman Paganism*, Tübingen: Mohr Siebeck.

Corti, A. (2014), *L'Adversus Colotem di Plutarco. Storia di una polemica filosofica*, Leuven: Leuven University Press.

Courcelle, P. (1974), «*Connais-toi toi-même*» *de Socrate à S. Bernard*, Paris: Études Augustiniennes (3 vols).

Creed, J. L. (ed.) (1984), *Lactantius. De mortibus persecutorum* (Oxford Early Christian Texts 1), Oxford: Clarendon.

Crystal, I. M. (2002), *Self-Intellection and its Epistemological Origins in Ancient Greek Thought*, Aldershot: Ashgate.

D'Ancona Costa, C. (2000), 'Syrianus dans la tradition exégétique de la *Métaphysique* d'Aristote', in M.-O. Goulet-Cazé (ed.), *Le commentaire, entre tradition et innovation, Actes du colloque international de l'institut des traditions textuelles, Paris-Villejuif, 22–25 sept. 1999*, Paris: Vrin, 311–327.

―― (2005), 'Il neoplatonismo alessandrino: alcune linee della ricerca contemporanea', *Adamantius* 11, 9–38.

De Lacy, P. (1945), 'The Stoic Categories as Methodological Principles', *Transactions and Proceedings of the American Philological Association* 76, 246–263.

De Vita, M. C. (2011), *Giuliano imperatore filosofo neoplatonico*, Milan: Vita e Pensiero.

Des Places, E. (1971), Oracles Chaldaïques, *avec un choix de commentaires anciens. Texte établi et traduit*, Paris: Belles Lettres.

Deuse, W. (1983), *Untersuchungen zur mittelplatonischen und neuplatonischen Seelenlehre*, Wiesbaden: Steiner.

Dillon, J. (2009), *Iamblichi Chalcidensis in Platonis dialogos commentariorum fragmenta (Iamblichus: The Platonic Commentaries)*, Westbury: The Prometheus Trust.

—— (2011), 'The Ideas as Thoughts of God', *Études Platoniciennes* 8, 31–42.

Dodds, E. R. (2004), *Proclus: The Elements of Theology. A Revised Text with Translation, Introduction, and Commentary*, Oxford: Clarendon Press.

Donini, P. (1988), 'The history of the concept of eclecticism', in Long and Dillon (1988), 333–370.

Donini, P. L. (1982), *Le scuole l'anima l'impero: la filosofia antica da Antioco a Plotino*, Torino: Rosenberg & Sellier.

—— (1994), 'Testi e commenti, manuali e insegnamento: la forma sistematica e i metodi della filosofia in età postellenistica', *ANRW* II.36.7, Berlin–New York: De Gruyter, 5027–5100.

Dörrie, H. (1976), 'Der Platonismus in der Kultur- und Geistesgeschichte der frühen Kaiserzeit', in *Platonica Minora*, München: Fink, 166–210.

Drake, H. A. (1998), 'Firmicus Maternus and the Politics of Conversion', in G. Schmeling and J. D. Mikalson (eds), *Qui miscuit utile dulci: Festschrift Essays for Paul Lachlan MacKendrick*, Wauconsa, Ill.: Bolchazy-Carducci, 133–149.

Duhot, J.-J. (1991), 'Y-a-t-il des catégories stoïciennes?', *Revue Internationale de Philosophie* 45.178 (3), 220–244.

Edwards, M. (2000), *Neoplatonic Saints: The Lives of Plotinus and Proclus by their Students*, Liverpool: Liverpool University Press.

—— (2007), 'Socrates and the early Church', in M. Trapp (ed.), *Socrates from Antiquity to the Enlightenment*, London: Aldershot, 127–141.

Eijk, P. van der (2014), 'Galen and Early Christians on the Role of the Divine in the Causation and Treatment of Health and Disease', *Early Christianity* 5, 337–370.

Erler, M., Heßler, J. E. and Petrucci, F. M. (eds) (2021), *Authority and authoritative texts in the Platonist tradition*, Cambridge-New York: Cambridge University Press.

Eshleman, K. (2012), *The Social World of Intellectuals in the Roman Empire: Sophists, Philosophers and Christians*, Cambridge: Cambridge University Press.

Falcon, A. (ed.) (2016a), *Brill's Companion to the Reception of Aristotle in Antiquity*, Leiden-Boston: Brill.

—— (2016b), 'Aristotelianism in the First Century BC', in Falcon (2016a), 101–119.

Fédou, M. (1988), *Christianisme et religions païennes dans le* Contre Celse *d'Origène*, Paris: Beauchesne.

Ferrari, F. (2001), 'Struttura e funzione dell'esegesi testuale nel medioplatonismo: il caso del *Timeo*', *Athenaeum* 89, 525–574.

—— (2010), 'Esegesi, commento e sistema nel medioplatonismo', in A. Neschke-Hentschke (ed.), *Argumenta in dialogos Platonis, Teil 1: Platoninterpretation und ihre Hermeneutik von der Antike bis zum Beginn des 19. Jahrhunderts*, Basel: Schwabe, 51–76.

——— (2012a), 'Quando, come e perché nacque il platonismo', *Athenaeum* 100, 71–92.

——— (2012b), 'L'esegesi medioplatonica del *Timeo*: metodi, finalità, risultati', in F. Clelia and A. Ulacco (eds), *Il Timeo. Esegesi greche, arabe, latine*, Pisa: Plus, 81–131.

——— (2014a), 'Materia, movimento, anima e tempo prima della nascita dell'universo: Plutarco e Attico sulla cosmologia del *Timeo*', in E. Coda and C. Martini Bonadeo (eds), *De l'Antiquité tardive au Moyen Âge. Études de logique aristotélicienne et de philosophie grecque, syriaque, arabe et latine offertes à Henry Hugonnard-Roche*, Paris: Vrin, 255–276.

——— (2014b), 'Gott als Vater und Schöpfer. Zur Rezeption von *Timaios* 28c3–5 bei einigen Platonikern', in F. Albrecht and R. Feldmeier (eds), *The Divine Father. Religious and Philosophical Concepts of Divine Parenthood in Antiquity*, Leiden-Boston: Brill, 57–69.

——— (2014c), 'Le système des causes dans le platonisme moyen', in C. Natali and C. Viano (eds), *Aitia II. Avec ou sans Aristote. Le débat sur les causes à l'âge hellénistique et impérial*, Louvain-La-Neuve: Peeters, 185–205.

——— (2014d), 'Lucio Calveno Tauro e l'interpretazione didascalica della cosmogenesi del *Timeo*', in R. L. Cardullo and D. Iozzia (eds), *ΚΑΛΛΟΣ ΚΑΙ ΑΡΕΤΗ. Bellezza e virtù. Studi in onore di Maria Barbanti*, Roma–Acireale: Bonanno Editore, 321–333.

——— (2015), 'Metafisica e teologia nel medioplatonismo', *Rivista di Storia della Filosofia* 70, 321–337.

——— (2020), 'Il Bene e il demiurgo: identità o gerarchia? Il conflitto delle interpretazioni nel medioplatonismo', in M. L. Gatti and P. De Simone (eds), *Interpretare Platone. Studi di filosofia antica*, Milan: Vita & Pensiero, 239–261.

Festugière, A. J. (1971), *Études de philosophie grecque*, Paris: Vrin.

Fiedrowicz, M. (2005), *Apologie im frühen Christentum: Die Kontroverse um den christlichen Wahrheitsanspruch in den ersten Jahrhunderten*, 3., aktualisierte und erweiterte Auflage, Paderborn–München–Wien–Zürich: Schöningh.

Finamore, J. (2014), 'Iamblichus on Soul', in P. Remes and S. Slaveva Griffin (eds), *The Routledge Handbook of Neoplatonism*, London–New York: Routledge, 280–292.

Fleet, B. (2002), *Simplicius: On Aristotle's Categories 7–8* (Ancient Commentators on Aristotle), Ithaca, NY: Cornell University Press/London: Duckworth.

Flemming, R. (2017), 'Galen and the Christians: Texts and Authority in the Second Century AD', in J. Carleton and S. Lieu (eds), *Christianity in the Second Century*, Cambridge: Cambridge University Press, 171–187.

Frede, M. (1981), 'On Galen's Epistemology', in V. Nutton (ed.), *Galen: Problems and Prospects*. London: Wellcome Institute for the History of Medicine, 65–86 [repr. in *Essays in Ancient Philosophy*, Oxford: Oxford University Press, 1987, 279–298].

——— (1987), 'Numenius', *ANRW* II 36.2, 1034–1075.

——— (1999), 'Epilogue', in K. Algra *et al* (eds), *The Cambridge History of Hellenistic Philosophy*, Cambridge: Cambridge University Press, 771–791.

Fredouille, J.-C. (1981), 'Götzendienst', *Reallexikon für Antike und Christentum* XI, 828–895.

Frend, W. H. C. (1987), 'Prelude to the Great Persecution: The Propaganda War', *Journal of Ecclesiastical History* 38.1, 1–18.
Funke, H. (1981), 'Götterbild', *Reallexikon für Antike und Christentum* XI, 659–828.
Gamble, H. Y. (1979), 'Euhemerism and Christology in Origen, Contra Celsum III 22–43', *Vigiliae Christianae* 33.1, 12–19.
Gassman, M. P. (2020), *Worshippers of the Gods: Debating Paganism in the Fourth-Century Roman West*, Oxford-New York: Oxford University Press.
Gavray, M.-A. (2011), 'Confronter les idées: un exemple de conciliation litigieuse chez Simplicius', in P. d'Hoine and A. Michalewski (eds), *Études Platoniciennes* VIII, *Les Formes platoniciennes dans l'Antiquité tardive*, Paris: Les Belles Lettres, 145–160.
Gazziero, L. (2008), *Rationes ex machina: la micrologie à l'âge de l'industrie de l'argument*, Paris: Vrin.
Gero, S. (1990), 'Galen on Christians: A Reappraisal of the Arabic Evidence', *Orientalia christiana periodica*, 56, 371–411.
Gerson, L. P. (2005), *Aristotle and other Platonists*, Ithaca: Cornell University Press.
——— (2013), *From Plato to Platonism*, Ithaca: Cornell University Press.
——— (2016), 'Plotinus and the Platonic Response to Stoicism', in Sellars, J. (ed.), *The Routledge Handbook of the Stoic Tradition*, London-New York: Routledge, 44–55.
Gibbons, K. (2015), 'Moses, Statesman and Philosopher: The Philosophical Background of the Ideal of Assimilating to God and the Methodology of Clement of Alexandria's Stromateis 1', *Vigiliae Christianae* 69.2, 157–185.
——— (2017), *The Moral Psychology of Clement of Alexandria: Mosaic Philosophy*, Abingdon: Routledge.
Gill, C. (2007), 'Self-knowledge in Plato's *Alcibiades*', in S. Stern-Gillet and K. Corrigan (eds) *Reading Ancient Texts: Essays in Honour of Denis O'Brien*, Vol. 1, Leiden: Brill, 97–112.
Glucker, J. (1978), *Antiochus and the late Academy*, Göttingen: Vandenhoeck & Ruprecht.
Golitsis, P. (2016a), 'Simplicius and Philoponus on the authority of Aristotle' in Falcon (2016a), 419–438.
——— (2016b), 'John Philoponus on the third book of Aristotle's *De anima*, wrongly attributed to Stephanus', in *Aristotle Re-Interpreted: New Findings on Seven Hundred Years of the Ancient Commentators*, R. Sorabji (ed.), London: Bloomsbury.
Goulet, R. (1977), 'Porphyre et la datation de Moïse', *RHR* 192, 137–164.
——— (2001), *Études sur les Vies de philosophes de l'Antiquité tardive*: *Diogène Laërce, Porphyre de Tyr, Eunape de Sardes*, Paris: Vrin.
Gourinat, J.-P. (2009), 'The Stoics on Matter and Prime Matter: "Corporealism" and the Imprint of Plato's *Timaeus*', in R. Salles (ed.), *God and Cosmos in Stoicism*, Oxford: Oxford University Press, 46–70.
Graeser, A. (1972), *Plotinus and the Stoics: A Preliminary Study* (Philosophia Antiqua 22), Leiden: Brill.
——— (1978), 'The Stoic Categories', in J. Brunschwig (ed.), *Les stoïciens et leur logique. Actes du colloque de Chantilly, 18–22 septembre 1976*, Paris: Vrin, 199–221.

Graf, F. (1996), *Gottesnähe und Schadenzauber. Die Magie in der griechisch-römischen Antike*, München: Beck.

—— (2011), 'Myth in Christian Authors', in K. Dowden and N. Livingstone (eds), *A Companion to Greek mythology*, Malden, MA: Wiley-Blackwell, 319–338.

Granieri, R. (2021), 'Xenocrates and the Two-Category Scheme', *Apeiron* 54, 261–285.

Grant, R. M. (1983), 'Paul, Galen and Origenes', *The Journal of Theological Studies* 34, 533–536.

Greenwood, D. N. (2016), 'Myth in Christian Authors', *Ancient Philosophy* 36, 197–207.

Griffin, M. (2014), 'Pliable Platonism? Olympiodorus and the Profession of Philosophy in Sixth-Century Alexandria', in R. C. Fowler (ed.), *Plato in the Third Sophistic*, Boston-Berlin: De Gruyter, 73–97.

—— (2015), *Aristotle's Categories in the Early Roman Empire*, Oxford: Oxford University Press.

—— (2016), 'Why Philosophy Begins with the *Categories*: Perspectives from the 1st-century Greek Commentators', *Documenti e studi sulla tradizione filosofica medievale* 27, 19–42.

Guyomarc'h, G. (2015), *L'Unité de la métaphysique selon Alexandre d'Aphrodise*, Paris: Vrin.

Haas, F. A. J. de (2000), 'Recollection and Potentiality in Philoponus' in M. Kardaun and J. Spruyt (eds), *The Winged Chariot: Collected Essays on Plato and Platonism in Honour of L.M. de Rijk*, Leiden–Boston: Brill, 165–184.

Hadot, P. (1968), 'Philosophie, exégèse et contresens', *Akten des XIV. Internationalen Kongresses für Philosophie*, Wien, 333–339 [repr. 2010 in *Études de philosophie ancienne*, Paris: Les Belles Lettres, 3–11].

Hadot, I. (1978), *Le problème du néoplatonisme alexandrin. Hiéroclès et Simplicius*, Paris: Etudes augustiniennes.

Hadot, P. (1987), 'Théologie, exégèse, révélation: écriture dans la philosophie grecque', in M. Tardieu (ed.), *Les règles de l'interprétation*, Paris: Editions du CERF, 13–34.

Hadot, I. (1991), 'The Role of the Commentaries on Aristotle in the Teaching of Philosophy according to the Prefaces of the Neoplatonic Commentaries on the *Categories*', in H.-J. Blumenthal and H. Robinson (eds), *Aristotle and the Later Tradition: (Oxford Studies in Ancient Philosophy Suppl.)*, 175–190.

—— (1996), *Simplicius: Commentaire sur le Manuel d'Épictète. Introduction et édition critique du texte grec* (Philosophia Antiqua 66), Leiden–New York–Köln: Brill.

—— (2003), *Simplicius: Commentaire sur le Manuel d'Épictète. Chapitres I–XXIX.* 2nd ed., Paris: Les Belles Lettres.

—— (2014), *Le néoplatonicien Simplicius à la lumière des recherches contemporaines. Un bilan critique*, Sankt Augustin: Academia.

—— (2015), *Athenian and Alexandrian Neoplatonism and the Harmonization of Aristotle and Plato*, Leiden: Brill.

Hankinson, R. J. (1992), 'Galen's Philosophical Eclecticism', *ANRW* II 36.5, 3505–3522.

—— (1994), 'Galen's Concept of Scientific Progress', *ANRW* II 37.2, 1775–1789.

—— (1997), 'Natural criteria and the transparency of judgement. Antiochus, Philo and Galen on epistemological justification', in B. Inwood and J. Mansfeld (eds), *Assent and Argument. Studies in Cicero's Academic Books. Proceedings of the 7th Symposium Hellenisticum*, Leiden: Brill, 161–216.

—— (ed.) (2008), *The Cambridge Companion to Galen*. Cambridge: Cambridge University Press.

—— and Havrda, M., (eds) (2022), *Galen's Epistemology: Experience, Reason, and Method in Ancient Medicine*. Cambridge: Cambridge University Press.

Harnack, A. von (1916), *Porphyrius, »Gegen die Christen«, 15 Bücher. Zeugnisse, Fragmente, und Referate, Abhandlungen der königlich preussischen Akademie der Wissenschaften, philosophisch-historische Klasse*, Berlin: Georg Reimer.

Harven, V. de (2022), 'The Metaphysics of Stoic Corporealism', *Apeiron* 55.2, 219–245.

Hatzimichali, M. (2011), *Potamo of Alexandria and the emergence of eclecticism in late Hellenistic philosophy*, Cambridge: Cambridge University Press.

—— (2016), 'Andronicus of Rhodes and the Construction of the Aristotelian Corpus' in Falcon (2016a), 101–119.

Hauer, M. (2016), 'Simplicius on the relation between quality and qualified', *Méthexis* 28, 111–140.

Havrda, M. (2015), 'The Purpose of Galen's Treatise *On Demonstration*', *Early Science and Medicine* 20, 265–287.

—— (2020), 'Intellectual independence in Christian and medical discourse of the 2nd– 3rd centuries', in L. Ayres and H. Clifton Ward (eds), *The Rise of the Early Christian Intellectual* (Arbeiten zur Kirchengeschichte 139), Berlin: De Gruyter, 81–100.

Helle, R. (2021), 'Self-Causation and Unity in Stoicism', *Phronesis* 66.2, 178–213.

Helmig, Ch. (2012), *Forms and Concepts, Concept Formation in the Platonic tradition*, Berlin: De Gruyter.

Heuten G. (1938), *Julius Firmicus Maternus*, De errore profanarum religionum, *traduction nouvelle avec texte et commentaire* (Travaux de la Faculté de Philosophie et Lettres de l'Université de Bruxelles, t. VIII).

Hicks, R. D. (1907), *Aristotle, De Anima*, Cambridge: Cambridge University Press.

Hirsch-Luipold, R., Görgemanns, H. and von Albrecht, N. (eds) unter Mitarbeit von Thum, T. (2009), *Religiöse Philosophie und Philosophische Religion der frühen Kaiserzeit: literaturgeschichtliche Perspektiven*, Tübingen: Mohr Siebeck.

Hoek, A. van den (1988), *Clement of Alexandria and his use of Philo in the Stromateis: an early Christian reshaping of a Jewish model*, Leiden: Brill.

Hoffmann, Ph. (2014), 'Science théologique et foi selon le commentaire de Simplicius au *De Caelo* d'Aristote', in *De l'Antiquité tardive au Moyen Âge. Études de logique aristotélicienne et de philosophie grecque, syriaque, arabe et latine offertes à Henri Hugonnard-Roche*, Paris: Vrin, 277–363.

—— (2001), *Simplicius, Commentaire sur les Catégories d'Aristote: chapitres 2–4*, Paris: Les Belles Lettres.

―――― (2006), 'What was Commentary in Late Antiquity? The Example of the Neoplatonic Commentators', in M. L. Gill and P. Pellegrin (eds), *A Companion to Ancient Philosophy*, Oxford: Wiley-Blackwell, 597–622.

―――― (2012), 'Un grief antichrétien chez Proclus: l'ignorance en théologie', in A. Perrot (ed.), *Les chrétiens et l'hellénisme: identités religieuses et culture grecque dans l'Antiquité tardive*, Paris: Éditions Rue d'Ulm, 161–197.

Hoheisel, K. (1972), *Das Urteil über die nichtchristlichen Religionen im Traktat De errore profanarum religionum des Firmicus Maternus*, Diss. Bonn: Rheinische Friedrich-Wilhelms-Universität.

Hoine, P. d' (2016), 'Syrianus et Asclépius: deux réponses néoplatoniciennes au *De Ideis* d'Aristote', Colloque *Le traité perdu d'Aristote sur les Idées*, organisé par M. Crubellier et L. Gazziero, Univ. Lille 3, 16–17 juin 2016.

Hübner, W. (1997), '§ 515 Firmicus Maternus (Iulius Firmicus Maternus iunior). B. Das Werk. a. Astrologische Werke', in R. Herzog and P. L. Schmidt (eds), *Handbuch der lateinischen Literatur der Antike* IV, München: Beck, 85–88.

Igal, J. (1981), 'The Gnostics and "Ancient Philosophy" in Porphyry and Plotinus', in H. J. Blumenthal and R. A. Markus (eds), *Neoplatonism and Early Christian Thought. Essays in honour of A. H. Armstrong*, London: Variorum Publications, 138–149.

Irwin, T. H. (1996), 'Stoic Individuals', *Philosophical Perspectives* 10, 459–480.

Isnardi Parente, M. (1986), 'Simplicio, gli stoici e le categorie', *Rivista di storia della filosofia* 41.1, 3–18.

Itter, A. C. (2009), *Esoteric teaching in the* Stromateis *of Clement of Alexandria*, Leiden: Brill.

Jaulin, A. (2016), 'Contexte et développement du premier argument du «De Ideis»: le statut des formes', Colloque *Le traité perdu d'Aristote sur les Idées*, organisé par M. Crubellier et L. Gazziero, Univ. Lille 3, 16–17 juin 2016.

Johnson, A. P. (2010), 'Rethinking the Authenticity of Porphyry, *c. Christ.* fr. 1', *Studia Patristica* 46, 53–58.

Johnston, S. I. (2008), 'Animating Statues: A Case Study in Ritual', *Arethusa* 41.3, 445–478.

Jones, C. P. (2014), *Between Pagan and Christian*, Cambridge, MA: Harvard University Press.

Joosen, J. C. and Waszink, J. H. (1950), 'Allegorese', *Reallexikon für Antike und Christentum* I, 283–293.

Joosse, A. (2014), 'Dialectic and Who We Are in the *Alcibiades*', *Phronesis* 59, 1–21.

Jourdan, F. (2014a), 'Woher kommt das Übel? Platonische Psychogonie bei Plutarch', *Ploutarchos* 11, 87–122.

―――― (2014b), 'Materie und Seele in Numenios' Lehre vom Übel und Bösen', in F. Jourdan and R. Hirsch-Luipold (eds), *Die Wurzel allen Übels*, Tübingen: Mohr Siebeck, 133–210.

Kahlos, M. (2004), 'Incerti in between. Moments of transition and dialogue in Christian polemics in the fourth and fifth centuries', *La parola del passato* 59.1, 5–24.

―――― (2007), *Debate and Dialogue: Christian and Pagan Cultures c. 360–430*, Aldershot-Burlington: Ashgate.

―― (2009a), *Forbearance and compulsion: The Rhetoric of Religious Tolerance and Intolerance in Late Antiquity*, London: Duckworth.

―― (2009b), 'The Rhetoric of Tolerance and Intolerance: From Lactantius to Firmicus Maternus' in J. Ulrich, A.-C. Jacobsen and M. Kahlos (eds), *Continuity and Discontinuity in Early Christian Apologetics*, Frankfurt: Lang, 79–95.

―― (2011), 'The Shadow of the Shadow: Examining Fourth- and Fifth-Century Christian Depictions of Pagans', in M. Kahlos (ed.), *The Faces of the Other: Religious Rivalry and Ethnic Encounters in the Later Roman World*, Turnhout: Brepols, 165–195.

Kalbfleisch, C. (1907), *Simplicii in Aristotelis Categorias commentarium* (Commentaria in Aristotelem Graeca VIII), Berlin: Reimer.

Karamanolis, G. E. (2006), *Plato and Aristotle in Agreement? Platonists on Aristotle from Antiochus to Porphyry*, Oxford: Clarendon Press.

―― (2013), *The Philosophy of Early Christianity*, Durham: Acumen.

Kehl, A. (1988), 'Hekate', *Reallexikon für Antike und Christentum* XIV, 310–338.

Kinzig, W. (2000), 'Überlegungen zum Sitz im Leben der Gattung Πρὸς Ἕλληνας / Ad nationes', in R. von Haehling (ed.), *Rom und das himmlische Jerusalem: Die frühen Christen zwischen Anpassung und Ablehnung*, Darmstadt: Wissenschaftliche Buchgesellschaft, 152–183.

Kledt, A. (1999), 'Der Mythos von Demeter in der Deutung des Firmicus Maternus', *Latomus* 58.3, 626–634.

van Kooten G. H. (ed.) (2005), *The Creation of Heaven and Earth: Re-interpretations of Genesis I in the Context of Judaism, Ancient Philosophy, Christianity, and Modern Physics* (Themes in Biblical Narrative 8) Leiden: Brill.

Krueger, P. (1980), *Fragmenta Vaticana. Mosaicarum et Romanorum legum collatio. Recognovit T. Mommsen. Consultatio veteris cuiusdam iurisconsulti, codices Gregorianus et Hermogenianus, alia minora* (Collectio librorum Iuris Anteiustiniani III), Berlin: Weidmann.

Kupreeva, I. (2003), 'Qualities and Bodies: Alexander against the Stoics', *Oxford Studies in Ancient Philosophy* 25, 297–344.

Kytzler B. (ed.) (1992), *M. Minuci Felicis, Octavius*, Stuttgart–Leipzig: Teubner.

Lang, H. S. and Macro, A. D. (2001), *Proclus: On the Eternity of the World (de Aeternitate Mundi)*, Berkeley: University of California Press.

Lautner, P. (1992), 'Philoponus, *in de Anima* III: Quest for an author', *Classical Quarterly* 42, 510–522.

Lecerf, A. and Saudelli, L. (2016), '«Sources» et «principes»: universalité et particularité dans les *Oracles Chaldaïques*', in H. Seng and G. Sfameni Gasparro (eds), *Theologische Orakel in der Spätantike*, Heidelberg: Winter, 47–88.

Lefebvre, D. (2008), 'Le commentaire d'Alexandre d'Aphrodise à *Métaphysique* A9, 990a34-b8. Sur le nombre et l'objet des Idées', *Les Études Philosophiques* 86, *Alexandre d'Aphrodise. Commentateur d'Aristote et philosophe*, ed. M. Rashed, 305–322.

―― (2016), 'Aristotle and the Hellenistic Peripatos: From Theophrastus to Critolaus', in Falcon (2016a), 13–34.

Lévêque, P. (1959), *Aurea Catena Homeri: Une étude sur l'allégorie grecque*, Paris: Belles Lettres.

Levieils, X. (2007), *Contra Christianos: La critique sociale et religieuse du christianisme des origines au concile de Nicée (45–325)*, Berlin–New York: De Gruyter.

Lévy, C. (1992), *Cicero Academicus: Recherches sur les* Académiques *et sur la philosophie cicéronienne*, Rome: École Française de Rome.

Lewis, E. (1995), 'The Stoics on Identity and Individuation', *Phronesis* 40.1, 89–108.

Lewy, H. (1956), *Chaldaean Oracles and theurgy: Mysticism Magic and Platonism in the Later Roman Empire*, Le Caire 1956: Imprimerie de l'Institut français d'archéologie orientale [3rd ed. by M. Tardieu, Paris: Études Augustiniennes 2011].

Lilla, S. (1971), *Clement of Alexandria: a study in Christian Platonism and Gnosticism*, Oxford: Oxford University Press.

Linguiti, A. (2015), 'L'etica medioplatonica', *Rivista di Storia della Filosofia* 70, 359–379.

Lloyd, G. E. R. (2005), 'Mathematics as a Model of Method in Galen', in R. W. Sharples (ed.), *Philosophy and the Sciences in Antiquity*, Aldershot: Ashgate, 110–130.

Long, A. A. (1982), 'Soul and Body in Stoicism', *Phronesis* 27.1–2, 34–57.

—— (2006), 'Timon of Phlius: Pyrrhonist and Satirist', in A. A. Long, *From Epicurus to Epictetus. Studies in Hellenistic and Roman Philosophy*, Oxford: Clarendon Press, 70–95 (first published in 1978).

—— and Dillon, J. (eds) (1988), *The Question of "Eclecticism"*, Berkeley: University of California Press.

—— and Sedley, D. (1987), *The Hellenistic Philosophers. 2 volumes. Vol. I: Translations of the Principal Sources, with Philosophical Commentary. Vol. 2: Greek and Latin Texts with Notes and Bibliography*, Cambridge: Cambridge University Press. (= LS)

Lumpe, A. (1959), 'Elementum', *Reallexikon für Antike und Christentum* IV, 1073–1100.

Luna, C. (2000), 'Syrianus dans la tradition exégétique de la *Métaphysique* d'Aristote', in M.-O. Goulet-Cazé (ed.), *Le commentaire entre tradition et innovation*, Paris: Vrin, 301–309.

—— (2001), *Trois études sur la tradition des commentaires anciens à la* Métaphysique *d'Aristote*, Boston: Brill.

Madigan, A. (1986), 'Syrianus and Asclepius on Forms and Intermediates in Plato and Aristotle', *Journal of the History of Philosophy* 24, 149–171.

Majercik, R. (1989), *The Chaldean Oracles* (SGRR 5), Leiden: Brill.

Männlein-Robert, I. (2001), *Longin, Philologe und Philosoph. Eine Interpretation der erhaltenen Zeugnisse*, München-Leipzig: Saur.

—— (2014), 'Ordnungskonkurrenz: Polemik und Feindbild in konkurrierenden Ordnungen. Der platonische Philosoph Porphyrios und sein Kampf gegen die Christen', in E. Frie and M. Meier (eds), *Bedrohte Ordnungen als Thema der Kulturwissenschaften*, Tübingen: Mohr Siebeck, 117–138.

Mansfeld, J. (1994), *Prolegomena: Questions to be Settled before the Study of an Author, or a Text*, Leiden: Brill.

Marmodoro, A. and Cartwright, S. (eds) (2018), *A History of Mind and Body in Late Antiquity*, Cambridge: Cambridge University Press.

Massa, F. (2013), 'Confrontare per distruggere. Firmico Materno e l'origine diabolica dei culti orientali', *Studi e materiali di storia delle religioni* 79.2, 493–509.

McGowan, A. (1994), 'Eating People: Accusations of Cannibalism Against Christians in the Second Century', *Journal of Early Christian Studies* 2.3, 413–442.

Méhat, A. (1966), *Étude sur les "Stromates" de Clément d'Alexandrie*, Paris: Seuil.

Menn, S. (1999), 'The Stoic Theory of Categories', *Oxford Studies in Ancient Philosophy* 17, 215–247.

―――― (2003), 'The Discourse on Method and the Tradition of Intellectual Autobiography', in J. Miller and B. Inwood (eds), *Hellenistic and Early Modern Philosophy*, Cambridge: Cambridge University Press, 141–191.

―――― (2018), 'Andronicus and Boethus: Reflections on Michael Griffin's *Aristotle's Categories in the Early Roman Empire*', *Documenti e Studi sulla Tradizione Filosofica Medievale* 29, 13–43.

Michalewski, A. (2014), *La puissance de l'intelligible. La théorie plotinienne des Formes au miroir de l'héritage médioplatonicien*, Leuven: Leuven University Press.

―――― (2016), 'The Reception of Aristotle in Middle Platonism: From Eudorus of Alexandria to Ammonius Saccas', in Falcon (2016a), 218–237.

―――― (2021), 'Writing in the Soul. On some Aspects of Recollection in Plotinus', in V. Decaix and C. Thomsen Thörnqvist (eds), *Memory and Recollection in the Aristotelian Tradition*, Turnhout: Brepols, 45–65.

―――― (à paraître), 'Les Formes séparées et la participation dans le commentaire à *Met.* A6–9 et B2 d'Asclépius de Tralles', in P. d'Hoine and A. Michalewski (eds), *Le commentaire d'Asclépius sur la Métaphysique d'Aristote (A-Γ). Recueil d'études et d'extraits commentés* (Cahiers de philosophie ancienne), Bruxelles-Paris: OUSIA.

Michel, A. (1984), 'Humanisme et anthropologie chez Cicéron', *Revue des Etudes Latines* 62: 128–142.

Mitchell, S. and Van Nuffelen, P. (eds) (2010), *Monotheism between Pagans and Christians in Late Antiquity*, Leuven: Peeters.

Molland, E. (1936), 'Clement of Alexandria and the Origin of Greek Philosophy', *Symbolae Osloenses* 15–16, 57–85.

Mondésert, C. (1944), *Clément d'Alexandrie. Introduction à l'étude de sa pensée religieuse a partir de l'écriture*, Paris: Aubier.

Moore, C. (2015), *Socrates and self-knowledge*, Cambridge: Cambridge University Press.

Moore, E. and Turner, J. D. (eds) (2000), 'Gnosticism', in L. P. Gerson (ed.), *The Cambridge History of Philosophy in Late Antiquity*, Cambridge: Cambridge University Press, 174–196.

Monat, P. (1973), *Lactance. Institutions divines. Livre V. Vol. 2: Commentaire et Index*, Paris: Éditions du Cerf.

―――― (1992–1997), *Firmicus Maternus. Mathesis*, Paris: Belles Lettres.

Moraux, P. (1973), *Der Aristotelismus bei den Griechen: Von Andronikos bis Alexander von Aphrodisias*, vol. 1, Berlin–New York: De Gruyter.

Moreschini, C. (1987), 'Note ai perduti *Stromata* di Origene', in L. Lies (ed.), *Origeniana quarta*, Innsbruck: Tyrolia, 36–43.

―――― (2015), *Apuleius and the Metamorphoses of Platonism*, Turnhout: Brepols.

Morlet, S. (2004), 'Eusèbe de Césarée a-t-il utilisé les *Stromates* d'Origène dans la *Préparation évangélique?*', *Revue de philologie* 78, 127–140.

―――― (2009), *La Démonstration évangélique d'Eusèbe de Césarée. Étude sur l'apologétique chrétienne à l'époque de Constantin*, Paris: Institut d'Études Augustiniennes.

―――― (2013), 'La *Préparation évangélique* d'Eusèbe et les *Stromates* perdus d'Origènes: nouvelles considérations', *Revue de philologie* 87, 107–123.

―――― (2014a), *Christianisme et philosophie: les premières confrontations (Ier–VIe s.)*, Paris: Le Livre de Poche.

―――― (2014b), 'Mentions et interprétations du tétragramme chez Eusèbe de Césarée', *Revue des études augustiniennes et patristiques* 60, 213–252.

Mortley, R. (1976), 'The Mirror and I Cor. 13,12 in the Epistemology of Clement of Alexandria', *Vigiliae Christianae* 30, 109–120.

Mras, K. (ed.) (1982–1983), *Eusebius. Werke VIII. Die Praeparatio evangelica*, 2., bearbeitete Ausgabe von É. des Places, Berlin: Akademie-Verlag.

Mußner F. (1988), *Der Galaterbrief*. 5th ed., Freiburg-Basel-Wien: Herder.

Müller, G. (2011), 'La doctrina de los principios en Numenio de Apamea', *Cuadernos de Filosofía* 56, 51–75.

Müller, I. Von (1897), 'Über Galens Werk vom wissenschaftlichen Beweis', *ABAW*, München 20, 403–478.

Murrin, M. (1980), *The Allegorical Epic: Essays in Its Rise and Decline*, Chicago–London: The University of Chicago Press.

Muscolino, G. and Girgenti, G. (eds) (2009), *Porfirio. Contro i cristiani*, Milano: Bompiani.

Narcy, M. (1981), 'L'homonymie entre Aristote et ses commentateurs néoplatoniciens', *Les Études Philosophiques*, 35–52.

Nautin, P. (1977), *Origène. Sa vie et son œuvre*, Paris: Beauchesne.

Nawar, T. (2017), 'The Stoics on Identity, Identification, and Peculiar Qualities', *Proceedings of the Boston Area Colloquium in Ancient Philosophy* 32.1, 113–159.

Nehamas, A. and Woodruff, P. (tr.) (1997), '*Phaedrus*', in J. M. Cooper (ed.), *Plato: Complete Works*, Indianapolis: Hackett, 506–556.

Niehoff, M. (2007), 'Did the *Timaeus* create a Textual Community?', *Greek, Roman and Byzantine Studies* 47, 161–191.

Noethlichs, K. L. (1991), 'Heidenverfolgung', *Reallexikon für Antike und Christentum* XVI, 1149–1190.

O'Meara, D. J. (2005), 'The Metaphysics of Evil in Plotinus: Problems and Solutions', in J. Dillon and M. Dixsaut (eds), *Agonistes. Essays in Honour of Denis O'Brien*, Williston: Ashgate, 179–185.

Opelt, I. (1974), 'Schimpfwörter in der Apologie De errore profanarum religionum des Firmicus Maternus', *Glotta* 52.1/2, 114–126.

―――― (1980), *Die Polemik in der christlichen lateinischen Literatur von Tertullian bis Augustin*, Heidelberg: Winter.

Opsomer, J. (1998), *In Search of the Truth. Academic Tendencies in Middle Platonism*, Bruxelles: Koninklijke Academie voor Wetenschappen.

―― (2004), 'Syrianus on Homonymy and Forms', in G. Van Riel and C. Macé (eds), *Platonic Ideas and Concept Formation in Ancient and Medieval Thought*, Leuven: Leuven University Press, 31–50.

―― (2005), 'Demiurges in Early Imperial Platonism', in R. Hirsch-Luipold (ed.), *Gott und die Götter bei Plutarch. Götterbilder – Gottesbilder – Welbilder*, Berlin–New York: De Gruyter, 51–99.

―― (2008), 'Weshalb nach Julian die mosaisch-christliche Schöpfungslehre der platonischen Demiurgie unterlegen ist', in C. Schäfer (ed.), *Kaiser Julian „Apostata" und die philosophische Reaktion gegen das Christentum*, Berlin–New York: De Gruyter, 127–156.

―― and Ulacco A. (2016), 'What is epistemic authority? A Model and Some Examples from Ancient Philosophy', in S. J. Boodts, J. Leemans and B. Meijns (eds), *Shaping Authority: How Did a Person Become an Authority in Antiquity, the Middle Ages and the Renaissance?*, Turnhout: Brepols, 21–46.

Osborn, E. F. (1957), *The Philosophy of Clement of Alexandria*, Cambridge: Cambridge University Press.

―― (1959), 'Teaching and Writing in the First Chapter of the "Stromateis" of Clement of Alexandria', *The Journal of Theological Studies* 10, 335–343.

―― (1972), 'La vraie dialectique selon Clément d'Alexandrie', in J. Fontaine and C. Kannengiesser (eds), *Epektasis. Mélanges patristiques offerts au Cardinal Jean Daniélou*, Paris: Beauchesne, 375–383.

―― (2005), *Clement of Alexandria*, Cambridge: Cambridge University Press.

Pastorino, A. (1956), *Iuli Firmici Materni, De errore profanarum religionum*, Firenze: La nuova Italia.

Pépin, J. (1966), 'Porphyre, exégète d'Homère', in *Entretiens sur l'antiquité classique XII: Porphyre: Huit exposés suivis de discussions*, Genève: Fondation Hardt.

―― (1971), *Idées grecques sur l'homme et sur Dieu*, Paris: Les Belles Lettres.

―― (1976), *Mythe et allégorie: Les origines grecques et les contestations judéo-chrétiennes*, Paris: Études Augustiniennes.

―― (1982), 'Réactions du christianisme latin à la sotériologie metroaque', in U. Bianchi and M. J. Vermaseren (eds), *La soteriologia dei culti orientali nell'Impero Romano: Atti del Colloquio Internazionale su La soteriologia dei culti orientali nell'Impero Romano. Roma 24–28 Settembre 1979*, Leiden: Brill, 256–275.

Perkams, M. (2003), 'Doppelte Entelecheia. Das Menschenbild in "Simplikios" Kommentar zu Aristoteles' De Anima', *Elenchos* 24, 57–91.

―― (2008), *Selbstbewusstsein in der Spätantike*, Berlin–New York: De Gruyter.

―― (2019), 'The Date and Place of Andronicus' Edition of Aristotle's Works According to a Neglected Arabic Source', *Archiv für Geschichte der Philosophie* 101, 445–468.

Petersen, A. K. and Kooten, George van (eds) (2017), *Religio-philosophical discourses in the Mediterranean World: from Plato through Jesus to Late Antiquity*, Leiden-Boston: Brill.

Petrucci, F. M. (2015), 'L'esegesi e il commento di Platone (a partire dall'esegesi della cosmogonia del *Timeo*)', *Rivista di Storia della Filosofia* 70, 295–320.

——— (2018), *Taurus of Beirut. The other Side of Middle Platonism*, London–New York: Routledge.
Pilhofer, P. (1990), *Presbyteron kreitton. Der Altersbeweis der jüdischen und christlichen Apologeten und seine Vorgeschichte*, Tübingen: J.C.B. Mohr.
Polansky, R. (2007), *Aristotle's De Anima*, Cambridge: Cambridge University Press.
Potter, D. (1993), 'Martyrdom as Spectacle', in R. Scodel (ed.), *Theater and Society in the Classical World*, Ann Arbor: University of Michigan Press, 53–88.
Rashed, M. (2004), 'Priorité de l'ΕΙΔΟΣ ou du ΓΕΝΟΣ entre Andronicos et Alexandre: vestiges arabes et grecs inédits', *Arabic Sciences and Philosophy* 14, 9–63.
——— (2007), *Essentialisme: Alexandre d'Aphrodise entre logique, physique et cosmologie*, Berlin: De Gruyter.
——— (2013), 'Boethus' Aristotelian Ontology', in M. Schofield (ed.), *Aristotle, Plato, and Pythagoreanism in the First Century BC*, Cambridge: Cambridge University Press, 53–77.
——— (2016), 'Traces d'un commentaire de Simplicius sur la *Métaphysique* à Byzance?', in *L'héritage aristotélicien*, Paris: Les Belles Lettres [originally published in *Revue des sciences philosophiques et théologiques* 84 (2000), 275–284].
——— (2020), 'Les relatifs', in R. Chiaradonna and M. Rashed (2020a), 179–212.
——— (2021). *Ptolémée «al-Gharīb». Epître à Gallus sur la vie, le testament et les écrits d'Aristote. Texte établi et traduit*, Paris: Les Belles Lettres.
Reesor, M. (1954), 'The Stoic Concept of Quality', *The American Journal of Philology* 75.1, 40–58.
——— (1957), 'The Stoic Categories', *The American Journal of Philology* 78.1, 63–82.
——— (1972), 'Poion and Poiotes in Stoic Philosophy', *Phronesis* 17.3, 279–285.
Reichardt, S. (2002), 'Feindbild und Fremdheit. Bemerkungen zu ihrer Wirkung, Bedeutung und Handlungsmacht', in B. Ziemann (ed.), *Perspektiven der historischen Friedensforschung*, Essen: Klartext Verlag, 250–271.
Reinhardt, T. (2007), 'Andronicus of Rhodes and Boethus of Sidon on Aristotle's Categories', in R. Sorabji and R. W. Sharples (eds), *Greek and Roman Philosophy. 100 BC-200 AD*, vol. 2, London: Institute of Classical Studies, 513–529.
Renaud, F. and Tarrant, H. (eds) (2015), *The Platonic Alcibiades I: The Dialogue and its Ancient Reception*, Cambridge: Cambridge University Press.
Resch, A. (1906), *Agrapha: aussercanonische Schriftfragmente*, 2nd ed., Leipzig: J. C. Hinrichs.
Reydams-Schils, G. (2020), 'Platonism and Stoicism in Clement of Alexandria: "Becoming like God"', in L. Ayres and H. C. Ward (eds), *The Rise of the Early Christian Intellectual*, Berlin: De Gruyter, 129–143.
Richard, M. (1950), '*Apo phōnēs*', *Byzantion* 20, 191–222.

Riedweg, C. (ed.) (2017), in Zusammenarbeit mit R. Füchslin, C. Semenzato, Ch. Horn and D. Wyrwa, *Philosophia in der Konkurrenz von Schulen, Wissenschaften und Religionen: zur Pluralisierung des Philosophiebegriffs in Kaiserzeit und Spätantike*, Akten der 17. Tagungs der Karl und Gertrud Abel-Stiftung vom 16.-17 Oktober 2014 in Zürich, Boston–Berlin: De Gruyter.

Rieth, O. (1933), *Grundbegriffe der stoischen Ethik. Eine traditionsgeschichtliche Untersuchung* (Problemata. Forschungen zur klassischen Philologie 9), Berlin: Weidmannsche Buchhandlung.

Rinaldi, G. (1997), *La Bibbia dei Pagani*, vol. I, Bologna: EDB.

Rist, J. M. (1969), *Stoic Philosophy*, Cambridge: Cambridge University Press.

Rizzerio, L. (1996), *Clemente di Alessandria e la «φυσιολογία veramente gnostica». Saggio sulle origini e le implicazioni di un' epistemologia e di un' ontologia «cristiane»*, Leuven: Peeters.

Roscher, W. H. (1890), *Ausführliches Lexikon der griechischen und römischen Mythologie*, I 2, Leipzig: Teubner [reissued Hildesheim: Olms 1978].

Roselaar, S. (2014), 'The cult of Mithras in Early Christian Literature – an Inventory and Interpretation', *Klio* 96.1, 183–217.

Rowe, C. K. (2016), *One True Life: The Stoics and Early Christians as Rival Traditions*, New Haven: Yale University Press.

Ruahala, M. (2011), 'Devotion and Deviance: The Cult of Cybele and the Others Within', in M. Kahlos (ed.), *The Faces of the Other: Religious Rivalry and Ethnic Encounters in the Later Roman World*, Turnhout: Brepols, 51–82.

Runia, D. T. and Share, M. (eds) (2008), *Proclus Commentary on Plato's Timaeus* (vol. 2), Cambridge: Cambridge University Press.

Russell A. A. and D. Konstan (eds) (2005), *Heraclitus, Homeric Problems*. Edited and translated by, Leiden–Boston: Brill.

Saffrey, H. D. (1975a), 'Les extraits du Περὶ τἀγαθοῦ de Numénius dans le livre XI de la *Préparation Evangélique*', *Studia Patristica* 13, 46–51.

—— (1975b), 'Allusions anti-chrétiennes chez Proclus, le diadoque platonicien', *Revue des sciences philosophiques et théologiques* 59, 553–563.

—— (1987), 'Comment Syrianus, le maître de l'école néoplatonicienne d'Athènes, considérait-il Aristote?', in J. Wiesner (ed.), *Aristoteles, Werk und Wirkung*, Berlin: De Gruyter, 205–214.

—— (1990), *Recherches sur le néoplatonisme après Plotin*, Paris: Vrin.

—— and Segonds, A.-Ph. (eds) (2001), *Marinus. Proclus ou sur le bonheur*, Paris: Les Belles Lettres.

—— and —— (eds) (2012), *Porphyre, Lettre à Anébon l'Égyptien*, Paris: Les Belles Lettres.

—— and —— (2013), *Jamblique, Réponse à Porphyre (De Mysteriis)*. Texte établi traduit et annoté par H. D. Saffrey et A.-P. Segonds † avec la collaboration de A. Lecerf, Paris: Belles Lettres.

—— and Westerink, L. G. (eds) (1974), *Proclus. Théologie Platonicienne* II, Paris: Les Belles Lettres.

Sághy, M. and Schoolman, E. M. (eds) (2017), *Pagans and Christians in the Late Roman Empire: New Evidence, New Approaches (4th-8th centuries)*, Budapest: CEU Press.

Salas, L. A. (2020), *Cutting Words: Polemical Dimensions of Galen's Anatomical Experiments* (Studies in Ancient Medicine 55), Leiden: Brill.

Saloustios (1960), *Des dieux et du monde*. Texte établi et traduit par G. Rochefort, Paris: Belles Lettres.

Sambursky, S. (1959), *Physics of the Stoics*, London: Routledge and Kegan Paul.

Sandbach, F. H. (1985), *Aristotle and the Stoics*, Cambridge: Cambridge University Press.

Sanzi, E. (2006), *Firmico Materno. L'errore delle religioni pagane*. Introduzione, traduzione e note a cura di E. Sanzi, Roma: Città Nuova Editrice.

Sarian, H. (1992), 'Hekate', *LIMC* VI 1, 985–1018.

Scarborough, J. (1981), 'The Galenic Question', *Sudhoffs Archiv* 65, 98–111.

Schadewaldt W. (1975), *Homer, Ilias*, Frankfurt: Insel Verlag.

Schäfer, C. (2002), *Unde malum. Die Frage nach dem Woher des Bösen bei Plotin, Augustinus und Dionysius*, Würzburg: Königshausen & Neumann.

────── (2015), '"Scheinbare Extravaganz". Pagane und christliche Platoniker über die Wunderlichkeit des Mythos', in Leppin, H. (ed.), *Antike Mythologie in christlichen Kontexten der Spätantike*, Berlin: De Gruyter, 93–114.

Schofield M. (ed.) (2013), *Aristotle, Plato and Pythagoreanism in the First Century BC: New Directions for Philosophy*, Cambridge: Cambridge University Press.

Schott, J. (2005), 'Porphyry on Christians and Others: "Barbarian Wisdom", Identity Politics, and Anti-Christian Polemics on the Eve of the Great Persecution', *Journal of Early Christian Studies* 13.3, 277–314.

Schubert, C. (2014), *Minucius Felix. Octavius*, übersetzt und erklärt, Freiburg-Basel-Wien: Herder.

Scott, D. (1995), *Recollection and Experience*, Cambridge: Cambridge University Press.

Sedley, D. (1982), 'The Stoic Criterion of Identity', *Phronesis* 27.3, 255–275.

────── (1989), 'Philosophical allegiance in the Greco-Roman world', in M. Griffin and J. Barnes (eds), *Philosophia Togata*, Oxford: Clarendon Press, 97–119.

────── (1997), 'Plato's auctoritas and the rebirth of the commentary tradition', M. Griffin and J. Barnes (eds), *Philosophia Togata II*, Oxford: Clarendon Press, 110–129.

────── (1999), 'Hellenistic physics and metaphysics', in Algra, K. et al. (eds), *The Cambridge History of Hellenistic Philosophy*, Cambridge: Cambridge University Press, 355–411.

────── (2003), 'Philodemus and the Decentralisation of Philosophy', *Cronache Ercolanesi* 33, 31–41.

────── (2012), 'Antiochus as Historian of Philosophy', in D. Sedley (ed.), *The Philosophy of Antiochus*, Cambridge: Cambridge University Press, 80–103.

────── (2018), 'Stoics and their Critics on Diachronic Identity', *Rhizomata* 6.1, 24–39.

Share, M. (2005a), *Philoponus. Against Proclus On the eternity of the world 1–5*, London: Bloomsbury.

—— (2005b), *Philoponus. Against Proclus On the eternity of the world 6–8*, London: Bloomsbury.
Sharples, R. W. (2010), *Peripatetic Philosophy, 200 BC to AD 200. An Introduction and Collection of Sources in Translation*, Cambridge: Cambridge University Press.
Simmons, M. B. (2000), 'Graeco-Roman philosophical opposition', in P. F. Esler (ed.), *The Early Christian World* II, London–New York: Routledge, 840–868.
Sleeman, J. H. and Pollet, G. (eds) (1980), *Lexicon Plotinianum*, Leiden–Leuven: Brill–Leuven University Press.
Sluiter, I. (2013), 'The Violent Scholiast: Power Issues in Ancient Commentaries', in M. Asper (ed.), *Writing Science: Medical and Mathematical Authorship in Ancient Greece*, Berlin: De Gruyter, 191–213.
Smith, A. (1993), *Porphyrii philosophi fragmenta edidit A. Smith: Fragmenta Arabica D. Wasserstein interpretante*, Stuttgart-Leipzig: Teubner.
Sorabji, R. (1990), 'Infinite Power Impressed: The Transformation of Aristotle's Physics and Theology', in R. Sorabji (ed.), *Aristotle Transformed, The Ancient Commentators and their Influence*, 181–198.
Staden, H. von (1982), 'Hairesis and Heresy: The Case of the *haireseis iatrikai*', in Ben F. Meyer and E. P. Sanders (eds), *Jewish and Christian Self-Definition. Vol. III: Self-Definition in the Graeco-Roman World*, London: SCM Press Limited, 76–100.
Stählin, O., Früchtel, L. and Treu U. (eds) (1970/85), *Clemens Alexandrinus* vols 2 and 3, Berlin: Akademie Verlag.
Steel, C. (1987), 'Proclus et Aristote sur la causalité efficiente de l'intellect divin', in J. Pépin and H. D. Saffrey (eds), *Proclus lecteur et interprète des Anciens*, Paris, éditions du CNRS, 213–225.
—— (2016), 'Matter and Soul as "place of the forms"', in *Seele und Materie im Neuplatonismus*, J. Halfwassen, T. Dangel and C. O' Brien (eds), Heidelberg: Universitätsverlag, 233–257.
Steinmetz, P. (1994), 'Die Stoa', in Flashar, H. (ed.), *Die Philosophie der Antike*, IV 2 Basel: Schwabe, 491–716.
Stempflinger, E. (1912), *Das Plagiat in der griechischen Literatur*, Leipzig: Teubner.
Stenger, J. (2009), *Hellenische Identität in der Spätantike: Pagane Autoren und ihr Unbehagen an der eigenen Zeit*, Berlin–New York: De Gruyter.
Stöcklin-Kaldewey, S. (2014), *Kaiser Julians Gottesverehrung im Kontext der Spätantike*, Tübingen: Mohr Siebeck.
Tanaseanu-Döbler, I. (2013), *Theurgy in Late Antiquity: The Invention of a Ritual Tradition*. Göttingen-Bristol (Conn.): Vandenhoeck & Ruprecht.
—— (2016), '"Denn auf der Erde können sie sich nicht aufhalten, sondern nur auf heiliger Erde": Bemerkungen zum Verhältnis der Götter zur Materialität in Porphyrios' *Philosophia ex oraculis haurienda*', in H. Seng and G. Sfameni Gasparro (eds), *Theologische Orakel in der Spätantike*, Heidelberg: Winter, 171–204.
Taormina, D. P. (1989), *Jamblique, critique de Plotin et de Porphyre, quatre études*, Paris: Vrin.

——— (1993), 'Dynamiques de l'écriture et processus cognitif dans le néoplatonisme', in M. Dixsaut (ed.), *Contre Platon I. Le platonisme dévoilé*, Paris: Vrin, 215–245.

Tarrant, H. (1985), *Scepticism or Platonism? The Philosophy of the Fourth Academy*, Cambridge: Cambridge University Press.

——— (2000), *Plato's First Interpreters*, London: Duckworth.

Tempelis, E. (1998), *The School of Ammonius, son of Hermias, on Knowledge of the Divine*, Athènes: Ekdoseis Philologikou Syllogou Parnassos.

Thome, F. (2004), *Historia contra Mythos: Die Schriftauslegung Diodors von Tarsus und Theodors von Mopsuestia im Widerstreit zu Kaiser Julians und Salustius' allegorischem Mythenverständnis*, Bonn: Borengässer.

Thraede, K. (1966), 'Euhemerismus', *Reallexikon für Antike und Christentum* VI, 877–890.

Tieleman, T. (1996), *Galen and Chrysippus on the Soul. Argument and Refutation in the De Placitis Books II–III*, Leiden: Brill.

——— (2003), *Chrysippus' On Affections. Reconstruction and Interpretation*, Leiden: Brill.

——— (2005), 'Galen and Genesis', in G. H. van Kooten (ed.), *The Creation of Heaven and Earth: Re-interpretations of Genesis I in the Context of Judaism, Ancient Philosophy, Christianity, and Modern Physics*, Themes in Biblical Narrative 8, Leiden: Brill.

——— (2011), 'Galen on Perception', *Antiquorum Philosophia* 5, 83–97.

——— (2013), 'Miracle and Natural Cause in Galen', in S. Alkier and A. Weissenrieder (eds), *Miracles Revisited. New Testament Miracle Stories and their Concepts of Reality*, Studies on the Bible and its Reception, vol. 1, Berlin: De Gruyter, 101–115.

——— (2018), 'Galen and Doxography', in J. Mansfeld and D. R. Runia (eds), *Aetiana IV. Paper of the Melbourne Colloquium on Ancient Doxography*, Leiden–Boston, 453–472.

——— (2022), 'Presocratics and Presocratic Philosophy in Galen', in M. Jas and A. Lammer (eds), *Received Opinions. Doxography in Antiquity and in the Islamic World*, Leiden: Brill, 120–150.

Timotin, A. (2012), *La démonologie platonicienne. Histoire de la notion de daimon de Platon aux derniers néoplatoniciens*, Leiden–Boston: Brill.

Tornau, C. (2006), *Zwischen Rhetorik und Philosophie: Augustins Argumentationstechnik in De civitate Dei und ihr bildungsgeschichtlicher Hintergrund*, Berlin–New York.

Torres, J. (2009), 'Emperor Julian and the veneration of relics', *Antiquité Tardive* 17, 205–214.

Trabattoni, F. (2011), 'Boeto di Sidone e l'immortalità dell'anima nel *Fedone*', in T. Bénatouïl, E. Maffi, and F. Trabattoni (eds), *Plato, Aristotle, or Both? Dialogues between Platonism and Aristotelianism in Antiquity*, Hildesheim: Olms, 1–15.

——— (2020). 'Boéthos de Sidon et l'immortalité de l'âme dans le Phédon', in Chiaradonna and Rashed (2020a), 337–359.

Tsouni, G. (2019), *Antiochus and Peripatetic Ethics*, Cambridge: Cambridge University Press.

Tsouna, V. (2001), 'Socrate et La Connaissance de Soi: Quelques Interprétations', *Philosophie Antique* 1: 37–64.

Turcan, R. (1975), *Mithras Platonicus: Recherches sur l'hellénisation philosophique de Mithra*, Leiden: Brill.
—— (1982), *Firmicus Maternus. L'erreur des religions profanes*. Texte établi, traduit et commenté par R. Turcan, Paris: Les Belles Lettres.
—— (1996), 'Attis Platonicus', in E. N. Lane (ed.), *Cybele, Attis and related cults*: Essays in memory of M. J. Vermaseren, Leiden–New York–Köln: Brill, 387–404.
Turner, J. D. (2010), 'The Platonizing Sethian Treatises, Marius Victorinus's Philosophical Sources, and Pre-Plotinian *Parmenides* Commentaries', in J. D. Turner and K. Corrigan (eds), *Plato's* Parmenides *and its Heritage volume 1: History and Interpretation from the Old Academy to Later Platonism and Gnosticism*, Atlanta: Society of Biblical Literature, 131–172.
—— (2012), 'The Curious Philosophical World of Later Religious Gnosticism: The Symbiosis of Antique Philosophy and Religion', in K. Corrigan, J. D. Turner, and P. Wakefield (eds), *Religion and Philosophy in the Platonic and Neoplatonic Traditions: From Antiquity to the Early Medieval Period*, Sankt Augustin: Academia, 151–181.
Ulacco, A. (2016), 'The Appropriation of Aristotle in the Ps-Pythagorean Treatises', in Falcon (2016a), 202–217.
—— (2020), 'The Creation of Authority in the Pseudo-Pythagorean texts and their Reception in Late Ancient Philosophy', in E. Gielen and J. Papy (eds), *Falsification and Authority in Antiquity, the Middle Ages and the Renaissance*, Turnhout: Brepols, 184–214.
Vegetti, M. (1986), 'Tradizione e verità: Forme della storiografia filosofico-scientifica nel *De Placitis* di Galeno', in G. Cambiano (ed.), *Storiografia e dossografia nella filosofia antica*, (Biblioteca storico-filosofica 2), Torino: Tirrenia, 227–243 [slightly revised English version in Ph. Van der Eijk (ed.) (1999), *Ancient Histories of Medicine*, Leiden: Brill, 333–357].
Vermander, J.-M. (1980), 'Un arien d'Occident méconnu: Firmicus Maternus', *Bulletin de littérature ecclésiatique* 81, 3–16.
Verrycken, K. (1990), 'The Metaphysics of Ammonius son of Hermeias', in R. Sorabji (ed.), *Aristotle Transformed*, London: Duckworth, 199–231.
Völker, W. (1952), *Der wahre Gnostiker nach Clemens Alexandrinus*, Berlin: Akademie-Verlag.
Wallraff, M. (2011), 'Die antipaganen Maßnahmen Konstantins in der Darstellung des Euseb von Kaisareia', in J. Hahn (ed.), *Spätantiker Staat und religiöser Konflikt: Imperiale und lokale Verwaltung und die Gewalt gegen Heiligtümer*, Berlin–New York: De Gruyter, 7–18.
Walter, J. (2016), '*Interpretatio pagana* des Christentums: Liebeslyrik, Adonis-Kult und christliche Heiligenverehrung in den theologischen Orakeln bei Porphyrios (De phil. ex or. p. 183 f.180–182.185 f. Wolff = fr. 343F; 345F; 346F Smith)', in H. Seng and G. Sfameni Gasparro (eds), *Theologische Orakel der Spätantike*, Heidelberg: Winter, 205–226.
Walzer, R. (1949), *Galen on Jews and Christians*, Oxford: Oxford University Press.
Waszink, J. H. (1950), 'Aether', *Reallexikon für Antike und Christentum* I, 150–158.

Weaver, B. H. (2011), 'Synthesis of Cultic and Mythic traditions in Firmicus Maternus' Stoicising Dionysiac Aetiology', *Mythos* 5, 149–171.
Weisser, S. and Thaler, N. (eds) (2016), *Strategies of Polemics in Greek and Roman Philosophy*, Leiden-Boston: Brill.
Werth, N. (2006), *Hekate: Untersuchungen zur dreigestaltigen Göttin*, Hamburg: Dr Kovač.
Wilamowitz-Moellendorf, U. von (1900), 'Ein Bruchstück aus der Schrift des Porphyrius gegen die Christen', *Zeitschrift für die neutestamentliche Wissenschaft* 1, 101–105.
Wilkins, E. G. (1917), *"Know Thyself" in Greek and Latin Literature*, diss. Chicago.
Winiarczyk, M. (1991), *Euhemeri Messenii reliquiae*, Stuttgart-Leipzig: Teubner.
—— (2013), *The Sacred history of Euhemerus of Messene*, tr. from Polish by W. Zbirohowski-Kościa, Berlin-Boston: De Gruyter.
Wischmeyer, O. and Scornaienchi, L. (eds) (2011), *Polemik in der frühchristlichen Literatur. Texte und Kontexte*, Berlin–New York: De Gruyter.
Wlosok, A. (1989a), '§ 569. Arnobius', in R. Herzog and P. L. Schmidt (eds), *Handbuch der lateinischen Literatur der Antike* V, München: Beck, 365–375.
—— (1989b), '§ 570. L. Caecilius Firmianus Lactantius', in R. Herzog and P. L. Schmidt (eds), *Handbuch der lateinischen Literatur der Antike* V, München: Beck, 375–404.
—— (1989c), 'Zur lateinischen Apologetik der constantinischen Zeit (Arnobius, Lactantius, Firmicus Maternus)', *Gymnasium* 96.2, 133–148 [= Wlosok, A. (1990), *Res humanae – res divinae. Kleine Schriften herausgegeben von E. Heck und E. A. Schmidt*, Heidelberg: Winter, 217–232].
—— (1997), '§ 515 Firmicus Maternus (Iulius Firmicus Maternus iunior). B. Das Werk. b. Christliche Werke', in R. Herzog and P. L. Schmidt (eds), *Handbuch der lateinischen Literatur der Antike* IV, München: Beck, 89–93.
Wolter, M. (1993), *Der Brief an die Kolosser. Der Brief an Philemon*, Gütersloh–Würzburg: Gütersloher Verlagshaus Gerd Mohn–Echter Verlag.
Wyrwa, D. (1983), *Die christliche Platonaneignung in den Stromateis des Clemens von Alexandrien*, Berlin: de Gruyter.
—— (2017), 'Philosophie in der alexandrinischen Schule', in Riedweg (2017), 193–215.
Zambon, M. (2002), *Porphyre et le moyen-platonisme*, Paris: Vrin.
——, (2019), *'Nessun dio è mai sceso quaggiù'. La polemica anticristiana dei filosofi antichi*, Roma: Carocci.
Ziegler, K. (1953a), *Iuli Firmici Materni, V C De errore profanarum religionum* mit Einleitung und kritischem Apparat herausgegeben von K. Ziegler, München: Max Hueber.
—— (1969), 'Firmicus Maternus', *Reallexikon für Antike und Christentum* VII, 946–959.

General index

Modern names are listed only when they are discussed in the main text. Footnotes appear only when the entry does not occur in the main text of that page.

Academy
   Old   10, 19–21, 25–26, 111
   Sceptical   10, 31–36
   see also   Platonism
Agreement   9–10, 21–22, 25, 40–41, 49, 53, 55, 57n32, 58, 69n32, 71–72, 87–88, 112, 115, 120
   see also Disagreement, *Symphônia*
Akrasia   119, 122
Alcibiades   9, 62–63, 78–79, 120
Alcinous   11n10, 32, 34–35, 37–38
Alexander of Aphrodisias   12n19, 19–20, 22–23, 26–27, 152–154, 161–165, 172n7, 178n29
Alexandria   25, 47, 104, 144, 152, 167
Allusions   12, 61, 64, 67, 74n43, 74n44, 75, 86, 105, 120n37, 156n22, 170n4
Ambiguity   114, 122, 154, 164–165
   see also Homonymy
Ambition (*philotimia*)   10, 47–48, 62n9, 112
Ammonius Hermeiou   151–167
Ammonius Saccas   25
'Ancients'   8, 13, 19–21, 24–26, 40, 47, 51–52, 55, 57
Andronicus of Rhodes (Peripatetic)   13–14, 19–24, 26, 27n32, 30
Antiochus of Ascalon   9, 13, 19, 25, 31–35, 44, 58, 58n33
   incorporation of Stoicism   9, 32, 39n29, 58
Antiquity, as evidence of truth   8, 19, 51–52, 61, 68–69, 73

Aphrodite, *see* Venus
Apollo   61, 63–64, 65n21, 66, 69, 136, 141
Apologetics   60, 86–88, 105, 107, 125–127, 129, 134n78, 136, 147–148
Apostasy   25, 81–82, 127
Appropriation   11, 12n19, 13, 59, 76n54, 111, 118
Apuleius   32, 34–35, 38
Arcesilaus   8, 32–33, 112
(Ps.-) Archytas, *On the Universal Account*   26, 29
Ariston of Alexandria   21, 25
Aristotelian/-ism (school)   9, 19–30, 32n6, 50–51, 152–155, 158, 162–163, 166
Aristotle   8, 19–20, 23–26, 30, 32, 51–52, 53n21, 57, 63, 69, 76, 88, 99, 106, 115, 119, 151–167, 171n5
   categories   11–13, 17, 19–24, 26–30, 169–173, 176–179, 181, 183–184
   criticism of Plato   11–12, 40, 151–153, 157–158, 162–164, 166–167
   hylomorphism, *see* Hylomorphism
   Platonizing reading of   12, 25–27, 29–30, 33, 37, 44, 151–167
Aristoxenus of Tarentum   23, 26
Arnobius   126
Artemidorus   99
Astrology   127, 141
Athenodorus (Stoic)   21, 172n6

GENERAL INDEX

Athens 8, 23–24, 62, 70, 152, 156n22, 167
Atticus 25–26, 32–35, 37–39, 43–44, 112
Attis 131–132, 135, 137, 139, 148
Audience 42, 47, 66–68, 74–76, 78n61, 78n62, 79–80, 92, 97, 112, 120, 127n17
Authority 8, 12, 46, 47n9, 55, 57–58, 113n8, 140, 153, 160, 170
   of school founders 11, 20, 24–25, 112–113
   of texts 8, 12, 16, 19, 112–113
Baltzly, Dirk 112, 119
Barbarians, wisdom of the 68–70, 73, 76, 103, 107, 136, 148
   see also Moses
Bible 54, 76, 80, 84, 86, 88–89, 93–97, 100, 103–105, 107–108, 129
Bodies, physical 11–12, 34, 62, 64–65, 66, 72–73, 175, 181
Boethus of Sidon (Peripatetic) 12–14, 19–24, 25n3, 27–30
Carpocrates 102–103
Cause 42, 62, 73, 101, 145, 176, 181
   of disagreement *see* Disagreement
   efficient 54, 72–73, 75, 78, 152, 158, 166
   of evil 39
   final 118, 158
   Forms as —s 151–152, 158, 160–163, 166
   material 39, 54
   paradigmatic 152, 158
   Platonic theory of —s 36, 38–40, 42, 54, 118
   soul as — 22–23
   Stoic *pneuma* as — 175n19, 183
   theory of four —s 54
Celsus 13, 81–101, 103–108, 126n9, 138–139, 142n134, 144
Christian, -s 53–149 *passim*
   eschatology 84–85, 87, 89, 95

   philosophy 60, 66–68, 69n33, 70, 74, 76–77, 80
   vs pagan interpretation 53–56, 63–80, 81–109, 112–113, 115–117, 120–123, 129–146
Chrysippus 48n12, 49–50, 53, 177
Church 66, 90–91, 93, 95, 127n17
Cicero 60, 64–66, 72, 75
Clarity, (lack of) 11, 13, 40, 49, 51–52, 55, 73, 77–79, 95, 100, 114–116, 121–122, 155, 159–160
Clement of Alexandria 12, 26, 55n27, 59–80 *passim*, 98, 102–104, 107n64
Commentary 8–10, 19–30, 35–44, 100–101, 106, 111–123, 151–184
Common ground 8, 10, 12–13, 20, 25–26, 30–32, 34–36, 43–44, 49, 51, 53, 59, 68n32, 71, 87–98, 104–108, 115, 121–123, 129–147, 172–179
Community 9–10, 29, 47, 57, 66, 75, 102, 112–113, 121
   textual — 112–113
Consensus, *see* Agreement
Consistency 11, 22–23, 50, 95, 143n142, 148, 166
Constans 125, 127
Constantine 125, 127
Constantius II 125, 127
Convention 118, 120–121, 123
Conversion 10, 25, 50, 125, 127, 128n25, 128n30
Cornutus 88, 130n40, 144, 172n6
Cosmos 62, 64–65, 69, 70–72, 78–79, 94, 130, 132
   eternal vs created — 16, 40–42, 77–78, 121–122
Courcelle, Pierre 59
Crantor 40–43
Cratippus (as Peripatetic) 25
Creation, -or 8n4, 40, 54–55, 72, 75, 78–79, 92–93, 121, 143
   see also Cosmos, Demiurge
Critias 61

Curriculum, philosophical 20, 50, 65, 67, 70, 151–152, 171n5, 173n11
Cybele 130n45, 131, 135, 137, 148
Definition 21–22, 24, 27, 28n36, 49n13, 55, 70n35, 120–121, 153–160, 162, 164
    of soul, *see* Soul
Delphic oracle 59, 61–66, 69, 71, 77–78, 115, 126n14, 136
Demeter (Ceres) 140
Demiurge 14, 36–39, 43, 54, 75, 116–118, 120–121, 133, 151, 153n9, 157–158, 160, 163–166
    see also Creation
Democritus, -eans 10, 19n1, 99
Demons 138, 140, 143, 146–147
Devil 85, 101, 140, 143, 146
Dialectic 46n7, 53, 76–77, 79, 120–121
Dialogue 35–37, 62, 65n24, 66, 75, 111
Dicaearchus 23, 26
Dio Chrysostom 107
Diogenes Laertius 45, 99
Dionysus 128, 137, 140–141
Disagreement *passim*
    as evidence of textual richness 10–11, 13, 23, 35, 64–65
    between Plato and Aristotle 12, 25–26, 52, 151–153, 158–167
    caused by cognitive deficiency 9–10, 49-51, 54–56, 73–74, 84–109, 118–121
    caused by moral deficiency 10, 13, 47–48, 51–53, 55–57, 68, 82, 89, 113–123, 139–140
    interpretative — 26–30, 31, 35–38, 40–41, 43, 63–66, 76–79, 84–86, 92–97, 100, 102, 104, 106–107, 116–117, 121–123, 154–156, 160–166
    merely superficial 11–12, 49, 158, 161, 163–164
    strategies to resolve — 11–12, 35, 49-51, 54–55, 57–58, 73–75, 156, 160–167
    verbal vs substantial 9–10, 40–42, 49
    with authorities 11, 20–24, 51–52, 57, 122–123, 152, 155, 158,
    with predecessors 12, 21–24, 31–36, 40–41, 45–46, 49, 53, 81–82, 121, 152, 162–163, 167
Doctrine, as basis of tradition 20, 30, 34–36, 41, 43–44, 48–49, 55, 59, 80, 92, 113
Dogmatist (medicine) 46, 50, 53–55, 57n31, 58
Dörrie, Heinrich 32
Dyad, *see* Monad
Earth 88, 94, 120n37, 129n38, 131–132, 137
Egypt, -ians 76n54, 82, 100–101, 105, 107, 131, 136–137, 144
Elements 11–12, 20, 22, 52–53, 106, 129–140, 148, 175
Empedocles 119, 132
Empiricist (medicine) 45–46, 50, 53–55, 57n31, 58
Enigmatic discourse 61, 69, 85, 89, 105n58, 114–116
    see also Clarity
Epicurean, -ism 8, 19n1, 45–46, 48n12, 50, 54, 57, 69n33, 99n32, 99n33, 115
Epistemology 9–10, 49–52, 55, 57, 61, 63, 70, 72–78, 98, 101, 119–121, 151–167
Erasistratus of Keos, Erasistrateans, 45, 47, 48n10
Essentialism 14, 24, 26
Ethics 10, 47–57, 61, 63–64, 71, 76, 111–123, 130, 133–135, 139, 142, 171n5
Etymology 121, 144–146
Eudorus of Alexandria 19, 21, 25–27, 29–32, 38–39, 41–43
Euhemerism 135, 138, 140–141, 143
Eusebius of Caesarea 81–82, 104–107, 126, 147n166

GENERAL INDEX

Evil   37, 39, 52, 140, 146
Exclusion, of opponents   7, 15, 34–36, 45, 86, 97, 108, 112, 116–117
Exegesis   8, 11, 19, 21–30, 35–37, 40–43, 69–71, 77n58, 83–107, 111–123, 151–167
   allegorical — of myth   62, 85, 115, 130–146
   strategies of   35, 40–43, 70–72, 74–80, 96–98, 118–121, 157–159, 161–166
Explanation, -ory power   52, 55, 169–170, 175n18, 176, 183–184
Favorinus of Arelate   32, 45, 50n15
Fire   84–85, 95, 129n38, 133–134
Firmicus Maternus   125–149
Foreknowledge   73, 89, 90–91, 146
Form   11, 14, 17, 21–22, 24, 53, 61, 66n25, 117, 151–157, 159, 160–167, 173n11, 174, 175n20, 176–178, 182, 183
   immanent vs transcendent   17, 23, 36, 152–155, 157–158, 160–163, 173, 175
Frede, Michael   20, 57n31
Galen of Pergamum   11n10, 12, 45–58, 99
Gnostics   60n3, 66, 91–92, 94, 97, 101, 113–119
God (concept)   16, 29n37, 63–64, 69, 81, 92, 118–121, 157, 160, 164, 166
God (monotheistic)   54–55, 67–68, 72–80, 81, 84–87, 89–90, 92–94, 96, 102–103, 106, 118, 121, 129, 136–137, 139
Gods (polytheistic)   10, 78–79, 128–146
Good, Form of the   37–38, 118
Greekness (quality of discourse)   120–123
Hebrews, *see* Jews
Hekate   133–135, 137
Hera (Iuno)   132, 135, 137, 142n132

Heritage   23, 30, 32–34, 49n14, 58, 59, 112
Hermeneutic, *see* exegesis
Heterodoxy   7, 31, 33, 34, 40, 46
   of limited value as interpretative concept   22, 34, 36, 37
Hippocrates   12, 45–47, 52–53, 55, 57–58
Historiography   8, 31–34, 51–52, 61, 64n18, 66, 68–71, 73, 100
Homoiôsis theôi   39n29, 93, 119, 142
Homonyms/Synonyms/Paronyms   21, 25n23, 140, 141, 162, 163, 176–177n21
Hylomorphism   11–12, 21–23
Iamblichus   28–29, 65n24, 67n29, 134, 144, 145n153, 146n159 and n160, 151, 156, 170–171, 173
Identity (sameness)   174, 177n23
Identity (social concept)   13, 45, 121, 127n17, 147n167
Idolatry, accusation of   136, 146
Ignorance, *see* Knowledge, lack of
Innovation   9, 39, 57–58, 108, 114, 146, 171
   accusation of (*kainotomia*)   81–82, 107
Integration (of ideas and traditions)   11, 12n19, 25, 30, 32, 37, 39n29, 44, 47, 49, 51, 58, 66, 86, 108, 145, 151–152, 175n20, 176
Intellect (*nous*)   17, 37, 44, 49, 52, 61n7, 65, 75, 79, 116–119, 141, 151–166 *passim*
Interpretation   36–39, 59–62, 70–72, 74–75, 78–80, 90, 94, 97, 105, 111–123, 129–146, 151–167
   forced   111n2, 112–113, 116–117, 122–123, 142
   literal   40–43, 72, 121–123
   see also Exegesis
Irrationality, *see* Rationality
Isis   131, 135, 137

Jargon, *see* Terminology
Jesus   73n41, 74n48, 75–79, 95, 138, 139, 141
Jews   8n4, 14, 46, 53, 55, 56, 67–71, 76, 136, 138
    see also Moses
John Philoponus   41–42, 113, 121–123, 153n9, 154, 156–158, 166
Julian (emperor)   104–105, 126n7, 132n53, 132n54, 143n142, 144, 148
    Hymn to Helios King   141
Knowledge   9, 10, 33–34, 41, 48–51, 55, 58, 63, 64n17, 65, 66–67, 69–80, 82, 84, 88–92, 96–104, 115–117, 119–123, 125–127, 146, 156n22, 157, 166, 182
    lack of   9–10, 61, 76, 78, 97, 112, 115–123, 125–126
    of oneself   59–80, 115
Lactantius   126
Lang, Helen   121
Lecture notes   47, 153, 161
Lefebvre, David   23
Liber and Libera, *see* Dionysus, Demeter
Literary criticism   184
Logos (part of the soul)   119
Logos (Stoic principle)   182
Longinus   35
Love of honour (*philotimia*), *see* Ambition
Macro, A.D.   121
Martialos   47–48
Mathematics   11, 38n26, 119
Matter   38, 39n27 and n28, 54, 121, 137
    as cause of evil   39
Maximus of Tyre   39
Medicine   12, 14, 45–47, 50, 55, 57–58, 123
Menn, Stephen   177, 180n32
Metaphysics   14, 17–18, 26–27, 29n37, 30, 36, 42–43, 67, 118, 171n5, 173, 175
Methodist (medicine)   45–46, 50, 53

Microcosm, human as   65, 72
Middle Platonism   10, 14, 31, 32n4, 33–39, 41, 43–44, 69
Mirroring   63, 73–76, 80
Misunderstanding   15–16, 29, 111, 116
    accusation of (*parakoê*)   10, 13, 15, 16, 82–108 *passim*
Mithras   133, 135, 148n170
Monad   27–30, 36
Moon   140
Moraux, Paul   27
Moses   54–55, 76, 78n60, 100, 104, 116
    as source of Greek wisdom   67–70, 76, 88–89
Mysteries   74n44, 112, 116, 127–128, 142, 148
Myth   62, 84–85, 87–89, 100–101, 107, 112, 115, 127
    allegorical interpretation of, *see* Exegesis
    critique of   10, 128–149
    deformation of   84–85, 88, 101
Name   21, 47, 53, 61n6, 76, 118–119
    —ing oneself after a founding figure   46, 57, 58
    understanding of –s   120–121, 133, 144–145, 175n18
    see also etymology
Neoplatonism, *see also* Platonism   100, 105n58, 111–115, 118, 120n38, 121–123, 151–152, 154, 155–158, 165–166, 169–170, 171n5, 173, 178n29, 179
Nile   131n52, 136
Numenius   32–35, 37–39, 55n27, 88, 112, 116
Origenes   83, 85–108 *passim*, 126n9, 138–139
Originality, *see* Innovation
Orthodoxy   13, 14, 21—23, 31–34, 36–37, 39–41, 43–44, 46, 48, 113n9
    see also Heterodoxy
Osiris   85, 101, 131, 135, 137, 139

Pagan   7, 9n6, 10, 13, 15–17, 43, 111–113, 116, 121–123, 125–128, 138, 141, 144–148, 174
Participated/unparticipated/participant   173–174, 176, 181
Paul (Apostle)   69n33, 74–75, 80–81, 88, 93, 95–97, 107
Pedigree   8, 15–17, 57, 58
   see also Tradition
Peripatos, *see* Aristotelianism
Persecution   56, 125–126, 142n139, 147
   see also Tolerance
Persephone   140
Persia, -ns   62n9, 126n7
Philo of Alexandria   101, 104
Philodemus   25, 33
Philosophy
   deformation of   69, 114, 116
   gift from God   68, 77n57
   parts of   58, 65n24, 68–69, 71, 76
Phronêsis   118–119, 121
Plagiarism   82, 89, 114–117
Plato   8, 9–21, 24–27, 30, 32–36, 38n26, 39–42, 44–46, 48n12, 49–57, 60, 63, 66n24, 69–70, 76, 78, 80, 85–89, 98, 102, 104–106, 111–118, 120–123, 151–153, 158, 160–164, 166–167, 171n5, 181n34
   interpretation of –'s dialogues   32, 36, 41, 43n35, 44, 121, 123, 163
   polyphony of –'s philosophy   35, 44
   Phaedo   24, 37
   Phaedrus   37, 60–63, 68, 71–72, 111–113, 115
   Protagoras   60–61, 70, 98
   Seventh Letter   36, 37
   Theaetetus   10, 15, 119
   Timaeus   11, 13, 36–38, 40–41, 43–44, 119
   and see index locorum
Platonic, -ism   7, 11–12, 14–15, 17, 22, 24–26, 31–33, 34n11, 36–37, 39, 43, 46n7, 48n12, 50, 57–58, 60–61, 63, 74, 77n58, 112, 114, 121, 129, 130, 134, 144, 147, 170
   'system'   31–32, 34, 37, 40, 44
   see also Middle Platonism
Plotinus   11n10, 16, 25, 31, 35, 39, 44, 58, 65n22, 100, 105, 112–122, 155, 165, 170, 172n7, 173, 176, 179, 184
Plutarch of Athens   99, 100, 156
Plutarch of Chaeronea   14, 26, 32–41, 43–45, 63–66, 74n44, 182n36
Poetry, philosophical use of   46n7, 67, 77–79, 84–85, 86n11, 87–88, 100, 107, 134, 136, 140, 144–145
   see also Myth
Polemic   8, 13, 15–17, 23, 29, 32, 34, 39, 44–45, 66, 81–83, 86, 91, 99, 101, 103–105, 107–108, 113–114, 116, 125, 128n30, 129, 137, 140–142, 144, 146–147, 160, 163, 184
   serves to clarify own identity   39, 44, 99, 127, 130, 132n54, 148, 160, 170, 172n7
   see also Disagreement
Pompous (style of discourse, see *typhos*)
Posidonius of Apamea   48n12, 49–50, 82n7
Praxagoreans   47
Principles   36–40, 118, 162, 166, 175, 176, 183
   Theory of (*Prinzipienlehre*)   36, 38–40
Proclus   9–10, 13, 16, 65n24, 112–113, 118, 120–123, 152, 155, 158, 167, 173
Protreptic   62n9, 65–66, 69, 71, 76, 77n58, 79
Pythagoras, -eanism, -izing   11–12, 14, 19, 25–26, 29–30, 32–33, 39n29, 100
Quality (metaphysical)   11, 39, 41, 52–53, 162–163, 169–184
Quality (of persons)   76, 115, 118, 120
Rashed, Marwan   22, 23
Rationality   57, 115, 119, 134, 175

GENERAL INDEX

discursive 119
lack of 10, 15, 82, 98, 103
Reversion, of criticisms and arguments 86–87, 89–98, 106–107, 121–123, 136, 138–140, 145–147
Ritual 16–17, 136, 139–140, 143, 146
  see also Mysteries
Runia, David 120
Salustius 132, 137, 148
Sambursky, Samuel 177
Sarapis 143–144
Scholia 100, 104, 123
Sect, -arianism 14, 45–57, 91–92, 113–114
Seven Sages 67, 69–71, 73
Share, Michael 120–121
Silence (of an author) 9–10, 52–53, 55, 173n11
Simplicius 11–12, 17–18, 21–22, 27–29, 106, 151–152n1, 157n24, 163, 169–184
  appreciation of Stoics 169–184
Socrates 9, 15, 51, 61–63, 65, 70–72, 74n44, 76, 78–79, 81, 98, 115, 120
Sossianus Hierocles 126, 139n110
Soul 11, 22–23, 26, 38–41, 48, 61–67, 78–79, 116–117, 119, 156n22, 160, 164–165, 175
  capable of receiving Forms 17, 149–167
  definition 17, 23–24, 157–160, 163–166
  divine aspect of 72, 73n41, 119, 164–165
  as harmony 22–24, 26
  (im)mortality of the 43
  parts of the 49, 76, 116, 119
  precosmic 38–39
  as *tabula rasa* 156
  undescended 112
Sparta 61, 62n9, 69–70
Speusippus 21, 25, 27–28, 32, 40

Stoics, -ism 8, 19, 21, 23, 25n23, 32n6, 43, 48n12, 49–50, 63–64, 76n55, 115, 134n71, 169–184
  appreciation of 49–50, 53, 87–88
    see also Antiochus, Simplicius,
  attacks on 24, 26, 30, 45, 48n12, 49–50, 69n33, 99
  categories 169, 177–178
    comparable to Aristotelian 11, 169–170, 176–179
    Simplicius' criticism of 179–183
  concepts (*ennoiai*) 11n10
  pneuma 72, 175–176, 182–183
Style, of discourse 61, 69, 114–116
  see also Enigmatic, Pompous
Substance 11, 23–24, 27–30, 101, 154, 174, 177
  as a primary subject of inherence 21, 23
Sun 128, 137, 141, 148
Symphônia between Plato and Aristotle 12, 17, 25, 151–153, 156–161, 163–167
Syrianus 134n76, 145n153, 152–153, 162–163, 164n43, 167
System, -atization 11n10, 14, 20, 24, 26, 30–32, 34–37, 40, 44, 48, 60, 93, 129, 138, 141
Taurus, Lucius Calvenus 14, 26, 34–35, 41–43
Teacher (role of) 9, 19n3, 32–35, 44, 58n34, 63, 80, 112, 172n7
Terminology 9, 11n10, 12, 16, 65n19, 114, 116, 131n49, 169
Textual communities, *see* Community
Themistius 22, 152n6
Theodore of Asine 112
Theology 30, 36n19, 76, 107, 112, 125–126, 127n15, 129, 133, 138, 141, 151n1
Theophrastus, criticism of Aristotle 23
Thessalus of Tralles 46, 53

see also Methodist
Theurgy   135, 140–141, 144, 148
Time   41–42, 62, 84, 89, 115, 121
Tolerance/in–
  interpretative   10, 13, 22–24, 48n12, 112–113
  political and religious   56, 125–126, 147
Tradition *passim*
  ancient conceptualizations of –s   24–25, 32, 34–35, 46–58, 60–61, 67–70, 73, 76, 81–84, 87–88, 93, 101, 112–114, 117, 136–138, 170–171
  breaking with   32–33, 35–36, 51, 57, 68, 81–82, 86, 108, 112, 117
  differentiation of —s   31–36, 59, 75, 78–80, 106, 113–114
  grand — encompassing different views   25–30, 32–34, 44, 48–49, 51–53, 55, 57–58, 80, 86–87, 89, 108, 112, 156–159, 166–167
  reinforcing one's own   26, 30, 45, 47–48, 79–80, 112, 127–128, 147–148, 170, 183–184
  parallels between   8–13, 15–16, 59–80 *passim*

Transposition, Christian — of Platonic ideas   70, 75n49, 78–80, 85–87
Truth   8, 10–11, 13, 15, 47–50, 52–53, 56n30, 67–68, 73–74, 80, 82n7, 88, 94, 96, 98, 103–104, 108, 148n172, 160
  criterion of   49, 50n15
Typhon (divinity)   85, 101, 115, 131, 135, 137
Typhos/a– (quality)   115–117, 122
Unity (feature of entities)   117, 162
Unity (feature of traditions), *see* Agreement
Universe   37–38, 40, 43, 65, 71n39, 72, 77–78, 117
  see also Cosmos
Venus (divinity)   132, 135, 137, 142n132
Virtue   16, 40, 49, 56, 115, 118–120, 177n21
Water   73
Wilamowitz-Moellendorff, U. von   82
Xenarchus   20, 22, 154
Xenocrates   21–22, 24, 26, 27n32, 32, 40–42, 99, 112

Index locorum

Abu'l-Fida'
Universal Chronicle (ed. Fleischer)
108   56

Aetius
De placitis
1.7.33   175n19

Agrapha logia (ed. Resch)
144   74n44, 75

Albinus
Prologos
5   65

Alcinous
Didaskalikos (Didasc.)
163.11–14   38n26

Alexander of Aphrodisias
De Anima
84.25–85.5   154

De Mixtione (De mixt.)
225.1–3   175n17

In Aristotelis Metaphysica (In Met.)
76.21–23   161
85.5   161
93.1–7   162

In Aristotelis Topicorum libros (In Top.)
301.19–25   178n26

Ambrosiaster
Quaestiones Veteris et Novi Testamenti
82   149n178

84   149n178
114.1–16   149n178
114.2   129n32
114.3   141n127
114.6.11–12.26   135n87
114.29   129n32

Ammonius Hermeiou
In Aristotelis Categorias (In Cat.)
20.14–17   178n29
44.8–10   178n29
84.16–17   178n29

See also Asclepius

Ammonius Saccas
T. 15 Schwyzer   25–26

Anaxagoras
A73 Diels-Kranz   134n71

Anonymous
In Theaetetum
54.38–55.13   36n18

Apuleius
De Platone et eius dogmate (De Platone)
190   38n26

[Archytas]
Categoriae (Cat.)
30.23–31.5   26

Aristotle
Analytica Posteriora (A.Post.)
I.27, 87a36   28n36

Categoriae (Cat.)
6a36–37   21

De anima (De An./DA)
407b34–408a5   23
429a10–430a25   166
429a27–28   151–152, 156–157, 164
429a27–29   153
429b31–430a2   153
430a1–2   156
430a10–15   154
430a10–25   166
430a26–28   25n23
431b17   157, 164–165

De Caelo
270b24–25   134n71
278b3–4   106
279a7–9   106
306a20–26   11n14

Ethica Nicomachea (EN)
1147a10–24   119

Fragments (ed. Rose)
1   63, 65

Magna Moralia (MM)
1213a13   63n13, 66n25

Metaphysica (Met.)
990a34–b1   159, 164
990a34–b4   161
997b3   159, 164
997b5–8   161

Meteorologica (Mete.)
339b21–23   134n71

Politica (Pol.)
1274a28   58n34

Rhetorica (Rhet.)
1395a21   63n13
1404b1–4   115

Sophistici Elenchi (SE)
178b36   162n32

Artemidorus
Onirocriticon
IV.22   99

Asclepius of Tralles
In Aristotelis metaphysicorum libros (in Met.)
28.6   165
69.17–28   158–160, 164–165
69.17–70.13   161
69.18–20   151, 159
69.19–21   164
70.3   165n46
70.15–21   161
71.10–24   163
75.21–33   163
75.28   163n40
76.34   163n40
80.30   165n46
80.30–33   166
81.1–4   165n45
82.22–24   165n47
85.26–28   165n47
87.30–32   165n47
91.23–26   165n47
165.26–27   164
165.35–37   164
167.24–34   159–160, 164
167.30–31   151, 159

Athenagoras
Legatio
3.1.1–2   135n88
32.1   136n89

Index Locorum

Atticus (ed. Des Places)
Fr. 1.19–23   34
Fr. 1.32–37   34
Fr. 11.11–14   37n23
Fr. 12.1–14   37n23
Fr. 15.1–5   37n23
Fr. 16.1–12   37n23
Fr. 17.1–8   37n23
Fr. 18.8–13   37n23
Fr. 21.1–10   37n23
Fr. 22.1–5   37n23
Fr. 23   38n26

Augustine
Confessiones (Conf.)
10.15   62n8

De civitate dei (civ.)
2.7   142n137
3.3.5   142n137
4.9   142n137
10.9   144n149

Bible

Old Testament

Ecclesiastes (Eccl)
1.6   94

Genesis (Gn)
1   54
1.26   93
17.13   104

Psalms (Ps)
21.21   106–107

New Testament

Acts (Ac)
17.18   81

Colossians (Col)
2.8   69n33, 129n33
2.20   129n33

1 Corinthians (1 Cor)
3.19   97
13.12   73–74, 80
15.21–22   96
15.51–52   95

Galatians (Gal)
4.3   129n33
4.9   129n33

Matthew (Matth)
5.8   74n44

Romans (Rm)
5.12–14   96

1 Timothy (1 Tim)
4.1–3   96, 97

Chalcidius
In Timaeum (In Tim.)
293   175n17

Chaldaean Oracles (OC)
51–52   134n70
90   140n115

Cicero
Academica Posteriora (Ac. Post.)
13   32
17   35n14
1.39   181n34

De Finibus Bonorum et Malorum (Fin.)
5.44   64, 66

De Legibus (Leg.)
1.58   66
1.58–59   64

1.58–62   65n24
1.59   65, 72
1.61   65

De Natura Deorum (Nat. D.)
1.16   9n8
2.63–71   130n40, 144

De Re Publica (Rep.)
6.26   64, 66n25, 72n40

Tusculanae Disputationes (Tusc.)
1.52   64, 66
1.52–58   64n16
5.32   64n17
5.70–72   65n24

Clement of Alexandria
Protrepticus (Protr.)
114.1   78n61

Stromata (Str.)
1.15   107n64
1.16.2   67n27
1.18.1   67n27
1.20–59   68
1.28.176   26n30
1.50–51   69n33
1.59–60   70
1.60   67, 69–72, 75, 77–78
1.60.1–2   70n36
1.60.3–4   71
1.60.4   72
1.66.3–69.3   76n54
1.81–87   73
1.94   71, 73–76, 78, 80
1.94.3–7   73
1.151   76
1.151–182   76n55
1.165   76n54
1.176–179   76
1.177–178   77n57
1.178   72, 76–79

1.178.1–2   76–77
1.178.2   79
1.180.1   76n54
2.22.5   71n38
2.70.4   67
2.70.5   74n44
3.2.5.3   103n48
3.2.10.2   102n47
4.27.2   67
5.8.54.2   103n49
5.17.2   71n38
5.23.1   67
5.45.4   67
6.7.55.4   103n50
7.20.7–8   67
7.56–57   76n52

Codex Theodosianus
6.10.4   125n5

***Collatio Mosaicarum et Romanorum
legum***
6.4, 1.157.18–23   147n164

Commodianus
Instructionum libri ii
I.7   135n84
I.13   133n65

Cyril of Jerusalem
Catecheses
14.21   107n67

Damascius
In Phaedonem (in Phaed.)
I.433   24n19
I.422   24n19

Dexippus
In Categorias (In Cat.)
9.27–10.1   24n25
23.25–30   177n23
34.19–24   179n31

39.6-15   178n29

Diogenes Laertius
Vitae philosophorum
1.20   49n13
7.134   175n17
9.45   99

Epictetus
Diatribai
II.15.4   98n28

Epiphanius of Salamis
Panarion
27.5.9   97n3

Eudorus
3O Boys-Stones   29n37

Euhemerus (ed. Winiarczyk)
T91   135n81
T93   135n81
falsum 7   135n81

Eunapius
Vitae Sophistarum
1-5   105n57

Eusebius
Demonstratio Evangelica
X.8.92   107n62

Historia Ecclesiae
VI.2.15   104n51

Preparatio Evangelica (PE)
I.1.3d   56n30
I.2.1-4   82
I.2.3   126
I.2.6   104n54
II.1.53   107n63
III.13.22   135n79
IX.9-10   105n59
XI.10.14   55n27
XIV.20-10   107n65
XV.14.1   175n17

Firmicus Maternus
De errore profanarum religionum (err.)
1   136
1-5   129-140
2.1-3   135
2.6   131
2.7   135, 135n79
3.1   135
3.2   131, 131n49
3.3   135n79
3.5   130n45
4.1   132
4.1-3   135
4.3   137
5.1   133
5.2   133, 135
5.4   134
6-8   140-141
6.1-8   135n81
6.4   141
6.8   140n120
6.9   125n5
7.1-6   135n81
7.7   140
7.8   141n124
8.3   141
8.1-3   141
8.4   141
9-16   142-144
10.1   135n81
12.1-7   139n113
12.5   139
12.7   142n138
12.9   142
13   143-144
13.3   148n173
13.4   143-144
17   144-146
17.4   144-145
18   149n178

18–27   146–147
18.6   143n141
28   144
28.2–5   137n95
28–29   128n30
29.2   125n5

Mathesis
1.10.14   141
7.1.1   148n173

Galen
Adversus Iulianum (Adv. Iul.) (ed. Kühn)
XVI–IIA.246–299   45n1
XVIIIA.257–259   53n21

Adversus Lycum (Adv. Lyc.) (ed. Kühn)
XVIIIA.196–245   45n1

De Anatomicis Administrationibus (AA) (ed. Kühn)
II.620   58n34

De Causis Procatarcticis (CP) (ed. Hankinson)
1.1–3, 170.1–13 H.   51

De Differentiis Pulsuum (Diff. Puls.) (ed. Kühn)
II.4, VIII.579   55
III.3, VIII.657   54n26

De Indolentia (Indol.) (ed. Boudon–Jouanna)
58–59, 18–19.10   51n17

De Libris Propriis (Libr. Propr.) (ed. Boudon)
1.8–10, 138.6–21   47
1.11, 139.1–3   47
14.1–8, 164.1–165.23   51
19.3, 173.3   99n33

De Locis Affectis (Loc. Aff.) (ed. Kühn)
VIII.5, 158.17–159.9   49n13
VIII.314   48n12

De Methodo Medendi (MM)
Bk. 1, X.9–10 Kühn   53

De Naturalibus Facultatibus (Nat. Fac.) (ed. Kühn)
II.34   48n11
II.92   53n21
II.116–117   52

De Optima Doctrina (Opt. Doctr.) (ed. Kühn)
I.40–52   45n1

De Ordine Librorum Propriorum (Ord. Lib. Prop.) (ed. Kühn)
1.3–4, XIV.50–52   50

De Placitis Hippocratis et Platonis (PHP/De plac.) (ed. De Lacy)
II.2.4, 104.3–5   52
II.3.1, 108.21–25   52
II.4.3   46n7
II.5.65, 140.18   48n12
III.3.8–9   46n7
III.3.10–11   46n7
III.8.39, 232.25   48n11
IV.4–38, 258.19–25   50
V.3.8   175n19
V.6.5, 326.25–26   48n12
IX.7.5–6, 586.27–34   48

De Propriorum Animi Cuiuslibet Affectuum Dignotione et Curatione (Aff. Dig.) (ed. Kühn)
V.51   48n11

De Temperamentis (ed. Kühn)
I.523   99n31
I.535   99n31

I.622   99n31

De Typis (Typ.) (ed. Kühn)
VII.476   48n11

De Usu Partium Corporis Humani (UP)
XI, ch.14   54

In Hippocratis De Morbis vulgaribus, Commentarii (Hipp. Epid.) (ed. Kühn)
VIIIB.224   58n34

In Hippocratis De Officina Medici (Hipp. Off. Med.) (ed. Kühn)
XVIIIb.658   53n21

In Librum Hippocratis De Natura Humana (HNH) (ed. Kühn)
XV.2   58n34
XV.37   53n21

Quod animi mores corporis temperamenta sequantur (Quod animi mores) (ed. Bazou)
11.85.8–86.2   49
4.26.9–27.1   26

Gregory of Nyssa
In Canticum canticorum homiliae (In Cant. hom.)
2.2   62n8

Hippolytus of Rome
Refutatio Omnium Haeresium (Elenchos)
VII.32.8   97n22
6.135–137   140

Iamblichus
De Mysteriis (ed. Saffrey/Segonds/Lecerf)
I.9, 22.17–25.17   134n77
III.17, 104.11–107.18   146n159
III.31   146n160

In Categorias
Fr. 101   156–157

Homer
Ilias
5.127   78
5.128   77–79

Ibn al-Matran
Life of Galen
I.77 Müller (Ref. 1 Walzer)   55

Ireneaus
Adversus Haereses (Haer.)
I.26.6   97n22

Jerome
Epistolae
70.4   88n17

John Chrysostom
Adversus oppognatores vitae monasticae
II.10   107n66

Julian
Contra Galilaeos (ed. Masaracchia)
Fr. 25   138n101
Fr. 86   104n53

Contra Heraclium cynicum (Or. VII)
217C   130n48
219A   130n48
221D   143n140
222CD   130n48

Epistulae (ed. Bidez)
89a, 294BC–296D   144n151
89a, 304B–D   143n142
89b, 288B   140n116

In matrem deorum (Or. V [VIII Rochefort])
170AB   130n48

224 INDEX LOCORUM

In solem regem (Or. IV [XI Lacombrade])
144AB   141

Justin
Apologia
I.8.4   87
I.20.4   87
I.44.9   86n11
I.60.7   86.11

Cum Tryphone Judaeo Dialogus
56.1   87

Lactantius
De mortibus persecutorum
10   147n164
16.4   126

Institutiones (inst.)
5.2.12   126n10
5.3.4   139n110

Lucretius
De Rerum Natura
1.62–71   145n154

Marinus
Vita Procli
15   116n19

Minucius Felix
Octavius
9.2–10.2   135n848
9.4   135
30.1–31.4   136n89

Nemesius
De natura hominis (De nat. hom.)
78.7–79.2   181n34

Numenius
Fragments (ed. Des Places)
8.13   55n27, 116n20
21   38

24.10–14   112
24.57   33
52.92–93   29n27

Olympiodorus of Alexandria
In Alcibiadem (In Alc.)
92.5–7   10

In Aristotelis Meteora (In Meteor.)
4.5   151n1

Origenes
Commentary on the Gospel of John
XX.23.199   101n41

Contra Celsum (Cels./CC)
I.5   144n151
I.17.20   138n102
I.22   82
I.23   81
I.28   139n109
I.32   139n109
I.58   93
I.62   139n111, n112
I.71   139n111
II.4   81
II.5.10   139n108
II.23   142n134
II.30   83
II.46   139n112
III.16   84, 87
III.22–43   138n104
III.65   139
IV.11   84, 85, 88
IV.29   90
IV.30   93
IV.38   138n102
V.6   89
V.15   88n17
V.17   95
V.20–21   88n17
V.25   138n101
V.29   93

V.32   94
V.33   81
V.41   81
V.43   88n17
V.54   94, 97n23
V.57   88n17
V.61   90
V.64   95
V.65   83
VI.12   89n19
VI.7   85, 88, 88n17
VI.12   96
VI.15   85
VI.19   86
VI.24   90
VI.27   91
VI.34   91
VI.35   91, 95
VI.36   96
VI.38   91
VI.42   85
VI.51   92
VI.53   92
VI.62   94
VI.74   92
VII.3   88n17
VII.30   89n20
VII.30–31   88n17
VII.32   86
VII.36   139n107
VII.56   139n111
VII.68   138
VIII.14   93
VIII.35   88n17
VIII.41   142n134
VIII.56   126n9

De principiis (De princ.)
3.1.2–3   175n19

Pindar
Olympian
9.31   100

Scholia vetera in Pindarum (ed. Drachmann)
Ol. 9, scholium 46   100n35

Philo of Alexandria
De ebrietate
158   102

De migratione Abrahami (De migr. Abr.)
136–138   62n8
184–186   62n8

De plantatione
84   101

De somniis (De somn.)
1.54–58   62n8

De specialibus legibus
IV.53   102

De virtutibus
173   102

Quis rerum divinarum heres sit
109   102

Philodemus
Index Academicorum
XXXV.11–16   25

Philoponus
De Aeternitate Mundi (Aet. Mundi)
122.3–4   123
125.7–10   121–122
125.13–19   122
161.17–28   122
187.6–15   42

In Analytica Posteriora (In An. Post.)
242.26–243.26   157n24

In Categorias (In Cat.)
5.15–20   19n3
5.19–20   20

In De Anima
37.24–31   157
65–69   154
116.26–27   158
519.37–520.7   156
524.6   153n9
533.25–35   156

Photius
Bibliotheca
Cod.251, col. 461a24–39 (*Hierocles apud Phot.*)   25–26

Plato
Alcibiades maior (Alc. I)
111e11–112d3   9
124a8–b1   62n9
129a3   62
129a6   62
129e3–130c3   62
130c8–9   74n44
130d8–e5   62
130e8–9   62
132b4–5   62
132c–133c   75, 80
132c7–9   62
132c7   63
132c9–10   62
132e7–133a2   63
133b7–c3   63
133c4   72
133c4–6   63, 74
133c22–e3   65n19

Alcibiades minor (Alc. II)
150d6–e3   78–79
150d9   79
150e3   79

Anterastai (Anter.)
138a7   61n5

Charmides (Chrm.)
164c–175c   61
164d3–165b4   61
164e6   70n36

Epistulae (Ep.)
7.338d   98

Hippias maior (Hipp.)
228e2   61n5

Leges (Leg.)
923a4–5   61n5

Parmenides (Parm.)
132b   153n9

Phaedo (Phd.)
70a7   77n57
78b4–80c1   134n74
81a8   77n57

Phaedrus (Phdr.)
229e4–230a6   62
229e5–6   115
230a3–6   115
275d9–e5   111

Philebus (Phlb.)
48c10   61
48e8   61

Protagoras (Prot.)
330e   98
342–343   70
342a7–b1   61
342e2–4   61
343a6–b5   61
343b4   70n36
343b5   70n36

Respublica (*Resp.*)
377d5–378e3   130n43
436a8–b3   134n72
438a7–b1   21
510a1–2   74n43
517b5   154
580d3–581a1   134n72

Sophista (*Soph.*)
255d   21

Theaetetus (*Tht.*)
176b1–2   119
195a   98, 101, 103, 107n75
195c   10

Timaeus (*Tim.*)
22b4–8   76n54
28c3–5   38
29e4–30a2   118
30b   153n9
31b   106
46d   153n9
53b5–57d6   53n20
72a5   61n5

Plotinus
Enneads
I.1 [53]   65n22
I.2 [19], 1   118n29
I.2 [19], 4.17–28   155
I.6 [1], 9.40–41   154–155
II.9 [33], 6.5–10   114–115
II.9 [33], 6.14–24   116–117
II.9 [33], 10.19–33   114
II.9 [33], 15   118n29
II.9 [33], 15.32–40   119
III.6 [26], 13.18–20   155n14
III.6 [26], 2.20–32   119
IV.3 [27]   65n22
V.3 [49], 4.1–4   155
VI.1 [42] – VI.3 [44]   178n29
VI.1 [42], 25–30   179n31
VI.1 [42], 25.1–3   179n31
VI.1 [42], 25.1–6   177n22

Plutarch
Adversus Colotem (*Adv. Colotem*)
1118C   63, 65

Coniugalia praecepta (*Con. praec.*)
142E12–F3   182n36

De Animae Procreatione in Timaeo (*An. Procr.*)
1012B   40
1013A–B   40
1013D   41
1014D–1015F   39n27
1015A–B   38n26

De capienda ex inimicis utilitate (*De capienda*)
89A   60n4

De communibus notitiis (*De comm. not.*)
1083A–1084A   177n22
1083E7–8   178n25

De defectu oraculorum (*De def. or.*)
416D   74n44
435F–436F   37n23

De E apud Delphos (*De E*)
385D   65n23
392A   64
393A–C   38n23
394C   64

De Iside et Osiride (*De Is. et Os.*)
354A   100n40
354C   74n44
364AB   131n52
366A   131n52
370E–371A   38n26
372E–F   37n23

373E–F   37n23
374e   156n22

De Sera Numinis Vindicta (Ser. num. vind.)
550D   37n23

De Stoicorum repugnantiis (De Stoic. rep.)
1053F–1054B   175n19

Fragments (ed. Sandbach)
215d   156n22

Platonicae Quaestiones (Plat. quaest.)
II.1001B–C   38n25

Quaestiones Convivales (Quaest. Conv.)
VIII.2, 720A–C   38n26

Quomodo adulator ab amico internoscatur (Adulator)
49B   60n4
65F   60n4

Vita Alexandri (V.Alex.)
7.668A–B   26n30

Vita Demosthenis (Dem.)
3.2   66

Vita Dionis (Dion)
II.18.3   98n27

Porphyry
Ad Anebo (ed. Saffrey/Segonds)
11   134n77
13   130n42, 144n147
13a   130n42
44   146n159
59   141n122
62   141n122, 143n144
63   146n160
63a   146n160
64   130n42, 135n84, 144n147
65   135n84, 143n144
65b   143n144
65e   143n144
65j   143n144
65m   144n147
65o   143n144
65q–s   144n147
66   144n147
67   135n84
68   135n84
69   143n144
73   144n147
75   144n147

Ad Gaurum
9.4   100n38

Contra Christianos (ed. Harnack)
Fr. 1   126, 126n12
Fr. 39   116
Fr. 40   100n39

De abstinentia
2.42.2–3   143

De antro nympharum
18, 69.16   133n63

Fragments (ed. Smith)
58F   22
273F   66
274F   65
275F   63n13, 64–65
306F   144, 148n173
308F   134n73, 144n145
323F 8–14   136
324F 8–9   136n93
327F   143
343F   139
345F   138
345aF   138
347F   144n145
350F   144n145
351F 14–24   144n151

353F   135n79
355F   132n55
358F 22–29   132
360F 33–36   131
477–478F   141n127
488F 1   148n173

In Aristotelis categorias (In Cat.)
59.10–14   172n6
86.10–14   178n29
86.22–24   172n6
119.34–37   172n6
137.29–138.4   172n6

Isagoge (Isag.)
6.6–9   178n29

Vita Plotini
7   100n36
13.5–10   120
14.14–16   120
14.19–20   35n17
16.6   114
16.1–9   113
18.4–6   116

Vita Pythagorae
53   100n37

Posidonius
F 187 EK   48n12
T 58 EK   49
T 83 EK   50

Proclus
Elementatio theologica (ET)
23–24   173n9

In Alcibiadem (In Alc.)
5.1–6.7   65n24
30.6   157n25
258.15–259.21   120
264.3–6   10

268.12–16   9n7
277.20–278.1   155n18
280.26–281.16   155n18

In Cratylum (In Crat.)
94.16–95.23

In Parmenidem (In Parm.)
III.788.12–28   158n27
IV.842.26–35   158n27
IV.892.22–28   155n18
VI.1069.18–22   173n10

In primum Euclidis elementorum librum (In Eucl.)
14.24–15.9   155

In Remp.
I.90.19–91.6   134n76

In Timaeum (In Tim.)
I.152.10–155.2   145n153
I.266.28–267.1   158
I.266.29–267.11   158n27
I.295.20–26   152n5
I.369.12–19   118
I.369.19–25   118
III.107.31   157n25
III.108.7   157n25
III.234.8–235.9   134n76
III.235.9–238.26   134n76

Theologia Platonica
I.1, 6.16–18   112
II.11, 65.5–7   120n37
IV.10.195   155n17
IV.23, 69.5–70.17   112

Prodicus
B5 Diels-Kranz   145n152

Psellus
Philosophica Minora (ed. O'Meara)
II.40, 149.19–22   134n70

Salustius
De deis et mundo
2.2   130
3.4   130n48
4.1–3   137n96
4.3   131n52
4.7–9   131
10   134n71
14.1   142n133
18.3   135n80

Scholia vetera in Pindarum (ed. Drachmann)
Ol. 9, scholium 46   100n35

Seneca
Epistulae Morales ad Lucilium (Ep.)
58.13–15   178n26
65.2–10   38
108.23   35n16

Sextus Empiricus
Adversus mathematicos (Adv. math.)
8.263   181n34
10.218   178n26

Pyrrhoniae Hypotyposes (P.H.)
VIII.16–18   57n32

Simplicius
In Categorias (In Cat.)
2.5–6   171
2.8–9   171
2.9–25   170
2.13–3.1   170n4
3.2–4   170
3.4–10   170n4
3.10–17   170n4
3.13–17   171

4.28–5.1   173n11
5.3–6.5   171n5
10.8–19   178n29
18.26–19.1   172n6
19.13–14   176n21
36.28—31   21
38.7–9   176n21
38.19–24   25n23
38.19–39.2   21
41.28–29   25n23
48.11–16   177n23
62.24–30   172n6
63.22–24   21, 22
65.2–13   176n21
65.14   28
65.19–24   27
65.20   28
65.21   28, 29
66.32–37   177n22
66.32–67.2   178
67.2–8   179n30
67.15–18   179n30
67.17–68.31   179n30
69.4–71.2   173n12
78.4–5   28
78.4–20   21
78.20–24   22
82.35–83.16   173n12
169.10–15   21
159.32   21
192.30–193.2   172n6
206.3–7   176
207.27–35   176
207.28–208.20   177n21
208.16–17   176
209.1–3   170n3
209.10–29   170n3
211.5–15   178n29
212.12–28   179–180
212.12–213.1   170n3
213.1–6   181
213.8–10   174n13
213.8–214.2   176

213.29–214.2   174, 183n37
214.24–215.5   182
214.24–215.18   170n3
217.32–218.4   170n3
222.30–223.11   170n3
224.22–33   170n3
237.25–238.32   170n3, 172n6
242.12–15   170n3
264.33–36   170n3
269.14–16   170n3
271.20–23   170n3
276.30–32   170n3
284.32–285.1   170n3, 172n6
286.36–287.11   170n3
287.31–33   170n3
334.1–3   171n5

In De Anima (In De An.)
3.4–18   151n1
247.23–26   24n19

In De Caelo (In DC)
90.25–28   106
135.18–20   106
139.6–13   106n61
563.26–564.10   12n17
640.27–32   12n18

In Epicteti Enchiridion
192   171n5

In Physica (In Phys.)
181.7–30   29n37
295.15–18   163
1363.8–12   152n6

Stoicorum Veterum Fragmenta (*SVF*)
1.98   175n17, 181n34
1.518   181n34
2.310   175n17
2.329   178n26
2.331   178n26
2.332   178n26
2.363   181n34
2.369   177n22
2.371   177n22
2.374   177n23
2.398   177n23
2.449   175n19
2.580   134n71
2.771   53n21
2.841   175n19
2.988   175n19
2.1027   175n19
2.1067   134n71

Strato
Fragments (ed. Sharples)
80.8–11   24n19
80.33–35   24n19

Syrianus
In Aristotelis metaphysica (In Met.)
28.18–19   177n23
80.4–7   152
80.28   152, 152n3
114.35–115.1   162n36
195.9   152n3

Tertullian
Apologeticum
9   136n89

De Oratione
26   74n44

Themistius
In De anima (In De An.)
32.22–31   22, 24

[Timaeus Locrus]
De natura mundi et animae (de univ. nat.)
   (ed. Thesleff)
213.13–15   11n13

Xenocrates
Fragments (ed. Parente)
227   74n44

Xenophon
Memorabilia (Mem.)
2.8.1   58n34

Notes on Contributors

Riccardo Chiaradonna is Professor of Ancient Philosophy at Roma Tre University. His research focuses primarily on the ancient Platonic and Aristotelian traditions, on Plotinus and on Galen. Among his publications: *Sostanza movimento analogia: Plotino critico di Aristotele* (Naples 2002), *Plotino* (Rome 2009), *Platonismo* (Bologna 2017), *Boéthos de Sidon: Exègète d'Aristote et Philosophe* (Berlin and Boston 2020, with Marwan Rashed).

Franco Ferrari is Professor of Ancient Philosophy at the University of Pavia. The focus of his scientific research is Plato's philosophy (metaphysics, epistemology, cosmology and ethics) and ancient Platonism (middle Platonism and Plotinus). He has published translations with commentary of *Meno*, *Theaetetus* and *Parmenides*. He is the author of an *Introduction to Plato* and an *Introduction to Plato's Republic*.

Mareike Hauer works as a postdoctoral researcher in Jan Opsomer's ERC project *Not another history of Platonism. The role of Aristotle's criticisms of Plato in the development of ancient Platonism* (grant agreement No. 885273) at the KU Leuven, Belgium. Her main areas of research are ancient and especially late ancient philosophy of nature and metaphysics.

Albert Joosse is Lecturer in Ancient Philosophy at the University of Groningen. He is the author of articles on Platonic dialogues, the ancient reception of the *Alcibiades I*, self-knowledge and friendship in ancient philosophy and has edited *Olympiodorus of Alexandria: Exegete, Teacher, Platonic Philosopher* (Leiden, 2021).

Alexandra Michalewski is Research Fellow at the CNRS (Centre Léon Robin, Paris-Sorbonne), and Co-Director with Pieter d'Hoine of a funded research project on Asclepius' *Commentary on Aristotle's Metaphysics*. As a specialist of Plotinus and the ancient Platonic tradition, she focuses on the question of the nature and causality of intelligible Forms and on the reception of Aristotelianism in the context of the emergence of Platonic commentarism.

Sébastien Morlet is Professor at Sorbonne Université. His work is devoted to Late Antique and Christian literature in Greek (*Christianisme et philosophie. Les premières confrontations*, Paris, 2014; *Les chrétiens et la culture. Conversion d'un* *concept*, Paris, 2016; *Symphonia. La concorde des textes et des doctrines dans la littérature grecque jusqu'à Origène*, Paris, 2019).

Helmut Seng teaches classical philology at the universities of Frankfurt and Konstanz. His research focuses on Synesios of Cyrene and the Chaldaean Oracles. *Un livre sacŕe de l'Antiquité tardive: les Oracles chaldaïques* (Turnhout 2016) was awarded the 2018 médaille Le Fèvre-Deumier de Pons of the Académie des Inscriptions et Belles Lettres. He is series editor of the Bibliotheca Chaldaica, in which his latest publication is *Oracula Chaldaica Latine* (Heidelberg 2021).

Teun Tieleman studied classics and philosophy at Utrecht University, where he earned his PhD with highest distinction (1992). At the same university he holds a professorship in ancient philosophy and medicine (since 2015). His research focuses on Galen of Pergamum and his influence, Stoicism, theories of emotion as well as the ways in which philosophy was taught and transmitted in the Graeco-Roman world, the relation between ancient medicine and religion as well as ancient philosophy and early Christianity. He directed the research project 'Human Nature: Medical and Philosophical Perspectives in the Work of Galen of Pergamum' (2015–2021). He is a member of the governing board of the Gravitation-programme 'Anchoring Innovation' (2018–2028).

Angela Ulacco (PhD Pisa, 2010) has joined the ERC project 'Not another history of Platonism' in Leuven in July 2021. Prior to that she was postdoctoral fellow in Tübingen, Pisa, and Leuven, Juniorprofessor für griechische Philosophie at the Albert-Ludwigs-Universität Freiburg (2013–2019) and Senior Feodor Lynen Alexander von Humboldt Fellow at the University of Fribourg (2020–2021). Her research focuses on Plato and Ancient Platonism, in particular on the intersection between the Pythagorean and Platonic tradition. She has a special interest in metaphysics, the philosophy of nature, and methodology of the history of philosophy.

Robbert M. van den Berg is Lecturer in Ancient Philosophy at Leiden University. His research focusses on the Platonic tradition. His publications include *Proclus' Hymns: Essays, Translations, Commentary* (Leiden/Boston 2001); *Proclus' Commentary on the Cratylus in Context: Ancient Theories of Language and Naming* (Leiden/Boston 2008); *De Mythen van Plato* (in Dutch with Hugo Koning, Budel 2022).